THE SECRET LIVES OF SAINTS

DAPHNE BRAMHAM

THE SECRET LIVES OF SAINTS

CHILD BRIDES AND LOST BOYS
IN CANADA'S POLYGAMOUS MORMON SECT

Daphne Bramham (signature)

VINTAGE CANADA

Published in Canada by Vintage Canada, a division of Random House of
Canada Limited, Toronto, in 2009. Originally published in hardcover in
Canada by Random House Canada, a division of Random House of Canada
Limited, Toronto, in 2008. Distributed by Random House of Canada Limited,
Toronto.

Vintage Canada and colophon are registered trademarks of
Random House of Canada Limited.

www.randomhouse.ca

LIBRARY AND ARCHIVES CANADA CATALOGUING IN PUBLICATION

Bramham, Daphne
The secret lives of saints : child brides and lost boys in a polygamous
Mormon sect / Daphne Bramham.

Includes bibliographical references and index.
ISBN 978-0-307-35589-8

1. Blackmore, Winston, 1956–   . 2. Mormon fundamentalism—British
Columbia—Creston Region—History. 3. Polygamy—British Columbia—
Creston Region. 4. Child sexual abuse—British Columbia. 5. Freedom of
religion—Canada. I. Title.

BX8680.M535C3 2009   289.3'71162   C2008-903683-2

Printed and bound in the United States of America

2 4 6 8 9 7 5 3 1

For my parents, Donald and Lydia

CONTENTS

BLACKMORE FAMILY TREE

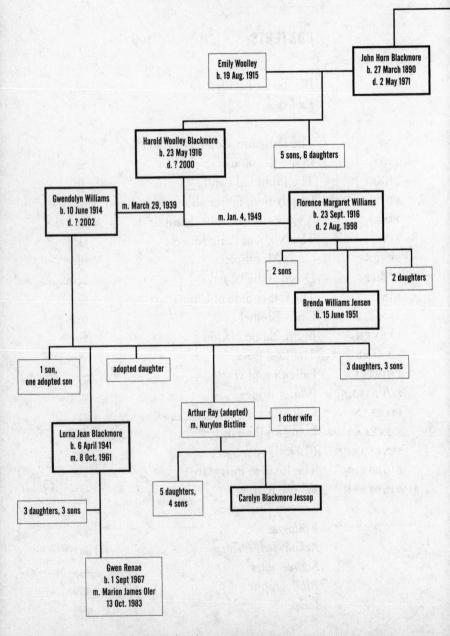

John Horn Blackmore
b. 27 March 1890
d. 2 May 1971

Emily Woolley
b. 19 Aug. 1915

Harold Woolley Blackmore
b. 23 May 1916
d. ? 2000

5 sons, 6 daughters

Gwendolyn Williams
b. 10 June 1914
d. ? 2002

m. March 29, 1939

m. Jan. 4, 1949

Florence Margaret Williams
b. 23 Sept. 1916
d. 2 Aug. 1998

2 sons

2 daughters

Brenda Williams Jensen
b. 15 June 1951

1 son,
one adopted son

adopted daughter

3 daughters, 3 sons

Arthur Ray (adopted)
m. Nurylon Bistline

1 other wife

Lorna Jean Blackmore
b. 6 April 1941
m. 8 Oct. 1961

3 daughters, 3 sons

5 daughters,
4 sons

Carolyn Blackmore Jessop

Gwen Renae
b. 1 Sept 1967
m. Marion James Oler
13 Oct. 1983

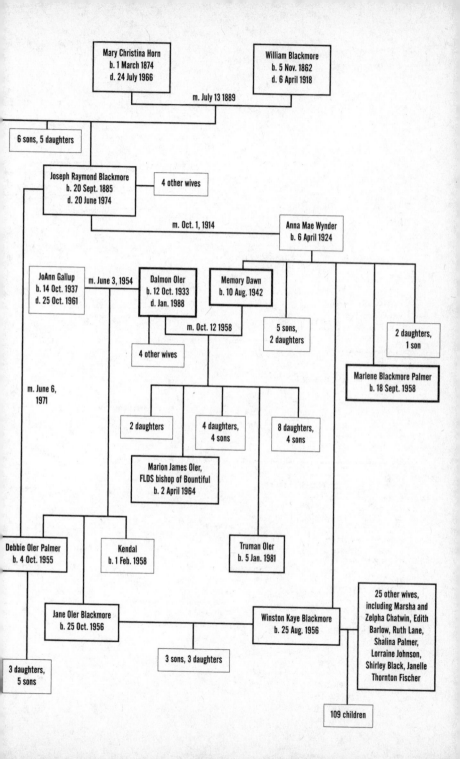

PROLOGUE

In early November 2001, a month after the United States, Canada and a coalition of countries attacked Afghanistan in search of Islamic terrorist Osama bin Laden, President George W. Bush talked about the kind of life women and children were leading under the tyranny of the Taliban.

"Women are imprisoned in their homes, and are denied access to basic health care and education. Food sent to help starving people is stolen by their leaders. The religious monuments of other faiths are destroyed. Children are forbidden to fly kites, or sing songs," he said. "A girl of seven is beaten for wearing white shoes."

A few weeks later, Laura Bush filled in for her husband on his weekly radio spot. "All of us have an obligation to speak out," she said. "We may come from different backgrounds and faiths—but parents the world over love our children. We respect our mothers, our sisters and daughters. Fighting brutality against women and children is not the expression of a specific culture; it is the acceptance of our common humanity—a commitment shared by people of good will on every continent."

That day, the U.S. State Department released a report that said the Taliban regime "systematically repressed all sectors of the population and denied even the most basic individual rights. It restricted access to medical care for women, brutally enforced a restrictive dress code, and limited the ability of women to move about the city . . . It perpetrated egregious acts of violence against women, including rape, abduction, and forced marriage." The report went on to say that women were allowed to work in only "very limited circumstances," noting that "restricting women's access to work is an attack on women today. Eliminating women's access to education is an assault on women tomorrow."

The State Department and the Bushes were referring to the Taliban in Afghanistan, but they might well have been talking about women and children in the United States and Canada living under the tyranny of the Fundamentalist Church of Jesus Christ of Latter Day Saints (FLDS), the largest polygamous sect in North America. Prophet Warren Jeffs controls every aspect of the lives of more than eight thousand people, from where they live to whom and when they marry. Jeffs has banned school, church, movies and television. He has outlawed the colour red and even forbidden his followers to use the word "fun." Along with his trusted councillors, Jeffs has arranged and forced hundreds of marriages, some involving girls as young as fourteen and men as old as or older than their fathers and grandfathers. Many of the brides have been transported across state borders as well as international borders with Canada and Mexico. He has taught racism and discrimination against "Negroes," which is why the FLDS is listed by the Southern Poverty Law Center as a hate group.

The roots of the FLDS are in Mormonism, although the name itself is a recent one. When the mainstream church renounced polygamy in 1890, dissidents splintered off and continued to practise plural marriage. Some men sequestered their illegal families, making contact with other fundamentalists only when they or their sons needed more wives. Others banded together to follow a "prophet" who claimed to hold the "keys to the priesthood," having received a revelation from God that he was to be a leader of men loyal to the Principle of Celestial Marriage. The fundamentalists believe they are the only true Mormons because they continue to hold to founder Joseph Smith's revelation that men must have multiple wives to enter the highest realm of heaven. There, in the "celestial kingdom," they will become gods, and their wives goddesses—albeit goddesses who must serve at the table of their gods for all eternity.

Polygamy has been illegal in Canada and the United States since 1890. But fundamentalist Mormonism is thriving in Utah, Arizona, Texas and British Columbia. There are dozens of different groups and thousands of so-called independents, which makes it impossible to know how many fundamentalists there are. Estimates range from thirty-seven thousand to one million across the continent, yet politicians have been loath to do anything about the people who call themselves Saints. Politicians have not just looked the other way, they have in many instances made it easier for the Saints' leaders to intimidate, control and abuse their followers. Nowhere is that more obvious than in Bountiful, British Columbia, and in the twin towns of Hildale, Utah, and Colorado City, Arizona.

In 1992, the B.C. government refused to enforce Canada's law by charging the bishop of Bountiful, Winston Blackmore, with polygamy. Citing studies by several leading legal experts, the B.C. government said the law would not withstand a challenge under the Canadian Charter of Rights and Freedoms, which, along with the national Constitution, guarantees freedom of religion and association.

Those rights, however, are not unlimited. Twice since its decision not to prosecute polygamy, the B.C. government has successfully gone to court to force children of Jehovah's Witnesses to submit to blood transfusions, even though that goes against their beliefs. The government's argument: religious belief cannot override a child's right to health.

There are other conflicting rights. In 1879, in a landmark case called *Reynolds versus United States*, the U.S. Supreme Court ruled that governments can intervene where the religious practice of polygamy undermines the rights of others.

"Suppose one believed that human sacrifices were a necessary part of religious worship, would it be seriously contended that the civil government under which he lived could not interfere to prevent a sacrifice? Or if a wife religiously believed it was her duty to burn herself upon the funeral pile [*sic*] of her dead husband, would it be beyond the power of the civil government to prevent her carrying her belief into practice?" The justices unanimously answered, "No."

Yet in 1992, the B.C. government effectively legalized polygamy. Since then Bountiful's population has more than tripled. In Utah and Arizona also, politicians have been loath to prosecute polygamists after a failed attempt to do so in 1953. The FLDS population in both states has doubled every decade since. To say that the Saints place a high value on large families is something of an understatement.

Unlike Christians, who believe that the soul comes to the body at birth and leaves the body at death, the Saints believe in both a pre-mortal existence and the "lifting up" of the earthly body into heaven. They believe millions of spirits are waiting to be born into earthly bodies. And, as God's Chosen People, they believe they have a responsibility to bring as many of those spirits as possible into the world as Mormons—rather than as something less worthy. As Joseph Smith's friend and apostle Orson Pratt wrote, "The Lord has not kept them [the spirits] in store for five or six thousand years past and kept them waiting for their bodies all this time to send them among the Hottentots, the African negroes, the idolatrous Hindoos or any other fallen nations that dwell upon the face of the Earth."

Emboldened by the failure of governments to prosecute, Canadian polygamist Winston Blackmore no longer hides. A second-generation leader and one of North America's best-known and wealthiest polygamists, Blackmore makes no secret of the fact that he has many wives. How many, he won't say. But some of his wives, those who have left him, say that he has been married twenty-six times and has more than one hundred children.

On at least two occasions, Blackmore—a spiritual leader, superintendent of a government-supported school and respected businessman—has publicly confessed to having sex with girls who were only fifteen and sixteen years old. That's a criminal offence in Canada. His first admission was in 2005 at a "polygamy summit" organized by his wives in Creston, B.C. Nobody said or did anything when he said he'd married "very young girls" because God and the prophet had told him to. Blackmore has yet to be charged.

Sexual abuse and exploitation of children by teachers and church leaders of all faiths usually lands on the front page of newspapers across North America, but Blackmore's confession did not make the national media and wasn't even reported in the Creston newspaper. Blackmore repeated his confession in December 2006 during an interview on the

Cable News Network (CNN) with Larry King. Blackmore said he hadn't realized that one of his wives was only fifteen when they'd married. She had lied about her age, Blackmore said. But all women do that, don't they? he asked King.

Girls may well lie about their age; middle-aged, balding men often do as well. But that's why there are laws to protect children. It's no defence for a predator such as a bishop or a school superintendent to say that he didn't know the girl was only fifteen. It's our society's shame that the laws are not always enforced.

After George and Laura Bush spoke out against the human rights abuses in Afghanistan, Utah's Attorney General Mark Shurtleff recognized the parallels and began calling the FLDS "North America's Taliban." After more than one hundred years of his state allowing them to hide in plain sight, he has promised to do something. Arizona's Attorney General Terry Goddard has also promised to end the theocracy that exists on his state's border. Both states began by laying charges against Warren Jeffs, first in Arizona and then in Utah. When Jeffs failed to appear in court to enter pleas, the Federal Bureau of Investigation (FBI) charged him with fleeing prosecution and put him on its Ten Most Wanted list along with Osama bin Laden. Jeffs was arrested on the outskirts of Las Vegas in August 2006, and went to trial in the fall of 2007. He has yet to be charged with polygamy. In Utah, he faced two counts of "rape as an accomplice" for having forced a fourteen-year-old girl to marry her nineteen-year-old first cousin. The penalty is five years to life in prison. In Arizona, Jeffs faces five counts of sexual conduct with a minor and one count of conspiracy to commit sexual misconduct with a minor.

A handful of men loyal to Jeffs have recently been convicted for having sex with minors. Several Hildale police officers, more loyal to the prophet than to the laws of the state and country, have been stripped of their badges and the Colorado City public school is in receivership. A Utah court—at the request of the states of Utah and Arizona— has placed the FLDS trust fund in receivership and reformed it to ensure that the people who contributed to it will benefit from it. And the states work jointly within the twin communities to try to prevent domestic abuse and to help victims of such abuse.

In British Columbia, the RCMP spent nearly three years investigating Bountiful. Lawyers in the attorney general's ministry recommended that no charges be laid because they didn't believe there was a substantial likelihood of conviction. Attorney General Wally Oppal didn't like that recommendation and hired a special prosecutor, who after two months recommended that the polygamy law be referred to the B.C. Court of Appeal, where justices could rule on whether the law would withstand a constitutional challenge. Oppal didn't like that answer either. A former Court of Appeal justice himself, Oppal believes it's not something the courts should do. So, he hired another special prosecutor—more of a pit bull—to give him the answer he wants. Charge one or more of them with polygamy, and send them to trial.

Meanwhile, Jeffs and Blackmore continue to direct and control almost every aspect of their followers' lives. With the increased prosecution, Jeffs has ordered many of his followers to leave Utah and Arizona and to move to several new communities, including the Yearning for Zion (YFZ) Ranch near Eldorado, Texas, where he consecrated the first fundamentalist Mormon temple while he was still a fugitive. Blackmore has moved many of his followers to Idaho and has made numerous trips to fundamentalist communities across the United States and Mexico to gather more faithful to his flock.

Girls are still being forced into marriages. Boys are still driven out to make the polygamous arithmetic work for the older men. Neither boys nor girls are getting an adequate education in either country. And Arizona's attorney general admits that reintegrating the communities into the mainstream after years of isolation and theocratic rule is still years away.

How is it that two nations, so clear-sighted in recognizing human rights atrocities in other countries and so fearless in taking on tyrannical rulers on the other side of the world, have been so blind to the human rights violations committed against their own women and children?

ONE

THE POLYGAMY CAPITAL OF CANADA

The community of <u>Bountiful</u> has been Canada's dirty secret for <u>more than sixty years</u>. Tucked away in the southeastern corner of British Columbia, it's out of sight and out of mind. As its founders had hoped in the mid-1940s, when they chose this remote location to raise their polygamous families, the neighbours don't really mind. They've got secrets of their own. So, they don't ask and the folks in Bountiful don't tell what really goes on out there under the cliffs of the Skimmerhorn Mountains.

Bountiful, B.C., is the polygamy capital of Canada. You won't find it on any map because it's a made-up name. The official name of the place you're looking for is Lister, but even with a detailed map of the Kootenay region, you'll have to search hard to find it. Lister was founded by First World War veterans, who, as they sailed home from Europe, dreamed of setting up a co-operative fruit farm. But there wasn't enough water and the land wasn't suitable for fruit trees. So, by 1923, their utopia in tatters, veterans began drifting away.

The closest town of any size is Creston—population 5,201 at last count. At the Creston Museum, you'll learn that this is a region with a history rich in dreamers, ne'er-do-wells, rounders, speculators, prospectors, hermits, murderers and even religious terrorists who emigrated from Russia.

It's little more than a ten-minute drive from Creston to the cluster of homes, schools, barns and trailers that Blackmore renamed Bountiful. According to the Book of Mormon, that's what an apocryphal character, Nephi, named North America when he arrived by sea from the Holy Land around 600 BC. The Mormons—mainstream and fundamentalist—believe that North America's aboriginal people are descendants of Nephi's brother, Laman. The Lamanites, as Mormons call native Indians, denied Christ, fell in league with the Devil and killed Nephi's descendants. Needless to say, Mormons had little time for Lamanites, until recently, when the mainstream Church of Jesus Christ of Latter-day Saints began to view American Indians as an opportunity for expansion.

The folks at the Creston Tourist Information office will give you directions to Bountiful, but they may do so grudgingly. The good burghers of Creston aren't happy that their pretty little town shares the infamy that comes with having twelve hundred polygamists living nearby. They'd prefer that people associate Creston with apples or cherries, or the local beer that's "brewed right in the Kootenays," as the company's slogan says. Or that Creston be thought of as a nice place to retire. If Creston has to be known for something, they'd rather it was for the first-rate marijuana—the "B.C. bud" that's grown only semi-surreptitiously throughout the lush valley—than polygamy.

Former Prime Minister Pierre Trudeau famously told Canadians that the state had no business in the bedrooms of the nation. Most people have forgotten that he said it during debates over a massive and controversial rewriting of the Criminal Code in 1967 that decriminalized "homosexual acts." A few years later, his government again stepped back from the private realm of sexual relations and legalized abortion. Finally, Trudeau tried—with a new Canadian Constitution and the Charter of Rights and Freedoms—to create a freer society where all men, women and children would have more choices open to them. Yet now Canadians—already burdened with the national characteristic of politeness—often repeat Trudeau's quote to justify not poking into other people's bedrooms even if it means ignoring abuse.

Certainly that's what Creston's elected representative to the regional district thinks. "We don't see the monsters that everybody else says are living among us," says John Kettle. He's more concerned about the Hells Angels taking over the regional drug trade than about men having more than one wife. Kettle admits he's been to Bountiful only a couple of times in the past twenty years, which is a bit surprising since he is the staunchest and most outspoken defender of Bountiful's former bishop Winston Blackmore. Kettle describes Blackmore as one of his close friends. They're also business partners.

In a letter to the local newspaper in 2004, local auctioneer Alex Ewashen gave full expression to the prevailing attitude about Bountiful:

> What I see are healthy women and young ladies who do not need artificial makeup to make them look attractive . . . But, the poor things, they do not have a smoke pit at their school, they are not brought up to deem it their right to pierce their belly buttons and whatever else—why they don't even have the freedom to show off their bare

midriffs and their cleavages. And, horrors above all horrors, they are taught life skills in school, like cooking, sewing, and keeping house. And, yes, they do know how to raise children . . .

And how about the boys? To my knowledge I don't know of any that didn't grow up with a good work ethic. I can't say that for the kids I used to be sent from the high school to introduce to the work force. Not long ago I saw a young Bountiful boy who I'm sure wasn't old enough to have a driver's license back up a 40-foot semi flat deck, I'm sure at 15 kilometres an hour in a perfectly straight line for a good 300 feet.

Ewashen concluded that many people are trying to return to simpler times. "Well, the Bountiful community doesn't have to do that, they are there. If you want to go way, way back, God told Adam and Eve to go forth and multiply—he didn't say to Eve to go forth and become a secretary, or a nurse, or a lawyer." Of course, there's no evidence that God told Adam to be a lawyer (or an auctioneer) either.

Polygamous communities might well produce some first-rate underage truck drivers. But they also have plenty of disadvantages that Ewashen overlooks. What goes on out there is not only illegal, it's anathema to the core values and principles espoused by Canadians. Even though polygamy has been illegal in Canada since 1890, men are marrying multiple wives. Some of Bountiful's men are in their forties and fifties when they marry girls as young as fourteen, which is Canada's legal age of sexual consent. The legal age for marriage in B.C. is eighteen, with the consent of a B.C. Supreme Court judge required for any child under sixteen. But before they are even of legal age to be married, a third of Bountiful's girls are impregnated by men who are at least a decade or more older than they are. Underage girls in Bountiful are two to seven times more likely to get pregnant than any other girls in the province.

Children—boys, mainly, but also girls—are frequently used as unpaid labourers in dangerous construction and forestry jobs. To ensure that those children don't have any other choices, the leaders encourage them to leave school well before high-school graduation to become either wives and mothers or indentured labourers. It's all done in the name of God and religion by men who are aiming to be gods with dozens of wives and hundreds of children serving them for all eternity.

—

Like most people in town, Creston's mayor, Joe Snopek, is uncomfortable about looking into the bedrooms of Bountiful. In 2004, he said polygamy "is no different than a gay lifestyle or being a Jehovah Witness or anything else . . . And I sure would hate someone investigating my lifestyle." But by the time B.C.'s attorney general ordered a Royal Canadian Mounted Police (RCMP) investigation into allegations of sexual abuse, child brides and polygamy in 2005, so many journalists had asked Snopek about Bountiful that he'd grown weary of defending it. He'd even begun openly talking about some of the other abuses.

Snopek recalled how he had reported a Bountiful company to the Workers' Compensation Board and the B.C. Labour Ministry a few years earlier because the contractor was using a crew of barefoot children—some as young as six and none older than thirteen—to pull shingles off the roof of a Creston home. "They [the WCB and Labour Ministry] didn't do anything," Snopek said. "The finding was that it was a family operation and they can do pretty much what they want. It puts us [the city] in a nasty position in one way. Where are the powers that be in government to shut down companies like that or do something about it?"

Snopek welcomed the RCMP investigation into the allegations of sexual abuse, child brides and trafficking of girls, and he urged police to look deeper into the community: "It's time they [the government] stepped in and took a good hard look and not just at the smoke and mirrors that Winston [Blackmore] has been playing for the media."

Still, many people in Creston do not want to get rid of the polygamists claiming to be "saints"—people who, much to the horror of mainstream Mormons, continue to assert that they are the only true members of Joseph Smith's church. Many Creston businesses are afraid to lose customers. A local hardware store that stocks a small selection of books along with the usual fare of nails, paint and lumber, had *Keep Sweet: Children of Polygamy* on its shelves. The book is former resident Debbie Palmer's gruelling account of the abuse and neglect she witnessed growing up in the fundamentalist community. The owners pulled the book off the shelves when people from Bountiful threatened to boycott their store.

Polygamists and their big families spend a lot of money on cars, trucks, gasoline, groceries, shoes and other necessities. Because of this, many people don't want them gone, but, at the same time, they don't want to know about polygamy. They don't want to talk about it or have anybody else talk about it. If that means becoming inured to the sight of pregnant teenagers pushing a baby carriage while they hold the hand of a toddler, so be it. If it means another year when the New Year's baby is the progeny of a polygamist, well, whatever. If the baby's mother is little more than a child and the father is old enough to be the mother's grandfather, well, let's not get

A *familiar sight around Bountiful and Creston: a young mother
in pioneer dress shepherding toddlers around.*
(*Ian Smith / Vancouver Sun*)

into that. And so what if everybody looks suspiciously similar
and most have the same few last names because cousins marry
cousins and stepfathers impregnate stepdaughters? They're
not hurting us.

But when Mayor Snopek recently had city staff calculate
the economic impact of Bountiful on the community, they
found that the Saints account for only about 10 per cent of the
total economy. Of course, Snopek hasn't really broadcast that
to his citizens. So maybe people don't know the limited extent
of the Saints' economic impact. Maybe they are only going on
the perceptions gained at the grocery checkout. But it's more
likely that it's not about the money at all. People just don't
want to see what's in front of them.

Even though the Saints stick mostly to themselves, there's
evidence of them all over Creston. Logging trucks emblazoned with the names of their companies—J. R. Blackmore

& Sons and Oler Brothers—frequently rumble along the wide street. Creston residents don't find it unusual when a couple of "sister-wives" push a grocery cart or two up to the checkout at Extra Foods and start unloading several dozen eggs, litres of milk and large sacks of flour for their family of thirty or more.

Several of Winston Blackmore's wives are on the local search and rescue team. And in the winter, a couple of nights a month, some of Blackmore's sons, nephews, cousins and other relatives rent ice to play hockey at the local recreation centre, wearing sweaters bearing the J. R. Blackmore & Sons name. Until recently Blackmore paid as much as forty thousand dollars a year to rent ice time so that his family and others from Bountiful could skate without having to mix with outsiders—"gentiles" as they call all nonbelievers. Of course, with more than one hundred children of his own, Winston has enough Blackmores to start his own league. Yet, while Blackmore doesn't want his sons, daughters and followers' children socializing outside the community, he sees nothing wrong with lacing up his skates and playing in the Creston old-timers' league alongside his good friend Chris Luke, the chief of the Lower Kootenay Indian band, which has leased thousands of acres of land to Blackmore Farms.

Creston businessmen may worry about losing Bountiful's trade, but few people ask how a man like Blackmore can support his twenty-some wives and all those children. Few wonder just how many of their tax dollars go to subsidize them. And, if you are an outsider who asks about it, the folks in Creston are likely to get their backs up and tell you to mind your own business. Which is exactly what Blackmore and the folks in Bountiful say when they're asked.

Many Creston residents will tell you that the Bountiful people don't do drugs. They'll say that they don't drink alcohol, that many won't touch even coffee or tea, for that matter. What lots of them say is that, from what they can see, the people look healthy and happy. What they don't realize is that the people in Bountiful are programmed by their prophets to look happy.

The Bountiful people are taught from birth to "keep sweet." Happiness is the only emotion that's allowed. Anger, frustration, depression and especially rebellion are not allowed. They're taught to suppress those emotions and to put all their energy into obeying the word of their prophet, who speaks directly to God.

Saints are also taught that it's okay not to tell the truth to outsiders, especially if it means protecting the secrets of how many mothers and how few fathers there are or of how the fathers are ripping off the evil government, a practice known as "bleeding the beast."

That's the problem: most of the townsfolk don't know much about Bountiful and neither do their politicians or police. Politicians have shamelessly curried favour with Bountiful's leaders, accepting campaign donations and appointing some of the community's members to government boards. To indiscriminant politicians, the Saints are just another group in Canada's vote-rich multicultural tapestry.

—

To get to Bountiful, you follow paved backroads through the settlements of Erickson and Canyon, past farms and rolling meadows where cattle and horses graze. At a T-crossing, the road to Bountiful goes straight towards the mountain. You'll know you're nearly there when you see the first NO TRESPASSING sign. You will not be welcomed in this community where all but one or two small parcels of land are owned by the church's United Effort Plan Trust (UEP). It is a tenet of the faith that land, labour and material goods are to be handed over to "the priesthood." In theory, the bishop and the elders then divide it up according to each person's individual needs. In practice, the bishops and elders get the biggest and best houses as well as the most—and prettiest—wives.

Once upon a time, at the sight of a stranger's car, flocks of children used to scatter like small birds, abandoning their bicycles or trampolines. It doesn't happen as much any more—even the people of Bountiful are getting used to being a tourist draw. But mothers are still likely to gather up their little girls in long dresses, pulling them into the bushes or the closest house. The boys—especially the bigger ones—cluster together and are likely to shout, "Go away! Leave us alone!" They'll all be dressed the same in jeans or black pants with long-sleeved shirts, even on the hottest days. They might gesture rudely. Occasionally, strangers have felt threatened when men in pickup trucks with gun racks follow closely behind them. That's rare, but it's happened often enough to keep most people from Creston from venturing out to see what their neighbours are up to.

Blackmore's house is at the entrance of Bountiful, where the road splits to circle the community. It's two storeys high and looks like a 1960s motel; it's flanked on one side by an enormous garage and on the other by a large building with a wide, covered porch. The kitchen and the dining room are located in the large building.

Outside the fenced compound, there are signs saying NO TRESPASSING and PRIVATE ROAD. The compound itself is set back from the road. A strip of grass that's usually littered with abandoned bicycles of all sizes, shapes and colours gives way to a huge gravel parking lot. Triangular concrete barriers keep the clusters of vans and trucks from parking too close to the house.

Beneath the surface of the sleepy cluster of sheds and houses that comprise the polygamist epicentre of Bountiful, B.C., a bitter feud simmers over who will control the money, the land, the faith and the wives of Canada's fundamentalist Mormons.
(Ian Smith / Vancouver Sun)

Next to the compound is the midwifery clinic where many of the community's babies are born, away from the prying eyes of gentile doctors and nurses at Creston Hospital. Its waiting room is lined with dated photographs that show the midwives and all the babies they've birthed.

Farther along is the first of the two government-funded private schools that are attended by nearly four hundred children. Blackmore's school is called Mormon Hills, the other school, controlled by his rival, Warren Jeffs, is called Bountiful Elementary-Secondary School. Jeffs is the prophet of the Utah-based Fundamentalist Church of Jesus Christ of Latter Day Saints. He thwarted Blackmore's attempt to become the prophet in 2002, and then promptly excommunicated him. About two-thirds of the Canadian Saints—eight hundred or so people—stuck with Blackmore and about five hundred transferred their loyalties to Jeffs.

Mormon Hills is a makeshift affair that Blackmore cobbled together after the split. The school consists of two buildings, with some of the classes held in a house that's been renovated for classroom purposes. On the hill above is the more established Bountiful Elementary-Secondary School. In front, spelled out in white-painted rocks is the community's motto: KEEP SWEET. Together, the schools get more than one million dollars a year in provincial government grants. At both, the provincial curriculum is taught through the filter of their questionable religious values and beliefs. But that's apparently okay with the government, whose inspectors are somehow supposed to enforce the prohibition on teaching hate without having the power to review the religious materials.

Beyond the big, older houses where the two school principals live, and past the creek, are the slums. There, when the weather is warm, shoeless children play in the dirt outside dilapidated trailers. Wood for the stoves is piled alongside the trailers. At the opposite end of the community are the "suburbs." Here, off the circular road, there are lovely, large, recently constructed log homes on huge lots. Some belong to Jeffs's followers and some to Blackmore's. While you can tell a Bountiful man's status by the size and quality of his house, you can't look at his house and determine which spiritual leader he follows.

The split between the two men came without warning. So neighbours, who a few years ago watched out for one another's kids, shared stories and gossip, now no longer even acknowledge one another. Mothers no longer speak to daughters or sons. Contact between grandmothers and grandchildren has been severed. Jeffs's followers have been told to limit their communication with outsiders. A general store opened recently, but it serves only people loyal to Jeffs. Blackmore's followers aren't welcome.

While Bountiful is the heart of Canadian fundamentalist Mormonism, not all the Saints live there. Hundreds are scattered throughout nearby communities in both British Columbia and Idaho, and there's a small outpost in Alberta where men and boys labour in mills and logging camps for companies owned by fundamentalists.

But, on weekends, all of the Saints converge on Bountiful for two separate church meetings where their preferred prophet will remind them that they are God's Chosen People, and that they owe their hearts, minds, souls and most of their worldly goods to the prophet, who is God's mouthpiece. All men, who become members of the priesthood when they are twelve, will be reminded of their duty to tithe a tenth of what little they earn to the church's United Effort Plan trust. They will be reminded that if they are obedient, they will be blessed with multiple wives, without whom their entry to the highest realm of heaven is uncertain. Women and girls will be told again and again that they are to give themselves mind, body and soul to their fathers and later their husbands, who are their priesthood heads and their pathway to heaven. And their prophets tell them that no matter what they do in God's name, they are safe. The Canadian Charter of Rights and Freedoms protects them.

TWO

IN THE BEGINNING

Deputy Marshal Garr rapped on Charles Ora Card's door at nine thirty in the morning on July 26, 1886, with a search warrant in his hand. Card was a respected sawmill owner, justice of the peace and former city councillor of Logan, Utah. As president of the large Church of Jesus Christ of Latter-day Saints congregation or "stake" in Cache Valley, he had overseen construction of both the Logan Tabernacle and the Temple.

Card had four wives, including the daughter of Mormon prophet Brigham Young, Zina Young Card. Four years earlier, the United States government had passed the Edmunds Act, which was aimed squarely at the Latter-day Saints (LDS)— Mormons, as they're more commonly called. When Garr finished searching the house, he handed subpoenas to some of Card's wives and children and arrested Card.

The plan to take Card to Salt Lake City's jail on the two o'clock train should have been kept secret. But Garr told a clutch of reporters and they raced to the telegraph office to get the news into their papers' afternoon editions. As the steam engine was being stoked to leave the station, Card asked Marshal E. W. Exum if he could get a drink of water from the fountain at the back of the car. Exum agreed and Card sauntered down the aisle. He kept going, right off the end of the train as it pulled out of the Logan station.

By coincidence, or more likely by design, a saddled horse was tied to a rail near the station. Although it was early afternoon, not a single soul was around to stop Card—a pillar of the community—as he galloped through the streets of the small Mormon town and headed for the wooded banks of the Logan River.

The train was at full speed before Marshal Exum figured out that perhaps Card wasn't coming back and before he asked the conductor to stop the train. The conductor refused. Card's disappearance wasn't his problem, he said. The railway had a schedule to keep. Official Mormon histories record that the conductor was not a Mormon, but they are silent on the religious affiliations of the marshals and the owner of the getaway horse.

Card hid along the riverbank until after nightfall, when he made his way to a friend's home. For the next two months, he kept ahead of the marshals, travelling at night and staying in a series of safe houses, where he was secreted away by other Mormons. Persecution had been a way of life for the church's leaders almost from the moment that Joseph Smith had published the Book of Mormon fifty-six years earlier, in 1830. Mormons know how to hide and they know how to keep secrets.

—

The Book of Mormon had caused a sensation in puritanical America. Early critics dismissed it as a romance that mixed superstition with swindle. They scoffed at its fantastical tales of escaped tribes of Israel coming by boat to North America around 600 BC and of Christ appearing before those early North American Christians right after his resurrection, repeating the Sermon on the Mount and appointing twelve disciples to baptize and administer bread and wine in remembrance of him.

Smith was an unschooled young man with a reputation as a treasure hunter. He was from a family of spiritualists who had broken with the mainstream churches and sought their God in a more personal way that included folk magic, visions, incantations, divining rods, amulets and hats containing special "peep" or "seer" stones that allowed them to make out what was normally invisible to the eye. Smith's formative teen years were spent in Palmyra, in western New York state, a place that had come to be known as "the Burned-Over District." In this area an unusually high number of preachers, evangelicals and mystics held raucous revival meetings where people were healed and spoke in tongues. So, as strange as it all seems now, Smith and his story fit right in. Even claiming to be a prophet in direct contact with God was fairly common. What's extraordinary is that his tale not only survived but metamorphosed into a mainstream religion with twelve million members worldwide.

Smith claimed to have used special eyeglasses made of two smooth, three-cornered diamonds called Urim and Thummin to translate the Book of Mormon from "reformed Egyptian" characters engraved on golden plates that the Angel Moroni had helped him find buried under a tree. The idea of a lost tribe of Christians on their very own continent was appealing to the pioneering spirit of Americans. Smith borrowed heavily from the King James version of the Bible, but some of his doctrine is radically different from Christianity.

His God has "a body of flesh." If this sounds vaguely pagan, so is Smith's idea of the afterlife and the bodily resumption of family life, which is the reason for Mormons' intense interest in genealogy.

Smith's heaven has three realms: the "celestial kingdom" or highest order, for the most righteous; the "terrestial kingdom" for those who were honourable but not the most righteous; and the "telestial kingdom" for liars, adulterers and others who would face Christ's judgment at the last resurrection.

In Smith's cosmology there is no hell anything like Dante's depiction of eternal torment—no fiery pit, no demonic legions. After Christ's judgment, according to Mormon faith, the liars, adulterers and those who had denied him in life, and who continue to deny him in death, are believed to spend eternity in eternal blackness.

It may not be orthodox, but neither is it highly original. What provoked such enmity in the minds of other Christians was Smith's contention that after the second century AD, Christ's church had been corrupted and had become offensive to God. With the Book of Mormon, Smith set out not simply to reform Christianity. He believed his mission from God was to found a new church based on the old ways and invigorated by newly revealed texts, new translations of the Bible and, of course, through orders given to him by God through revelations.

All of this was blasphemy to organized churches, their leaders and their adherents. But as Robert V. Remini writes in his biography of Joseph Smith, "The *Book of Mormon* . . . imbued believers with a sense that their faith had a power no other sect possessed: Divine authority."

Smith's new religion was, and remains, uniquely American. He told his followers that not only was Christ's Second Coming imminent, but Jesus would come to America, to a

New Jerusalem that Mormons would build in Missouri, where Adam sought refuge after his expulsion from the Garden of Eden. Superficially, Mormonism is highly democratic. Every person has the potential to speak directly to God and to become a god, which appealed to the revolutionary, democratic and highly individualistic American identity that was just emerging. In practice, however, Smith's church and Mormon society were extremely hierarchical; his promised land was a theocracy.

Before his murder in 1844, Smith was not only the church's prophet, president, seer and revelator. He was mayor of Nauvoo, Illinois; chief justice; trustee of a private university; and publisher of a newspaper. He was a real estate agent, a candidate for president of the United States and lieutenant general of a five-thousand-member militia that had modern rifles rather than the more common and cumbersome muskets of other Western pioneers.

Smith was a prolific writer and revelator. In addition to the Book of Mormon, he published two other books that are regarded as Mormonism's holy books. One is the Pearl of Great Price, which includes material Smith said was omitted from the Old Testament. The other is the Doctrine and Covenants, a compendium of revelations Smith compiled only after some of his closest advisers said God had been telling them about errors in Smith's work. It is one of the inherent problems with Smith's doctrine. There will always be too many potential messiahs. And who is to judge whether a man speaks the truth about God appearing in a dream or an angel appearing in a brilliant light to give him an order?

Smith's most troubling revelation was recorded in 1843. Doctrine and Covenants 132 is the New and Everlasting Covenant of Marriage, which proclaims that only men with multiple wives will reach the celestial kingdom. Anyone who knows about polygamy but doesn't practise it forfeits salvation: "then are ye damned; for no one can reject this covenant and be permitted to enter into my glory." In short, be a polygamist or go to hell.

The New and Everlasting Covenant of Marriage also supersedes God's commandment about adultery: "If any man espouse a virgin, and desire to espouse another, and the first give her consent, and if he espouse the second, and they are virgins, and have vowed to no other man, then is he justified; he cannot commit adultery for they are given unto him; for he cannot commit adultery with that that belongeth unto him and to no one else. And if he have ten virgins given unto him by this law, he cannot commit adultery, for they belong to him, and they are given unto him; therefore is he justified."

Doctrine and Covenants 132 was recorded twelve years after Smith claimed it was revealed to him. By the time it was written down, Smith already had plural wives and was well aware of the furor the revelation would cause. His first wife, Emma Hale Smith, was horrified by the revelation and the idea of polygamy. When rumours began to circulate that Smith was a polygamist, Emma refused to believe them. She gave speeches insisting on her husband's monogamy, expressing her revulsion towards plural marriage and defending Smith's good name. It seems even God was aware of Emma's feelings, because included in Doctrine and Covenants 132 is his warning to her, "If she will not abide this commandment, she shall be destroyed."

No one is certain how many wives Smith had. Historians have put the number at anywhere from twenty-eight to eighty-four. There is also disagreement over the ages and identities of the wives. Some say the youngest were fourteen and that they included the wives and daughters of some of his closest friends.

Smith's controversial new religion forced him to keep moving his family west in search of the New Zion. His hagiography is filled with descriptions of persecution. He was once tarred by vigilantes who broke into his house. He was arrested numerous times for disturbing the peace and other minor charges. It was no secret that several of his wives lived together in his house, but because polygamy was not illegal, Smith was never arrested for practising it.

In 1844, Smith was in custody in Carthage, Illinois, charged with inciting a riot after having ordered the destruction of the *Nauvoo Expositor*'s printing press. He said the newspaper's first and only edition aimed to destroy "the institutions of the city, both civil and religious. Its proprietors are a set of unprincipled scoundrels, who attempted in every possible way to defame the character of the most virtuous of our community."

The *Expositor* had a different view of the virtuous. Its stated aim was "to explode the vicious principles of Joseph Smith, and those who practice the same abominations and whoredoms."

The newspaper's owners also weren't keen on Smith's most recent pronouncement. Only a month earlier, according to biographer Richard Lyman Bushman, Smith had told his followers: "God was one of the free intelligences who had learned to become God. The other free intelligences were to take the same path . . . Souls were meant to grow from smaller to greater." What Smith was teaching was that all men (that is, not women) had the potential to be gods. In short, theological debate had sparked a religious riot.

Smith was arrested with his brother Hyrum and held in an unlocked and unbarred debtors' cell in the Carthage jail. With assassination rumours rife, supporters who had come to visit them had managed to sneak a six-shooter to Joseph and a single-shot pistol to Hyrum.

Late in the afternoon of June 27, 1844, a crowd of armed men gathered outside the jail. A few ran up the stairs, while others fired shots through the unbarred window of the apartment. Hyrum died first, of wounds from musket balls that had struck him in the face, thigh, torso and shin. Joseph fired into the hallway before trying to escape through the window. A musket ball from behind struck him in the hip. He was shot three more times in the chest. "O Lord, my God!" he cried before he fell from the window to the street. One of the mob propped his body up against a curb and, under orders from Colonel Levi Williams, four men fired at the prophet simultaneously. Smith died within seconds. Another of the men, John Taylor, was wounded in the thigh, but survived.

Brigham Young, president of the group of twelve apostles known as the Quorum of Twelve, quickly stepped in to take the prophet's place, even though Emma Hale Smith had argued that her eldest son, twelve-year-old Joseph Smith III, was the rightful successor. Young's leadership was confirmed at a meeting on August 8, where some people claimed they witnessed the miracle of Young transfigured into Smith, "clothed in a sheen of light covering him to his feet." "The mantle of Joseph had fallen upon" Brigham Young, said Wilford Woodruff, one of the twelve apostles, who would later also become the prophet.

Young was so committed to maintaining and practising polygamy that he married eight of Smith's widows. But he knew that Mormons were no longer safe in Illinois and, in 1846, led more than ten thousand Mormons on a long trek west that ended at the Great Salt Lake Basin in Utah. There he began building a Mormon theocracy.

Emma Smith never went to Salt Lake City. In 1860, she made a final break with Brigham Young and the LDS. She transferred her loyalty and support to her eldest son and his

Reorganized Church of Jesus Christ of Latter Day Saints, which rejected polygamy. Both Emma and her son believed that plural marriage had been Young's idea and that "Joseph, the Martyr" would have renounced it had he lived longer. The remnants of the reformed church survive as the Community of Christ.

Charles Ora Card's parents were among the pioneers who had followed Brigham Young west. By the time of Card's arrest in 1886, the territory that would became Utah was populated almost entirely by Mormons. They held all of the top positions in the government, the judiciary, the police, and the schools and businesses, as they do today. Despite that, Mormons were still subject to federal laws, including the antipolygamy law. Because of that law, hundreds of men were fugitives and hundreds more took those men in and kept them hidden.

In September 1886, after weeks of travelling at night from one safe house to another, Card bought a wagon and began gathering supplies. He planned to flee along a well-trodden fugitives' path to one of several Mormon colonies already established in Mexico. But as he prepared to head south, Card got a message from Prophet John Taylor, Smith's friend who had survived the shootout and succeeded Young as the church's third president, prophet, seer and revelator. Like Card, Taylor was a polygamist and a fugitive.

Taylor instructed Card to head north to Canada to seek "asylum and justice" in the British territory. Trained as a Methodist preacher, Taylor had emigrated from England with his parents to Toronto, where the young minister quickly fell under the spell of Joseph Smith's teaching.

Perhaps Taylor's British heritage led him to believe that Mormons might be more welcome in Canada than in the United States. However, there was nothing in English law that would have supported this belief. Bigamy had been outlawed in England since 1603—second marriages were not allowed "until their former Wyves and former Husbands be deade."

Taylor's desire to establish a Canadian colony was further influenced by Smith's prophecy that England—the most powerful country in the world at the time—would be the last to fall in the days of Armageddon before God destroys the earth. So, it would be from soil under British rule that Taylor believed the most righteous would be lifted up in the final days. There was a pragmatic consideration as well. Canada was so desperate for settlers to justify its recently completed national railway and to secure its sovereignty over the West that it was recruiting members of persecuted religious groups, such as the Hutterites and Doukhobors, to emigrate from Europe.

In mid-September, Card went north with two other men. Because Card was a wanted man, he and his companions travelled under assumed names. They went by train to Spokane Falls, Washington, where they bought saddle ponies and pack horses. They crossed the Columbia River by ferry and entered British Columbia on September 29, 1886. Card wrote in his diary that when they crossed the border he took off his hat, "swung it around and shouted 'In Columbia, we are free.'"

Despite his initial optimism, Card could not find what he was looking for in British Columbia. Settlers already occupied the best land and Card deemed the mountain valleys too rugged for agriculture. He and his companions crossed the Rocky Mountains into what is now Alberta. There, they found a buffalo plain only nine miles from the U.S. border, deemed it suitable for settlement, staked a claim and headed back to Utah.

When Card told Taylor about the site, the prophet ordered him to enlist colonists and return north that spring.

Forty-one names were on the list Card titled "Missionaries for the Land Desolation." These people moved north and founded the town of Cardston, which remains the heart of Canadian Mormonism.

Over the next three years, more than three hundred Mormons moved to Cardston and the villages clustered nearby. A few brought more than one wife, but most, like Card, brought only one. Almost invariably, Mormon historian Jessie Embry says, it wasn't the first wives or even the legal wives who the men brought; it was the youngest. The other wives and their children were left to survive on their own, with help from the church and occasional offerings from their pioneering husbands, who came on infrequent visits.

In 1888, Card went to Ottawa to meet with Prime Minister Sir John A. Macdonald along with two members of the Quorum of Twelve—the most senior advisers to the LDS president and prophet. They wanted permission to bring their plural wives and families to Canada. In their lengthy brief to Macdonald, they asked for "an abiding place in peace in Canada where they [Mormon men] can provide for their families, educate their children and not be compelled to cast them off and subject them to the charities of the cold world, thus breaking faith with their tender and devoted wives, innocent children and with God, our Father, from whose hand we received them."

Macdonald refused. Even though Canada had offered concessions to the Mennonites in 1874, including military exemptions and the right to teach their children the German language, there was no way the prime minister of Canada would agree to polygamy. After the Mormons left, Macdonald instructed the North West Mounted Police to watch out for any men practising polygamy.

Public opinion on Mormons and polygamy was divided. The *Lethbridge News* supported the settlers. In an editorial on

*Charles Ora Card's Alberta homestead. Polygamist Mormons
tended to bring only their youngest wives along for the difficult work
of settling in Canada.* (**Glenbow Museum**)

August 17, 1887, it concluded that attacks on Mormons were
"unwarranted." "It is characteristic of some of the eastern
papers in dealing with Northwest matters to jump at conclusions and make a mountain out of a mole hill. A recent example of this is the agitation which many of them are now
experiencing because some settlers from Utah have found
their way into southern Alberta." One of those eastern papers
was the *Toronto Mail*, which continued to warn of the dangers
of Mormons settling the west. In June 1889, it concluded that
the Mormons "must leave their superfluous wives behind
them or Canada must erect more gaols in the Territories."

North West Mounted Police officer Sam Steele wrote a
report on the Mormons to the prime minister in 1889. "The
Mormons are believed by almost all of the people in the district to be practising polygamy in secret." He said they were
"as perfect slaves to the Church and Elders as it is possible for
any community of people to be," adding "the intelligence of

the Mormon is far below the average intelligence of the set-tlers of any country." Still, Steele concluded that Mormons were "very industrious people and have made a better show towards success than any settlement in the district."

This was to be the first of more than a century's worth of contradictory and somewhat exasperated (and often exasperat-ing) assessments of polygamous Mormons. On the one hand, they were hard-working and good for the economy. On the other, they seemed determined to break the law. Such assess-ments have meant that, for more than one hundred years, the polygamous Saints have lived on society's fringes and created a culture of obfuscation and distortion.

Prime Minister Macdonald received many letters from concerned citizens. One of the letter writers, Robert Scott, had lived for fourteen years in Tooele County, Utah. Scott urged Macdonald not to let the Mormons get a foothold in Canada because they judge men by their "religious proclivi-ties," favour the brethren by establishing positions "unknown to the law" and then pay their appointees handsomely. He also warned: "There is no equality nor republican ideas among them for the priesthood is supreme in all things."

After Steele's report, Charles Card's assistant Orson Smith wrote to Macdonald in January 1890 denying that any Mormons were practising polygamy. "There has been nothing of the kind attempted or even contemplated. So far, not a sin-gle attempt has been made by any member of this colony to break the faith established between the Government and our representatives. Therefore, we can truthfully say that the charge is unfounded."

Despite the Mormon leadership's placating words and promises, the Canadian government could scarcely ignore the enthusiasm of recent convert Maitland Stenhouse and his high-profile promise to practise polygamy. He had ostensibly

Mormon leaders John A. Woolf, Henry L. Hinman and Charles Ora Card. Polygamist Mormons have been a problem for politicians and police from the moment they settled in Canada.
(Glenbow Museum)

resigned his seat in the B.C. legislature in 1887 to move to Salt Lake City and be baptized a Mormon. He never made it. Instead, he moved to Cardston and told reporters he planned to show up at the altar with two women and simultaneously marry them to prove his claim. He missed his chance.

In February 1890, the Canadian government criminalized bigamy and "any form of polygamy . . . what is among the persons called Mormons known as 'spiritual or plural marriage.'" What was striking about the legislation, however, was that bigamy was a felony with a penalty of up to seven years in prison, while "spiritual or plural marriage" of Mormons was only a misdemeanour with a penalty of up to five years in jail and a fine of five hundred dollars. Historian Brian Campion called the legislation "an unofficial, but workable relationship between the Mormons and the authorities." Not a single Mormon has ever been prosecuted.

That same year, with the U.S. government threatening to strip all Mormons—even those who were not polygamous—of their right to vote, the Mormon church buckled. The president of the Church, Wilford Woodruff, issued a Manifesto suspending the earthly practice of plural marriage until some later, unspecified date. The Manifesto repudiated one of the commandments that their prophet ostensibly got directly from God. Woodruff conceded on this crucial point to ensure that Utah would be granted statehood, to end the persecution and to begin the realignment of the Church of Jesus Christ of Latter-day Saints that would bring the LDS closer to mainstream society. Mormons call this change "the Great Accommodation." But, despite the Manifesto, the church hierarchy turned a blind eye to plural marriages that had been performed pre-Manifesto, and even privately sanctioned dozens of "celestial marriages" after it.

The LDS was so keen to gain the U.S. government's support for the statehood bid (which was finally granted in January 1896) that it had launched a public relations campaign in 1887, spending $144,000 to persuade key newspapers not to print negative items and, if possible, to publish positive ones. Immediately following the Manifesto, Woodruff ordered fugitives like Card to turn themselves in and be tried for the crime of polygamy. Card was acquitted in August 1890 because the jury—a majority, if not all, were Mormons—didn't believe the testimony of Card's first wife, Sarah Jane Birdneau.

Card returned to Alberta to live with his fourth wife, Zina Young Card. But he maintained conjugal relations with his other wives throughout his life, visiting them frequently in Utah. Card and most Saints originally from the U.S. complied with Canadian law only to the extent that they didn't bring their other wives into Canada. Mormon historian Jessie Embry's research indicates that the majority of the church's Canadian leaders had at least two wives. In 1895, the four most senior Mormons in Alberta were polygamists. Of the twelve men on the high council, ten were polygamists. More than half of the high priests were polygamists. Most of those plural marriages predated Woodruff's Manifesto, but not all.

In a report that proved to be remarkably accurate, almost prescient, the North West Mounted Police offered a warning to the government in 1899: "These people are up to all kinds of dodges for shielding polygamy which necessity taught them in the U.S.A. and if it gets a footing in Canada will be very hard to stamp out, perhaps next to impossible."

Meanwhile, Card's community was not only thriving economically, it was growing rapidly, urged on by an aggressive campaign by the Canadian government and the Mormon hierarchy. John W. Taylor, who had gone to Ottawa in 1888 with Charles Card and was the son of Mormon president John Taylor, had been appointed by the church to direct emigration to Canada. Even though John W. had six wives (and thirty-six children), he had managed to get on the Canadian government's payroll as a sub-agent for the immigration department. His job was to recruit settlers as well as investors to move to Alberta, dig canals and establish an irrigation system that would give rise to the lucrative sugar beet industry. The government rejected his initial request for $150 a month in expenses. Instead, Canada offered Taylor "$2 per head on every male adult and $2 per head on every female over 18 years of age and $1 per head on all under 18 years."

Taylor was sent a book of certificates that he was to fill out with the immigrants' names, ages and so on. Those certificates were to be collected and endorsed by the customs official and forwarded to Ottawa. "It need not be known by your people that you are being paid by the government, the certificate being something that the department would require anyway in order to keep a check on the number of people who come into the country both overland and by rail," W. J. White wrote from Ottawa in June 1899, soon after he'd returned from a meeting with Taylor in Salt Lake City.

It was a huge mistake. Over the next four years, the government's accounting of the number of Saints that Taylor had helped move north and Taylor's accounting never matched. He proved to be a splendid, if not entirely trustworthy, recruiter. Even after he and Card had given their word to the Canadian prime minister that Mormon settlers would obey the antipolygamy law, Taylor performed plural marriages in Alberta, possibly even on trips subsidized by the Canadian government. At least three are known to have occurred in 1903 alone.

In an undated invoice on letterhead from "the office of The First Presidency of the Church of Jesus Christ of Latter-day Saints," Taylor submitted a bill of nine hundred dollars. At the time, that was roughly equivalent to the full-time annual salary for an office manager. But the government had no evidence of settlers that matched that amount. Despite frequent letters from various bureaucrats, the certificates never seemed to arrive and the lists of certified settlers seem to constantly go missing. Taylor claimed he had delivered more than four thousand people, but the Canadian government was able to account for only 2,085.

In 1902, White was told by the deputy minister of immigration to try to sort it out. After "the most careful investigation," White determined that of 1,306 people Taylor claimed on one list, only a third had actually stayed in Canada. On another list, Taylor claimed 784 immigrants without providing any evidence.

After several years of claims and counterclaims, in 1903 the government paid Taylor far less than he'd demanded and terminated his contract. It's not clear whether one of the most powerful Mormon leaders had tried to trick the Canadian government into paying him nearly twice what he'd earned or whether a Canadian bureaucrat was pocketing the extra money. But the last communication the federal government sent to John W. Taylor, Esquire, in Salt Lake City was returned covered with stamps and notices to return to sender.

Taylor had fled. He was excommunicated in 1905 for performing plural marriages. But it's an indication of the continued ambiguity regarding polygamy within the mainstream Mormon church that Taylor's excommunication was posthumously rescinded not once, but twice. He was first reinstated by proxy a few months after his death in 1916. A year later that was declared null and void. But, in 1965, Taylor was again rebaptized by proxy and reinstated.

Although Taylor may have lied about the number of Mormons he'd helped immigrate, by 1901 Alberta's Mormon population had grown to 6,891. A decade later, there were 15,971 Mormons in Alberta, and among them was a young couple from Idaho. Mary Christina (Tina) Ada Horn and William Morris Blackmore rate no mention in the early public records. But their contribution was an extraordinary family that included a member of Parliament and a grandson named Winston, who would become one of the richest and most powerful polygamists in North America.

———

An unpublished family history of William Blackmore speaks glowingly of the hard-working patriarch. When he was only eleven or twelve, William ran away from his home in England

and joined the merchant marine. In the tales he later told his children, he was shipwrecked "more than once" and nearly killed several times in wicked storms. In the swashbuckling tradition of the high seas, William emerges in the history as stubborn and quick to anger. At one point he nearly kills a man on board—an event that his son John puts the best possible spin on, suggesting that the man had "persecuted" his father: "Father had wonderful self-control, but it was possible for him to reach a breaking point and he was then relatively only a boy."

Heavily tattooed on his arms, neck and chest, William jumped ship once in England, only to be found and returned. At nineteen, he deserted ship once more, this time in New York City. William escaped and headed to Idaho to visit his maternal aunt. He found work there and stayed on to help his uncle after his aunt died, leaving four young children, including Tina, who was twelve years younger than him. At one point, William went back to England to marry his childhood sweetheart, but the marriage was called off just days before the ceremony, after William had a fight with the bride's family over the serving of alcohol at the reception. By then William was a Mormon and had sworn not to drink alcohol, coffee or tea or to use tobacco. In his family history, William's son John muses about whether his father might have been like other sailors, drinking and whoring in every port of call: "Did he ever get drunk and if he did, did he do it again? More serious still, did he ever have any sexual relations with any girl or woman? The evidence that has come to me, indicates very strongly that he never did . . . [H]e had become a very devout, conscientious and scrupulous Latter-day Saint." Of course, by then, William was an elder in the church, and if he had memories of grog-sodden nights in the brothels of his many ports of call, they may not have been exactly the sort of thing he would have passed on to his young son.

Having left his childhood sweetheart at the altar, William returned to his uncle's home in Idaho and began courting his first cousin Tina. She was fifteen and he was twenty-seven when their marriage was sealed for time and all eternity. But because of William's temper, the Blackmores didn't stay long in Idaho.

After a fight with a neighbour over use of water in an irrigation ditch, William read a Canadian government ad for immigrants in the local newspaper. He sold his house for four hundred dollars, bought some tools and a wagon and set out for Alberta in May 1892, temporarily leaving behind his wife, two-year-old son and a baby.

Tina followed him to Cardston a few months later, arriving to find that William had broken his leg and that their home was far from finished. It was built of sod and tarpaper. The house had no windows, no insulation and not even chinking or daubing to keep out the howling prairie wind. With the help of neighbours, it was finished in time for winter. Still, it was rudimentary at best.

After the first snowfall that November, Tina took two-year-old John to visit their closest neighbours, who lived more than three miles away. While playing "horse," John was injured in a freak accident. According to one family history, John "made an abrupt turn on some ice and his legs were violently spraddled. A scream of pain brought everyone in haste to discover the little boy's leg was almost torn from his body. The open ends of the tendons and bleeding muscles confirmed the seriousness of the injury."

Tina rushed her toddler home. The next day, she sought the advice of Zina Card, who suggested a number of home remedies to take the stiffness away. But the little boy's leg was limp and wouldn't hold his weight. A few days later, William Blackmore readied his wagon for the fifty-mile trip to Lethbridge to pick up coal. There was a doctor there, but William decided not to take his son with him. William told Tina the trip was too rough for their injured son, that it required fording rivers. Besides, there was scarcely enough money for food, let alone doctors. He told Tina to pray for their son.

John survived. According to one account, he was so frail that he had to be carried around on a pillow. By the time he was seven, his mother was losing heart. Her second son had died at age two and she had just buried an infant daughter. Following the funeral, Zina Card suggested that everyone in the community fast and pray for three days before a special meeting at Bishop J. A. Hammer's home to seek the Lord's blessing on little John. (The practice of praying and fasting was common in the community. In 1897, Charles Card had called a special fast to make the snow melt. Whether it was divine intervention or just a chinook, a warm wind began blowing soon after the prayer meeting ended.)

At the beginning of the special prayer meeting for John, Zina upbraided William for failing to take his son to the doctor after the accident. Then she began speaking in tongues. John's third-person account of the family history, written nearly fifty years after the event, says two women translated as Zina spoke. Not only would John survive, Zina is reported to have said, "He will grow up and do great work and in due time will go back to the Halls of Congress in Canada and represent the Mormon people."

With that optimistic prophesy, John wrote that his parents set a strict regime of exercises and chores aimed at increasing his strength. When he was strong enough, William took his son to a Lethbridge hospital. William dropped him off, took the boy's clothes with him and left the hospital without saying goodbye. It was months before William and Tina returned to visit and then they only stayed one day. Doctors experimented with repairing the tendons and muscles. But even after sixteen months in hospital, there was no miracle cure. John was fitted with an iron brace, sent home and, at thirteen, finally started school.

Meanwhile, William was working the homestead, doing odd jobs and making quite a name for himself. He brawled with neighbours, got fired from his job shearing sheep ("The crew managed to get him fired," according to John) and rose in the LDS church to the position of elder. After his fifth child was born, William went on a church mission to England for eight months, leaving Tina behind with three children under nine and a farm to run. So much for Mormon family values.

John proved a quick learner when he finally started school. Ten years later, in 1913, the twenty-three-year-old was in the University of Alberta's first graduating class. Two years later, at the request of the Mormon stake president, John completed his teacher's training and was hired to teach at the church's Knight Academy in Raymond, Alberta. He worked there for twenty-one years, the last ten years as principal. In his son Harold's account of the family history, John was "a brilliant student" and a "superb athlete," despite his disability. According to Harold, his father won regional university wrestling and boxing championships by hopping about on his one good leg. If that's true, John didn't mention it in his own telling.

Soon after moving to Raymond, John went to the post office and met pretty young Emily Woolley, who worked there. Within a year, they were married in a temple ceremony in Salt Lake City. Temple marriages seal a couple for "time and all eternity," which means that husband and wife will be reunited in bodily form in heaven along with their children. And if they are reunited in heaven's highest realm (the celestial kingdom), they will continue to have children and expand their families. To have their marriage sealed this way, John and Emily spent all the money they had. The newlyweds returned in August with only one dollar left until John got his paycheque at the end of September. Money is a theme that runs through the Blackmore history in Canada.

In 1917, two years after John's marriage, William died suddenly at the age of fifty-five. He had no savings. William's wife, Tina, was left with a farm to run and nine children under the age of fifteen—the youngest was eleven months old. John did what he could to help his mother and siblings, but he had his own family of ten to take care of. Teachers didn't earn much, but their wages dwindled to almost nothing in the crippling depression of the 1930s. In 1932, even though he was the principal, John's salary was $1,633.10. Only a third of that was cash. The remainder was in promissory notes.

"Our family was steadily increasing while our income was rapidly decreasing," John's oldest son, Harold, wrote in his memoir. "In one year alone, doctor and hospital bills far exceeded the year's income—a birth, a death and a funeral, broken bones and numerous other problems put us desperately behind. Our little four-room house was woefully inadequate for 11 people so an addition was attempted. When only roughly boarded on the outside, our finances were depleted and we never could finish it."

In 1934, Harold persuaded his father to attend a meeting where William Aberhart was speaking. Aberhart was a radio evangelist whose show was broadcast on Sundays throughout the Prairies. Because Aberhart was also the leader of the Social Credit Party, a regional protest party, his sermons were a curious blend of religion and economics.

Social Credit was based on the notion that if there wasn't enough money, the government should simply print more and distribute it to stimulate the economy. The early Socreds, as they were called, were virulently anti-Communist and anti-Semitic, believing in a world economic conspiracy of "political Zionists," Jews like the Rothschilds.

Aberhart's message captured the despair and discontent of men like John Blackmore, who were suffering and near starving after years of drought. With the blessing of their stake president, lots of Mormons, including John, bought party memberships. Soon, the LDS leaders began encouraging Mormons to run for the party. Again, John was one of them. He'd belonged to a debating society during college, and as a student and LDS elder, he was a seasoned speaker. According to Harold's memoirs, Aberhart asked his father to run in the 1935 provincial election, offering him his choice of three ridings. John declined, but, the following year, he agreed to run in the federal election.

In 1936, the Socreds won every seat in Alberta. Earl Pingree Tanner, a prominent LDS elder, congratulated John Blackmore on his victory. "I have always looked forward to the time when we could send one of our own people back to Ottawa," he wrote. "While I feel you will have the interests of all electors at heart, yet I believe you will find time to explain some of the scientific [sic] aspects of Mormonism to the leaders of this great country of ours." Tanner wished him success and signed off as a friend and brother "in the Cause of Truth."

At age forty-five, John Blackmore fulfilled Zina Card's prophecy. He was the first Mormon elected to the House of Commons. He had also been chosen as the Social Credit Party's national leader, a role he filled until 1944, when he was replaced by another Alberta Mormon, Solon Low.

The Depression didn't only bring about political and social change. More than forty years after the Manifesto suspending the earthly practice of polygamy, Joseph Smith's church was experiencing its own upheaval and internal dissent. "A complete breakdown threatens the monogamistic order of marriage, the boast of modern civilization," Joseph Musser wrote on the front page in the first edition of a newsletter called *Truth*. "Gnawing at its very vitals, to which the glorious principle of marriage is slowly but surely succumbing, are the death-dealing agencies of infidelity, birth control and divorce." With a perverse kind of logic, Musser believed that the only way to save the very institution of marriage was to radically alter it. What he was proposing was a return to the practice of polygamy.

He wasn't the only one agitating for its return, and throughout the Mormon community, plural marriage was once again being seriously considered by other priesthood men. Musser's newsletter was their rallying point. Priesthood men, including John Blackmore, began holding clandestine "cottage meetings" where they questioned whether the leaders of the Church of Jesus Christ of Latter-day Saints were hypocrites, denying God's commandment to practise "the Principle" of plural or "celestial marriage." Blackmore often went to the meetings with his oldest son, Harold. Because Blackmore had difficulty walking very far even with canes, Harold literally took him there. John would perch sideways on the frame of his son's sturdy bicycle while Harold pedalled like mad.

THREE

THE PROMISED LAND

In 1947, John Blackmore was celebrating Christmas at home in Cardston with his wife, Emily, when he got word from Salt Lake City that he had been excommunicated. The Council of the First Presidency, the ruling body of the Church of Jesus Christ of Latter-day Saints (LDS), had ousted one of its highest-profile Canadian members for "teaching and advocating the doctrine of plural marriage." It's not clear whether Blackmore was invited to appear before the council to defend himself and didn't go or whether he was denied that opportunity altogether. However, accounts from others who have been excommunicated suggest that it wouldn't have mattered. The accused is given little chance at the church hearings to mount any kind of defence.

His excommunication meant that in the eyes of the church, Blackmore was worse than a nonbeliever; he was an apostate who had denied the One True Church. He was a man doomed to something worse than other Christians' perception of hell. Instead of going bodily to one of the three realms of heaven to live eternally with his family, Blackmore (and any of his family who didn't denounce him) would be ground into nothingness when he died and float in boundless blackness for eternity.

When a Canadian Press reporter called Blackmore at home on December 28, he said, "No comment is necessary." But in a public statement the following day, Blackmore said, "I deny the charge. I definitely declare I have done no wrong; that I have not consciously broken any of the Ten Commandments or violated any of the principles of the Sermon on the Mount; that I am the husband of only one wife and that to her I have always been scrupulously faithful. I have merely discussed and defended the doctrine of plural marriage as a biblical principle."

Blackmore's excommunication was front-page news in Canada and Utah, and was prominently featured in *Newsweek* magazine's Canadian edition. Even though Blackmore was convicted by his church of counselling illegal activity, the *Toronto Star* ran an editorial supporting him, praising him as a proper Mormon and oddly suggesting the path to infidelity and polygamy might be paved with tobacco and carbonated drinks. "He is not the sort of man to take his excommunication lying down," the *Star* editorialist wrote. "At 57, he is still full of fight. He conforms to the rule of his church that members should neither smoke nor drink; in fact even soft drinks are looked upon with disfavour."

Blackmore's expulsion from the church hurt him and his family deeply. It led to unpleasant jabs thrown at him by opposing politicians across the floor of the House of Commons. Worse, it cut him off from his own people, his community, the society in which he had grown up and the church that had not only provided for him spiritually but also paid his salary. Surprisingly, it never hurt him at the ballot box. Since Joseph Smith's time, Mormons have tended to vote as a bloc, supporting other Mormons if they run or the gentiles that the LDS priesthood deems most sympathetic to its interests. Blackmore was re-elected in general elections in the years 1949 and 1953. After nearly twenty-three years of representing Lethbridge, he was defeated in 1958, the year the Social Credit Party collapsed and failed to win a single seat in Parliament.

Blackmore revealed his undiminished devotion to Mormonism during his last two terms, when he persuaded the Canadian government to amend its antipolygamy law. In the 1952 updating of the Criminal Code, the reference to the religious or plural marriages of "persons commonly called Mormons" was deleted from the definition of polygamy. John Blackmore never took another wife in his eighty-one years of life. But, unlike John W. Taylor, Blackmore has never been rehabilitated in the eyes of the church. His name isn't mentioned in the LDS-sanctioned *History of the Mormon Church in Canada*. Blackmore rates a brief mention along with Solon Low, a Mormon who succeeded him as Social Credit leader, in *The Mormon Presence in Canada*, which was edited by Charles Card's son Brigham Young Card. In the book it's stated that "While these men did receive some publicity because of their status as leader of a small protest party, neither ever moved far from the obscurity of the opposition backbenches in Ottawa."

At the time of Blackmore's excommunication, the LDS had begun a massive expansion and recruitment program. Overseas missionary work that had been abandoned during the Second World War was resumed. Those efforts would have been at risk if people like Joseph Musser, Rulon Allred and the other fundamentalists were able to revive polygamy and stir up public enmity against the church. By excommunicating Blackmore, who was one of the highest-profile Mormons in the country, the LDS church sent a sharp warning to Canadian members that there would be no flirtation with fundamentalists, no debate over "the everlasting covenant of celestial marriage" and no challenges to the leadership.

That didn't put an end to the cottage meetings or stop the underground circulation of *Truth*. It certainly didn't dampen the enthusiasm of Blackmore's eldest son, Harold, or John's youngest brother, Joseph Ray, for polygamy. If anything, it may even have encouraged them. Both Harold and Ray were LDS members who had done their two years of unpaid missionary work for the church. After graduating from teachers' college in Calgary, Harold had gone to Ottawa as the mission's president the same year his father first took his seat in Parliament.

Dressed in his dark suit, white shirt and tie, Harold roamed the streets of Canada's capital looking for souls to save. His mission didn't go unnoticed. Soon local ministers began attacking Mormonism by raising the spectre of polygamy. They wrote letters to the local newspapers. Harold later said that it was because of their attacks that he began "a continuing and exhaustive study" of polygamy and its practice.

The tall, handsome young Blackmore made few converts in the capital. But one of the other missionaries certainly attracted his attention. Gwendolyn Williams was a petite, round-faced teacher from a devout Mormon family in Idaho. She was twenty-three and was wary of twenty-five-year-old Blackmore's evident interest in her.

"She was a faithful and diligent worker and [had a] sweet and friendly disposition," Blackmore later wrote in one of his many self-published pamphlets extolling the virtues of plural marriage. "It was not long before the thought occurred to me that she would make a wonderful wife. She was so circumspect that I had little opportunity to cultivate her friendship. When my time was up, I voluntarily stayed on four months longer

*Gwen Williams, future wife of polygamist
proselytizer Harold Blackmore.*
(Photo courtesy of Brenda Williams Jensen)

until her release [from the mission work] in order to plead my
case and beg her hand. She finally responded and I joyfully
returned home to prepare for her coming to be my wife."

After more than two years of unpaid work for the church,
Harold used his last five dollars to buy a wedding ring. Gwen
spent her last five dollars on the marriage licence. They were
sealed for time and all eternity in Cardston's Mormon temple
and moved into the basement of John and Emily Blackmore's
home. They stayed there for a few months before being hired
to care for "an old blind lady" in return for room and board.
After a full year with the blind lady, Harold and Gwen had
earned just $118.

At the end of that year, Harold began to seriously consider practising the Principle of plural marriage, and so did Gwen. According to Harold, they had been attending a temple marriage of a widower to a second wife when temple president E. J. Wood suddenly stopped and turned to Gwen. "Sister Gwen, do you realize that plural marriage is a correct principle and must be lived?" The young bride blushed and then stammered that the Manifesto had declared plural marriage was no longer applicable on earth. But Wood contradicted her and the church's directive. "No. No. No. I want you to know that it is required of us and must be lived."

Gwen didn't keep a diary or record her thoughts about polygamy. So we're left with Harold's memoirs and the stories Gwen told her daughters and nieces about the decision. Harold wrote that together they studied the stories of polygamy in the Bible, in the Doctrine and Covenants and in the writings of people like Musser. They concluded that any person who had ever participated in a Mormon temple ceremony had promised to live by every one of Smith's commandments set out in the Doctrine and Covenants.

If they believed Smith was a prophet and his revelations came directly from God, Harold asked, how could they pick and choose which were correct? And if Smith was God's voice on earth, were they willing to risk eternal damnation by not following the Principle, since Doctrine and Covenants 132 says "if ye abide not that covenant, then are ye damned; for no one can reject this covenant and be permitted to enter into my glory."

In his memoirs, titled *We Three in Polygamy*, Harold writes: "We resolved that if ever we found the opportunity and a way was opened up, we would live that commandment." Perhaps Gwen believed that day would never come. Heaven knows they had pressing temporal concerns. They had nothing.

No money. No jobs. No home. Besides, Harold was impulsive like his grandfather, William. A few months after they had resolved that polygamy was a possibility in the future, a new area about 150 miles from Cardston was being opened up for homesteaders. Land was cheap and poor people could buy on good terms. Harold and Gwen borrowed thirty-five dollars and secured a homestead.

They didn't stay long enough to even get settled. Within three months, Harold was hired to teach at a six-room Mormon school in Raymond, Alberta. For ten dollars, Harold bought a lot and some used materials to build their new home. The two-room shack was about the size of the average living room. Harold had never built anything before, but he began to learn the basics of what would become the one-time teacher's later job as a building contractor.

Even though Harold and Gwen had apparently decided that at some point they would defy Canadian law and their church by practising polygamy, they continued to be faithful Mormons whose devotion was rewarded with "temple recommends"—letters from their bishop attesting to their piety that granted them entry into the temple and allowed them to participate in various secret rituals. Harold advanced through the ranks. He was an elder, which meant he was able to baptize converts, invoke the Holy Ghost through the laying on of hands, and transform wine and bread into the Body and Blood of Jesus Christ in commemoration of the Last Supper.

They wanted and prayed for children, but Gwen had been unable to conceive and thereby become a "mother in Zion." No doubt, Harold frequently reminded her about the story of Sarah in the Old Testament—a Bible story much loved and often cited by polygamists. As the story goes, when Sarah was unable to conceive she instructed her husband, Abraham, to take her slave-girl Hagar as a second wife. (After Hagar's son was born, Sarah became pregnant, leading to one of the Old Testament's more awkward domestic arrangements.)

When Gwen was twenty-seven, the couple filled out adoption forms and were told that they would soon be getting a baby boy. But before the child arrived, Gwen became pregnant. They went ahead with the adoption and the baby arrived just a few months before their own son was born. When those two children were barely out of diapers, Gwen was pregnant again. Both Gwen and Harold wanted a big family. It was what their church urged them to do. So, even though he rarely changed a diaper throughout his life, Harold thought the experiment with the near-twins had gone so well that they should do it again. Just a few months before their daughter, Lorna Jean, was born, they adopted a baby boy.

Having outgrown the tiny shack, the Blackmores bought thirty-five acres of land near Rosemary, Alberta, and built a twelve-room house. Before the house was finished, Gwen was pregnant again. They now had four children under four, but Harold was enthusiastic about adopting again. It's possible that Gwen believed by giving Harold as many children as he wanted, she might stave off his desire for a second wife. It's also possible that by saddling Gwen with so many children, Harold hoped she would see the benefits of having another woman in the house to share the load. For whatever reason, Gwen went along with the madness.

Given their apparent enthusiasm for adoption, one might have thought the Blackmores would have worked hard to blend their family. But they didn't. Harold and Gwen always clearly differentiated between their own children and the ones they'd adopted. There were their "blood children" and the "other children." None of the children was ever spoiled, but the "other children" always got the least when food and favours were divided up. And they got the harshest beatings

when punishment was meted out. Gwen was a stern discipli-
narian who never spared the rod. All of the children were
beaten for the slightest offences, but the adopted ones always
got the worst of it.

As the family grew, Harold prospered. Not only was he
teaching as well as farming, he'd set up a grain-elevator company. But the history of Canadian polygamy might have been
very different had Harold not met a practising polygamist who
happened to be visiting relatives in Raymond. The man,
whom Harold did not identify in his memoir, gave him a copy
of Brigham Young's 1874 sermon on plural marriage that
urged Mormons to follow Joseph Smith's teachings regardless
of the repercussions.

The unidentified man was probably Owen Allred, a life-
long friend of Harold's who became the leader of a fundamentalist Mormon sect called the Apostolic United Brethren.
Allred wasn't the only fundamentalist missionary making
frequent visits to Canada. Joseph Musser's son, Guy, was also
busy proselytizing. And there were others who later set up different polygamous sects, including the murderous Church of
the Firstborn in the Fullness of Time and the Latter-day
Church of Christ, which preached incest.

It was no secret that after LDS President Wilford
Woodruff had signed the Manifesto he officiated at several
celestial marriages and even took several more wives for himself. Exactly how many wives Woodruff had isn't certain.
Biographer Thomas Alexander says he had nine, others have
suggested he had eleven. That Woodruff's Manifesto and subsequent actions had discredited him without in any way
redeeming polygamy as a viable doctrine apparently never
occurred to Harold and the other proselytizers.

Like all fundamentalists, Harold had also come to believe
that the apocalypse was fast approaching, which is why there

was added urgency to the immediate reinstatement of plural marriage. With the unbridled zealotry of the recently converted, Harold preached about plural marriage and Doctrine and Covenants 132 a few weeks after his meeting with the unidentified polygamist. He did this at the Sunday meeting of Raymond's LDS congregation. Immediately afterwards, he and his family were shunned. Harold was called before a church court—a public hearing attended by more than three hundred people—and threatened with excommunication. Both his and Gwen's temple recommends were withdrawn. Harold and Gwen had become pariahs. In addition to the public shunning, Harold began to be economically shut out of the community.

"Orders were given that no Mormon was to sell grain to my elevator company," Harold wrote. "The Mormons' finest tool of destruction, the economic blockade was put into action. The withering effects were soon seen. When harvest time came, not one bushel of grain came to my elevator from a Mormon except for one bigot who stooped to replacing 50 bushels of wheat I had loaned him to plant his crops that spring—not one bushel more. The message was loud and clear—either crawl and be subject or get out!" Harold seemed surprised that flouting social values in a small community turned out to be bad for business.

Already an outcast, Harold went to Salt Lake City to meet with Joesph Musser and other fundamentalist Saints in 1945. Before he left, Gwen had told her husband that she was ready to live the Principle. Whether she made the decision out of desperation because of the demands of caring for six children under the age of six or because it might mean eternal life in the higher realm of heaven, Gwen never confided in her children. The only thing she ever told them about her decision to become a plural wife was her insistence on one condition: If she had to share her husband, there was only one woman she would accept as her sister-wife: her younger sister, Florence.

Gwen came to this conclusion, she told her children, through fasting and prayer. But she also told her children that the truth had been revealed to her and Florence years earlier by a Ouija board—a message she said she had failed to understand at the time. Ouija boards were popular divination tools used by spiritualists in Joseph Smith's day, but they are also believed by some Christians to be an instrument of Satan.

A decade before Gwen went on her LDS mission to Ottawa, she and Florence visited a psychic in their hometown of Treasureton, Idaho. Like most young girls, the big question on their minds was the name of their future husband. Gwen, two years older than Florence, went first. They placed their fingertips on the three-legged pointer and closed their eyes.

The pointer is supposedly driven by spirits acting through the fingertips of the questioners. It is placed at the bottom of a board. The letters of the alphabet are arranged in an arc at the top of the board. After the pointer inches its way up the board to the first letter, it is then repositioned at the bottom of the board and the process begins again until the word or words are spelled out completely. Getting an answer can be a tedious process. Answering Gwen's question was a particularly slow process because the name was so long. H-A-R-O-L-D B-L-A-C-K-M-O-R-E. Curiously, they knew enough not to stop after Black even though neither Gwen nor Florence had ever heard of Harold Blackmore.

Then it was Florence's turn. The pointer again started with H, then A. Once again, the spirits spelled out HAROLD BLACKMORE. Although they were Mormons, Gwen and Florence later told their children that polygamy was so far from their thinking that the only conclusion they could draw was that Gwen was destined to die young and that Florence would step into her place to console her grieving husband and raise Gwen's children. Of course, as good Mormons they had no problem with the idea that they would all be reunited as a family in heaven, where polygamy is fully accepted.

When Harold went south in 1945, he didn't just go with the intention of meeting Musser and other polygamists. He didn't just go to spend time in the dusty stacks of the LDS library, poring over thousands of pages of records and documents to find, in his words, "abundant proof of the hypocrisy, deception and ruthless hate of the modern leaders." With Gwen's blessing, Harold Blackmore stopped in Treasureton, Idaho to begin his courtship of Florence.

Florence was a teacher like both Gwen and Harold. She was an attractive, independent-minded woman given to hijinks and practical jokes. Committed to Mormonism, she too had done missionary work. But she was thirty and single, which doesn't fit the patriarchal plans for women in the LDS. Women are men's helpers, whose roles Joseph Smith had narrowly defined as being within the domestic sphere as mothers and moral guardians of as many children as possible to grow the army of Christ. Florence's daughter, Brenda, says her mother had rejected many suitors who didn't measure up intellectually or spiritually. But the fact that Florence eventually ended up a polygamist sharing a husband with her sister is a rather harsh commentary on the quality of men living in Treasureton at the time.

What's mystifying, given the extrordinarily explicit prophesies and the fact that Gwen felt close enough with her sister to share a husband, is that Gwen apparently never told Florence why Harold was suddenly coming to meet her on his way back from Salt Lake City. Stranger still, if later reports of the Ouija board prophecy are to be believed, is the reception Harold got when he showed up on Florence's doorstep. Despite having been named as her husband many years before, Harold writes that Florence was "cool" to the idea of polygamy when he raised it during that first visit. Florence later told her daughter that she was so shocked by his suggestion that she threw a book at him and called him "a dirty liar." Even so, Florence found Harold sufficiently interesting that she agreed to correspond with him. And while plural marriage wasn't the only subject of their year-long correspondence, it was the subtext.

In his letters, Harold probably pressed his perception that these were terrible times and the end was nigh. The Second World War was over and it had taken a huge toll. More than 42,000 Canadians and 300,000 Americans had been killed. In addition to the eternal benefit of being a goddess in the celestial kingdom, Harold no doubt laid out for her all of the earthly "benefits" for women in what he called the "patriarchal family." He wrote in his later pamphlets that polygamy guarantees that women "shall not be deprived of motherhood," "shall never have to endure widowhood and shall have economic security within the family structure." Women can work full-time outside the home while a sister-wife looks after the children and takes care of the home. Household chores can be shared. Wives would provide comfort, support and company for each other on the far-flung farmsteads while their husband was away working. Of course, he didn't mention that the number of children the wives would look after would be at least double the size of a normal family, especially if the women lived up to their duties and had a child every second year. He probably also neglected to mention that prayer is not always a cure for jealousy or a salve for loneliness.

Even though Harold's study of celestial marriage had begun at cottage meetings he'd attended with his father, John Blackmore opposed his son's flirtation with polygamy. In

Florence, Harold and Gwen Blackmore. Harold was a tireless advocate of polygamy and believed it made women happy. His wives would eventually tell a different story.
(Photo courtesy of Brenda Williams Jensen)

early 1946, John wrote to Harold expressing his concerns that his son had apostatized and turned against the church. John's letter has been lost, although it is clear from part of Harold's response that John was anxious about Gwen's well-being and concerned that his son did not love his wife. Harold's impassioned—although disingenuous—four-page response, written after he'd begun courting Florence, survives. In it, he rails against "certain ignorant busy-bodies" who "exaggerate and stir up a mess."

"We cannot understand what all the bitterness is about as everything is peaceful and happy with us here. It seems strange indeed that Latter-day Saints who claim to pattern their lives after Christ should become so bitter over a little difference of opinion on points of doctrine," he writes on Gwen's behalf. "We are just as concerned about our exaltation as you are and, if you were here, you'd see that our works, testimony and lives will measure up to any standard you want to set."

Harold criticized his father for picking and choosing among the doctrines. He questioned why his father chose to believe Joseph Smith's controversial "Adam-God" doctrine when other Mormons did not. What Smith said was that Adam—who in the biblical creation story is forced out of the Garden of Eden after Eve tempts him to eat the forbidden fruit—became God, the creator of heaven and earth. The idea was so controversial even in Smith's time that some believe it was the tipping point that led to the prophet's murder.

"You do the same against plural marriage (which I believe) and which our beloved Joseph Smith, Brigham Young and hundreds of others say is an eternal principle. So what? We are not living it nor are we doing anything else against the rules of the church except *studying*, which is apparently a hellish sin," Harold wrote, underlining words for emphasis.

Harold goes on to suggest that many of the LDS hierarchy agreed with him and not with his father:

> It may be surprising to you that my stake President A. E. Palmer [the leader of the Alberta group, or stake] declared in a public meeting here that "*Plural marriage* and the *United Order* would have to be lived some day in the church but that the *crime* was to live it right now." Wow! Have I ever said anything worse than that? It seems strange that my stake President feels no anxiety over us here. We disagree on several points, but he feels most kindly toward us—if he can, why can't you?
>
> Just what hellish crime have I committed that you should hate and disown me? We go to church, live the word of wisdom, do good to those who hate

us, have regular family prayer, give financial and other assistance to our neighbours and what is more just last June I have sent $50 every month in support of a missionary in the Eastern Canadian Mission. Who is out preaching this gospel you claim I have apostatized from?

All I did was issue a warning to you people that I felt great events were going to come to pass in the church and that we should study and prepare ourselves so as to be able to stand the tests when they come.

Harold said the only real crime he could think he and Gwen might be committing was preparing for the apocalypse by storing large quantities of food, clothing and medical supplies so that "your grandchildren who love you and whom I hope you still love, will not suffer unduly if the world situation gets out of control."

Harold closed his letter with not so much a lie as an obfuscation, telling his father that he and Gwen have "done nothing and are doing nothing that you need be ashamed of."

Harold later claimed that, in the summer of 1946, he'd had a vivid dream about a valley where he established a community of like-minded families who would live the Principle, hidden away from prying eyes. In his dream, they worked together for the mutual good. Harold had recently taught at a Hutterite colony near Cardston and had admired the way that religious sect pooled their resources—money, labour and property—for the common good. However, Harold later wrote that the Hutterites' material wealth had come at the cost of "loss of agency and a very low cultural level." What he subscribed to was Joseph Smith's vision of a patriarchal family order that centres on plural marriage and a United Order, which calls upon the members of the community to work together, giving as much of their wealth and labour as they can to the church in the expectation that if they need help, the community will provide it.

Harold's dream was hardly unique. Joseph Smith had dreamed of a New Zion in Missouri and the fundamentalist prophet Joseph Musser had received a vision that resulted in the 1935 settlement of Short Creek on the desolate Utah–Arizona border, where he wrongly prophesied that the land would become so fertile that one acre would produce more food than ten acres of the best land in Utah.

Within weeks of his dream, Blackmore took the train to visit his aunt Zina Boehmer, John Blackmore's sister, in Creston. Tucked in the southeastern corner of British Columbia, Creston was a remote, rough-and-tumble resource town that was gradually converting into an agricultural centre. A single highway through Creston along its one paved street connected it to the larger logging town of Cranbrook in the north, at the edge of the Rockies, and to Idaho in the south.

The folks there were an odd collection of bootleggers, miners, loggers and farmers, attracted to the area as much by its solitude as by its rich resources. In addition to the minerals and forests, the area's temperate climate supported cattle, fruit trees, grain and, years later, some of the best marijuana crops in the province.

Harold wanted to know whether there was any farmland for sale, and his cousin Rupert "Spot" Boehmer took him to see Camp Lister, about nine miles south. They hiked in and, as they went over the hill to Camp Lister, Harold saw the valley he had supposedly dreamed of. The property backed on to the steep cliffs of the Skimmerhorn Mountains and ran almost to the Canada–U.S. border. Before he went home,

Harold paid two thousand dollars for the eighty acres. Forty acres were already cleared and ready for farming; the remainder was forest.

Thirty years earlier, another religious sect leader had spied the same property and deemed it a perfect place. Peter Veregin had tried to buy the property for his flock of Sons of Freedom Doukhobors, who were decamping from Saskatchewan. But once the owners found out that the dissident Doukhobors might buy the land, the price was jacked up and Veregin couldn't come up with the cash to pay the exorbitant cost.

Instead, the Freedomites moved into the next valley and began terrorizing the locals with bombing attacks that destroyed trains, power lines and government buildings. These attacks were celebrated with nude marches. By the time Harold secured the Lister site in 1946, the B.C. government estimated the Freedomites had destroyed more than one million dollars worth of public property. They were the perfect foil for the Blackmores and the fundamentalist Mormons who settled in the Creston Valley.

The Freedomites and fundamentalist Mormons did, however, share one thing. Both embraced polygamy. Veregin kept what author Simma Holt described as "a harem of maidens" and exercised the right to have sex with all brides on their wedding nights. His powerful lieutenant, John Lebedoff, had five wives at one time and more than sixty-four over his lifetime.

Of course, nobody in Creston had any inkling of Harold Blackmore's plans. Nor did the idealistic Harold have any idea at the time that his utopian dream of communal life would founder just as the Freedomites' would because of the absolute power claimed by its leaders.

With the Lister property secured, Harold rushed back to Alberta to get Gwen and the children ready for the move. He also suggested to both Gwen and Florence that the time and place were right to begin practising the Principle. Both sisters agreed. But even though the fundamentalist Mormons' sealing ceremony often includes the first wife taking the bride's hand and placing it in their husband's, Gwen did not do that. She wasn't even at the ceremony. She stayed behind in Alberta while her husband and sister went to Salt Lake City in September 1946. There fundamentalist Prophet Joseph Musser joined them in marriage for time and all eternity. After a brief honeymoon, Florence stayed behind in Idaho, while Harold went back to Alberta. Conscious that the new neighbours might not appreciate living next door to polygamists, Harold had decided that Florence should remain in Idaho until the rest of the family was already settled in Camp Lister.

Harold's eldest daughter, Lorna, was four when they arrived at the Creston train station. It was cold and overcast. She remembers being disappointed because the clouds obscured the towering mountain that her father had told them stood behind their farm. It was days before the clouds lifted. When they did, the little prairie girl had her first look at a real mountain, and Lorna recalls it being more oppressive than impressive. But she grew to love that mountain so much that, more than sixty years later, she continues to live in its shadow.

Nothing dampened Harold's optimism about the future — neither the dismal weather that greeted their arrival that November nor the urgent work that needed to be done before winter set in. At the station, the Blackmores loaded all of their belongings into a horse-drawn wagon and set out for Lister. There were four log houses on the property, built by First World War veterans who had been given the land as part of their payout when they returned home. The cabins had stood empty for a long time and were scarcely livable. Harold, Gwen and their children moved into the biggest one. There was a lot to be done. Enough wood to get them through the winter had to be chopped and stacked. Supplies needed to be brought in, not only because winter was coming, but because Harold wanted to minimize his contact with any potentially nosy neighbours.

In January, Florence Williams moved into a small cabin on the Lister property, which was where she lived until Harold built a house large enough for all of them. But her arrival wasn't the only cause for celebration.

That same month, Sons of Freedom leader Joe Eli Podovinikoff held a news conference in British Columbia's capital, Victoria. Podovinikoff renounced all private ownership, including the "private ownership of persons and families." Wives and children were common property, he said.

A few British Columbians were upset and wrote letters to newspapers demanding the attorney general do something about polygamy. But Attorney General Gordon Wismer had taken the public pulse and refused to do anything. He was supported by the *Vancouver Sun* newspaper, which said in an editorial, "If they wish to behave like cattle, it is probably their own affair."

FOUR

PERSECUTION, PROSECUTION AND BETRAYAL

B y 1949, Florence and Harold had had their first "covenant child," as children born into polygamous marriages are called. And while John Blackmore had disapproved of his son practising polygamy, he had made peace with Harold. Strangely, even though John had been excommunicated, Harold and both his wives were still members in good standing in the mainstream Mormon church. It would be three more years before Harold and his wives were called before a church court, charged with apostasy and accused of "teaching and advocating the present practise of plural marriage in violation of the rules, regulations and teachings of the Church of Jesus Christ of Latter-day Saints."

With things going so well in Lister, Harold Blackmore took some of his growing family back to Alberta that summer to visit family and friends. While he was there, Harold went to several cottage meetings to share his experience in patriarchal marriage. His uncle Joseph Ray Blackmore was at some of those meetings as well. Ray was John's youngest brother, and only nine months older than Harold. They were more like cousins or brothers than uncle and nephew. While Harold had done his two-year LDS mission in Ottawa and had few converts to his credit, Ray had gone to New Zealand where, he bragged, he had made more converts than any other missionary. After the mission, Ray had returned to Alberta and, in 1941, at the age of twenty-six, married seventeen-year-old Anna Mae Wynder. Years later, in a letter to one of her two hundred or so grandchildren, Anna Mae wrote, "I was 17-and-a-half and, believe me, I was too young. I should have been at least 18 or 19. We are so anxious to grow up, yet we do not know what we are doing."

Soon after their marriage, Ray had bought a dairy farm in British Columbia's Okanagan Valley along with his friend Charles Quinton. The dairy had gone bankrupt. But before Ray, his family and Charles Quinton moved back to Alberta and the embrace of the LDS community, Ray had taken a second wife, his twenty-eight-year-old niece Aloha. In the spring of 1949, fundamentalist Prophet Joseph Musser sealed Ray and his niece for time and all eternity in a celestial marriage ceremony in Salt Lake City. It was a convenient marriage for Ray. Aloha Boehmer, a sturdy, hard-working young woman, had gone with Ray and Anna Mae to work in the dairy.

Anna Mae had embraced the Principle, but grudgingly. Ray and particularly Anna Mae treated Aloha more like an indentured servant than a wife. Anna Mae made it clear to Aloha that she was the first wife, the alpha wife, and someone who would not be trifled with. It was *her* husband, *her* house and everything in it was *hers*, except for what Aloha had brought with her. That is, not much.

Harold Blackmore didn't approve of the way Ray organized his family and said so in his 1978 book, *All About Polygamy: Why and How to Live It!* Gwen, Florence and Harold had appeared on the *Phil Donahue Show* that year, after a handful of polygamists had been arrested in Utah for having sex with underage girls. They explained that *that* was a perversion of polygamy, which was a religiously sanctioned way of life chosen by consenting adults. In this chatty self-published book that aimed to answer questions sent to him after the show, Harold uses Ray and Anna Mae as an example of how *not* to live polygamy. He describes Ray as "blustery, arrogant and inwardly a coward" and Anna Mae as "shrewd."

Harold accuses his uncle and aunt of not being committed to polygamy as a religious principle. Rather, Harold writes, they courted the second wife as "an ego trip" and then failed to treat Aloha equally or fairly. But, as usual with Harold, it all went back to money.

"Some families, where some of the wives are too immature to live in harmony, occupy a duplex, four-plex or any other facility adequate for their needs," Harold wrote. "This is an extreme financial burden and deprives them of close family association. It is very difficult for the father to give the personal attention to each family member that should be had."

But Ray couldn't have cared less about any rational or complicated discussions about polygamy. He was just happy to live it, and he left the details of living it up to Anna Mae. As for money, Ray's bankruptcy was testimony to the fact that he wasn't the best businessman or the hardest worker. He was a showman and a cowboy. If he wanted the best horse, he bought it, even if he couldn't always afford it.

There was plenty for fundamentalist Saints to talk about in the summer of 1949. Joseph Musser was the patriarch of the fundamentalist movement in Salt Lake City. Although he had been excommunicated by the LDS in 1921, Musser claimed that his authority to practise polygamy and recruit others into the

The beards change, but the ideas do not. FLDS prophet Joseph Musser is in the middle. His eventual successor, Rulon Jeffs, is on the right. Jeffs's son, Warren, would succeed him in his turn.
(Photo courtesy of Brenda Williams Jensen)

Principle had come from the highest office of the Mormon church, more than a decade after Wilford Woodruff had issued his Manifesto renouncing its earthly practice.

Musser had only one wife when he claimed a messenger arrived to tell him that Lorenzo Snow—Woodruff's successor and the fifth LDS prophet—had selected him to be one of a small group of men to keep the Principle alive. It's a claim that the LDS hierarchy has always denied. Mathias Cowley, a member of the powerful Quorum of Twelve, performed the first of Musser's celestial marriages in 1901, and another one after that. As one of the apostles, Cowley was in line to become the LDS prophet. But he resigned from the Quorum in 1905. Cowley believed the Manifesto against plural marriage should apply only to the United States and not to Canada or the rest of the world. Because of his enduring belief in practising polygamy, Cowley was excommunicated in 1911, but reinstated twenty-five years later.

Musser claimed his third marriage had been sealed by Joseph F. Smith, the sixth LDS prophet. In 1915, Musser recorded in his journal that Smith had "conferred upon me the sealing power of Elijah, with instructions to see that plural marriage should not die out."

But by the summer of 1949, the seventy-nine-year-old Musser was physically and mentally weakened by the first of a series of strokes. His influence among the fundamentalist Saints was waning even though he was soon to succeed John Y. Barlow as the second prophet of the United Order, which was later renamed the Fundamentalist Church of Jesus Christ of Latter Day Saints. With both Barlow and Musser ailing, warring factions were forming that would eventually force the first schism in the fundamentalist movement. It was a scenario that would prove strikingly similar to a more public split between two men more than fifty years later.

Ever since Brigham Young had succeeded Mormonism's founder, the leadership had passed to the next most senior of the Quorum of Twelve. However, leadership challenges are hardly surprising. Joseph Smith's doctrine is a recipe for conflict, since every man is a potential prophet and god. Every man can speak directly to God, and if a man says an angel appeared in a brilliant light and gave him an order, well, who's to say that the angel didn't? There's a further complication. It's what Willa Appel calls "messianic etiquette." As she writes in *Cults in America: Programmed for Paradise*, "To establish his credentials, the messiah must officially demonstrate that he or she does not eagerly embrace such an exalted burden but only accepts it upon realization that there is no other choice." It's a difficult act—seizing the reins while appearing to thrust them away. But it's a standard rite in cult successions, and the fundamentalist Saints have proven no different. They're as adept at feuding as dissembling.

One of Musser's closest allies was Harold Blackmore's friend Rulon Allred. One of his bitterest opponents was his son, Guy Musser. Not only was Joseph Musser debilitated by a stroke, he lived in Salt Lake City, far from Barlow's home and power base in the growing community of Short Creek on the Utah–Arizona border. Barlow had written the first pro-polygamy pamphlet in 1927, and during his fourteen years as the United Order's prophet he had established what Saints have come to refer to as "one-man rule." He diminished the authority of the Priesthood Council by issuing orders and filling council vacancies without so much as a divine revelation to back his decision. His choice of LeRoy Johnson—a man whose family had lived and practised polygamy near Short Creek since first arriving in Utah—as a councillor, for example, was "inspired" rather than "revealed." It's an important distinction to those who believe they always know the difference between God's will and personal desire.

LeRoy Johnson helped Barlow undermine Musser's influence, as did Guy Musser. At a meeting in 1952, the depth of their enmity was apparent. Joseph Musser was not allowed to speak in his own defence—democracy and fair play are not the watchwords of church courts. According to notes that historian Ben Bistline obtained from the meeting, Johnson said, "If the Lord wants to use an incapacitated leader to lead some people astray, that is the Lord's business."

What Guy Musser said was more profane, damning and frightening: "Rulon C. Allred has used my father as a pissing post. If I wanted to use the same policy that Rulon is using we could get father to do whatever we wanted him to do. Certain of the Brethren have come to me and offered to take Brother Allred's life if he continues to maintain his stand."

The final break between the Musser/Allred group and the Barlow/Johnson group was still three years away. But the brewing feud provided plenty of fodder for the Alberta cottage meetings in the summer of 1949. Not only were there the personalities of the leaders to consider, the idea of one-man rule was highly contentious. Because one-man rule is strikingly similar to the Catholic notion of the infallibility of popes, men like Harold Blackmore argued that it ran contrary to Joseph Smith's doctrine of free agency, which potentially allowed all believers equal access to God's word.

There were other issues as well. Both Barlow and the Priesthood Council had increasingly used their authority to dole out "blessings"—code for additional wives—in exchange for money, property or services rendered. It's not clear whether this was sheer greed or a recognition that a potentially fatal flaw for a polygamous religion is simple arithmetic. Males and females of all species are born in almost equal numbers. Nature is about pairs, not multiples, so polygamy doesn't work even on paper, never mind in practice.

When Joseph Smith had his so-called revelation about plural marriage more than a century earlier, polygamy wasn't a crime. Smith was young, handsome, charismatic and powerful, with few concerns about attracting enough women willing to marry him for time and all eternity. But by the mid-twentieth century, with polygamy banned by both church and state, the inevitable shortage of women was becoming acute. The competition for women of child-bearing age was so fierce that historian Ben Bistline said it was commonplace for suitors to line up outside the door as soon as a girl reached her thirteenth birthday. By then, she was educated enough to cook and clean and old enough to bear children. Young girls, writes Bistline, were put under tremendous pressure by dozens of men, all trying to convince the girls that they had

had a revelation from God about the marriage pact made between them in the pre-existence.

Among the beliefs that set Mormons—both mainstream and fundamentalist—radically apart from other Christians is what they believe about the pre-mortal existence. Mormons believe there are millions of spirits waiting to be granted bodily forms, which they will take with them into the after-life. It is because of those millions of spirits waiting to be born that Mormons believe they should follow God's com-mandment to go forth and multiply prodigiously. This is their way of ensuring that those spirits are raised in the One True Faith.

While those spirits are waiting to be born, they are paired off; their marriages are arranged not just for their time on earth, but for all eternity. When the time comes on earth, the Saints believe God will reveal their marriage partners to them.

Bistline says the prophet and priesthood weren't prima-rily concerned about the theological confusion a rush of pro-posals provoked in young girls. "The other (and no doubt greater) problem was that the girls would invariably choose the younger men, making it almost impossible for the older Brethren to get new wives." It seems that as long as women have their choice of men, polygamy doesn't work, and it especially doesn't work for old men.

The buzz at the Alberta cottage meetings in 1949 was not only about leadership intrigues, revelations or even arithmetic. Harold Blackmore shared news of his dream valley, his grow-ing family and life in the Creston Valley. His enthusiasm was so infectious that Ray Blackmore and Eldon Palmer began making plans to join him there.

Harold was like his father, tall, thin, distant and austere. He was a bit of an intellectual snob, relatively speaking, who loved to show off by quoting from memory. He would quote from the Bible and the Book of Mormon, and from literary works by Emerson, Thoreau and Shakespeare. His eclecticism extended to music; he also loved to yodel. Perversely, however, Harold hated country music and its singers, whose twanging and poor enunciation offended him.

Despite believing in a religion based entirely on mysticism, revelations, dreams, visions and speaking in tongues, Harold professed to value reason over passion. "Love is not that romantic and ridiculous emotion that so often is called love," he wrote in 1974. "To love is to value. Only a rational, self-respecting person is capable of true love because he holds firm, consistent, uncompromising values."

But more than anything, Harold was frugal to the point of obsession. He was never above diving into a Dumpster at the back of a grocery store or restaurant to rescue a meal for his family. He worked his wives and his children hard on the farm and later in his construction business. Whatever his wives and children earned, they handed over to Harold, who in return gave them little in terms of material comforts.

Shorter and stockier than Harold, Ray was a man of action, a cowboy with no intellectual pretensions. He loved wrestling and rodeo and, when he was younger, frequently provoked Harold into fighting. Even though Ray was the aggressor, Harold would later claim that he was usually the winner. While Harold was a more proficient speaker, Ray was gifted and charismatic. He lived large, enjoyed the fruits of his labours and rarely denied himself or his family indulgences, without concerning himself unduly about the cost.

By miracle or twist of fate, Ray was able to buy a 350-acre farm adjacent to Harold's. By the end of 1952, he had built a big house for his two wives and nine children, and a large barn was under construction at the foot of the mountain.

Bountiful's founding fathers. Harold and Ray Blackmore are at the far right. Though they worked together to establish their polygamous outpost, they would soon be at each other's throats.
(Photo courtesy of Brenda Williams Jensen)

Eldon Palmer and his family were living in one of the houses on Harold's property.

The burgeoning community kept to itself as much as possible to keep the secret of the many mothers. Before all of Harold's family moved into the same house, Florence stayed in one of the small log cabins. The Blackmore children weren't allowed to go down to Auntie Florence's house. Of course, that didn't stop them.

Harold's eldest daughter, Lorna, and some of the others ran down one day and found a baby in a bassinet on the lawn. "Boy, were we ever in trouble," Lorna recalls. "Everybody started yelling that we had no right to go over there. I can't remember what happened. But I'm pretty sure we got a beating for that."

The baby was Lorna's half-brother Stephen. Too young and naive to know any better, the children accepted what their parents told them: Florence was looking after the baby for "a blind lady"—a ruse modelled on Gwen and Harold's experience with the blind lady in Alberta. Once the whole family was living together in the spartan "big" house, which was really only large enough for two separate bedrooms (one for each wife) and two dormitory-style bedrooms (one for the girls and another for the boys), Harold's family continued to go to great lengths to avoid discovery. Lorna remembers her tall, dignified "Auntie Florence" packing a baby in a suitcase to get past a gentile visitor sitting in the living room.

Only when the children were eight and baptized did Harold and his wives explain the family set-up to them. Until children are baptized at eight, Saints believe they are pure, incapable of sin and unaccountable for their actions. But, after that, they are responsible for their own sins and they begin to be treated as adults. For girls that means they begin training in earnest to be "mothers in Zion." For boys, it is the first step towards joining the priesthood at age twelve.

Following her full-immersion baptism in the icy pond water behind their house, Lorna was finally told the truth about the "blind lady's babies," who by then were arriving at regular intervals. Pointing to her aunt's rounded belly, Harold and Gwen gave their daughter the full extent of her sex education. Auntie Florence was pregnant and Harold was the baby's father. That was a secret and she must never tell anyone or her father might go to jail.

By 1953 the Blackmores and others in Lister realized that they were far from invisible. On July 24, R. Scott Zimmerman, the president of the Western Mission of the Church of Jesus Christ of Latter-day Saints, sent letters to ten or more people in Lister accusing them of apostasy. One letter was sent to Gwen

Blackmore and another to "Mrs. Leonard L. Blackmore," the pseudonym Florence used to explain her children's ancestry. (As a tribute to her non-existent husband, Florence named one of her sons Leonard.) The sisters were told that they would be excommunicated if the charges made against them were substantiated or if they failed to defend themselves in person.

News of the impending church trials was reported in local papers and by the Canadian Press newswire. Gwen and Florence never spoke about what happened before they were tossed out of the LDS, so Brenda and Lorna don't know whether their mothers defended themselves at a church hearing. How many others were also declared apostates isn't known because the LDS church denied that it had even held the trials. The story was reported across Canada, causing a sensation everywhere but in Creston, where the community quickly closed ranks against outsiders and charges of any wrongdoing in the sleepy little valley.

In its front-page exclusive on August 6, 1953, the *Creston Review* (which described itself as "a newspaper of national distinction") thundered that every other news agency had got the story wrong. There had been no trials, Zimmerman's visit had no connection to reports of polygamy and nobody in the Creston Valley was practising polygamy. The story was prefaced by an editor's note:

> In order that local members of the Mormon Church may be protected from the ill-timed, inaccurate public reports local and outside, relative to recent investigation held last weekend, *The Review*, in an effort to eliminate ridicule and embarrassment from these Creston Valley adults and especially children, sought and received personal interview from Mr. Zimmerman. From top-flight

sources, *The Review*, could find no evidence that
the Arizona Cult and the local church investigations tied together, but sensational dailies and others made a field day to the detriment of local
people and the valley's reputation.

The *Review* quoted Zimmerman as saying that there had
been no excommunications. He and his aides had visited in
order to investigate "certain members standing relative to
church beliefs and practices." The story went on to say, "A special detail of the RCMP who have spent considerable time
investigating rumours, direct and indirect relative to polygamy
and malpractices, reported nothing substantial in their investigations which terminated last weekend."

It seems the lengths to which the Blackmores and others
went to keep their secret had paid off. Their discretion meant
that the parochialism of the valley had now become part of
their protection from criminal prosecution.

Still, Canadian Saints realized how vulnerable they were.
Early in 1953, the RCMP swept into the nearby Sons of
Freedom community and rounded up members of a radical
Doukhobor sect whose relationship to other Doukhobors was
akin to that of the fundamentalists to mainstream Mormons.

In December 1952, Freedomite leaders had urged their
followers to burn their own homes. When the buildings were
razed, they set up a tent city and paraded nude in front of a
school. Police arrested 144 men and women that day.
Politicians and residents were fed up with the Freedomites,
who, over the years, had set one too many fires and bombed
one too many buildings. Over the weeks that followed, there
were a series of raids one hundred miles northwest of Lister
in the Slocan Valley. A total of 103 children were rounded
up and put in dormitories in New Denver—buildings that

only a few years earlier had housed Japanese Canadians interned during the Second World War. The B.C. government told the Freedomites that their children could come home only if the parents agreed to send the children to public schools. None would.

But it was the raid later that year, on Short Creek, Arizona, that holds iconic importance to fundamentalist Mormons. It began shortly after midnight on July 26, to coincide with the longest lunar eclipse of the twentieth century. The polygamists had been warned of the raid, but Prophet LeRoy Johnson told them not to run. "We will stand up to them and ask the Lord to fight our battles," he told them. As the police approached, the sentries posted at the outskirts of town detonated dynamite.

With sirens wailing and lights flashing, more than one hundred Arizona highway patrolmen, Mohave County sheriffs and Arizona National Guardsmen pulled into the schoolyard in a swirl of red dust. They got out with their guns drawn, carrying arrest warrants for thirty-six men.

Everyone from the community—except for about one hundred men who had hidden in the canyons on the Utah side of the border—was gathered around the flagpole, singing patriotic anthems. They continued singing as the officers went through the crowd arresting the men, separating them from their wives and children.

The men were taken before a judge in a makeshift courtroom set up in the school, charged and sent off to jail. Forty-three women and their children were taken before a juvenile judge, who declared them wards of the state. The women and children were then bused to Phoenix. They were initially housed in nursing homes and provided with welfare support payments and food stamps.

In a radio address the morning after the round-up, Arizona Governor Howard Pyle said it was necessary to combat "the insurrection within our own borders" by fundamentalist Mormons who are "dedicated to the production of white slaves who are without hope of escaping this degrading slavery." The governor said the raid was aimed at protecting "the lives and futures of 263 children," who were "the victims of the foulest conspiracy you could imagine."

In a statement of opinion that presaged what Arizona and Utah politicians would be saying fifty years later, Pyle said: "They are innocent chattels of a lawless commercial undertaking of wicked design and ruthlessly exercised power. This in turn is the co-operative enterprise of five or six coldly calculating men who direct all of the operations and reap all of the profits and are the evil heart of the insurrection itself."

Pyle said the evidence against the men included "alleged instances of statutory rape, adultery, bigamy, open and notorious co-habitation" as well as "marrying the spouse of another." The governor accused the men of contributing to the deliquency of minors by providing such abysmal examples. But that was not all. He said they were guilty of "an all-embracing conspiracy to commit all of these crimes along with various instances of income tax evasion, failure to comply with Arizona's corporation laws, misappropriation of the school funds, improper use of school facilities and falsification of public records."

But prosecutors couldn't prove those allegations. No witnesses came forward to testify and eventually the men were released and the families reunited. Pyle was trounced in the next election by voters who were horrified by the images of tearful women and children being pulled away from their husbands and fathers.

Despite his defeat and personal repudiation as a result of the raid, Pyle remained unrepentant. On the thirty-fifth anniversary of the raid, Pyle told the *Arizona Republic* that if he were still in office, "I would make another try to put an end to the polygamy, even though there's no state statute addressing it."

But the overwhelmingly negative public response to the raid and the state's failure to make its case against the polygamists poisoned the political will in Arizona and elsewhere. Pyle's strongly worded condemnation of the polygamists was the last time for nearly fifty years that any politician in either the United States or Canada would give so forthright an assessment of the community or attempt to bring the polygamists to justice.

In 1953, Lorna Blackmore was twelve. She remembers police cars sitting at the edge of their property for days following the Arizona raid. The RCMP had been warned to watch for polygamists coming over the border to escape the crackdown in Arizona. Her half-sister Brenda was only two at the time. But Brenda was told about the raid so often that she "remembers" it vividly. Like all of the kids in Lister and in Short Creek, Brenda grew up terrified that a raid could happen again if she slipped and inadvertently told the secret of her two mothers. Telling convincing lies is one of the most important skills that the Saints' children learn.

Brenda Williams Jensen was one of Florence's five children, but she and her siblings were primarily raised by Gwen. Florence always worked outside the home, either as a teacher or side by side with Harold in construction, logging or any other money-making venture he embarked on. Until Brenda was five, she was told she was to call her mother Auntie Florence whenever other people were around. That changed one winter when two of Brenda's fingers were accidentally chopped off by one of her brothers' friends who was cutting wood. Brenda had started to climb up the wood pile to get her gloves off the warming rack when the axe came down on her hand.

In 1953, these four families were the entire population of the commu-
nity that came to be known as Bountiful. The only one missing is
Florence Williams, who took the photo.
(Photo courtesy of Brenda Williams Jensen)

As she was rushed to hospital, her parents admonished
Brenda not to say anything about their family and not to speak
to anyone. Florence was the only one who came to the hospital to visit her so as not to raise suspicions. But after her fingers
had been reattached, Brenda chattered away to a nurse about
her brothers and sisters and mothers and father. "My parents
took [the nurse] as an enemy agent who would put my father
in jail. But I think she was just trying to make me feel more
comfortable," Brenda says.

It must have broken Florence's heart to have her children
deny her, because after Brenda went home from the hospital,
Florence told her children that they no longer had to call her
Auntie Florence. From then on she would be Mother. But
when they were asked about their father, they were drilled to
say that they had none. Even so, Brenda says, "We always

messed up. There was so much pressure on us. We were supposed to take on the role of an adult and keep secrets."

Gwen, the legal wife, was the primary caregiver, cook and housekeeper. In contrast to Florence, who was light-hearted, spirited and preferred literature to reading the Bible, Gwen followed the rules as she read them in the scriptures. She never spared the rod, and certainly never spoiled any of the seventeen children. Both Lorna and Brenda recall being whipped and beaten often. Girls, they said, were more likely to be punished than boys. Boys had a higher status. They were gods in training—at least the Blackmore progeny were. The adopted boys were treated even more harshly than the girls. In one letter to Harold, Gwen asked whether she should beat one of the boys—she didn't say which one—for some minor offence or wait for Harold to do it when he got home. The only thing surprising to her daughters about the letter is that she suggested waiting until Harold got home. Gwen rarely waited for permission or for him to mete out punishment.

Harold and his wives always differentiated between their own thirteen "blood children" and the four who were adopted. The adopted children were frequently reminded that they were not real Blackmores. Gwen also singled out Florence's five children for more frequent and more brutal punishment than her own eight. Whether it was simple mothering instinct to protect her own or a means of getting back at Florence, who spent so much time with Harold, no one ever knew. Nobody ever asked either.

The house was cramped. There was no running water, no indoor plumbing and no washing machine. It's hard to conceive how Gwen was able to feed the whole family with what she could grow in the garden, get from the goats or buy with the meagre grocery allowance Harold gave her.

Harold Blackmore's children. With this many children, there was no money for luxuries and sometimes not even for staples like sugar. There was also no time for the individual attention they craved.
(Photo courtesy of Brenda Williams Jensen)

Some of Gwen's burden was passed on to Lorna, the oldest girl in the family. Lorna is built like her mother, compact and strong, with hands callused and rough from nearly sixty years of work. She is pragmatic and plain-spoken. Work is almost all she can remember from the time she was seven or eight; her chores included milking the goats, making the butter and cheese, and tending the other children. Because she was the oldest, she had less schooling than the others. Even though all three of her parents were teachers, initially they were too busy building up the farm to worry about home-schooling their children. Lorna remembers envying Ray and Anna Mae Blackmore's kids, who had bicycles and horses. But that's not what she envied most. It was that they had eggs and sugar, which were both luxuries in Harold's home.

Neither Lorna nor her half-sister Brenda, who is ten years younger, remember having tender moments with either of their mothers or their father. No one ever got any individual attention—not even the littlest ones. No one was ever told they were special. "Everything was mass," says Brenda. "There was mass love, mass eating, mass discipline and no room for individuality. We were read Bible stories after dinner and then it was everybody to bed. Even when we finally got electricity, we couldn't use the lights because it cost too much. We walked carrying kerosene lamps to the barn to milk the goats."

While Lorna remembers wishing for sugar and eggs, Brenda remembers jealously eyeing the yellow rubber duck squeaky toy that three-year-old Debbie Oler carried when she and her family arrived in Lister in 1957. "I'd never seen any-thing like it," Brenda said nearly fifty years later.

Dalmon and JoAnn Oler and their three children—Debbie, two-year-old Jane and baby Kendal—initially moved into one of the small houses on Ray Blackmore's property. Since the Blackmores owned all the property in Lister, Oler eventually bought land and built a big house a few miles down the road in Canyon. Like the Blackmores, Oler was from Alberta and had attended some of the same cottage meetings there. But those discussions weren't what con-vinced Oler to become part of the polygamous community in Lister—it was his father-in-law, Amos LeRoy Gallup. Gallup received his "testimony" about the correctness of plural mar-riage before Dalmon did. But it was years before Gallup told his family that he had embraced the idea of polygamy and it wasn't until the 1960s that he took a second wife.

JoAnn had been raised in the mainstream Mormon church and had been only sixteen when she married twenty-year-old Dalmon. Because of her father's secrecy about his testimony and her church upbringing, when Dalmon suggested taking a second wife, JoAnn was shocked. After prayer, fasting and, of course, her husband's insistence, JoAnn yielded and accepted that it was something that had to be done in exchange for a chance to reach the highest realm of heaven.

Her decision stunned both Oler's father (who disowned Dalmon) and JoAnn's maternal grandparents, whose Mormon roots extended back to the early days of Smith's ministry. "I hope we have not caused you to feel badly over the course that we have taken," JoAnn wrote to her grandparents at Christmas in 1957. But her letter shows how completely her re-education as a polygamist had taken root: "We feel that this has been a wise move for us. I have felt the spirit of the Lord here, more than I ever have in my life. I love these people here and appreciate all that they have taught me. It's wonderful to know what your aim in life is and the purpose in life.

"The only thing that remains is to live the things that we know to be right and pleasing in the eyes of the Lord. We have lots of things to study and learn about and pray about and I pray that our desire to learn will continue to grow."

JoAnn was slim and pretty, with short, stylishly curled hair when she arrived in Lister. She had brought some beautiful dresses with her; dresses that she soon put away permanently in a trunk. When there had been a split between the Musser/Allred group and the Short Creek group, the people in Lister had sided with the "Crickers" and their new prophet LeRoy Johnson. The group headed by the man known as "Uncle Roy" would eventually be named the Fundamentalist Church of Jesus Christ of Latter Day Saints and would become the largest polygamous group in North America.

Uncle Roy was not shy about imposing his will—with or without revelation—on all manner of things from metaphysics to women's fashion. He had decreed that women must dress modestly, although he stopped short of requiring they revert to the pioneer styles worn by Mormon women on the long trek to Utah. That was left to a later prophet. But it wasn't only women who needed to keep their arms and legs covered, so did little girls. Uncle Roy forbade women and girls from cutting their hair, which he said was their crowning glory. All women and girls—wives, sisters, mothers, daughters—were to wear their hair either in braids or swept up in a simple chignon.

All those directives chafed on Harold Blackmore, who believed in Joseph Smith's promise of free agency and resented the one-man rule of LeRoy Johnson or anyone else. But Harold was not ready to leave his valley or his utopia just yet. He had children to raise. He had sons who needed wives and daughters who needed husbands, in order to secure their salvation. Ray Blackmore, on the other hand, had no qualms about Uncle Roy's directives; by 1957, he was the one giving and enforcing them. His loyalty and service to LeRoy Johnson were well rewarded. Ray had four wives and was Johnson's Canadian lieutenant.

As Johnson's lieutenant, Ray didn't necessarily agree with everything the prophet said. He was cocky and arrogant and gave the people in Lister every impression that he too talked directly to God. He was also a showman, an entertainer who could mesmerize a crowd with the wild Maori dances he'd learned during his Mormon mission in New Zealand. And, unlike Harold, who was more given to quoting Shakespeare, Ray was known for his renditions of Robert W. Service's poem *The Cremation of Sam McGee*. With great flourishes and dramatic pauses, he'd reel off from memory the lurid ballad about a Yukon prospector's surprise when he consigns a friend's corpse to the flames.

Ray was no businessman, but he had the best horses in the valley. He never stinted on their cost. He loved his horses so much that his detractors (some in his own family) say that the horses were better treated than his children.

Ray frequently went to Harold for money; in fact, when he died, Ray still owed Harold close to fifty thousand dollars. Frugal Harold had established a successful construction company that did work both for the brethren in Lister and in the nearby town of Creston. With three teachers in his family, Harold got government approval to home-school not only his own children but the others in the community as well.

But Ray's loyalty and service to the prophet trumped all of that, and Ray's appointment as leader rekindled the long-standing intra-family rivalry. Church meetings were raucous and tense. "We thought the religion was terrible because all we heard at the church meetings was criticism [and] bitching. And there was such oppression," says Lorna, who was sixteen when her uncle became leader. Brenda, who is a decade younger, remembers the animosity, but not the source of it. "We were not allowed to be rude and unkind words in our family were a rarity. But the things that were done and said at those meetings were unspeakable."

The disagreements weren't confined to the meetings or the adults; they spilled out of church and into the kids' realm. After one particularly angry church meeting, the sons of Harold and Ray escalated the debate to a fistfight. Rather than chastising his sons for attempting to devolve a theological debate into fisticuffs, Ray was delighted with his sons for having stood up for him.

LeRoy Johnson was radically altering Joseph Smith's teachings and taking more and more power for himself and staunch loyalists like Ray. While Harold lived by the principle of "do unto others as you would have them do unto you," Johnson and Ray were becoming bullies. They were grabbing power and authority for themselves—and by arrogating to themselves the exclusive ability to to have revelations and inspirations, they were attempting to take away the fundamentalists' right to have a direct relationship with God. They wanted to control not only the doctrine but the money, the property and the distribution of wives who guaranteed men's salvation.

The prophet may not have appreciated Harold's challenges to his authority. But Harold had two things that LeRoy Johnson wanted. Johnson, over the years, had become a sly and skilled manipulator. People in Short Creek were living in appalling conditions in shacks, sheds and even abandoned cars. In 1963, Johnson appealed to Harold's pride. He noted that Harold was not only a successful contractor but a dedicated teacher. If Harold moved to Short Creek, the prophet promised to put him in charge of building new homes there. After the 1953 raid, the town had been split in two and was now officially designated as Hildale, Utah, and Colorado City, Arizona. Johnson also promised Harold that if he were to move there, he could set up a new, private, church-funded academy where fundamentalist boys would be taught the building trades.

Harold had gone to Guy Musser in the early 1950s and offered to gather up like-minded Canadians and move them to Short Creek. Musser had dissuaded him, telling him that there was work to be done in Canada and that his group was best able to accomplish it. He told Harold that when the apocalypse came—and he believed it would be soon—powerful prayer circles of fundamentalist Mormons stationed along the Rocky Mountains would save the earth from ruin.

But by 1963, when Johnson approached him, Harold was reluctant, but flattered. "I disliked the idea of going down there very strongly because the looks of that desert just did things to me after what I was used to," he said years later. "I don't see how anyone could live in that environment. And I had no desire to go down there." So why did he go? "Because I was asked to help them."

Initially, Harold took his wives and oldest sons to Colorado City to build a house for his family, leaving the girls and youngest children behind with twenty-four-year-old Lorna. Two years earlier, Lorna had been convinced by her parents to accept the prophet's assigning of her as a plural wife. She was married in a celestial ceremony to her forty-one-year-old uncle Charles Quinton, Ray Blackmore's good friend and former business partner. The marriage was so secret that not even Quinton's first wife knew about it. Quinton and his first wife didn't live in Lister, they lived in Rosemary, Alberta, where he returned after the wedding and remained a member in good standing in the LDS church.

After Harold arrived in Colorado City, LeRoy Johnson set to work getting the other thing that he wanted—the title to Harold's property in Lister. Through a company called the National Land Corporation, two of the prophet's closest advisers told Harold that they wanted to help him develop the Lister property into a hunting lodge or guest ranch to attract rich executives. They offered to raise US$100,000 for the venture if Harold signed over his property to the company as collateral. In exchange, Harold would have a 51 per cent share in the company and would be the manager of the lodge.

But Johnson's two advisers lied to Harold about the hunting lodge, just as Johnson had lied to him about the building academy. Neither materialized. Harold never got any shares in the National Land Corporation. After he transferred the title to the Lister property to the company, his two "partners" transferred the property into the United Effort Plan (UEP) trust, which they also controlled, ostensibly for the betterment of all fundamentalist Saints.

Two weeks after the land was transferred out of the shell company and into the UEP, Johnson went to Lister and told the people that the land now belonged to the church; he

then promptly turned it all over to Ray Blackmore to administer. Immediately, Ray began issuing orders to Harold's children who remained in Lister under Lorna's care, making
clear he was now in charge. That's how Harold learned he
had been swindled. Ray initially ordered the children out of
the house, but later relented, allowing them to stay until
Harold had finished building his house in Colorado City.
When the last of the children had snuck across the U.S. border, taking an old smuggler's route through the forest into
Idaho, Ray evicted Lorna Blackmore and began moving
some of his wives and children into Harold's house and the
other cabins on the property. He took over the operation of
the oil refinery, the ten sheds and the barn. Lorna Blackmore
took shelter at Dalmon Oler's house.

"I want it understood that I had no intention of staying
there when I went down," Harold said twenty-five years later.
"I went down to help them. I was trapped there. I intended to
go back [to Lister] . . . When I found that they had taken the
property and given it to the UEP, I had nowhere to go."

Furious, but refusing to repent and follow the prophet's
orders, Harold packed up his family again and moved twenty
miles or so up the road to Hurricane, Utah. He cut all ties
with the United Order and no longer referred to its leaders as
the priesthood or brethren. Instead, Harold referred to them
as "priestcrafters," an amalgamation of the words *priesthood*
and *witchcraft*. But his departure didn't mean that the priestcrafters had heard the last of him. As historian Ben Bistline
wrote, Harold may have lived for only a short time in Colorado
City, but "of all the apostates who have lived there and left, he
has probably had more of an impact on the community and
the cult than any other person."

FIVE

A CHOSEN SON AND A CHILD BRIDE

The year after Ray Blackmore was named leader of the fundamentalists in Lister, Winston Kaye Blackmore was born. Round-faced, with bright blue eyes and a ready smile, he was the chosen son destined for greatness. All the mothers doted on him, but nobody loved him more than his mother, the formidable Anna Mae.

Winston was neither their first-born child nor their first-born son. He wasn't even their first "covenant child," as children born into polygamous families are called. Winston was Anna Mae's fifth son, the ninth of her thirteen children, and the fourth child born after she and Ray had embraced the Principle. Even though Ray eventually had thirty-one children, almost everybody in the family and nearly everyone in the community believed that Winston was their Nephi, the Book of Mormon's golden boy. No one believed it more strongly than Anna Mae.

Obedient and devout, the apocryphal Nephi was the fourth son of Lehi and Sariah, who rescued the Plates of Brass containing the writings of Moses from Jerusalem. The plates are the ones Joseph Smith claimed to have found twenty-five hundred years later buried under a tree in Palmyra and translated into the Book of Mormon. According to the Book of Mormon, Nephi brought the plates to America (which he called Bountiful) around 590 BC, when he came with his brothers. At first all was well in Bountiful. But, eventually, the brothers and their families had a falling out. Nephi and his descendants followed God, while another brother, Laman, and his descendants, fell in with the Devil. The Lamanites were cursed with "a skin of blackness," and Mormons believe that North American Indians are Laman's descendants, and are thus one of the lost tribes of Israel.

Even without being likened to Nephi, Winston had a lot to live up to. His uncle John Horn Blackmore had been a member of Parliament. His namesake was John's son, Winston Woolley Blackmore, a fighter pilot killed at age twenty-three during the Second World War. But the towering presence in Winston's life was his father, an autocrat and the most powerful man in the cloistered community, with the authority to direct both the spiritual and earthly lives of everyone who lived there. Ray directed everything, from who married whom to who lived where, on the property that was now largely controlled by the church's trust fund, the United Effort Plan. Ray did it all, supposedly, according to God's explicit instructions. Winston wanted to be just like him.

Ray never minded that Winston frequently skipped school to spend time with him or to play hockey. Although Winston loved the farm and the horses, his dream was to be a professional hockey player. Ray indulged him, allowing him to play in the valley's organized league, even though it meant having to mix with gentiles, a privilege denied most other Saints. After Winston learned to drive, he became his father's unofficial chauffeur and missed even more school.

Like all Mormon boys, Winston was initiated into the priesthood—the fundamentalist priesthood—when he was twelve. Already cosseted and confident, Winston grew more arrogant with the certitude that as a man, specifically a fundamentalist Saint, he was one of God's chosen, with the potential to be a god. But the same year that he joined the priesthood, Winston also became aware of his nemesis. She was one of his classmates, a pretty and feisty thirteen-year-old named Debbie Oler, who had attracted the attention of his fifty-three-year-old father.

Debbie was the oldest child of Dalmon and JoAnn Oler, who were the last family to join the community. Only four years after moving to Lister, JoAnn died of complications from an untreated heart condition. The church leaders, including Winston's father, Ray, had told JoAnn that faith healed better than gentiles' drugs. Her faith was strong; her belief in the correctness of living the Principle never wavered, even though her sister-wife had made her domestic life a trial, if not a living hell. But faith alone didn't heal her. JoAnn Oler died on October 25, 1961, her middle child's birthday. Jane was five that day. Debbie was six and JoAnn's son, Kendal, was only two.

JoAnn's children were like orphans in the midst of a chaotic family that eventually grew to include forty-eight children. They were raised primarily by Oler's second wife, Memory, who was barely sixteen when she married twenty-five-year-old Dalmon in 1958. Memory was Winston's sister, and Ray and Anna Mae's eldest daughter. Even though she was a princess born into the equivalent of Saints royalty, she was a pawn in the polygamist game, given by her father to Oler to secure his loyalty to him and the prophet and, perhaps, to secure Oler's place in the celestial kingdom. Even log-and-tarpaper communes have their dynasties.

The pairing of Memory and Dalmon Oler was a fruitful one that eventually produced fourteen children, including a son, Jim, who would later become the FLDS bishop in Bountiful. Eighteen-year-old Memory brought all of the cruelty of adolescence to her role as stepmother to the three grieving children. Debbie, the eldest, who had been especially close to her mother, bore the brunt of her stepmother's frustrations, anger and resentment. As JoAnn's health worsened, Debbie frequently came up with excuses to stay home rather than go to school or play with other children. When JoAnn died, Debbie was nearly inconsolable. Without her mother to protect her, Debbie says, Memory frequently beat her. To spare her siblings, Debbie often took their punishment as well.

As ill-prepared as Memory was to raise JoAnn's children and her own babies, her burden was exacerbated by Dalmon's taking two more teenaged brides soon after JoAnn's death. One of them was Memory's fourteen-year-old cousin Wanda, whom Ray and Anna Mae had adopted a few years earlier. Apparently the child protection agency hadn't heard the rumours about polygamists in Lister, and the social workers didn't notice anything odd about the Blackmore household. Nobody raised any objection to putting a young girl, whose parents were not polygamists, into a polygamous family and a polygamous community.

But police and child protection authorities were very interested and concerned when fifteen-year-old Wanda had a baby. Both she and her son were held for a few weeks before being allowed to return to Oler's home. No charges were ever laid against Oler. A few months after Wanda returned, Oler was assigned sixteen-year-old Andrea. She was another of Ray's daughters and Memory's half-sister. With all the young brides, babies were soon arriving in the Oler home at a rate of two or more a year. There were so many babies that "cribs" had to be created from filing cabinets; perhaps this is what inspired Dalmon to use the same first letter of the alphabet for each baby born in a particular year. One of Oler's babies was born on July 1, 1967, and was probably the only polygamous child to get a gold medallion from the Canadian government for the coincidence of being born on the country's one hundredth birthday.

Even though Memory was a teacher at the community's Hope Private School, she frequently enlisted Debbie and Jane to skip school and look after the children instead. "We took care of hordes of children," Jane recalls. "At 5 a.m., I got the kids up. I got breakfast for them. I did their hair. I made their lunches. And somewhere between 4:30 a.m. and 7:30 a.m., I practised my music. I resented others in my peer group that didn't have to take care of children. But we [Debbie and I] were the oldest in the family."

Memory told Debbie that she was stupid, and when tests showed Debbie to be exceptionally bright, Memory accused her of cheating. No matter how hard Debbie and Jane tried to please Memory, it was never enough. Both were good students, but it was made clear to them that their highest purpose in life was to be wives and mothers in Zion. Their glory would come from having as many babies as possible for the greater glory of God. That was the whole point of celestial marriage. It was reinforced at school and at the church meetings, especially when the prophet came to speak.

"The Lord is sending to the earth right now, through the law of plurality, spirits who have been held back purposely to take part in the establishment of a righteous generation in the earth," LeRoy Johnson explained in a sermon he gave on June 4, 1967, in Lister.

Because covenant children—the progeny of plural marriages—are so special, Uncle Roy said young people must be taught from an early age to curb their sexual desires and feelings. But he also told the children that they were so special, so filled with the spirit of God that when they told the wind to stop, it would cease. When they asked for rain, it would come. And when they told a fierce storm to calm, it would.

But, if any of the girls were under the misapprehension that women had the right to more than one husband or the prospect of being exalted in their own right, the fundamentalist prophet, seer and revelator set them straight on that. "Polygamy has no place in the Latter-day Saint religion. If you will define the word polygamy, you will find that it is just as lawful for a woman to have more than one husband as it is for a man to have more than one wife. We don't believe in any such doctrine! Plural marriage is a sacred ordinance designed to take a man into the eternal worlds and exalt him and make a God out of him . . . You desecrate it by linking it up with the worldly idea of polygamy." It's an interesting rhetorical sleight of hand that attempts to separate religious polygamy from other, supposedly baser, plural marriages and ensure that fundamentalist women don't get any wrong ideas about what their place is for time and all eternity.

In the spring of 1969, when Debbie Oler was graduating from Grade 8, the world was in upheaval. Both Martin Luther King and Robert Kennedy had been assassinated. America's first manned mission to the moon was set for that summer, overshadowing the news from Vietnam, where Americans had been fighting for close to four years. Families still watched television together, but, rather than tuning in to the sitcoms, many were increasingly tuning in to the dark humour of *Laugh-In*. The Mafia was the year's most talked about phenomenon because of Mario Puzo's bestselling book, *The Godfather*. And while The Fifth Dimension were singing about the dawning of a new age of Aquarius, Peggy Lee was asking "Is That All There Is?"

But that was a world away from Lister, where Debbie and the other girls were still dressing like pioneers and marrying their uncles and friends' fathers for the glory of God. The big event in Lister that year was the first high-school graduation at Hope Private School, which had just been accredited by the B.C. government to issue Grade 12 diplomas. Government officials saw nothing wrong with accrediting a school whose superintendent, Dalmon Oler, had five wives and forty-eight children, whose teachers were polygamists and whose religious curriculum centred on teaching the Principle.

Gaining the government's seal of approval—to say nothing of the graduation of the school's first students—was worthy of a huge celebration that brought the prophet back for another visit. But the speech Debbie recalls was her father's:

> "Our children are being prepared and will be turned over to the Lord's prophet when the boys turn twelve and the girls turn fifteen. These children no longer belong to me. They belong to the Lord. If I can take my daughter to the Lord's servant and put her hand in his and say here is a vessel ready to be a mother in Israel, this is the sole purpose of my life. When my sons turn twelve and are given the priesthood of the living God, then I no longer have any right trying to control their lives unless I present them to the prophet and tell him we are as clay in the hands of the Potter."

There may have been no one there that night more ready to become clay in the Potter's hands than Debbie. She was yearning to place her trust in the Lord and the prophet and become a mother in Zion.

Following the speeches, there was a dance outside. Electric lights supplemented the moonlight. Debbie had sewed a new dress from a bold Hawaiian print; underneath the thirteen-year-old wore a new crinoline and her first bra. On that clear night under the stars, she danced for the first time with the man who would be her husband. As they danced, he recited the Song of Solomon in her ear:

> Thy two breasts are like two young roes that are twins, which feed among the lilies . . . My dove, my undefiled is *but* one; she *is* the *only* one of her mother, she *is* the choice *one* of her that bear her. The daughters saw her, and blessed her; *yea*, the queens and the concubines, and they praised her. Who is she *that* looketh forth as the morning, fair as the moon, clear as the sun, *and* terrible as *an army* with banners?

The man who romanced her with biblical poetry was fifty-three-year-old Ray Blackmore. He was eighteen years older than her father and was her stepgrandfather, the father of two of her stepmothers. He had a dozen children older than Debbie and twenty-one children who were younger, including his favourite son, Winston, who was a year younger than Debbie. And Ray Blackmore was the father of one of Debbie's closest friends, Ruth, whose birthday was five days after Debbie's.

It's almost impossible for anyone born outside the community to understand why Debbie felt so privileged to have attracted the attention of a man who was older than her father and already riddled with the cancer that would eventually kill him. But having been routinely told that she was worthless by her stepmother, having been denied a proper education and schooled instead to believe that her best hope for salvation was to serve, Debbie was vulnerable and insecure, easy prey for any man, but especially for a man like Ray Blackmore. He was the most important and influential man in her world, and he had singled her out. With that one dance, she glimpsed heaven.

With the benefit of hindsight, experience and therapy, Debbie wrote to federal Justice Minister Anne McLellan more than thirty years later, begging the government to take action against the fundamentalist Saints. She explained that when leaders constantly talk about "about being married and giving birth like it is [equivalent to] winning Olympic gold, by the time you are a 14-year-old girl, there are no words or concepts for anything else." Girls are anxious to marry and have babies because that's the dream they are allowed; it's constantly reinforced both at school and at church, where girls are frequently read aphorisms from the fundamentalist prophets and the most respected elders of early Mormonism, which are collected in a book called *Purity in the New and Everlasting Covenant of Marriage.*

"A man who obeys the ordinances of God and is without blemish or deformity, who has sound health and mature age, and enjoys liberty and access to the elements of life, is designed to be the head of a woman, a father and a guide of the weaker sex and of those of tender age, to mansions of eternal life and salvation," says one quote from Elder Parley Pratt, one of Smith's contemporaries.

"A woman, under similar circumstances is designed to be the glory of some man in the Lord; to be led and governed by him, as her head in all things, even as Christ is the head of the man; to honour, obey, love, serve, comfort and help him in all things, to be a happy wife, and if blessed with offspring, a faithful and affectionate mother, devoting her life to the joys, cares and duties of her domestic sphere," he continued.

A quote from another early Mormon elder, Heber Kimball, suggests even women know how incapable they are of being anything but a chattel. "Ladies, there is not one of you that has common sense but would leave the man that would suffer you to lead him; you would rightly consider that he was not following his calling, if he would bow to your mandates." Pity the poor woman who learns this after finally convincing her husband to take out the garbage, fold the laundry or change a diaper.

But girls aren't only taught to aspire to marriage. They are taught to aspire to *plural* marriage. In a sermon to the folks in Lister in 1965, Rulon Jeffs (who was the fundamentalists' prophet from 1986 to 2002) preached about celestial marriage, "the highest and most sacred law." "Without it we cannot become Gods. Without it we cannot redeem Zion and build up the Kingdom of God . . . we are not going to build up the Kingdom of God or establish His Priesthood in the earth and God will have to go on and get another people."

By his own admission, Winston Blackmore was "a busybody," keen to listen in on semi-whispered schoolgirl conversations. He either knew intuitively or had learned by watching his father that knowledge is power. Nothing is more powerful than knowing secrets in any community, but this is especially true of a closed community like Lister, where little more than four, very large families were becoming ever more intertwined.

"I needed to know who the girls had a crush on and what their favourite singers were singing and who were their favourite movie stars. Well, I knew those statistics about these girls [Debbie and Jane Oler] as well as the other girls in my school class," Winston wrote years later. "None of the boys would do. They were all no good. We were Blackmores, Palmers and the odd Oler boy and the girls just knew that no one was right for them . . . but Deb focused on my father. I thought she must have been crazy, and so did he, for there were no secrets kept long in our society. She had scarcely reached 14 before she was overly anxious to get married."

It wasn't just the exhortations and expectations of the priesthood leaders that made Debbie Oler anxious to marry. She also believed in the power of revelation, and that by fasting and praying she would come to know God's plan for her. And what she came to believe was that God not only had chosen her to be Ray Blackmore's wife, but that he would tell her how to cure Ray of his leukemia if she loved him enough, was obedient enough and prayed hard enough. That fall, after her fourteenth birthday, Debbie told her father about her revelation and how she felt about Ray. Dalmon Oler approached the prophet LeRoy Johnson on his next visit to Lister. The prophet listened but said nothing. Debbie was heartbroken and, in her distress, poured out her heart to her friends, and Ray's busybody son heard almost every word.

"Oh what an uproar at school," Winston wrote in his questionable account of the strange romance:

> The girls sobbed their hearts out . . . In her mind, she [Debbie] was mature, desperate and time was running out for my father had been diagnosed with cancer and he was in the fight for this life. She seemed to be driven by the belief that if she could just marry him then she could somehow prolong his life, and she seemed driven to get out of her own father's home. Her tears and fuss at school brought on a whole new scene of wonder among the students . . .
>
> Deb was a pretty girl and it did not go unnoticed. Among the other men who were nonstudents, her focus on father sparked some debate as many I suppose could not understand why any girl

would want to commit to a man soon to be dead.
The kind of cancer that father had was final in 95
per cent of all those who contacted [*sic*] it. I am
sure that it seemed such a waste of a pretty girl's life
to be locked on a man who was terminally ill, while
there were others who in their minds were handsome, ready, willing and able. Father could not
understand it either and the thought had no appeal
to him. Time went by for him and as it happened,
she eventually got her wish, as father was called to
come and have her become his wife.

It seems that even years later, after Winston himself had
taken several fifteen-year-old wives, he was unwilling to believe
that his father had seduced Debbie.

Some former Lister residents have speculated that
Winston's intense interest wasn't just in knowing secrets.
They suggest Winston and some of his older brothers had
their eyes on Debbie and were upset that their father might
take her, but knew that they were no competition for their
powerful father or for any older men who paid special tithes
or used their connections to the prophet to get the smartest
and most beautiful girls.

It wasn't until 1971, when Debbie was fifteen, that the
prophet had his own "revelation" confirming Debbie's—and
perhaps Ray's—fervent wish. The only hint that Debbie got
from her father of her impending marriage was a new suitcase and the thirty dollars that he gave her a few weeks before
the June priesthood meeting in Cardston, which was still fertile ground for attacting converts to polygamy. She wasn't certain if the money was for her wedding dress and trousseau, but
she used it to buy material for two dresses, including a soft
cornflower-blue print that would be suitable for a wedding.

Debbie wore her blue dress to the June meeting. She sat through hours of sermons preached in one of the rented meeting rooms before Uncle Roy took her hand and told her to wait for him in the hallway. Together they went into another room set aside for the secret sealing ceremonies. Ray and Anna Mae were already there along with Joseph Musser's son Guy, one of the prophet's senior councillors. Musser took one of Anna Mae Blackmore's hands and placed Debbie's hand in hers. With their hands intertwined, their middle fingers resting on the pulsing veins of one another's wrists, Anna Mae followed the example of Sarah. In the Old Testament story of Sarah and Abraham, the childless Sarah placed the hand of her servant-girl Hagar in her husband's as a sign of her consent that he take another wife to give him children. And that's what Anna Mae did. She placed Debbie's hand in Ray's. Ray was nearly forty-one years older than his bride. He was just a few months shy of his fifty-sixth birthday.

After Anna Mae had joined the hands of Debbie and Ray, one smooth and girlish, the other wrinkled and worn, she stepped aside. Musser asked "Brother Ray" to "receive her unto yourself to be your lawful and wedded wife and you to be her lawful and wedded husband for time and all eternity, with a covenant and promise, on your part, that you will fulfill all the laws, rites and ordinances pertaining to this holy bond of matrimony in the new and everlasting covenant, doing this in the presence of God, angels and these witnesses of you." Then Debbie vowed to be Ray's "lawful and wedded wife for time and all eternity." Musser invoked the authority of the "Holy Priesthood" and sealed them together with the blessings of Abraham, Isaac and Jacob and "with all other blessings pertaining to the new and everlasting covenants."

When the ceremony concluded, the men went back to their priesthood meetings and the new bride, Ray's sixth wife, found herself alone outside in the shade, uncertain what to do next. It gave her time to contemplate the complex family genealogy that had just become even more complicated. She was Winston's stepmother and stepmother to her own two stepmothers which, most confusingly of all, made Debbie her own stepgrandmother.

When it was time to return to the motel, Anna Mae ceded her spot next to Ray in the front seat of the truck. But Debbie was about to learn that Anna Mae lived what is called the "Law of Sarah"; she was like Sarah in many ways. In the Old Testament story, a few years after Hagar's marriage to Abraham and the birth of their son Ishmael, Sarah became pregnant at age eighty-eight with the son she named Isaac. After Isaac was born, Sarah demanded that Abraham cast out both Hagar and Ishmael, telling him, "The son of this bond-woman shall not be heir with . . . Isaac." Like Sarah, Anna Mae never gave up believing that she was the one true wife and that her favourite son, Winston, was Ray's only true heir.

Ray didn't consummate the marriage that night. Despite Anna Mae's symbolic approval of the marriage, her weeping in the room next to the newlyweds' was so loud and went on for so long that Ray left his child bride and spent the night comforting forty-seven-year-old Anna Mae. It was a prophetic start to Debbie's lonely, difficult and even dangerous life as a sister-wife.

Inside Ray Blackmore's home, there was no one more powerful than Anna Mae and no one more protective of him as he grew weaker, both from the cancer and from the intensive treatments that he had opted for rather than depending on faith alone. Anna Mae was the alpha wife and Mother Superior. Even though all the wives did not live in the same house, Anna Mae doled out their chores and responsibilities. She disciplined the sister-wives, and reminded them of their duty to obey their husband and her. The other wives had to make appointments through her to see their husband. Anna Mae had insisted that Ray's bedroom be in the house where she lived, and she kept the schedule of whose turn it was to sleep with him.

She charted the wives' menstrual cycles to ensure that they were only having sex with Ray when they were most fertile, since sex for pleasure without the goal of procreation is a sin. Anna Mae didn't only regulate the wives' access to Ray, she was his sleeping dragon. She spent nights on the floor outside her husband's room while one of the other wives slept with Ray.

Ray's thirty-one children were also scattered in several different houses and Anna Mae acted as gatekeeper to them as well, regulating their access to their father. That, of course, meant that the door was always open for Winston to spend as much time as possible with his father. Still, arranging time alone wasn't simple. Everybody wanted a few minutes with Ray—his children, his wives and priesthood men, who were becoming increasingly dependent on Ray, not only for their salvation but also for their homes and their jobs. Plus, Ray had a ranch to run in order to pay for food and clothing for six wives and thirty-one children.

Debbie was as spirited, insecure and demanding as any teenaged girl. She was also beautiful, and Ray was not unaware of that. His attentiveness to his child bride upset Anna Mae's rigorous schedules, and Debbie's inability to blend sweetly into the family angered the matriarch—and inflamed her son Winston. Debbie had a miscarriage six months after the wedding. Ray—and, no doubt, Anna Mae—blamed Debbie for it. Ray and Debbie had broken the celestial covenant and had sex while she was pregnant. Ray told Debbie that she had tempted him into sinning and Debbie believed him when he told her she was wicked. Debbie fell into a depression and had only begun to recover when she was pregnant again. Debbie's daughter was born in November 1973. Surprisingly, Debbie agreed to name the girl Memory, even though that was the name of her stepmother, who had been so hard on her.

By then, Debbie says, Winston had begun a campaign against her. She says he spied on her, and she found menacing handwritten notes, including a particularly chilling one that read:

> You are a murderer and innocent blood will be on your hand forever because of it. We were all told by the prophet that the Good Father would be healed and restored to full health if his wives and children would keep sweet and be obedient. You are guilty of the sin of gossip and stirring up wicked and vile spirits to destroy the peace and healing power in the Good Father's family.
>
> You will pay before the judgment bar of God for the sins you have committed. You will know the pain of the damned in this life for destroying the prophecy of our prophet, LeRoy Sunderland Johnson — the prophecy that our Good Father would be healed and live forever without ever tasting death. Watch yourself, because I am watching you. From this day forward, someone will always be watching and recording every act you commit, so beware! You will know me. Never forget this day.

It was signed "the Protector of the Faith and the Good Father."

Debbie had reason to be frightened. Mormons are taught that there are sins for which the atonement of Jesus does not apply and for which the spilling of blood is justified. This controversial concept is called blood atonement. Brigham

Young, the second president of the LDS church, outlined it in 1856: "There are sins that men commit for which they cannot receive forgiveness in this world or in that which is to come, and if they had their eyes open to see their true condition, they would be perfectly willing to have their blood spilt upon the ground that the smoke thereof might ascend to heaven as an offering for their sins; and the smoking incense would atone for their sins, whereas, if such is not the case, they will stick to them and remain upon them in the spirit world."

Throughout Mormon history, there have been murders in the name of cleansing sin. But in the 1970s, a fundamentalist Mormon leader named Ervil LeBaron had gone on a killing spree, murdering or ordering the deaths of as many as thirty people. LeBaron had had a revelation that he was the rightful successor to Joseph Smith, and anyone who refused to pledge their full allegiance to him was in danger from his roving hit squads. Among the most spectacular and brazen of these murders was the shooting of chiropractor Rulon Allred. Allred was Harold Blackmore's old friend who had taken over from Joseph Musser after the 1952 split between fundamentalists in Salt Lake City and those in Short Creek who later became the FLDS. At the time of Allred's murder, he had an estimated five thousand followers—the second largest polygamous group in North America after the United Effort in Short Creek.

Eighteen-year-old Rena Chynoweth—LeBaron's thirteenth wife and the leader of a commando group that the LeBarons called the United Women of Zion—walked into Allred's waiting room, which was filled with patients, on the afternoon of May 7, 1977. When Allred came out of his office, Chynoweth emptied the six-shot magazine of a .25 calibre automatic pistol into Allred. She and her accomplice, Ramona Marston, left. But Chynoweath returned a few minutes later, placed the muzzle of a .38 calibre revolver against Allred's head, and fired a final shot.

Chynoweth was nearly nine months pregnant when a Utah jury acquitted her of the murder. Despite her acquittal, Ervil LeBaron was convicted in 1981 of ordering his wives to kill Allred. And Chynoweth later wrote a book admitting to it. Marston also admitted to the murder, but jumped bail and disappeared before she had her day in court.

Seven years later, after Allred's murder in 1978, Ron and Dan Lafferty slit the throats of their twenty-four-year-old sister-in-law, Brenda Lafferty, and her eighteen-month-old daughter, Erica. Brenda had refused to agree to her husband, Allen, taking a second wife. His brothers were acolytes of another polygamist prophet called Brother Onias, whose real name was Robert Crossfield. Crossfield had grown up in Cardston and spent several years living in Lister before he began having revelations that he was the true prophet.

There have been other blood atonements since and, as recently as 1997, Rulon Jeffs preached to the eight thousand or so members of the Fundamentalist Church of Jesus Christ of Latter Day Saints that sometimes blood atonement was not only permissible, but necessary:

> I can refer you to plenty of instances where men have been righteously slain in order to atone for their sins. I have seen scores and hundreds of people for whom there would have been a chance . . . if their lives had been taken and their blood spilled on the ground as a smoking incense to the Almighty, but who are now angels to the Devil . . . The wickedness and ignorance of the nations forbid this principle being in full force, but the time will come when the law of God will be in full force.
>
> This is loving our neighbour as ourselves; if he

needs help, help him; and if he wants salvation and
it is necessary to spill his blood on the earth in order
that he might be saved, spill it.

Debbie was never faced with a gun or a knife, but the
threat was always there. And, before long, with the family
becoming more and more discontented, Debbie and her
newborn daughter were banished from Blackmore's big
house and sent to live in an unheated room over the meeting
hall. She stayed there for a few months until Ray asked the
prophet to order Debbie and her daughter to return to
Dalmon Oler's home.

On June 17, 1974, fifty-eight-year-old Ray Blackmore died.
Just a few days after her third wedding anniversary, eighteen-
year-old Debbie was a widow.

SIX

THE NIGHT OF LONG KNIVES

Not long before Ray Blackmore died he gave his sons some advice: "If you boys will just stay together, this valley will fall into your hands one piece at a time and there will be nothing anyone can do about it." But his favourite son, Winston, who has always claimed to revere his father, ignored that advice. He was too intent on claiming power and doing whatever it took to get it. After all, that's what his father had done.

Only a few days before Winston was to write the first of his Grade 12 provincial exams, his father had finally told him that it was unlikely he would live up to his promise. He was not going to live forever and was not likely going to be able to beat cancer. On June 17, 1974, Winston should have had his head down, writing his exam. Instead he stayed home as his father weakened. Winston never took that test, and never sat through another school exam. Ray Blackmore died that afternoon. He was fifty-eight.

Winston's grief was histrionic. The favourite son acted

as though he was the only one who felt the loss, even though there were six widows and thirty other children. Winston began writing letters to his dead father, which he bizarrely published years later on the Internet. "I am the loneliest boy in the world," he wrote in one. In another he continued the theme: "When he [Ray] died, I could have died too, as he was the one dear thing I had in my life. . . . My heart was broken by my father's passing, I could not think nor barely function. Jane and Miriam [Winston's sister] took their finals, did their usual well and prepared for their graduation day. I disappeared."

Well, not exactly. Winston moved into his father's bedroom in the big ranch house and Anna Mae made it clear to the family, and everyone else in the community, that they were to go to Winston, not to his older brothers, for advice and counselling. His brothers didn't like it and some of the older members of the community initially balked at the idea, but, in the end, they all complied. The younger ones grew up to worship Winston.

Since Anna Mae was Ray's legal wife, she was the only one with inheritance rights. Nothing prevented Ray from providing for all of his wives and children in his will, but he chose not to. Instead, his single-page will signed on November 21, 1970, said simply: "I give, devise and bequeath all my property of every nature and kind and wheresoever situate, including my property over which I may have general power of appointment to my wife, Anna Mae Blackmore, for her use absolutely."

Ray designated Dalmon Oler—Debbie's and Jane's father—as sole executor. Oler was a slow-talking man known for helping everyone. His outlook on life was summarized on a plaque in the family kitchen that read: "The most important word is 'We.' The least important word is 'I.'"

Ray's will shocked some of the wives and children, especially his older sons. Fundamentalist Mormons may have different beliefs from other Christians about the afterlife, but they're like everyone else when it comes to squabbling over the worldly goods left behind. Some of Ray's family challenged the will in court, claiming Ray had written another, separate will "designating the distribution of his estate." Some claimed each of the surviving children had been promised a ten-acre parcel of land; others believed they would get title to the homes they were living in. Still others believed that all of the family property was to have been put into a family trust overseen by Anna Mae, with all of them as beneficiaries.

Oler, in addition to being designated the referee of the Blackmore family feud, was appointed the community's spiritual leader by Prophet LeRoy Johnson. As Winston wrote in one of his posthumous missives to his father, the appointment was to last "until the Lord decided otherwise." Both seemed wise appointments since Oler had a reputation as a peacemaker. "Dad was honest and very sincere," his daughter Jane says. "I find it incredible that he could maintain the faith that brought him into the community throughout the first few years there. There was incredible discord from the beginning. I don't really even remember peaceful [church] meetings or Sunday school until after Harold Blackmore left, Winston's father died and Charles Quinton quit coming to the meetings. That's when my father was in charge and I remember it as being the happiest time of my childhood."

Not that relations in the easygoing polygamist's home were always congenial. The jealousy and tension among the Oler wives was not only palpable, it was dangerous. When Dalmon took his wives and children to the drive-in, the kids spread blankets on the ground in front of the car and the wives sat in the car. Dalmon stood outside. He watched the movies leaning on the car. "He didn't dare sit next to one of them because the others would get jealous," says Jane. "The mothers didn't get along at all. It's another of the reasons I'm dumbfounded that my father lasted as long in the religion as he did."

Winston described Oler's appointment as community leader in a letter to his dead father. Although Winston was very comfortable sliding into his father's role, he described Oler's appointment as the community's religious leader as "quite a relief to lots of us and it made some others very mad." In a somewhat disingenuous letter—if such a thing is possible when one writes to a dead man—Winston continued, "I remember when you told me that there were people just waiting to pick your bones. I see what you mean. It seems like Dalmon is the only peaceful one of the lot. Everyone else just seems to be mad. It doesn't make any sense to me."

Winston's brothers were fighting over the 350-acre ranch that sits under a jutting cliff called the Devil's Seat. "We are having an awful time," Winston wrote to his father in August. "Mac [Winston's oldest brother] wants to divide your things up. The other day Brandon [the second eldest] got some spray paint and started over at the southwest corner and measured out each of the boys an equal portion of the property all the way to the west meadow. Some of us don't want that to happen. They are having meetings down at Oler's to try to decide what to do with your property. I haven't gone to any of them because it just makes me sick."

Winston was busy tending cattle on the family farm and working three days a week at Oler's Ford dealership. He'd earned a spot on the Canyon Cougars team in the local hockey league in the fall of 1974. But, after three games and no ice time, he quit, perhaps recognizing that his future lay not in the National Hockey League, but in filling his father's shoes. "It was a waste of my time," he wrote to his father. "Besides, you are not standing on the bench [coaching]." Although Winston hung up his skates for a while, he has long since been back on the ice, skating with his many children and playing in old-timers' pickup games.

It wasn't only that Winston was too busy to get involved in the family fight over property. He didn't need to. His mother had title to it all and could do what she wanted with it, regardless of what her sons, Oler or anyone else said. More important, Anna Mae trusted Winston, her "Nephi," to handle it and keep them all on the right path. While most seventeen-year-olds would find it a burden to be thrust into their father's role, Winston revelled in it. Soon almost everybody in the community believed as Anna Mae did. Winston had been born to lead them.

One of the first problems Winston had to resolve was the care and feeding of his father's other wives and children. Ray had left no money for them in his will and no indication of how they should be supported. In addition to the economic imperative, there was a spiritual imperative. Saints believe wives and children must be ruled by men, their "priesthood heads." Without a man to guide them, wives and children had no moral centre, no one to rule their baser instincts and keep them from going astray. The women and children would have to be reassigned.

In fundamentalist Mormon belief, women are not allowed to have multiple husbands, either on earth or in any of the three realms of heaven. To get around the theological dilemma posed by widows wandering aimlessly and without a priesthood head, Joseph Smith had come up with a solution that—depending on your point of view—is either elegant in its simplicity or simply inane.

When widows remarry, they can do so simply "for time" and not for all eternity. For example, a woman whose husband had been a prophet or senior member of the priesthood, such as Ray Blackmore, is reassigned to a second husband, but only "sealed" for her remaining time on earth. For eternity, she rejoins her first husband, presumably in the celestial kingdom. However, if the second husband is a more righteous man and a better candidate for heaven's highest realm, the widow can ask for a divorce from her dead husband. With the posthumous divorce, she can then be sealed to a better man for time and all eternity, leaving the first husband who knows where.

Although Winston would later defend his marriages to fifteen- and sixteen-year-olds by claiming he was only following the orders of God and the prophet, he took personal credit for arranging the marriages of two of his father's wives to Dalmon Oler. One of the wives was Allaire, his adopted sister and stepmother.

"Allaire didn't want to get married, but we had a few good talks and I encouraged her to get on with her life," Winston wrote to his dead father. "The Boss, as I have dubbed Dalmon, is a good man and a good example and I know that is the right thing to do."

That left him with the tougher problem of what to do with headstrong Debbie Oler and her young daughter. Because of the furor she had caused in the Blackmore household before Ray died, Debbie had been sent back to live under the direction of her father. Even though her father's house was large, there was no room for Debbie and her baby now that Oler had taken in two of Ray's widows and their children. What Winston suggested (with no apparent disagreement from Oler) was that Debbie be reassigned as the fifth wife to fifty-four-year-old Charles Quinton. Quinton, who had been Ray's partner years earlier in a failed dairy farm, was abusive and well-known for his cruelty.

Debbie's marriage to Quinton was sealed by Prophet LeRoy Johnson a few weeks before Christmas, not that Christmas was celebrated that year or any subsequent year in the Blackmore household. Winston claimed to be so distraught over his father's death that he refused, that year and ever again, to celebrate one of the two most important dates on the Christian calendar. That year, some people in Lister celebrated Smith-mas instead— making Joseph Smith's December birthday a time of exchanging gifts and feasting. But, the following year, most reverted to celebrating Christ's birthday.

As Winston began playing a greater role in the community, it became apparent that he needed a wife and a family. For years, everyone in the community had assumed that Winston would marry Jane Oler. Everyone thought that it was a love match that happened to match the blessing of God and the prophet. Winston has even said that his father had prophesied the marriage—not that it was a big stretch to make such a prediction. There were few other girls of marriageable age in Lister and, at eighteen, Jane was already considered an old maid.

Winston was just two months older than Jane and they had been the only two in their grade all the way through Hope Private School. Shy, self-contained, quiet and studious, Jane tried to be invisible. What she recalls of growing up in Lister are anger, hostility and tension. The Oler home roiled with the wives' jealousy and frustration as they vied for their husband's attention. Their quarrels filtered down to the children, who often bore the brunt of their mother's offence against a sister-wife. At church meetings, there were also the quarrels and disputes that stemmed from the growing insistence that men should not only tithe 10 per cent of their earnings but consecrate all of their property to the priesthood leaders and the United Effort Plan Trust.

Jane was the polar opposite of genial Winston, who was so confident of his place in the community. But Dalmon Oler encouraged the pairing of his daughter with young Blackmore, who seemed destined to a bright future for time and all eternity. In January 1975, Dalmon invited Winston on a snowmobiling trip with him, his new bride Allaire (Winston's sister), Jane and her brother, Kendal. A few months later, Dalmon asked Winston to join them at the spring conference in Utah, which is one of the high points of the religious and social calendar. The spring conference is the time when young men and women often get their "patriarchal blessings," written documents in which the prophet outlines what God has in store for them. Men get promoted within the priesthood ranks, assignment marriages are discussed and celestial weddings are performed.

It was the first time Winston had been invited and it was his first opportunity to have a private meeting with the prophet who had so blessed his father. LeRoy Johnson was impressed with the ambitious young man. He too referred to Winston as being like Nephi. Having confirmed what Anna Mae and Ray Blackmore had prayed for—that Winston might one day become a prophet and later a god in heaven—Johnson told Winston to pray for a revelation about whom he should marry.

The following month, there was another church conference in Rosemary, Alberta, a small Mormon settlement near Cardston. It seems unlikely, but Winston claims he had no plans to go to the meeting, no idea that Jane had gone with her father and no inkling that they were to be married in Rosemary that weekend: "On Saturday about noon, my brother Brandon and his wife LaRee came and found me and invited me to go to conference with them. I told them that I had no money to go, so I couldn't. But they wanted me still to go with them and they offered to pay my expenses," Winston later wrote in an article about Debbie and Jane in his newsletter, titled "A Tale of Two Sisters."

On May 4, Winston and his brother went to Amos Gallup's home, where the meeting was being held. Gallup was Jane's maternal grandfather, who had convinced Dalmon Oler to take up the Principle. "Uncle Roy [Johnson] was sitting on the couch and when he saw me, he beckoned me to come into the side room with him," Winston wrote. "He then told me of his intention of having Jane stand with me as my wife. I was speechless and he told me to go take a walk and think it over."

Winston walked down the muddy road and ended up at another fundamentalist's home where Dalmon was visiting. "He [Oler] was cordial, talkative, and obviously enjoying himself. I went into the next room, came face to face with Jane, turned around and left. Twenty minutes later, we were married in a private ceremony with her folks, grandparents, my brother and his wife, President [of the priesthood council] Marion Hammon and a couple others as witnesses."

Following the ceremony, the men went back to their meeting and Winston was called on to speak; a speech, he said, that could not possibly have made any sense because he was so overwhelmed by his marriage. Jane and Winston drove back to Lister together. They married, Winston claims, because "at last Jane decided that she wanted to get married. In her mind it was time."

That's not the way Jane tells the story. She didn't welcome the prophet's news that she was to marry Winston. When Jane was fifteen, she had had her testimony from God and the prophet and had been told that she would be a mother in Zion. But the prophet also told her that she had been singled out to provide medical help to the community. It fuelled her dream to become a doctor and her eagerness to do well in her studies. But Jane knew that marriage would delay, if not quash, that.

Jane also had someone other than Winston in mind. "I cared deeply for a certain young man, I didn't think God would see it that way. It did not turn out that I was a spiritual young woman," she says wryly. Far from her marriage to Winston being a love match as so many in the community believed, "He was the last person I wanted to marry. I knew Winston. I knew him."

But, in 1975, Jane believed in God and the prophet. She accepted that it was God's will that she should marry Winston Blackmore. It was far from the happiest day of her life. Thirty years later, Jane claims no memory of either the religious ceremony or the later civil ceremony. She doesn't recall whether she had a wedding dress or even a new dress for either the religious ceremony in Rosemary or the civil ceremony a month later in Bonner's Ferry, Idaho. Jane can't recall why they married in Idaho and not in British Columbia. However, other people from Creston say that before terrorism and border concerns, it was a common practice to get married in Idaho. There, unlike in British Columbia, there was no waiting period. You bought your licence and said your vows.

The marriage telegraphed to the faithful that Winston was a man to watch with his impressive lineage, his alliance with the Olers and a bond with the prophet. But if Winston was grateful to his father-in-law for anything—for setting up and initially financing J. R. Blackmore & Sons Limited, which grew into a multi-million-dollar transportation, logging and manufacturing business, or for his daughter—Winston didn't show it. He was too busy currying favour with Uncle Roy—LeRoy Johnson—and trying to get a place on the Priesthood

Council. Oler, the trusting peacemaker, gave Winston ample opportunity to do that by making sure that his gregarious son-in-law had access to the religious leaders. But it was his mother who gave Winston the means to grasp for glory.

In the early spring of 1984—a decade after his father's death—Winston received a commission as clerk for the Priesthood Council. That meant monthly trips to Colorado City to record the high council's decisions and maintain the church's history. His diligence was rewarded a few months later, when he was sworn in as the bishop for Canada, pushing aside Oler, who was ordained as patriarch and presiding elder. Oler's titles were impressive, but meaningless. He had been stripped of influence and humiliated in the culmination of what Jane described as "a power struggle and some devious alliances." There was no question that Winston was in charge. Following the example of Nephi, who had named America "Bountiful" on his arrival, the new bishop renamed his community Bountiful.

It was a fitting name since the community was multiplying at a rapid rate. Only forty years earlier, Harold and Gwen Blackmore and their eight children were the only Saints in the valley. By the 1980s, pioneers Ray Blackmore and Dalmon Oler together had fathered seventy-nine children, and now their sons and daughters were having large families of their own.

Winston had cemented his position by persuading Anna Mae to sign over all 350 acres of J. R. Blackmore's land to the United Effort Plan trust for one dollar on March 8, 1985. Rather than owning the entire valley, Ray Blackmore's sons were now only beneficiaries of a trust. It meant that they were now beholden to the prophet and his closest allies, who controlled virtually all of Bountiful's townsite, in addition to most of the property in Colorado City, Arizona, and Hildale, Utah.

The only security that Anna Mae or anyone else had was Winston, who was given one of the coveted seats as a UEP trustee a few months after the property was transferred. He was the first and only Canadian director of the trust, which at its apex was estimated at more than US$400 million. Nearly twenty years later, Winston claimed in a lawsuit that at least some of the property he had signed over was in the J. R. Blackmore Trust, and that it had been given on the condition that it was to be returned to the family if the church failed to operate a private school for all of the children in the fundamentalist community.

The 1942 document that Salt Lake City accountant and priesthood councillor Rulon Jeffs drew up establishing the United Effort Plan trust is a bizarre blend of faith and legalese. "The United Effort Plan is the effort and striving on the part of Church members toward the United Holy Order," it says, citing a passage from the Doctrine and Covenants. "This central principle of the Church requires the gathering together of faithful Church members on consecrated and sacred lands to establish as one pure people the Kingdom of God on Earth under the guidance of Priesthood leadership."

A consecration is defined as "an unconditional dedication of a sacred purpose." "Consecration of real estate to the United Effort Plan trust is accomplished by a deed of conveyance. Church members also consecrate their time, talents, money and materials to the Lord's storehouse to become the property of the church and, where appropriate, the United Effort Plan Trust." What this means is that the Saints turn over their money, labour and property to the church in the hope that they'll derive some benefit from the trust—and from its administrators, who also dole out wives.

The trust document is littered with religious quotes and includes one from Doctrine and Covenants 82:17–21, which says the trustees "in their sole discretion, shall administer the trust consistent with its religious purpose to provide for Church members according to their wants and their needs, insofar as their wants are just."

All young FLDS men yearn and pray for the day that they will be able to build a house on UEP land—sacred, consecrated ground. They are taught that to advance in the priesthood and gain their salvation, they needed to live on God's land. Ross Chatwin was one of the men who felt privileged to be able to do that. "It's quite an exciting time for a young man," he said years later. "He knuckles down and puts everything he has into building his home, all the while anticipating the possibility of marriage and of getting to start a family. When I was young, impressionable, a little ignorant and maybe even a little overly zealous, I wanted more than anything to build a home . . . The excitement I felt as a seventeen-year-old boy at receiving a building lot from the UEP can only be matched by the dread of finally realizing the UEP might be used as an instrument to forcibly take my home from me."

The UEP was largely the creation of Rulon Jeffs, who became the prophet after LeRoy Johnson's death in 1986. Jeffs, an accountant and successful businessman in his own right, had drafted the original trust document. But in 1998, he oversaw a massive revision of it that reduced faithful Saints from beneficiaries of the trust to tenants-at-will. The amendments were unanimously approved by the trustees, including Winston Blackmore, after an unsuccessful lawsuit filed by Harold Blackmore and other disaffected members. Far from Harold's utopian vision of a communal society, the UEP's cabal of directors now had the power to do whatever it wanted, including evicting men from the houses they had built.

"The privilege to participate in the United Effort Plan and live upon the lands and in the buildings of the United Effort Plan Trust is granted and may be revoked by the Board of Trustees," the revised document reads. It continues as follows:

> Those who seek that privilege commit themselves and their families to live their lives according to the principles of the United Effort Plan and the Church and they and their families consent to be governed by the Priesthood leadership and the Board of Trustees. They must consecrate their lives, times, talents and resources to the building and establishment of the Kingdom of God on Earth under the direction of the President of the Church and his appointed officers. All participants living on United Effort Plan Trust land must act in the spirit of charity (Moroni 7:6–10, 45–48). They must live in the true spirit of brotherhood (Matthew 22:36–40) and there shall be no disputations among them (3 Nephi 18:34).

With these amendments, the trustees claimed the power to evict anyone who they deemed was not living up to the principles of the trust and the church. They gave themselves the power to throw individuals and families out of homes they'd built or from property they'd signed over to the trust. They claimed the power to force individuals and families to share their accommodations. Finally, the trustees revoked "any obligation whatsoever to return all or any part of consecrated property back to a consecrator or to his or her descendants."

The president/prophet and the priesthood now controlled every aspect of people's lives: where they slept at night, whom they slept with and where they spent eternity. It was no longer enough to be righteous and to follow the laws of God; the prophet or Bountiful's bishop could now use material needs as both carrot and stick to discipline and demand obedience. If a young man didn't pay his tithes or the increasingly regular demands for additional "donations," he wouldn't get a plot of land to build a house. He wouldn't get a single wife, let alone the trio he would need to save his soul.

The church leaders were even able to determine where a man could work. Most had companies in their own names, despite the exhortations to followers to consecrate their worldly goods to the UEP. Using money and property tithed to the UEP, Rulon had established companies involved in everything from grain farming to cattle ranching to manufacturing aerospace components to mining tin in Bolivia.

Dalmon Oler was among those who became a tenant-at-will. With the heavy demands for tithes and additional contributions, his once-flourishing business went bankrupt. Winston Blackmore never offered to help his father-in-law. Instead, he hired Oler's sons to work for his own companies. Some of Oler's wives abandoned him. Near the end of his life, the man who had once been the most powerful man in the community and who had once run the school was driving the school bus. His boss was the school's superintendent, Bishop Winston Blackmore, a Grade 12 dropout.

"Father lost his position and was disgraced. He lost his sons [who sided with Winston]. He lost his homes. He lost his family and his property. He paid rent on our own home until 1997," says Jane, adding, "It was unpleasant to be the wife to one and the daughter to the other."

Being alienated from much of his family, disgraced and financially ruined—all due in no small part to his son-in-law—destroyed Dalmon's health. He died of a heart attack in 1998, at the age of sixty-four.

As Oler declined, Winston grew in stature, not only among Saints but also among residents in the nearby community of Creston. It was partially his charm. But it was also due to a confluence of events that he might attribute to God. Others might say it was good luck.

After becoming bishop and a UEP trustee, Winston had commandeered the basement of Oler's home as a school. But with six school-aged children of his own and dozens more anticipated (he now had six wives), Winston was determined to build a new school. The land he wanted was on the edge of the community. It was the ten-acre site of the old Creston garbage dump, which was owned by the provincial government. Winston got a bank loan for $23,000 and bought the property in April 1985.

At about the same time, British Columbia's Social Credit government passed legislation granting private schools access to public funding for the first time. Accredited schools were now eligible for up to half the amount that public schools received annually for operations. Administering the new Independent School Act were many of the same people from fundamentalist Christian schools who had lobbied so hard for the legislation and the money for their parochial schools.

The government's independent school officials encouraged Blackmore to apply for accreditation for the recently completed Bountiful Elementary-Secondary School. With the prophet's approval, Blackmore incorporated a non-profit society that would establish, maintain and operate schools for "those persons who practice the Fundamentalist Church of Jesus Christ of Latter Day Saints religion."

One of the society's other goals was to "solicit, collect, deal in and dispose of used and salvaged goods and articles of every kind for the purposes of the association." For some reason, no one in the office of the provincial government's Independent

School Inspector questioned the junk-collection and garbage-disposal goals of the society, or the wisdom of building a school next to a garbage dump. No one seemed concerned that the religious curriculum included teaching polygamy or that the science curriculum would be augmented with the prophet's beliefs that dinosaurs never existed and that the moon landing was a hoax. And no one seemed to mind that once the school was accredited the money began flowing to a society that had an American "prophet" as its president.

In 1988, the school's grant amounted to nearly $350,000 for the 184 children registered at BESS that year. By 2007, Bountiful's population of school-aged children had nearly doubled, and B.C. taxpayers were sending more than one million dollars a year to Bountiful's two schools.

By the mid-1980s, Winston Blackmore had forged a friendship with Howard Dirks, a local businessman who had worked in the Texas oil patch long enough to have acquired a drawl. Dirks ran for the B.C. Social Credit Party in 1986. The bishop of Bountiful told his followers to vote for Dirks and the party that John Blackmore had once led nationally.

"I was in church when the colony leader, Winston Blackmore, told everyone to vote Social Credit because they'd fund our new school," a Bountiful resident told a *Vancouver Sun* reporter. "The impression everyone got that day was that we would go to hell if we didn't obey him on how to vote. Directions on how to live your life always came from the pulpit."

Dirks won by 131 votes. Dirks denied making any promises about funding the Bountiful school. But, after he was appointed provincial secretary, Dirks approved a $4,700 grant for the school's playground. The government defended the grant, saying that the playground is open to the public when, in fact, the only road to Bountiful is lined with NO TRESPASSING signs.

But Dirks helped Blackmore and the community in another, much more substantial way during his tenure as a member of the legislative assembly. He was on the committee that had recommended breaking the virtual monopoly that big lumber companies had on timber lands. What that did was make it easier for small, independent logging contractors like J. R. Blackmore & Sons to gain access to Crown-owned forest resources. J. R. Blackmore & Sons began to prosper.

Local staff at the B.C. Assessment Authority also helped Blackmore. They advised Blackmore to transfer all the property the school sat on to the School Society, which would lower the tax bill.

With Blackmore's growing affluence and influence, social workers and the RCMP were either so unaware or willfully blind to the rising number of child brides in Bountiful that, in 1989, they signed a child-abuse protocol with Blackmore, the school's superintendent, and FLDS prophet Rulon Jeffs. Rather than teachers reporting suspected abuse directly to the police or to the provincial child protection service, they were to report first to the school principal, Merrill Palmer, who would in turn advise Blackmore.

In other words, the foxes were in charge of the henhouse. Blackmore, Jeffs and Palmer were all polygamists. They not only believed that any abuse should be handled internally, they had been taught since birth to distrust outsiders and to have as little as possible to do with gentiles. All of them eventually had teen brides, including some who were students at the school that they operated.

If government officials and politicians had expected that all of this help would eventually bring Bountiful into the mainstream, they were wrong. If they believed that by supporting the school that Bountiful's children would get a better education, they were wrong. Over the next few years, so few children graduated from high school that the school quit offering Grades 11 and 12.

If officials trusted that Blackmore, the school's superintendent, was committed to education, they were wrong. Even as Blackmore battled the bureaucracy to get more money for his school, he was encouraging and even ordering boys to leave school to go to work for his companies. As for the girls, he was either assigning them to marriages or sending them off to work as cooks at his company work camps.

His undervaluing of education had led to almost continual skirmishes in Winston's own home with his wife Jane—over her own education and their children's. Jane had accepted her role as one of God's chosen women whose job it was to populate the earth with the faithful in advance of Jesus Christ's coming again. She had tried to keep sweet as the bishop's first wife. But when she had received her patriarchal blessing at fifteen, the prophet had told her that she would be called on to minister to the sick. Because of that, Jane had not given up on her dream of becoming a doctor. Her father refused to allow it. So did her husband.

Yet Winston constantly asked Jane to tend to people in the community who had minor injuries and illnesses. With no formal training, she was frustrated by her lack of knowledge and afraid that she might do more harm than good. She kept asking her husband and the prophet to at least let her go to nursing school. But they had more important things on their minds. Finally, when Jane's sixth child was only fifteen months old, she had waited long enough. As she recalls, "I decided that God helps those who help themselves and I enrolled in college." Jane defied her husband and the prophet. She knew Winston too well to believe in him or his revelations.

First, she had to take the high-school science classes she'd been denied when she was in high school. Jane finished those easily, overcoming some of the homegrown "science" she'd been taught in Bountiful, and went on to qualify as a registered nurse with a specialty in obstetrics.

In 1995, Winston asked Jane to start delivering babies at home for his twelve or more American wives, who didn't qualify for Canada's universal health care. Jane asked Winston for permission to take additional training as a midwife. According to her, "He said no, time was too short. The world was going to end." Once again, Jane defied him and went anyway, even though it put her in the extraordinary position of having to attend at the births of more than half of her husband's one-hundred-plus children born to his teenaged wives—and at one particularly gruelling birth of a baby to a fourteen-year-old.

Jane got her education the only way most women are allowed to within this closed group. They must first be mothers. If they need to go away to school, they have to leave their children behind to be cared for by sister-wives; the children are insurance that the mothers will come back.

Of course, Winston remembers it all very differently. After Jane had left him and Bountiful, he wrote the following:

> We just knew she needed to be a nurse and so we enrolled her in Selkirk College. Our family included others by now and it was convenient, to say the least. But the very real struggle of doing your lessons was all her own. Eventually she graduated, got a job at the hospital and literally assisted hundreds of people in hundreds of ways. As our family increased, she would welcome the mothers and children in a gifted, inspired and friendly manner.
>
> Eventually she added the midwife program to her agenda and like the student she has always been, tackled it and graduated. She was the mother

> to hundreds, loved by thousands and admired by
> saint and sinner alike. I was a 24-hour-a-day bishop
> and Jane a 24-hour-a-day mother of a community.

It's the kind of revisionism that seems essential to fundamentalist leaders intent on proving their own wisdom and infallibility. And while there has never been any doubt that Winston loved being the 24-hour-a-day bishop, Jane had never aspired to be the mother of the community. In fact, as Winston and the community were soon to find out, Jane didn't want to be part of the community at all.

SEVEN

GOD'S MOUTHPIECE

W inston Blackmore wasn't the only young prince rising as aging polygamous leaders looked to the future in the 1980s. There was another man with the prospect of becoming like Nephi. His name was Warren Jeffs and his bona fides as a polygamist were even more impressive than Blackmore's.

Warren's grandfather David Jeffs was among the first men to point out the impossibility of the church or state stamping out polygamy simply by outlawing it. Short of a revelation—a direct commandment from God that Smith had been wrong about celestial marriage—David Jeffs and others just kept on marrying as many girls and young women as they could. Fundamentalists have always asserted that Wilford Woodruff's Manifesto was not a revelation from God but a pragmatic decision aimed at earthly—not spiritual—gain. They point out as well that Woodruff didn't call for an end to polygamy but a suspension of its earthly practice. What fundamentalists have argued since 1890 is that without a revelation from God to the prophet that Doctrine and Covenants 132 is wrong, they will ignore not only the Manifesto but also laws made by states, provinces and countries. Until God tells them explicitly to stop practising polygamy both now and in the hereafter, they intend to continue to follow what they are certain are His laws, which take precedence over everything else.

Warren's father, Rulon, was born in 1909 and raised in polygamy. But he rejected the Principle as a young man and fully embraced the mainstream church. Rulon served a two-year mission for the Latter-day Saints in England during the Depression and managed to save enough money to go on a European tour when his mission was completed. But when Rulon's twenty-four months were up, the mission president asked him to stay on for a few months longer. Rulon not only used up all of the money he'd saved for his European travels, he had to borrow money from the mission president, who demanded repayment.

"It had a souring effect on him," Rulon's son Dick Hodson told a *Salt Lake City Tribune* reporter in 1998. Hodson was estranged from his father, whom his mother divorced because of polygamy. Rulon Jeffs returned to Salt Lake City to work as an accountant with the Utah State Tax Commission for US$185 a week. His office in the Capitol building overlooked the Mormon Tabernacle. While Rulon was working there, he began courting Zola Brown. Her father, Hugh B. Brown, was an apostle and one of the thirteen most powerful men in the LDS church. He spent seven years as the first councillor to the church's president.

Both Brown and his wife were Canadians. A lawyer before he volunteered to serve in the Canadian army during the First World War, Brown was promoted to major, but claimed further advancement was denied him because he was a Mormon. His wife, Zina Young Card, had an impressive Mormon lineage, counting among her ancestors both Brigham Young and Charles O. Card, the founder of Cardston, Alberta.

Following his marriage to Zola Brown, Rulon seemed on track for a senior post in the LDS church. His own mission service, coupled with the family connection, made him a likely candidate. However, after the birth of his first son, Rulon began inviting his father for Sunday dinners. Polygamy was a frequent topic and, over the dinner table, the old man convinced his son of the hypocrisy of the mainstream church's position and the correctness of following all of Joseph Smith's revelations, not simply the ones that gentiles allowed.

Rulon and Zola argued about it for weeks. It was anathema to all that she believed. Finally, on a hot July night in 1940, Rulon Jeffs crawled into bed with his wife after weeks of sleeping apart. Rulon told Zola he'd had a vision of the woman God wanted him to marry. He'd had this vision while on a trip to the mountains, according to court records from their 1941 divorce. The woman in the vision just happened to work at a store in Provo.

Rulon told his wife he was going to take a second wife. If Zola couldn't accept that, he said, things could never be the same between them. Zola cried seemingly non-stop day and night, while Rulon began building a suite in the basement of their new home for his second wife. Because of the stress, Zola's milk dried up and she could no longer nurse her infant son. Finally, she packed up their two sons and moved to Pasadena, California, where she filed for divorce. Two weeks after the divorce was finalized, Rulon was excommunicated by the mainstream Mormon church. But he'd already moved on by then. Rulon had married the girl in his vision and their home had become a centre for polygamist activity.

Rulon's credentials as a loyal priesthood man were further established after his arrest in 1944 in a Utah roundup of polygamists. Rulon spent several months in the Salt Lake City Jail before his case was dismissed. Others, including John Y. Barlow, the first fundamentalist prophet, signed papers renouncing polygamy, even though they promptly went home to their plural wives and resumed life as before. Undeterred, Rulon also went back to polygamy and his accounting practice. He worked hard to enrich himself as well as the polygamous group known then as the United Order. (After Rulon became the group's prophet in 1986, he registered the church as the Fundamentalist Church of Jesus Christ of Latter Day Saints or FLDS.)

Although Rulon oversaw an extensive financial empire of his own, managed the church's growing portfolio of real estate and companies, and lived on an estate in one of Salt Lake City's most expensive neighbourhoods, he maintained a low profile. One of the few times his name was mentioned in the media was in 1958, when he was ousted as president of the Federated Insurance Company. Rulon had solicited shareholder proxies to fire all of the other directors. But they found out and fired him instead.

His name was mentioned again in 1986, after the U.S. *Challenger* space shuttle exploded, killing seven astronauts. He was a director of Hydrapak, which manufactured the faulty O-ring that allowed fiery gas to escape and ignite the shuttle's liquid fuel tank. (Bizarrely, for a director of a company with aerospace contracts, after Rulon became the prophet he told his followers that the 1969 moon landing was a hoax.)

Over the years, Rulon accumulated more than sixty wives. Two young girls, sisters named Edna and Mary, are said to have been given to him by their father as a gift on his ninetieth birthday. But Marilyn Steed—his fourth wife—was Rulon's favourite, and Warren Jeffs is her second son.

Warren was born prematurely on December 3, 1955, in Sacramento, California. When he was about six months old,

Warren and his mother moved to the Salt Lake Valley. He struggled with school for his first seven years, but not because of any particular learning problems. Rather, Warren claims he simply preferred to stay at home. At least that's what he told a court-appointed psychologist in 2007.

Unlike in Ray Blackmore's family, where Winston was the unchallenged favourite, things were not as clear-cut in the Jeffs family. Warren was never adored by his siblings or the other mothers. Tall, skinny and awkward, Warren was unpopular at school. "He was a poor, picked-on individual. He was clumsy and always in his brothers' faces. Four or five of them always made fun of him and picked on him," says Ross Chatwin, who was kicked out of the FLDS by Warren. "He's made a vendetta and got back at everybody who ever took advantage of him."

Warren was not even his father's clear favourite. It was Warren's older brother, Leroy, who was sent to study accounting and who took over his father's business in 1983. Still, Warren was always closer to his father than many of the other sixty or so children in his family.

Despite a slow start at school, Warren began doing better after Grade 6, graduating from a public high school in Jordan, Utah, in 1973. He was reportedly in the top 3 per cent of his class, although no one has ever said how many were in the class. Rulon sent Warren to teach at Alta Academy, the private school for fundamentalist Mormon children set up within the family's large compound in Little Cottonwood Canyon, which was large enough to accommodate two hundred students.

The compound also had steel grain silos and five houses, including a twenty-two-room house that Rulon's business partner Lloyd Wall and his family lived in. Rulon's own 8,300-square-foot home had two kitchens equipped with industrial-sized fridges, ovens and appliances, ten bathrooms, four fireplaces and twenty-three bedrooms for twenty-three wives, who all kept an identical photo of Rulon on their bedside table.

Although Warren had only a high-school diploma, he taught math, science and computer programming. Alta Academy's science curriculum taught students that dinosaurs, the moon landing and subsequent spacewalks were fictional. Evolution was largely ignored and creationism was taught as the only true theory. Biology lessons were cursory and left chasm-sized blind spots for teenagers—there was no explanation of where babies come from, for example, or why girls menstruate. After three years of teaching, Rulon promoted his son to principal. In this role, Warren oversaw the religious instruction, preached daily homilies, taught family life classes and enforced the school's motto: "Perfect obedience produces perfect faith, which produces perfect people."

Some former students remember him as a dedicated and even encouraging teacher. But what others recall of Alta Academy is the abuse. One former student told the *Deseret News*, "I witnessed Warren Jeffs taking a young second grader and hanging him upside down by the ankles in order to shake the evil out of him."

Sworn affidavits in a civil suit launched in 2004 allege that Warren had a history of sexually abusing boys, starting when he was fourteen. Church leaders were aware of that, according to unchallenged court filings. Yet his father not only allowed Warren to continue teaching children, he left him in charge of teaching ethics and morality. Rulon Jeffs gave his son ultimate authority over the children in his care.

The elders—most, if not all, of whom had children going to Alta Academy—covered up Warren's history of abuse and did not report it to police. And according to the lawsuit, the FLDS leaders, including Jeffs and his brothers, terrorized the young

Warren Jeffs with some of his seventy or more wives, sitting down to dinner in Salt Lake City in the 1990s. "Perfect obedience produces perfect faith, which produces perfect people," was his motto.
(Photo courtesy of the HOPE organization)

victims, threatening them with "eternal damnation" if they went to the authorities. And because no one reported the sexual abuse at the time it occurred, there is no way that those earlier claims can now be criminally prosecuted. Utah legislation doesn't allow for it. Unlike in Canada, where there is no time limit for a victim to report a sexual assault—something that has been key in the successful prosecution of teachers, priests, ministers and others—victims in Utah have only four years from the time of the assault to report it. Even children must report abuse within that time period, which helps explain why so few pedophiles and rapists from polygamous communities or any others are convicted in Utah. Up until 2002, Arizona's statute of limitation gave victims only seven years to report abuse. In 2002, the state legislature removed the time limit.

Warren Jeffs's victims have no other recourse but to file civil suits, and in July 2004, one of them did. Brent Jeffs,

Warren's nephew, has alleged that, beginning in 1980, when he first attended Alta Academy, he was "repeatedly sodomized and otherwise sexually abused" by Warren and two other uncles, Blaine and Leslie Jeffs. During Sunday church services at the academy, children were sent to the basement for two hours of religious training. On repeated occasions, Brent alleges that Warren and his brothers would come down, take him to the nearby lavatory and tell him to take off his clothes. When he was naked, Brent says, one or more of his uncles would tell him it was God's will that he submit to them. Then they would take turns sodomizing him, telling the boy that they were doing "God's work" and that it was all part of their effort to make him "a man."

Brent says they told him it was also "God's will that he never disclose the abuses to anyone and that if he did, it would be upon pain of eternal damnation." Brent alleges he wasn't the only boy who was repeatedly sexually assaulted by Warren, Blaine and Leslie Jeffs. Brent's two brothers were victims as well. He says the pressure of keeping that terrible secret eventually drove his brother Clayne to commit suicide in January 2004. Clayne's suicide was the catalyst for Brent's filing the civil suit.

Ward Jeffs, who is Brent's and Clayne's father and Warren's brother, told a television reporter, "I have no doubt our son's death was due to Warren. He would put the fear of God into people, telling them that perfect obedience assures heaven . . . Eventually the man will have to pay for doing such bad things to people."

So far, Warren Jeffs has not responded to his nephew's claims.

—

Warren Jeffs remained principal at Alta Academy until 1998, when the school closed. Rulon had had a revelation that Salt

Lake City was soon going to be destroyed in the apocalypse. He moved his family—including Warren—to Colorado City to await the lifting up of the righteous from the land that they believed was sacred, having been consecrated for the use of the Lord.

Warren Jeffs has never consented to an interview, so the only glimpses of him come from court appearances following his arrest in 2006, and from videos, recordings and written texts of his sermons. A videotape of a 1993 school perform-ance, obtained by the *Deseret Morning News*, shows Warren dressed in a dark suit and large, thick glasses presiding as master of ceremonies for a program that included skits and musical performances. He says a prayer before the curtain parts and a choir comprising teenaged girls in pioneer-style floral dresses and boys in checkered long-sleeved shirts and dark denim pants sings a few songs. After the singing, he introduces a couple of skits about the evil of eating too much, as well as performances of "Cinderella" and "Goldilocks and the Three Bears."

Midway through the program, Warren makes an unex-pected appearance, popping through the curtain wearing a ball cap tilted on his head and a Groucho Marx nose, with matching glasses and eyebrows. He pulls out a toy violin and leads the children through "Twinkle, Twinkle, Little Star." "Sing it! Louder! Louder!" he shouts as they go through "Mary Had a Little Lamb" and "Frère Jacques."

There are reports about other school shows where Warren did spoofs of Sherlock Holmes and impersonations of Jerry Lewis. He's said to be quite musical, having written hymns and rewritten some well-known LDS hymns to suit the funda-mentalist doctrine.

But it's his taped sermons and lectures that go back to his time as principal that are most revealing and chilling. All are delivered in a droning monotone, whether it is hate-filled rants about "Negroes" and homosexuals, admonitions about obedience, or threats to those who question the prophet. In one of his weirdest rants, Warren condemns not only "Negroes" and homosexuals, but links them to the Beatles and all of rock and roll:

> I was watching a documentary one day and on came these people talking about a certain black man. In the program it was revealed that this black man was homosexual, immoral on drugs, the worst kind of person. And then it showed the modern rock group, the Beatles. It shows them as pingy-pangy, useless people who no one would hire.
>
> And so the manager of the group called in this Negro, homosexual, on drugs, and the Negro taught them how to do it. And what happened then, it went worldwide. And all other music has followed that pattern. The most famous of what we call the rock groups. So when you enjoy the [rock] beat, which may be even toned down with an orchestra, you are enjoying the spirit of the black race and that's what I emphasize to the students. It is to rock the soul and lead the person to immorality, corruption, to forget their prayers, to forget God. And thus the whole world has partaken of the spirit of the Negro race, accepting their ways.

In another recorded sermon, Warren rails against "the black race" as the people "through which the devil has always been able to bring evil unto the earth." In another, he tells the schoolchildren, "If you marry a person who has connections with a Negro, you would become cursed." In still another sermon, Warren says, "Today you can see a black man with a white woman, et cetera. A great evil has happened on this land because the devil knows that if all the people have Negro blood, there will be nobody worthy to have the priesthood."

Homosexuality, Warren says in another sermon, is "the worst evil act you can do, next to murder. It is like murder. Whenever people commit that sin, then the Lord destroys them."

But his most frequent topics are obedience to the prophet, who is "God's mouthpiece on Earth," and women's obedience to their husbands. He told the students in a home economics class in November 1997 that a man must have more than one wife, but women can only be married to one husband. "A faithful priest must have faithful wives in order to raise a family. Women must have a faithful husband," he said. "We cannot go to the kingdom on our own. This holy ordinance binds women to a man in such a manner that they are to be one. He is their Lord and as he is like God, he is God over them and they are to love and build him up and as a result will bring children unto the Lord."

In another lesson, he reminds students "marriages must be by revelation through the prophet. Appointed through him; the Lord speaking through the heavens to him on your behalf. Those kinds of marriages are eternal." But if an assignment marriage fails, Warren says, it cannot be the prophet's fault, because the prophet is infallible. "It's the people who lived it wrong . . . The prophet does right in the appointment of marriage and if the people live right, blessings will come . . . and then they shall be gods because they will have no end."

As for young men who attempt to court their own brides, Warren said he had been instructed by his father, the prophet, that that they will be cast out "even before they destroy the girl." But he saves his fiercest warnings for the girls. Not only are young girls forbidden from having friendships with boys, Warren tells them they can't hold on to friendships with other girls either:

> If you hold on to friendship with your girlfriends you will not love your sister-wives. Your sister-wives must be your best friends because they are part of your husband. Your preparation for this is in your father's home. A girl learns to love all her mothers. And you must love every mother and call them "Mother." Don't date secretly with boys, you're just tricking yourself, ladies. You want a husband who is close to the prophet. A girl who wants eternal life will want this kind of man. You must be a family in heaven, you can't get there alone, so don't play around with your eternal salvation, turn to the prophet who can read the hearts of the men. The prophet will lead you to a man who will exalt you, and when temptation comes into your mind you must pray to the Prophet.

One of the extraordinary things about this group is that, in the name of God, the prophets have forced women to cede the very essence of motherhood. They do not protect their children. In deference to the prophet's will, fundamentalist mothers have allowed their daughters to be raped, abused, traded, humiliated. They have allowed their sons to be abused, exploited and even cast out alone into the world when they're barely teenagers.

History suggests that women are hard-wired to protect their children. Over the millennia, women have heroically proven under the most unbearable of circumstances, including wars, famines, plagues, depression and economic hardship, that they will sacrifice everything for their children. But whether hard-wired or socialized, it doesn't really matter. Over the centuries, even philosophers and psychologists such as Aristotle, St. Augustine and Carl Jung, who had little regard for women, acknowledged that this trait of protective motherhood grants women a small measure of superiority over men. In Christian theology, it is motherhood and the care of children that has lessened the sting of Eve's sinning in the Garden of Eden.

From Greek times until today, there seems to be something so inherently evil in mothers who do not protect their children that Euripedes' play from 431 BC about Medea, who kills her two children in her distress over her husband abandoning her to take another wife, still seems no less shocking than the news reports in 2002 that Andrea Yates had murdered her five children in Texas. Perhaps it is for this reason that almost every person who leaves polygamy saves the harshest criticism for his or her mother and not the father.

All Mormons believe that their leader is a prophet with a direct connection to God. Unlike Catholic popes, Mormons believe that their presidents or prophets don't just interpret scripture, they have new commandments revealed to them by God. These revelations are then added to the Doctrine and Covenants, one of the Mormon holy books. But as the LDS church has become more mainstream, the flood of revelations has become a trickle. By the twentieth century, doctrinal changes were rare, but often revolutionary, such as Spencer Kimball's 1978 revelation to lift the ban on black men joining the priesthood. But if God speaks less frequently now to mainstream LDS prophets, he works overtime revealing new commandments to fundamentalist prophets. Over the past twenty-five years, they have recorded countless predictions about one thing alone — that the world is about to end. The frequency of those predictions only accelerated as the millennium drew closer.

"We only have until the year 2000 to do this work and the Prophet Joseph, the one mighty and strong, will take over and carry this Gospel to the world," Prophet LeRoy Johnson revealed in 1984. "There will be a period of peace upon this continent for a thousand years."

That revelation didn't pan out, nor did Johnson's revelation that he would live well into the twenty-first century and see the establishment of the New World Order. He died in November 1986 at the age of ninety-eight, but only after he'd helped establish a theocracy in Colorado City and Hildale.

When Arizona and Utah agreed to incorporation of the two towns in 1985, Hildale resident J. M. Pipkin said in a letter to the editor of the *St. George Spectrum* that what the state governments had done was help "establish and finance the first papal state within the United States of America . . . Yes, now with the official establishment of the city codes by rubber-stamp councils having a private (papal) security force (law enforcement) all that there is left to accomplish is to convince the States of Utah and Arizona to finance at taxpayers' expense, an Iron Curtain around Short Creek!"

Rulon Jeffs, the most senior member of the priesthood council, succeeded Johnson, and took over not only spiritual leadership of the approximately eight thousand people, but full control of the civil and legal institutions in the twin towns as well, just as Joseph Smith did in Nauvoo, Illinois. Almost everyone in Hildale and Colorado City belonged to the FLDS, lived on UEP property and pledged obedience to the prophet. That included the doctors and nurses in the hospital, the teachers, the police and even the local judge. They pledged their loyalty to the prophet's laws, not to the state's or to the nation's. As a result, anyone who dared question the prophet could be arrested, tried, punished, medicated,

*FLDS prophet Rulon Jeffs with
the last two brides he'd ever
marry. Edna and Mary Fischer
were given to him as a ninetieth
birthday present.*
(Photo courtesy of HOPE Organization)

declared insane and hospitalized, stripped of his wives and
children and evicted from the twin towns.

The Fundamentalist Church of Jesus Christ of Latter Day
Saints—as Rulon Jeffs had named it—had all the attributes
that anthropologist and author Willa Appel ascribes to messianic cults in her book *Cults in America: Programmed for
Paradise*. They are groups, she writes, that "hold themselves
apart in some way from the rest of the world." Appel goes on
to say, "They are by nature antagonistic toward society, their
members bound by a fervent ideology and belief in a spiritual
leader. The classic structure of messianic cults is authoritarian; followers, subjugated to an all-powerful leader or hierarchy of leaders, are dependent and submissive, believing that
their salvation is contingent on abject obedience."

Rulon used that power over his followers almost from the
moment he took over as prophet. He announced frequent

revelations, invoking God's authority to ensure he was obeyed. And these revelations weren't just about big things like the end of the world. "Leave television alone! Do away with videos! Do away with the headphones, the listening to radio, hard metallic music. It is of the devil," he told followers in 1991. "That is how he is getting into our homes. Believe me, dear people, leave it alone!"

He told them to stop reading novels and stick to Mormonism's holy books—the Book of Mormon, the Doctrine and Covenants, and the Pearl of Great Price. "Put these thoughts in your mind in place of all these devilish and satanic media operations. Media is television. Pornographic books and magazines. Leave them alone! If there are any in the community, get them out! We don't want them here! They must not be here!"

In August 1997, when Rulon was eighty-seven, he had a major and debilitating stroke. Over the next five years, the line began to blur between Rulon and his ambitious son Warren, who increasingly spoke on behalf of his father. But if Rulon had trouble communicating with his followers, it seemed he had no trouble hearing the word of God. Among the most revolutionary things that God told him in 1998 was that men must have at least three wives if they aspired to the celestial kingdom. Joseph Smith's revelation had never specified numbers. All that Doctrine and Covenants 132 says is that men must accept multiple wives if God tells them to, because that will be their salvation.

Men having two wives causes an arithmetical problem. Setting three as a minimum made the shortage of women even more acute. There were now far too many men for the number of available women, and with the end of the world in sight, time was running out. Boys and young men needed to be culled from the flock. So, Rulon began revealing even more rules and regulations, more reasons to cast them out.

Another serious, but unacknowledged, problem inherent in a closed, polygamous community was revealed during Rulon's reign. By the 1980s, the insular community was becoming inbred. Increasing numbers of babies were being born with acute mental and physical disorders. Theodore Tarby, a Phoenix pediatric neurologist, had grown used to seeing a wide range of serious childhood deficiencies.

But, in 1980, when a child from Short Creek was brought to him with severe physical problems and acute mental retardation, Tarby had no idea what had caused it. He sent urine samples to Dr. Steve Goodman, a pediatrics professor at the University of Colorado whose laboratory detects rare genetic diseases. Goodman concluded that the patient had fumarase deficiency, which is so rare that only a handful of cases had been reported worldwide. Because of a recessive gene, victims lack the fumarase enzyme, an essential component in a biological process called the Krebs cycle, which converts food into energy within each cell. Not enough of the fumarase enzyme can lead to severe mental retardation and physical deformities. As a result, victims suffer a range of symptoms including severe epileptic seizures, inability to walk or even sit upright, severe speech impediments, strokes and failure to grow at a normal rate.

Children with the deficiency have an IQ of less than twenty-five, although most can say a few words. They have bigger than normal heads and coarse, thick features. Tarby says their brains are "strangely shaped" and are frequently missing large areas of brain matter, which has been replaced with water. An MRI (magnetic resonance imaging) of one child's brain showed that more than half the brain was missing.

With that diagnosis in hand, Tarby asked the parents whether there were other children with the same problem. They brought in their son. He had it as well. At least two other families had children with fumarase deficiency.

By the late 1990s, Tarby discovered that Colorado City, Arizona, and Hildale, Utah, had the highest concentration of fumarase deficiency in the world. The recessive gene that triggers the deficiency was found in two of Short Creek's founding families, the Barlows and the Jessops. Nearly half the eight thousand people in the twin towns are blood relatives, and several thousand people are believed to carry the recessive gene.

The gene-related deficiency may have been another reason for the sharp increase in bride trading between Colorado City/Hildale and Bountiful, starting in the late 1980s. So far, there have been no reported cases of fumarase deficiency in Bountiful.

The shallow gene pool also explains the preponderance of children with thick glasses and "Babyland" cemetery, where in 2005 there were 180 marked and 58 unmarked graves. Since then many more children—most of them under the age of ten—have been buried. After antipolygamy advocate Flora Jessop publicly criticized the Mohave County, Arizona, coroner for signing off on many of those deaths without ever examining the bodies, the county changed the rules for coroners.

But it's more likely the orgy of cross-border bride trading was fuelled not by Rulon's concern for children, but by his desire to reward his loyalists. Fundamentalist Saints don't put much stock in modern medicine, especially when they're not directly affected. If a child is born with a physical or mental handicap, the male leaders blame the mother. She must not be a righteous woman. She must have sinned, either by having sex with her husband while she was pregnant, by failing to be blindly obedient to his every wish or by being unfaithful to him in some other way. In fundamentalist Mormon communities, women—the daughters of Eve—are almost always the root cause of sins and sickness.

—

EIGHT

DOWN AT THE "CRICK"

The twin towns of Hildale, Utah, and Colorado City, Arizona, blend seamlessly into one another as they hug the highway before edging back into the starkly beautiful canyons. Beneath rich red cliffs that rise from the austere and harsh desert landscape, even the massive houses seem insignificant. And there are lots of big homes for families of forty or more children and multiple wives. Not surprisingly, the prophet's house, worth an estimated three million American dollars, is the biggest.

Little can be seen of it or the other houses because of the high brick walls surrounding the compound. At the prophet's house, there's an Enterphone to limit the traffic to family, friends and those with appointments or invitations. The compound's eight-foot-high exterior wall once had cameras tucked into every post. They're gone now because the prophet doesn't live there any more.

But, in the heady days at the end of the twentieth century while Rulon Jeffs was prophet, the compound was the nerve centre of the Fundamentalist Church of Jesus Christ of Latter Day Saints, and the twin towns were home to slightly more than half the FLDS's estimated eight to ten thousand members. It's where "Uncle Rulon" lived with some of his sixty or more wives. His son Warren and some of his seventy or more wives also lived within the compound. Rulon, who was born just nine years into the twentieth century, travelled in motorcades driven by white-shirted bodyguards in white sports utility vehicles. His car was a Cadillac and, wherever Rulon went, he took along some of the younger wives from his ever-increasing harem. Some of them were as much as seventy years younger than their husband.

Rulon had modernized the Saints' businesses and hidden many of them through a series of numbered companies. He and his advisers had grown wealthy and lived in mansions, while many of the followers still lived in dilapidated trailers and half-finished homes both in Short Creek and in Bountiful. Many of the homes had no interior doors, so wives' bedrooms were separated from one another and from the children by curtains. There were no secrets in those homes and no privacy. According to the *Salt Lake Tribune,* more than a third of the residents of Hildale and Colorado City were on welfare in 1998. Many families relied on Medicaid and used food stamps. The average family's income was so low that area residents paid the least income tax of any community in Utah—US$651.

Rulon had grown skilled at getting money from the government. Using federal grants, he'd managed to build the community's airport into the largest one in southern Utah. For the airport, he received a start-up grant worth US$1 million, which was followed by another US$1 million in 1990. In 1992, the runways were paved with a US$800,000 grant. Two years later, there was a grant worth nearly US$200,000 for the airport's water system and in 1995 a US$150,000 grant paid for the airport's terminal building.

It was quite an accomplishment, considering that the twin towns have no bus service and that their residents place a high value on isolation and anonymity. But the plundering of government funds wasn't limited to an airport that was used almost exclusively by the prophet and senior priesthood men, such as Winston Blackmore, who flew in regularly on private planes.

Part of the US$4 million that Colorado City got annually to operate its public schools was used to purchase a US$220,000 Cessna 210 that "school district personnel"—all senior priest-hood men—used to fly to cities across Arizona. And there were lots of staff to fly in the plane. The district had more than one hundred full- and part-time employees for three hundred students, although there were only thirty teachers. The average Arizona public school district had one employee for every twenty-six students.

In violation of state law, the school district bought vehicles, including Ford Excursions, F-350 pickups and Chevy Suburbans, for Warren and Rulon Jeffs's closest friends and advisers. The school district had an illegal slush fund that allowed FLDS board members, administrators and principals to charge personal expenses to school credit cards. There was a grand jury investigation of the school district initiated in December 2000 by Janet Napolitano, who was attorney general before she was elected governor. No charges were ever filed.

Whatever money the FLDS needed and couldn't get from the various levels of government, the leaders got from tithes and from the increasingly frequent and increasingly high additional monthly payments that they demanded of their followers. For everything else, they borrowed. Rulon had encouraged them to borrow what they could, to max out credit cards and to remortgage their homes. It was money that they were told they would never have to repay. They wouldn't need to. They would be lifted up at the millennium. In Canada, Winston Blackmore did his best to follow the prophet. He had a plane, as well as a silver Cadillac.

These were heady days for the leadership in other ways as well. Public sentiment seemed to be swinging in the polygamists' favour. In Utah, Arizona and British Columbia, government officials and the courts were "normalizing" polygamy. The antipolygamy laws hadn't been enforced since the 1953 raid. Utah's highest court had ruled that polygamists could adopt. Child protection services in both Utah and Arizona were returning runaways to their polygamous parents.

The prophet's Colorado City compound was a swarm of action in the 1990s with family members coming and going, children playing, women tending to the cooking, cleaning or child-raising. There was a steady stream of visitors coming to ask for the prophet's advice. Rebecca Musser, one of Rulon's young wives, watched it all from the kitchen window. She had gone to school at Alta Academy in Salt Lake City and taught there, which is how she came to the prophet's attention. It was supposedly the Lord who had inspired Uncle Rulon to take the stunningly beautiful teen as a wife. Musser's father, Lloyd Wall, who lived within the prophet's compound, readily agreed, even though Rebecca was eighteen when Warren married her for time and all eternity to his eighty-three-year-old father.

From her viewpoint at the window and from her place at the prophet's table, Musser says she learned that God didn't always reveal placement marriages to the prophet. Often, they were worked out by church elders over a meal at the long table in the banquet-sized dining room.

Priesthood men made monthly appointments for their families to meet with the prophet. "People clung to him as their lifeline. People would call and ask if they should go on a trip. If somebody was sick and the doctors were saying this is what they should do, he [Rulon] would give guidance and counsel on what they should do. And some people just came, met him and talked with him," Musser says.

That changed in August 1997, after eighty-nine-year-old Rulon Jeffs had the first of a series of strokes. "It was severe enough that for the following weeks, his speech . . . he would use words that did not make sense. We were told he was tired, stressed from dealing with so many people," Musser says, adding that Rulon also couldn't remember the names of his wives. "For a month after the stroke, the brethren didn't realize what had happened. People didn't realize how severe it was. I remember Warren instructing Brother Isaac [Jeffs] that if anyone called or wanted to talk to Father, to say absolutely not. He said, 'We can't let them know how serious it is. They have to talk to me.'"

Efforts to meet with the prophet were blocked. Warren began taking all of his father's appointments and was ostensibly the mouthpiece for God's mouthpiece. But, in fact, Warren was becoming the prophet. Occasionally, he consulted his father on issues, giving him options and then suggesting what the best option would be. Mostly, Warren acted on his own, even taking it upon himself to discipline some of his father's wives, like Rebecca, who refused to do as Rulon commanded in the bedroom. Warren reprimanded her for not being sufficiently submissive and ordered her to cut all ties to her family and submit to his father's will.

By 1999, Rulon Jeffs had suffered another stroke and, for a while, was reported to be on oxygen twenty-four hours a day. He rallied enough to give the occasional sermon. But by then, Warren had become his puppet master even though he continued to preface his remarks with "This is what Father wants me to tell you."

In one of his occasional sermons in 2001, Rulon mentioned Ruth Stubbs. Ruth had been only sixteen when she was forced, in 1998, to marry thirty-two-year-old police officer Rodney Holm. Ruth had left him and was seeking sole custody of their two children. "God bless that girl," Rulon said. "No, no, no, Father," Warren whispered loudly enough to be overheard by many people. "She is fighting against us." Corrected, but still confused, Rulon called twice more for God to bless Ruth. Twice more Warren corrected him.

(Ruth won the custody case, and her testimony against Rodney in 2003 resulted in his conviction and jailing for bigamy and two counts of sexual misconduct. In 2007, the U.S. Supreme Court refused to hear his appeal that the bigamy charge was unconstitutional. But by then, Holm had been charged in Arizona's Mohave County with sexual conduct with a minor and conspiracy to commit sexual conduct. Charges against him were dismissed in August 2007 after the prosecutors determined that Ruth was involved in a blackmail plot that involved Holm and Warren Jeffs.)

Rebecca Musser recalls only once hearing Rulon rebel against Warren's control. It was over lunch just a few months before he died in September 2002. "Rulon was very quiet. Then he leaned forward on the table and pleaded, 'I want my job back. I want to take care of my people.' After he said that, somebody brought Warren into the room and he tried to calm him [Rulon] down, saying we're just trying to take care of you."

It would have surprised rank-and-file followers to know that the prophet felt he was unemployed, since so many revelations were being issued in his name and they were following all of them without question. His order to borrow as much money as possible resulted in his followers bankrupting the ninety-nine-year-old Bank of Ephraim. All of the hastily made end-of-the-world loans totalled US$18 million and accounted for 90 per cent of the bank's portfolio. One loan was for a watermelon farm that never saw a single watermelon seed. Another was for a company that salvaged military barracks to convert them into motels. It went broke when it was discovered that the barracks all contained lead paint, asbestos and other hazardous materials.

But the knockout punch was twenty-four years of embezzlement by the head cashier and a partner, who together stole more than US$5 million. When the Federal Deposit Insurance Corporation finally sorted it out, U.S. taxpayers were on the hook for close to US$40 million in insured deposits.

Meanwhile, FLDS followers obediently threw their televisions in the dump, even though Warren and others in his family still watched theirs. School was banned and mothers were told to home-school their children using Warren Jeffs's tapes from Alta Academy and his more recent sermons as the curriculum. Reading books other than the Bible, the Book of Mormon, the Pearl of Great Price, the Doctrine and Covenants and the collected speeches of the prophets was discouraged. The colour red was banned. Thanksgiving was banned. People were warned against laughing, based on Warren's reading of an obscure tenet in the Doctrine and Covenants that says laughing causes the spirit of God to leak from people's bodies. Even the word *fun* was banned.

"There came a time when we couldn't say fun any more, we had to say enjoyment," said Ethan Fischer, who had been the youngest man ever appointed an elder before he was expelled in 2003. "We were also discouraged from saying negative words. So we couldn't say 'water fight.' So at first we called it water fun. But when fun was banned, we had to call it water enjoyment. The thought was that if you had too much fun, you'd lose sight of what was important. The focus should be on God and on the Prophet."

When the United Effort Plan trust was reformed in 1998, men, women and children had their inheritances stolen. In a legal document that contains Rulon Jeffs's shaky signature as well as the signatures of Winston Blackmore, Fred Jessop and the other three trustees, the beneficiaries were relegated to the status of tenants in homes they'd built and paid for. They had no rights. If they slipped from grace, they could be evicted. At the time, the change went largely unnoticed. Rulon's devotees were focused on the millennium and on Rulon's predictions that the world was soon going to end, that the "One Might and Strong" would come to preside over a thousand years of peace.

On one occasion before 2000, Rulon called a select group of twenty-five hundred people. He instructed them to buy food and clothes and come to a designated plot of ground from which they would be lifted up to heaven. But, before the time came, Rulon called it off. God had decided that the select were not righteous enough and that they needed more time to prepare.

He called them again on June 12, 1999. According to Colorado City historian Ben Bistline, the select gathered in the parking lot of the meeting house at 6 a.m. They formed a prayer circle, held hands and prayed before they formed a procession and walked about two blocks to Cottonwood Park, where they spent the day celebrating.

"However," Bistline reports, "before the day ended, word came down from the prophet that the people lacked the faith for this event to take place. They were told that another date would be set for it to happen, thus giving them a little more time to repent."

These millennial predictions were hardly original or even surprising. A premillennial report on doomsday cults by the Canadian Security Intelligence Service estimated that 35 per cent of Americans believe that an apocalypse similar to what is predicted in the Bible will take place at some point. Although it was a Canadian report, it provided no estimate for how many Canadians hold the belief.

Along with other so-called millenarian groups, fundamentalist Mormons believe that the two-thousand-year reign of Christ will soon end. They believe it will occur as it is described in Revelations. The final days will be marked by a battle between Good and Evil, God's people and Satan's people, saints and sinners. The fundamentalist Mormons believe the righteous will be lifted up and saved. Nonbelievers, sinners and apostates will be destroyed, cleansing the earth for the Second Coming of Christ, which will be followed by one thousand years of peace.

Prior to January 1, 2000, national security agencies considered the possibility that some of these apocalyptic cults might actually initiate a war. They wondered where to draw the line between dangerous and benign "millennialists" and they concluded that it was largely dependent on the leader. In its premillennial Megiddo report, the U.S. Federal Bureau of Investigation identified a number of "militias, adherents to racist belief systems such as Christian Identity and Odinism and other radical domestic extremists" that posed a threat to national security because they were focusing on the millennium as a "time of action." It noted there were "several religiously motivated groups [that] envision a quick, fiery ending in an apocalyptic battle."

While the FBI report admitted that it is "extremely difficult and imprecise" to predict which groups are prone to violence, one key factor is determining whether there is a "cultic relationship" between the leader and his followers. A cultic relationship, it says, is one where the followers are totally or nearly totally dependent on the leader for almost all major life decisions because that leader has convinced them that he or she possesses some special talent, gift or knowledge.

The report urged law enforcement officers to consider several other attributes when assessing the group's risk of violence. Is it a sequestered group with no access to the outside world, making it difficult for followers to critically evaluate the leader and the ideas he espouses? What are the leader's fantasies, dreams, plans and ideas? These, it said, are important because they are likely to be assimilated by his or her followers. Is the leader a "charismatic psychopath" or someone with "narcissistic character disorder"? Has the leader's personality changed as the result of a death or illness?

The FBI report suggested that groups be evaluated on whether the language used to espouse their ideology was becoming increasingly violent and whether the leader's speeches were seeded with language that followers might interpret as a directive to violence. It suggested evaluating people within the leader's inner circle to determine whether there had been recent changes and to determine whether there were now more people within that sphere of influence who either had military backgrounds or were familiar with the use of weapons. Finally, the report warned, "The longer the leader's behaviour has gone unchecked against outside authority, the less vulnerable the leader feels."

The FLDS was not among the apocalyptic cults identified by the FBI. But it's hard to ignore how many of its characteristics matched those singled out for having a high potential for violence. The FLDS is sequestered. It has been allowed to carry on largely unchecked since the 1953 raid. Rulon had suffered a traumatic and debilitating illness and Warren was in control. His reported arrogance, lack of empathy and sense of superiority appear to fit with the clinical definition of narcissistic character disorder, a common disorder among psychopaths and cult leaders.

Sam Brower, a private investigator who has spent close to a decade working on cases involving Warren Jeffs and the FLDS, says, "I'm convinced [Warren] is a sociopathic narcissist who is extremely cunning."

Reports indicated that people within the group had not only stockpiled money and food, they had also hidden guns in caves in the mountains behind Short Creek and Bountiful, B.C. People who have left the group have reported witnessing cruel demonstrations of animals being killed.

Despite the revelations and preparations the new millennium dawned as any other day. There was no violence in Short Creek or Bountiful, where, as usual, the first baby born in Creston was a polygamist's baby. But Hildale and Colorado City are different and are much more volatile than Bountiful because they are so insular. In 2006, the Utah Supreme Court finally booted the town's polygamous judge off the bench—twenty-six years after he'd been appointed by the Hildale city council.

The mayors and city councillors are all FLDS men—most, if not all, are polygamists. All of the law enforcement officers in the twin towns were polygamists until 2004, when Arizona appointed a special investigator to Colorado City. Municipal policing continued to be done exclusively by FLDS men until 2006, when Utah's Washington County Marshal's Service finally posted a gentile to work with the polygamists policing Hildale and Colorado City.

The doctor who runs the local hospital is a polygamist. All of the nurses and assistants at the government-funded hospital are FLDS. In town, the pharmacist, the dentist, the accountants, the bankers and the teachers are all FLDS.

Not only is everyone in town FLDS, they all dress the same. Despite the scorching summer heat, boys and men wear long-sleeved, Western-styled shirts and dark jeans. Girls and women wear their hair in braids or chignons with high swoops off the forehead. They dress in long sleeves with ankle-length skirts that barely conceal full-length temple garments—holy underwear—and sneakers. The women are like Stepford wives with bad hair and clothes, not just because of the prophet's edict to keep sweet, but because so many of them are on Prozac or other antidepressants.

But that's not all that's odd about the twin towns. In its 2005 intelligence report, the Southern Poverty Law Center notes: "Because everyone is related, there's a sense of déjà vu with each high forehead, pointed nose, and reddish-gold mane. In Short Creek, it's not uncommon for your sister to be your cousin or your uncle your stepfather. The lack of new blood—this is a sect you must be born into—explains the recurring facial structures."

Although these towns have no signs warning people to stay away as Bountiful does, strangers are not welcome in Colorado City and Hildale. They're not welcome in the drugstore, the grocery or the restaurant. Until 2007, when the intriguingly named Merry Widows Café opened, there was no coffee shop in either town, and, of course, no bar. Coffee, tea and alcohol were all banned by Joseph Smith. Fundamentalists largely ignore the so-called Words of Wisdom, but the mainstream Mormons don't, which makes it hard enough to get a good cup of coffee in Utah, let alone a beer or a cocktail. In Short Creek, it's almost impossible to get alcohol, unless you're a kid with connections. But then, those connections may not last long. Many of the several hundred young men known as the Lost Boys, who have been kicked out the FLDS in the last decade, were expelled after beer parties up in the canyons.

The boys who aren't partying are the Sons of Helemon—Jeffs's private armed militia of boys as young as twelve who patrol the streets. They're the religious police on the lookout for strangers—particularly journalists—and for any one who might be disobeying the prophet. They're armed because it's America, where private militias are legal and carrying guns a constitutional right. And they're armed because they're in Utah and Arizona, which have the laxest gun laws in the country. In both, surrendering $119 and your fingerprints gets you a permit to carry a concealed weapon. There are no limits on how many guns you can buy in a month, no waiting period for the purchase of guns, no restrictions on assault weapons and ammunition and no requirement that guns be stored away with child-proof locks.

Of course, stricter laws, restrictions and waiting periods for buying firearms wouldn't change the reason people buy and hoard weapons or even stop them, especially if they believe the end of the world is nigh. There is little governments can do to legislate rational behavior. But they can compel legal behavior, and that means not only preventing millenarian fantasies from turning into religious violence, but also enforcing laws to protect those vulnerable to the capricious authority of an isolated patriarchal sect. Armed cults feverishly awaiting the rapture may be alarming to those on the outside looking in, but for women and children, the everyday experience of polygamy, with its violence, privation and internecine strife, is far more dangerous.

NINE

THE OTHER SIDE OF UTOPIA

Harold Blackmore never once acknowledged the havoc his faith wreaked on his family. He never knew that after fifty-one years of sharing her husband, Gwen Williams Blackmore breathed a sigh of relief when Florence died, even though Florence was her sister whom she loved. "Finally, I am the only wife," Gwen told Florence's daughter Brenda Williams Jensen.

Harold never knew that for years Florence had toyed with the idea of leaving him and their plural marriage. "I tried and I tried to get her to leave," says her daughter Brenda. "But she loved both Harold and Gwen. She always said that their marriage was like a three-legged stool. If you take one leg away, it falls."

If Harold regretted his choice to live on the margins of society, always waiting for a knock at the door, or doubted his faith, he never let on. Even though he experienced swindling and the stealing of his land, was thrown into poverty and developed a festering anger at priestcrafters,

Harold could never bring himself to admit that polygamy had been a mistake.

In 1990, Harold wrote to the Creston RCMP urging them to investigate the crimes being committed in Bountiful—everything but the crime of polygamy, that is. He likened the FLDS to the Mafia and suggested the police investigate tax and welfare fraud. He suggested the police consider charges of conspiracy to commit a long list of violations, including "the selling of girls into marriages they don't want because they are told they will be damned if they don't"; "deliberate deprivation of personal rights by brainwashing"; and "the promotion of plural marriage for personal and monetary gain" by the prophet, bishops and elders who took money or young girls from fathers desperate to buy wives and a way into the celestial kingdom. But don't pursue polygamy, he told the RCMP. "Plural marriage is not bad, but the abuse and perversion of it is."

Harold died in 2000 without ever saying sorry to his daughters, granddaughters and grandsons for the life that he'd dragged them into, for the molestation and abuse that bred more abuse, for the alcoholism and for the loss of so many dreams.

For nearly fifty years, Brenda Williams Jensen has struggled to forgive her father and her mothers for their devotion to the Principle and its devastating legacy. She was four when the molestation began by some of the older boys in the community. After a while, they left her alone.

By then, Brenda says, it scarcely mattered. She was numbed to it: "I was already on the road to hell because I was damaged goods. But I didn't dare tell because I knew I was less than nothing. I was irredeemable. Part of the reason I never told was because I was less than nothing. But the other part of it was that my parents, and especially Mama Gwennie [Brenda's aunt and "other mother"], were very harsh disciplinarians. Punishment was very, very extreme . . . I was afraid of the ramifications of telling. I knew it [the abuse] would have been [regarded as] my fault."

Brenda kept the secret through twenty years of alcoholism, until one night, drunk and on the verge of her fiftieth birthday. She called her mother. She screamed at Florence, blaming her for not having stayed at home to raise her and protect her from the sexual abuse. When Brenda was done, Florence said she was glad Brenda had kept silent. If Brenda had said anything, Florence said, it would have upset Gwen and Harold. Brenda hit rock bottom. A few weeks later, she went into alcohol rehabilitation. Brenda has been sober ever since, but the wounds of her childhood have yet to fully heal.

Brenda lived in Bountiful until 1965. She was fourteen when she and her younger siblings finally rejoined their father, two mothers and other siblings in Colorado City, where the Blackmore/Williams clan believed they were "building the Kingdom of heaven." When Brenda and the other children snuck across the border to the United States, taking the smugglers' route through the mountains, they left behind Harold and Gwen's oldest daughter, twenty-four-year-old Lorna. Lorna had taken care of them for nearly two years. They'd lived in the house that Harold had built soon after founding the polygamous community in 1946.

Six years earlier, Lorna had been assigned to marry her forty-one-year-old uncle, Charles Quinton. It was a loveless, joyless and, up until then, childless match. It was bad enough that Quinton was married to Harold's sister and was twenty-three years older than Lorna. But Harold's sister had frequently complained to Harold and his wives how abusive Quinton was. Still, when Prophet LeRoy Johnson told Harold that Lorna was being assigned to Quinton, Harold didn't say no. Then he lacked the courage to break the news to Lorna. He left that to Gwen. "I don't think he [Quinton] knows how to be kind," Gwen told her daughter. But Gwen was adamant that the marriage had to go ahead. Lorna had no choice, her mother told her. To refuse the marriage was to refuse a direct order from God.

Lorna was terrified. She'd heard stories from her aunt about Quinton, but she'd also heard them from her best friend, Quinton's daughter. "She really hated her dad. And I felt there had to be something wrong with him," Lorna says. "I couldn't understand why anyone could hate their dad."

Lorna begged her father to spare her from the marriage. "I went to my father and told him, 'I don't feel good about this.' My Dad and I went to speak to the prophet LeRoy Johnson. Dad said I wanted some time to pray and think and Uncle Roy just looked at me and said, 'This is the Lord's will.' I was crying my eyes out."

Harold caved in to the prophet then and again when another of his daughters was assigned in marriage. Years later, Harold gave interviews and wrote propolygamy screeds insisting that plural marriage was great only as long as women have free choice, but it was no consolation to Lorna or another sister whose husband was also abusive. "Marriage must be a voluntary association of equals who choose to pursue common objectives together of their own free will and choice," he wrote in *All About Polygamy: Why and How to Live It!* Yet, when put to the test, Harold obeyed the prophet, not his conscience.

With her father abandoning her and her mother insisting that she must obey, Lorna had no options left. "I was thinking, 'I can't go against the Lord.' I also thought anybody can go through a ceremony . . . It is something I lived to regret."

Neither Harold nor Gwen even had the courage to show up at the wedding. Lorna stood alone when the prophet married her to Quinton for time and all eternity. As Lorna explains, her parents "didn't ever want to have to testify that they witnessed my marriage." Strangely, Lorna believes that her husband was just as terrified as she was. "The second he got married, he took off in a streak." He drove back to Cardston and to his wife Eleene and their seven children. He resumed his attendance at the mainstream Mormon church, where for years he remained a member in good standing. No one knew that he had embraced polygamy, not even Eleene and certainly not their children. Lorna was depressed and disillusioned by the marriage:

> I was crying and I walked the fields for hours and hours. I just felt so bad that I wanted to die . . . He was old enough to be my dad. His daughter was the same age as me and she was petrified of her father as well. It just creeps you out. A girl wants to be a wife to someone she has something in common with. I was looking forward to life and he was looking at retirement.
>
> I felt like [my parents] had just sold me down the river. I didn't feel like I was fulfilling a wonderful mission from God. I had been taught that you were married by revelation to somebody who you had been promised to in the pre-life. You were just supposed to know the person you were meant to be with. I thought how beautiful that would be. I don't believe any of that any more. I don't think those men have the "Spirit of God" or any revelations at all. I have come down from belief to non-belief.

Lorna didn't tell anyone outside her immediate family that she was married. She lived with her parents, teaching the younger kids and doing the familiar round of chores until they moved south. Quinton occasionally came for visits, but Lorna didn't want to be with him: "He scared the living daylights out of me . . . I was terrified of him. He was always quite harsh. His voice would just put you through trembles and fears. I was always afraid of him. I never got over that."

But it didn't suit the prophet that, after a couple of years of marriage, Lorna still had no children. Uncle Roy ordered her to move to Cardston to live with Quinton and his other family. Aunt Eleene wasn't thrilled to share her husband with her niece. Her seven children had no idea their father was a polygamist until after Lorna arrived and, finally, after being asked for the millionth time what she was doing there, she told one of her cousins that she was their father's second wife. It was so uncomfortable for all of them that Lorna was relieved to go back to Lister to look after her four youngest siblings while their parents got settled in Colorado City.

Quinton gave her no money and her parents were stretched for cash because of the move to Arizona. Lorna struggled to feed the children. They often lived whole weeks on a box of macaroni and cheese, supplemented with tomatoes and cheese made from goat's milk. The children tended the goats while Lorna did most of the other chores, such as cooking, gathering firewood for the stove and carrying water. She tended the garden and sold whatever extra produce there was for a little cash to buy clothes or shoes or flour. It was only because of the goats that Lorna and then Harold learned he had been swindled by the prophet and priesthood men. Lorna's great-uncle Ray Blackmore stalked up to the house one day and demanded that the goats, which had always wandered freely, be tethered. It was UEP property now, he told her. And he was in charge.

Ray evicted Lorna right after the last of her siblings started their trek across the mountain. Brenda felt bad for leaving Lorna behind, but she was kind of glad that she wasn't going to be there the following year — 1966 — when, according to Ray Blackmore, the moon would turn red and the world would end. Everybody in Lister believed that. Some of Brenda's friends were even excited. It meant they would be going to heaven soon. But Brenda knew she wouldn't be. The fourteen-year-old believed she was a harlot, a fallen woman, who could never be allowed into heaven. Everything she'd been taught led her to conclude that she was raped and molested not only because she deserved it, but because she had asked for it with some inadvertent wanton behaviour.

Even had Brenda been able to set aside her self-loathing, her childhood would still have been far from idyllic. "There was no hope in our lives, no loving God, no doing unto others. And when you get that every day of your life, you have a dread that drags you down emotionally . . . What happened to me was that I would get so discouraged, I would think why try? I even got to the point sometimes where I would say, why should I even bother to plant a tree?"

Dalmon Oler took Lorna in. In an arrangement straight out of Dickens, Lorna helped his wives and looked after his brood of children in exchange for room and board. By Christmas 1965, Lorna had given birth to her first child, a little boy. Quinton had gone to Colorado City for the holidays, but he didn't bother taking his young wife and baby with him, even though it had been more than two years since Lorna had seen her parents and many of her siblings. On December 26, she wrote to her parents: "I've been thinking how much it would mean to me to see you all again. He was just going to be there for such a short time, I knew there really wasn't much sense in my wishing. But I really would have like[d] to go."

"I had Christmas with the Oler family. They are very good to me. They bought me a beautiful wrist watch and a clock and Dalmon gave Darren [her son] a little John Deere tractor . . . Anyways, they seem grateful for my help with the children and I'm glad to have a place to stay where I don't have any worries."

It was two more years before Quinton finally took Lorna to visit her family, in 1967. They stayed one night. Lorna wanted to stop in Salt Lake City, but as she wrote in a letter to her parents before they set out, "I'll try to get the folks to stop, but I don't dare be a pest or I'll lose my privileges."

Lorna lived with and worked for the Olers until 1969. By then she had three children. Quinton still lived in Cardston and only came occasionally for well-timed visits. By 1969, Quinton had evidently got over any qualms he had about polygamy or about offending Eleene and the children. He took a third wife, Cherene. She was the favourite. Quinton bought her a nice house in Cardston, where his first family lived, and spent most of his time with Cherene. Together they eventually had fourteen children. When Quinton died in 1978, he left everything he had to Cherene. There was nothing in his will for any of the other wives or children. (Soon after Cherene received her inheritance, Winston Blackmore decided that he should be her priesthood head. He married her even though he already had more than twenty wives.)

In 1969, Quinton bought Lorna a place to live. It was a ramshackle, wood-heated farmhouse near Lister. As Lorna recalls, "He'd come with a sack of flour, a bag of sugar, rice or some potatoes and think he was providing for us." With three children under five, Lorna continued to struggle to get by. The only money she had was the two or three dollars a day she made selling milk. Most of the time, she was exhausted. But she makes no excuses for what happened.

After supper, she placed her month-old daughter tummy-down on a towel on the kitchen table. Lorna had planned to bathe her after she'd washed up the supper dishes. Although babies that age usually can't roll over, Lorna's daughter did, banging her head hard when she hit the floor. Lorna was scared and ashamed that she had let it happen. She didn't mention the accident to anyone, even though her daughter cried all through the baby shower held in her honour a few days later.

That night, Lorna discovered a lump and swelling on the back of the baby's head. She asked her neighbours to take her and her baby to Creston hospital. By the time the baby went into surgery that night, she was in a coma. She survived the surgery, but died later that night. The police came to Lorna's home the next day to investigate. Because her son was the only witness, Lorna agreed to let the officers speak to her five-year-old alone. They asked him if he had killed his sister. They asked him if he'd pushed his sister off the table. "They scared him so badly that he pulled all of his hair out. He kept saying to me, 'Why did they ask me if I had killed her?'"

The police eventually concluded that the death was accidental. But the interrogation continues to haunt Lorna's son and Lorna. "I can't explain how hard it was for me to go on with my life. I felt so terrible and couldn't forgive myself for what had happened to my baby. I wasn't much good for a long time after this happened. My other children needed me and I gradually came out of my depression."

Charles Quinton was no help. He didn't even come to his daughter's funeral. Instead, he became more verbally abusive, telling Lorna that she was "unworthy to carry his seed." "He would tell me that I would end up looking at my son through the bars of prison and that I wasn't fit to be a mother." He also began physically abusing his children. Lorna soldiered on.

She had another baby, a third daughter, in 1971. It helped lift her from her depression. But, the following year, the chimney, which had never been cleaned, caught on fire. The old farmhouse burned to the ground.

Quinton gave her no choice. Lorna had to take her children to live in Alberta with Quinton, his third wife and their family. "She would spy on me and tell him. He was often cruel to my children, especially my oldest son." The third wife was no happier than Lorna with the arrangement. It was so dreadful for all of them that, after a few months, Quinton bought a small grocery store in Creston with an apartment in the back for Lorna and her children. For a while, Quinton lived there and ran the store—all the while hectoring Lorna to take a job to support the children. Lorna had been home-schooled and never finished high school. But she got a job at a government-run institution for severely handicapped children. She handed every paycheque and every family allowance cheque to her husband.

Compared to Bountiful, everything about the twin towns of Hildale and Colorado City was big and even a bit frightening to Brenda Williams. But, just as she was starting to make a few friends and get settled into the high school there, her eldest brother Stephen came back from his "work mission"—unpaid labouring—in the home of fundamentalist prophet Marion Hammon, with news that the prophet planned to take Brenda as his next wife. Brenda's half-sister Nola was already married to Hammon, who was in his sixties. Nola had been sixteen when she became Hammon's eleventh wife. "Dad told Nola a million times, you don't have to marry him," says Brenda. "But she said, 'I have to. He's a priesthood man.' Dad told her it was nothing but a pack of lies . . . Dad said she didn't have to marry him, but nobody told her to run for her life."

After she was married, Nola told Brenda that one night Hammon had brutally raped her. "She couldn't walk the next day," Brenda says. "He left her bleeding and crying. She [Nola] told Gwen about it. But Gwen told her she had to go back. Gwen was consumed with this. She was a zealot and so was Nola . . . Nola went back and gutted it out."

Harold had no idea what had happened to Nola. No one told him about the rape. Not Nola. Not Gwen. Not Brenda. But Brenda told her father that she would commit suicide by jumping off El Capitan, the red-rock cliff above Colorado City, rather than marry Hammon. "You have a choice," her father told her. "You're promised a choice."

This time, Harold went to Hammon and told the prophet that there was no way that his daughter would marry him. It was the tipping point for Harold. Having already had his Canadian property stolen by the priesthood, Harold was through with the prophet and his gang. He began making plans to leave Colorado City. But when Harold asked that the United Effort Plan buy his home from him for the US$6,000 cost of the materials, the prophet refused. Furious, but not about to repent or seek absolution from men who had cheated him, Harold, his wives and the five youngest children moved to Hurricane, about half an hour's drive north of Colorado City. "We had a one-ton truck, some canned fruit, a couple of blankets and very little else," says Brenda.

Some of the older children (including Nola) remained in Colorado City. A couple of Harold's sons became polygamists. But over time, they either drifted away or were excommuni-cated. Arthur remained there the longest. He was not a "blood" Blackmore. He'd been adopted as a baby in 1945, just before Gwen gave birth to Nola. Arthur ran the co-op in Colorado City and had two wives. His children grew up not knowing that they had grandparents and aunts and uncles just up the road. They weren't told about them because the other Blackmores were apostates.

In Hurricane, Brenda was enrolled in Grade 12 at the public high school. As she says, she might as well have been a refugee from a different planet: "We had one comb amongst us. We had terrible clothes and finally Stephen [her oldest brother] bought me a tube skirt to replace the flouncy skirts I had. But I didn't have nylons. I didn't have the right kind of shoes and we used lye soap and vinegar for washing our hair . . . The boys were off working, so they had money. But the girls had nothing and the mothers had nothing."

She begged Harold to let her go back to Colorado City. He told her to wait three months, and if she still wanted to go back, she could. She never did. "He was a crafty old guy. Hurricane was horrible, but it was way less horrible than Colorado City. I had a hard time because of the terrible loneliness." But she wasn't always lonely. "There were still a couple of guys from Colorado City who would come by courting us [Brenda and her three younger sisters]. But I said no way. Never. I was never going to be a polygamist."

Harold's contracting business did well. He took on every job he could, putting his young children to work shovelling cement and cinders onto the muddy roadbeds and other menial tasks. When there was no construction work for them, Harold found them jobs picking fruit or doing other manual labour. Harold kept the money they earned. Florence Williams worked full-time as a teacher and Gwen Blackmore took a part-time job at a restaurant, just to have a little money for things like sugar that Harold deemed frivolous. Harold was so frugal that he wasn't above Dumpster diving at the back of restaurants to put food on the table.

When Brenda graduated, Florence gave her daughter one hundred American dollars that she had managed to hide from Harold—enough for the round-trip airfare to Spokane, where Lorna had arranged for someone to pick her up and drive her to Creston. In Creston, Brenda spent the summer living in the cramped apartment behind the grocery with Lorna and Charles Quinton, their children and Charles's new wife, Debbie Oler. There wasn't an inch of space in the apartment that wasn't covered with something or someone. But Brenda recalls having had a happy time with her sister and some of her old friends before going back to Utah that fall to the Mormon-run Dixie College in St. George.

After Christmas, Harold took Brenda to Mexico to visit his friends, fundamentalist Mormon colonists whose families had lived there since the late 1880s. Harold was trying to find an acceptable husband for her, preferably a polygamist. "Dad was a firm believer in polygamy and he wanted his children to have good marriage partners in polygamy. In that sense, he wanted his children cared for." The men in Mexico were eager for fresh blood and young wives. One of them took Brenda horseback riding to a ridge overlooking his ranch. He promised to build her a house there. She asked how he would manage that when he couldn't afford to take care of the three wives and children that he already had.

When Brenda went back to Utah, her brother Stephen introduced her to his friend Kim Jensen. Kim was the same age as Brenda. Years earlier, he'd run away from the Mexican colony that Brenda had just returned from. His father had been one of the men courting her. "We didn't hate each other," Brenda says of their first meeting. "We didn't fall in love right away either. But finally, I thought here was somebody single."

Over their year-long courtship, Kim came every Sunday for baked beans and bread served with a heaping dose of Harold preaching the virtues of polygamy—this added a whole new dimension to the age-old embarrassment suffered by teens when their parents talk to their boyfriends and girl-friends. Kim's sister was there for the dinners and sermons as well. Judy was dating Brenda's half-brother Lane. "I wanted to believe in it [polygamy]," says Brenda. "I didn't want to be an outcast, but I didn't want to be asleep either. I saw the neglect. I saw the sadness and the abuse. I saw nothing that sparked anything in me that was good."

In 1973, in a double wedding ceremony, Brenda married Kim, and her half-brother Lane married Judy, for time and all eternity. Harold officiated at the ceremony since he still claimed to have God's blessing to perform religious rituals. These were "religious" marriages, not legal ones.

Before the wedding, Kim and Brenda had agreed that polygamy wasn't for them. But, while Brenda was pregnant with their first child, Kim proved he was clearly not a master of timing. He started talking about the possibility of a second wife, using many of Harold's arguments that he'd heard over Sunday dinner. Kim even suggested they emulate Harold's family; Brenda's sister Marla could be her sister-wife. Brenda refused to even consider it. She vowed never to live polyga-mously or to raise her children that way.

Mothers never love all children as if they are their own, Brenda told Kim. She knew that for a fact: "I was always the kid whose mother was always gone. There was never any time for me. Kids, at a certain point in their lives, need to believe that the world centres around them. I never had that. Nobody ever had time for me." Kim wisely gave up the idea and, more than thirty years later, Kim and Brenda are still together.

Meanwhile, in Creston, Lorna was dealing with an abusive husband, four children under the age of nine and another dif-ficult sister-wife, Debbie Oler. Ray Blackmore's eighteen-year-old widow had been assigned to Charles Quinton in 1974.

Initially, things were okay. Lorna had looked after Debbie when she was a child and had felt sorry for her when she had married Ray. "He [Ray] was so mean to her. He treated her like dirt so much that even I got after him." But Lorna says Debbie soon became her nemesis. "I fell into it because Debbie was really nice to me. I told her how I felt about things and she used it against me. I was probably the dumbest person on the block."

With Lorna working full-time, Debbie insisted that she needed something of her own to do. She took over the running of the house. "She was trying so hard to get Charles to see her in a kindly way and he took advantage of her because she would do anything." Debbie reported on Lorna's every misdemeanour and every criticism to Quinton. It was only later that Lorna realized that Debbie was having a mental breakdown.

She'd come home some days to find Debbie sitting in the dark. Finally, one day in 1976, while Lorna was at work, Debbie set some boxes of paper on fire. "She figured that the store was the problem. We all figured the store was the problem because Charles felt it was more important than the family," says Lorna. The store was damaged, but not destroyed. Labelled a troublemaker once more, Debbie was forced to move back to her father's house. The prophet and Winston Blackmore released Debbie from the marriage to Quinton.

Soon after the fire, Quinton sold the store and the trailer that he had promised Lorna could live in with their five children. Once again, Dalmon Oler rescued Lorna as he had his own daughter. He let Lorna and her children move into an old house that he owned in Lister that was in desperate need of repair. Lorna had had enough of Quinton. She told him she was done being his wife, but he could see the children whenever he wanted. He never came to see them. He also initially refused to provide for Lorna and the children in any way.

It was only because of Lorna's Aunt Florence that she got anything from Quinton. She insisted that Harold asked his son, who was living in Idaho, to track down Quinton and threaten to sue if Lorna didn't get some child support or some sort of settlement from him. It worked. "He [Quinton] wrote a letter saying that he would give me $150,000 and a blue van and he would never have any more financial or moral responsibility towards me or the children. He made me sign it before he would give me the money," says Lorna. That's all twenty years of her life was worth to him, $150,000 and an old van.

"I had been with him 20 years and through this time, he had done everything to break me. I might have had a breakdown too, only I was too much of a fighter," she says. "I feel like I spent most of my married life fighting for myself and my children . . . I had always felt that people who were not part of the group were very unlucky as they did not have a chance to know the fullness of the gospel. I was so wrong."

Not only was Lorna done with Quinton, she was done with the religion. But again it was Lorna's Aunt Florence—not her father or her mother Gwen—who made sure that her niece finally had some security. Florence took her own savings from the bank and gave it to Harold to buy Lorna some property in British Columbia. Lorna chose a little farm almost within sight of Bountiful. Her oldest son and two daughters were married and chose to stay behind, and Lorna wanted to be close in case they needed her. Harold bought the property she had picked out and put his name (not Florence's) and Lorna's on the title.

Six years before he died, seventy-eight-year-old Harold handwrote and had notarized a letter stating his intent that Lorna have sole ownership of her little farm. Florence sent an accompanying letter warning Lorna that "there is still a threat [to the title of the property] from the 'Brethren' and followers of Winston . . . they are working through your kids to try to get it." In the letter, she tells Lorna that her children in Bountiful are "so 'nice' and 'sweet' but they'd kick you off if they got on the property," Florence wrote. "*Don't* trust *any* of them. They've declared their allegiance several times and it's always back to Winston and the group not to [their] mother . . .

"These kids have been programmed all their lives. But you were too and you got free and stayed free with Dad's help. Be careful. Women are gullible and men know it. They'll offer you the moon, but follow up with nothing. Love you dearly, Aunt Florence"

A year later, Harold wrote Lorna again saying that he had asked her brother Lane to make sure that the title transfer was completed. But he had instructions for Lorna as well: "I direct you never to sell or deal with anyone in that polygamous group. Use caution in any dealings with your children who are associated with them."

As it turned out, Florence and Harold should have warned Lorna and the other daughters about their brothers, who had learned all too well the priestcraft ways.

One brother managed to get title to half of Lorna's farm before trying to pressure her into signing over the other half. When she went to court to clarify what she owned, her brother didn't show up and she won a default judgment. But that wasn't the end of it. Lorna, Brenda and their sisters are still in court with some of their brothers, fighting for a share of their parents' estate. It's worth fighting for. All those years of Dumpster diving, going without sugar and wearing thrift-store clothes paid off. Together, Harold, Gwen and Florence had saved $1.5 million. The money had been secreted away, first by Harold and his wives, and then by their sons, in various trusts—the Saguaro Company Trust, the Sodell Company Trust, the Tom Willie Trust—and in a non-profit corporation called the Patriarchal Society.

The Blackmore infighting is every bit as bitter as it was a generation ago, except now it's also about gender. At every step of the process, the sisters have had their history thrown back in their faces. They are constantly reminded of the priesthood's arrogant belief that women are nothing and that only men can inherit heaven and earth. The depth of the inculcated misogyny, the grotesqueness of the men's greed and the sheer depravity of their actions in this cult is stunning.

In 2007, the case had yet to go to trial. But the examination for discovery phase rekindled their old feelings of powerlessness and the taunts that girls could never be as good as boys. Remaining deep in some hidden parts of their souls were the old lessons that they had been taught in church and at home about the superiority of men and their own God-given mission to be submissive, obedient and sweet. With the memories of all of the abuse they'd suffered came tears. Then, for the first time, the sisters shared with each other what they had suffered, including sexual abuse. What came next, especially for Brenda, was the anger.

She had been molested first in Bountiful and later in Utah, where the laws make it almost impossible for sexual assault victims to get justice. There is only a small window of four years after the rape occurs for victims to report to police. The only remaining legal remedy is for victims to file civil suits, as Blaine Jeffs has had to do against Warren Jeffs, his uncle and FLDS prophet. But Canada's laws are different. There is no statute of limitations for sex crimes. In early 2007, Brenda filed a complaint with Creston RCMP about her own sexual abuse as a child. She did it for herself, but also to show her sisters that there could be some measure of justice. So many years after the fact, Brenda doesn't really expect her molester will be punished. But after police knocked on his door to question him, Brenda hopes he has at least begun to recognize that what he did was not just wrong, but evil.

—

Eighteen-year-old Carolyn Blackmore was teaching Grade 2 in the Colorado City public school when she was assigned to marry fifty-year-old Merril Jessop in 1987. She had no choice and no options, despite what her grandfather was telling reporters and people like Phil Donahue. "They [polygamists] make claims that it is all about free choice and consenting adults. But women don't have a choice," says Carolyn. "I don't know of one woman there [in Colorado City/Hildale] who has not been pushed to the point that she would do something different if she had options. But they don't have options . . . And if the government is not going to prosecute polygamy, then at least they should make sure that women do have free choice."

Growing up in Colorado City, Carolyn had been allowed very little contact with anyone outside. Her father, Arthur, was one of the boys whom Gwen and Harold Blackmore had adopted as a baby back in Cardston. He had severed relations with them long before Carolyn was married. Arthur wanted nothing to do with apostates. He was intent on making his own way through the priesthood hierarchy and had done well for himself. He'd been assigned two wives and was making a success of the Foodtown Co-operative in the twin towns.

Arthur had never given Carolyn or his other children any reason to believe that their grandparents would welcome them in their home, which was less than an hour away. He also said very little about their aunts, Lorna and Brenda, who had left the group twenty or more years earlier. As a result, Carolyn had no access to people who might counteract "that crap that they tell you about women who leave ending up on the street as prostitutes."

Carolyn didn't want to marry Merril Jessop. But the prophet said it was God's plan for her—what choice did she have? She was eighteen. Her husband was fifty, and on his way to becoming one of the most powerful men in the FLDS. One of his uncles was the former prophet LeRoy Johnson, another was Colorado City bishop Fred Jessop. Fourteen of Merril's daughters were married to Prophet Rulon Jeffs and eventually became Warren Jeffs's brides after the son became prophet. Merril is so loyal to the priesthood and the prophet that he oversaw the construction of the new community in Eldorado, Texas, where in 2006, Warren—the fugitive prophet—consecrated the first fundamentalist Mormon temple that's patterned after Joseph Smith's temple in Nauvoo.

Carolyn was Merril's fourth wife, and from the time she married, she had tried to figure out how she could leave the marriage and the community. By 2003, when Warren Jeffs was tightening his control over his nearly ten thousand followers, thirty-three-year-old Carolyn was more than ready to go. After fifteen years of an abusive marriage, she had eight children and was determined not to leave any of them behind: "I had to have a window of opportunity because I was doing something that had never been done before. I was going to take all of my children. Women had left before, but they only took their younger kids. But I had decided if I left, they were all coming with me."

It was complicated. Her husband frequently went away during the week, but was almost always home on the weekend. And her oldest child, fifteen-year-old Arthur, had been working on construction crews outside the community since he was twelve and only came home on weekends. But, at 10 p.m. on April 21, Carolyn's window opened. Arthur was at home for a dental appointment and Merril had just left for Salt Lake City.

Still it was a huge risk. She had to get past the local police, who were all FLDS priesthood men, and the well-armed Sons of Helemon, known as the God Squad. "It's not a situation that you can try [to escape] and fail because the consequences are horrific," says Carolyn. Had she been caught, she believes her children, aged two to fifteen, would have been taken from her. Not only would she have been shunned by the community, Carolyn believes that the doctor, another priesthood man, would have diagnosed her as mentally ill and either drugged her—Carolyn estimates at least a third of the women in the community are on Prozac—or consigned her to a mental institution in Flagstaff, Arizona, where several other "rebellious" women from the community had been locked away.

Carolyn went to her sister's house to make telephone calls to ensure that her sister-wives could not eavesdrop. First, she called the police outside the twin towns, asking for help. "They said it was outside their jurisdiction and some other things. But it was just excuses." She called people who had previously said they would help any women leaving the cult. "That was bogus. Nobody wanted to help." Finally, desperate, she called her brother in Salt Lake City and begged him to come and rescue them. If he left immediately, he would be there by 5 a.m. But there was one condition: he refused to risk getting caught by the local police or the God Squad. Carolyn and her eight children had to meet him at Canaan Corners, three miles out of town.

Her kids slept scattered throughout the big house with some of Merril's other forty-six children. Carolyn needed to wake them, dress them and put them into the van, without her sister-wives raising the alarm with either their husband or the local police. Through the night, she quietly gathered two days' worth of clothes for herself and her children. But things didn't go quite as planned: "I had $20. I decided I was just going to make a run for it . . . I started getting the kids up at 4 and told them to dress quietly. But I got caught. I was getting my oldest daughter up when one of the other wives asked what I was doing. I said I was taking them to town to get family pictures taken. I said that Harrison [her second-youngest son] had a doctor's appointment and I decided that because Arthur was home as well, we'd have pictures taken."

The sister-wife didn't buy the story. Even though Harrison was born with cancer and is multiply handicapped, women can't take their children to the doctor without their husband's permission. Carolyn's sister-wife called Merril in Salt Lake City, and at 4:20 a.m., Merril called Arthur Blackmore, demanding to know what his daughter was up to. Arthur said he had no idea. Merril then called his home and demanded to speak to Carolyn. Another wife paged Carolyn on the large home's intercom as Carolyn was frantically pushing the children into the van.

"The last thing I remember was taking Harrison off the oxygen and his feeding pump, putting him in the van and getting ready to drive away when I realized that Betty [her oldest daughter, who was fourteen] was gone. I just sat there for a moment: Do I take the seven kids and save them or do I go back in the house and try to get her? I decided that it had to be all or nothing. I went in and grabbed her. She was in her room sobbing. She said there is something wrong in what you're doing. She asked why hadn't I told Father. I just grabbed her. She was fighting me and crying."

As Carolyn struggled to get Betty into the van, there was chaos in the Jessop home. But somehow in all the confusion, nobody called the police. If someone had, the police would have arrested Carolyn. She did have one advantage. Unlike almost all of the women in Colorado City and Hildale, Carolyn's van was licensed. Usually, the men don't license the women's vehicles. It's a way to keep them enslaved. If men suspect their wives or daughters are trying to get away, they only have to call the FLDS police and the officer can arrest them. Otherwise, the FLDS police ignore the infraction.

When Carolyn started the van, the fuel gauge never moved off empty. She drove as fast as she could to reach Canaan Corners. As she describes it, behind her, "Betty went completely ballistic. She told the other children, 'She's stealing us. We belong to the prophet, we don't belong to you.' And I just told her, 'In the real world, you belong to me.'" By then, some of other children were crying.

As the lights of her brother's vehicle came into view, the van coughed to a stop. There was no more gas. Once again, Carolyn started grabbing her children. Carrying Harrison, she ran the last few hundred yards. "It was like jumping off a cliff."

She had no idea where they were going or how they would survive. The only certainty was that her husband would come after her and demand custody of the children. Forty-five minutes out of Salt Lake City, Carolyn phoned Dan Fischer, a dentist who had left the group more than a decade before. Since leaving, he had made a small fortune with his patented chemical teeth-whitener and used some of that money to help others leaving polygamy.

Fischer invited Carolyn and her children to stay at one of his five guesthouses. But he told her they couldn't stay long. Merril Jessop would come looking for them, and Fischer's home was one of the first places he'd look. After a few days, Carolyn and her children went into hiding. With Fischer's help, Carolyn got a meeting with Utah Attorney General Mark Shurtleff, who helped her get a lawyer and a protective order against her violent and abusive husband. With that order in place, Carolyn and her children returned to Fischer's guesthouse for five weeks, until there was room for them at a transition house. In June 2003, Carolyn was granted sole custody of her children.

But the judge granted her husband standard visitation rights, which concerned Carolyn since she was convinced

Jessop would try to lure the children away, if he didn't simply kidnap them. Again with help from Shurtleff, Carolyn was able to hire a lawyer to get that order changed.

Since her dramatic dash for freedom, life has been a struggle. Carolyn gets no child support from Jessop. Because the Mormon church has its own welfare system, people on welfare in Utah get less than almost any other welfare recipients in the United States. Not surprisingly, Utah's child poverty rate is one of the country's highest. State assistance is barely enough to cover Carolyn's rent. To cover other costs, she's had to rely on donations of clothes, gift cards and money. Month to month, she has struggled to make it through.

One of the few safety nets Carolyn has is Harrison's handicap. Utah state law requires that handicapped children have safe places to live, which means Carolyn gets additional money to ensure that there is electricity, heat and a roof over his head. It's perhaps fitting, because it was Harrison's illness that helped Carolyn gain the courage to escape.

Merril Jessop and others in the community blamed Carolyn for Harrison's illness, telling her it was because she wasn't righteous enough or obedient enough. Born with cancer, her son spent most of his first four years of life in a hospital outside Colorado City. There, the gentiles who Carolyn had grown up believing were evil were the only ones who were kind to Harrison and to her.

That experience gave her some idea of what to expect in the outside world, but her children had no idea: "I wanted it so bad, but for the children, they had their world ripped apart. I was an apostate and I was insane. That's what they were told. And things were very terrifying for them."

Two weeks after leaving Colorado City, Carolyn enrolled her children in a public school. All of them are bright, and counsellors said the best thing would be to put them into age-appropriate classes, regardless of how they did on the skills testing. At first, her oldest son, fifteen-year-old Arthur, hated it. He'd been working full-time alongside men for three years. Suddenly he was back at school with children in a strange city. He didn't know how to act around gentiles and he often didn't have a clue about what he was being taught. When Arthur refused to go to school, Carolyn called the police. Utah law requires children to go to school until they are eighteen. So, for the first weeks, Arthur went to high school with a police escort. But soon he was on the honour roll. He learned how to fly before graduating from high school. His goal is to be a commercial pilot.

Three years after leaving, Carolyn's oldest daughter, Betty—Harold Blackmore's great-granddaughter—still wanted to go back to Colorado City and to the religion she was raised in. Her mother promised her that if she still wanted to go back when she turned eighteen, Carolyn would let her. Even if Betty does return, Carolyn finds solace in the fact that she's saved Betty from becoming a child bride, provided her a high-school education and given her the security of knowing that she has a mother on the outside to rescue her if necessary.

Betty made it as difficult as possible to fit in at her suburban Salt Lake City high school. She insisted on wearing the "polyg dresses," which invited the taunts of classmates. "Polyg" is the derogatory name Utahns and others call the fundamentalist Saints. Although the fundamentalists keep to themselves as much as possible, there are 37,000 polygamists in Utah and the surrounding states, so it's hard not to see them. Attorney General Mark Shurtleff recalls going to school with polygamists. Women in "polyg dresses" are a common sight in discount stores from Salt Lake City in the north to St. George in the south. Brenda Williams Jensen sees them frequently in Wal-Mart in Mesquite, Nevada, where she lives just a half-hour's drive from St. George. They are tolerated, but barely. Some mainstream Mormons, who make up the majority in Utah, despise them for ruining the good name of their church, for the abuse of boys and the child brides. Still, many LDS members find it difficult to fully condemn them, because they too have polygamous ancestors.

Carolyn says her first priority is doing the best she can for her children. It's a struggle. "But," she says, "as bad as it's got, there's never been a moment or a second that I have considered going back. The worst thing out here can never be as bad as what I experienced there." Carolyn also tries to be a role model for other women considering leaving polygamy, because she can't forget the people she left behind. "I taught Grade 2 there for seven years and since I've walked away many of those precious little girls are married, many were married at 14 and I'm just sick about that."

She has written a book, done hundreds of interviews and spoken at conferences, always pushing her belief that education is the key to ending polygamy, a destructive and abusive way of life that demands strict obedience, not just from women, but also from men.

She has chided the Utah and Arizona governments for failing to provide adequate services—particularly housing—for people coming out of the cult. She is an adviser to Bruce Wisan, a court-appointed fiduciary who is trying to ensure that the appropriate people benefit from the US$110 million United Effort Plan that all FLDS members contributed to for years.

Her activism has led her back to her family. Carolyn was invited to speak at a human rights conference in Creston in 2006. Her aunts—Brenda and Lorna—had read the harrowing story of her escape and they'd seen her interviewed many times on television. When they found out she was going to the conference, the aunts went to meet Carolyn at the Spokane airport.

During the three-hour drive to Creston, Lorna and Brenda did for Carolyn what their father had never done for them. They apologized for not having been able to help her escape. And they told her how sorry they were that their parents had got them into the unholy mess in the first place.

But Harold's legacy doesn't end there. Despite all of Carolyn's attempts to keep her oldest daughter, Betty, in mainstream society, she went back to Colorado City in July 2007, right after her eighteenth birthday. So committed is Betty to proving her faith to the FLDS that her name was on the defense's list of witnesses in the 2007 case against Warren Jeffs on two counts of rape as an accomplice. Carolyn Jessop was on the witness list for the prosecution. Neither was called to testify, but just by being on opposite sides, they bore silent witness to the horrific toll their forebear's fascination with polygamy has had on their family.

TEN

GOD'S BROTHEL

Ever since Joseph Smith had his revelation about celestial marriage, the Saints' prophets have always known, directly from God, exactly what a woman's role should be. They have spent an inordinate amount of time telling girls and women just how important it is that they submit to and obey their priesthood heads, whether their fathers or their husbands.

"How is it with you sisters?" Rulon Jeffs asked in one of his sermons in 1970. "Are you upholding and honouring and sustaining the Priesthood of your husband and head? We hear a lot in the nation today about the liberation movement of women. I want to tell the world and anybody who is interested, the only true freedom of woman is in the abiding and holy Celestial Law of Marriage, submitting herself to her husband and head, and living his law as he lives and abides the law of God."

In one of his sermons in 1977, Prophet LeRoy Johnson warned women of the consequence of not obeying their husbands. "Some girls who have been set by good men will not take their place. The Lord says there is nothing left for them but to be destroyed. And to be destroyed is something that cannot be explained by men . . . Give them a chance to repent and if they will not repent, you are to chase them out of your midst."

When Debbie Oler was fifteen, she believed that she was special because her marriage to Ray Blackmore had been ordained by God. But Ray quickly shattered her girlish dreams of romance and intimacy. After she had a miscarriage, and even after the birth of their daughter, there was no tenderness. She never felt close enough to her husband to call him by his first name, let alone a pet name. And, instead of feeling like a goddess, as she'd believed she would as a mother in Zion, Debbie felt like a prostitute in God's brothel.

"He never talked to me. I thought sex was love. And I had to be so close to someone and have a penis in me or I didn't think anyone loved me," she wrote years later to her father, Dalmon, only after he was dead. "I was so special to be married to Uncle Ray . . . He loved to have sex with me! He was even willing to bypass the Law of Chastity [that forbids sex for pleasure] so that he could have sex with me. But he blamed me and I felt wicked."

Widowed at eighteen, Debbie's second placement marriage to Charles Quinton was no improvement. Quinton was a man that Dalmon Oler wouldn't have given a dog to. That's what he told his daughter later. But it didn't matter. When the prophet commanded, Oler handed over his oldest daughter in accordance with the prophet's will. Quinton had orders of his own from Prophet LeRoy Johnson. Get Debbie pregnant as quickly as possible. It's how women are dealt with. Get them pregnant, keep them pregnant and, if they're still not obedient, exile them to the edges of the community, drug them or have them committed to the psych ward.

Cruelly, after their son was born, Quinton took the baby. Frantic weeks passed. Debbie had no idea where Quinton had taken the baby. When he returned the child, Quinton told Debbie she'd passed the test—a test seemingly aimed at weakening the bond between mother and child. He told her she was ready to get pregnant again.

The seven-year marriage was punctuated by his abuse and her suicide attempts. She took all kinds of pills to ward off the pain of depression; she often sat in the house with the lights out. In the spring of 1982, after Debbie set fire to Quinton's store—and forced her sister-wife Lorna Blackmore and her children to find a new home—Prophet LeRoy Johnson released Debbie from the marriage. She was committed to the psychiatric ward in Creston for treatment.

While she was recovering in the hospital, thirty-seven-year-old Marvin Palmer started visiting her. Ignoring the prophet's prohibition on courting, Marvin spent long hours at Debbie's bedside. He told her she was beautiful and he listened to her. After telling him about her dream of soaring like a bird over the Creston Valley, Marvin took her flying when she was released from hospital. After years of yearning for it, Debbie was in love with the first man who had ever treated her kindly. Unfortunately, her Prince Charming was a polygamist who already had two wives—sisters Marlene and Miriam, daughters of Ray and Anna Mae Blackmore. That is, Winston's sisters.

Even though Marvin had disobeyed the edict forbidding courting, Uncle Roy agreed to let him take a third wife, who would open the gates to the celestial kingdom to him. The prophet sealed their marriage in August 1982. For a while, it was everything that Debbie had hoped and dreamed of.

"Marvin was so good to me," Debbie said later. "He treated me as if I was worth something besides sex. He valued my opinion and he stuck up for me, sometimes." She took his name and adopted it for her three children. Debbie felt safe and appreciated. "It was the first time that I made love with somebody. Before that it was somebody was doing sex to me. It was making love when I was with him. It was such a different experience than it had been before."

Over the next few years, Marvin came under increasing pressure from Bishop Winston Blackmore and the prophet to dedicate his property to the United Effort Plan. He eventually signed over a backhoe and some logging equipment worth $150,000. But it didn't go to the UEP; Blackmore had him sign it over to one of his companies. Marvin was promised shares in the company and a place in the Kingdom of God. But, it was the same kind of deal that the church leaders had done to cheat Harold Blackmore out of his farmland in Bountiful. When Marvin tried to collect his shares, he was told that he'd been voted out of the company. He got nothing.

After that, Marvin became a dangerous, perverted parody of the man Debbie thought she knew. He was abusive and had begun fondling and inappropriately touching some of the children, including Debbie's thirteen-year-old daughter, Memory. Memory burst sobbing into the kitchen one night while Debbie was making dinner. "I'm going to hell," she told her mother. "I'm going to hell." The young girl was terrified that because her stepfather had fondled her, she would be forced to marry him. That was the priesthood's solution to child molesting. The victims became the molesters' brides.

Marvin blamed his abuse of Memory on the terrible nightmares he'd begun having and on the severe beatings he'd taken as a child. Still in love, and in the thrall of the FLDS, Debbie didn't go to a social worker or to the police. Once again, she mistakenly believed she could cure the man she thought she loved. Debbie believed that if she could relieve some of his work pressure, Marvin would return to what he had been. She took an air brakes course and went out on the long hauls with him in the eighteen-wheeler.

If Marvin had ever been the loving and tender man whom Debbie had fallen in love with, he wasn't any longer. In the fall of 1987, he raped and sodomized her in a motel room. Six weeks later, after twenty hours of driving, they finally stopped for the night. Inside the motel room, Marvin grabbed Debbie and rolled her onto her stomach. He held her down with one arm, and jammed his fist into her with the other. He changed hands, did it again and then turned her onto her back and raped her.

It was the last time Debbie went on the road with him. But she didn't leave him or go to the police. Instead, she went to her father, the patriarch, and to Winston Blackmore, the bishop of Bountiful. She begged them to get help for Marvin. They refused. They told her it would be dealt with internally; there was no need to involve gentiles. That was the last thing that Winston wanted.

Winston had been appointed bishop three years earlier by Prophet LeRoy Johnson. But Johnson died at age ninety-eight in November 1986, and was replaced by Rulon Jeffs, who had his own set of allies and his own ambitious son. Jeffs's favourite dictum was one that is spelled out in white stones outside the Bountiful Elementary-Secondary School, written on posters thoughout the school and framed on the walls of many homes: KEEP SWEET. It was the code for blind obedience. Followers must simply smile and do what they are told. They needed to subjugate their will, their needs and their desires to those of the prophet. Winston Blackmore was eager and willing to prove that he could enforce that dictum.

Blackmore's increasing economic clout allowed him to nurture friendships outside Bountiful. He played oldtimers' hockey with some of them at the community arena and guided some on hunting trips through the rugged mountains. He befriended the local member of the legislature, Howard Dirks; a succession of mayors; John Kettle, the representative on the regional district's board; and Chris Luke, who for twenty-seven years was the elected chief of the Lower Kootenay Indian band and for much of that time was the band's manager as well.

If Blackmore's guests and friends disapproved of his "lifestyle" or envied his growing harem of young wives, they seemed willing to tolerate it. Even though the wives and mothers were getting younger every year, as long as they and their children smiled sweetly when they came to town, nobody was going to interfere.

Luke is a hockey player, a goaltender who still often literally faces down Blackmore, a forward, rushing in to shoot. Luke claims he mostly shuts out the polygamist leader, but not often enough. They still often wager on whether Blackmore will score. Luke says they've become "real good friends" as well as business partners. Luke brokered the deal that gave Blackmore a long-term lease on nearly 2,600 acres of rich farmland in the Creston Valley that the band secured only after a long and costly fight for a treaty settlement.

Raised in a Catholic residential school, Luke has little regard for organized religion and distrusts the way government treats minorities. Yet he's not bothered by Blackmore's particular brand of faith. He accepts that it's just something Blackmore was born into.

As for his friend's practice of taking underage brides, Luke says Blackmore has admitted it and has taken responsibility for it. Besides, "It's a matter of nature and maturity. If the girls are ready to have a relationship and they're capable of having children, then it's all right."

This live-and-let live attitude is the hallmark of a community that has seen more than its share of the unusual, including several bizarre and often violent cults, in comparison to which the polygamous fundamentalist Mormons look positively mainstream.

Luke's extreme tolerance gives a hint of how content Valley residents were to accept Winston's word that everything was fine in the community, Blackmore preferred not to have to answer any questions at all. Rather than getting outside help for Marvin or alerting the police, the bishop convened a religious court. Marvin and all of his wives and children were put through a series of "repentance and obedience tests." But the strictest instruction was that they were to keep Marvin's sexual assaults a secret within their community. Blackmore ignored the laws that require him as a spiritual leader and as superintendent of a school to report what had happened to the provincial social services ministry and to the RCMP.

In her book, Debbie says Blackmore told her that he knew everything about her, everywhere she went and every person she talked to. He tried on several occasions to take away Debbie's daughter Memory. (Memory's father is also Winston's father, making Debbie's daughter Winston's half-sister.) Winston told Memory that God and the prophet had directed her to move into his home and come under his authority so that he could direct her on the path to salvation. He didn't make the same offer to Debbie's other children.

"I was numb and exhausted," Debbie told a documentary filmmaker about that period of her life. She tried to drown herself in nearby Goat River. "I felt it was better for the children. If there was no place left for us to go, I felt I had to do this." After the suicide attempt, Debbie was again treated in the psychiatry ward of Creston Hospital. She called the only

people she could think of who might be able to help her—
ranchers Faye and Steve Street.

Faye Street—a strapping, strong woman—had worked on
the same forest-fire-fighting team as Marvin had in the mid-
1980s. She liked Marvin and, on one of their days off, she had
invited him to stay at their ranch outside Cranbrook. While
they were still up at the firefighters' camp, Marvin had started
talking about his wives. Faye, a plain-spoken woman with a
sharp tongue, thought he was joking. But he soon convinced
her that it was true and told her more about his wives and
Bountiful.

Although the whole idea of polygamy made Faye more
than a bit uncomfortable, Marvin brought Debbie to meet
her and her husband after the fire season ended: "I could tell
she [Debbie] was head over heels, passionately in love with
the guy. But I started talking to Debbie about the polygamy
crap. She told me all that stuff about how wonderful it is and
all that. But I could tell the whole time she was lying and trying to convince herself."

The Streets visited Marvin and Debbie in Bountiful a few
months later and were appalled at the living conditions. "The
boys were sleeping in a granary with the beds stacked up
against the wall. It was cold and dirty." Inside the house, the
atmosphere was also frosty. "I could feel the daggers between
the women," says Faye. "I told Debbie that this is crap."

The friendship with Marvin and Debbie ended abruptly.
During a visit at the ranch, Marvin asked the Streets' fifteen-
year-old foster daughter if she would be willing to be his fifth
wife. "I told him to stay away from her or I'd neuter him,"
says Faye.

But Faye stayed in touch with Debbie. So, when Debbie
called from the hospital begging for help, the Streets went.
They listened to her story about her daughter's molestation

and Debbie's own rape. They convinced Debbie to report the abuse to the RCMP; in January 1988, a social worker and a police officer arrived at Marvin's home. Alerted to their arrival (likely by one of the other wives), Winston Blackmore had taken Memory from the house. "They took me over to the school real quick and told me not to tell them [the social worker and RCMP officer] anything. Not to tell them one single thing," Memory said later. After a slow-speed car chase through the tiny community, the social worker and the RCMP officer eventually interviewed Memory, along with the other wives and children. Soon after that, Marvin was charged with five counts of sexual abuse and molestation.

When Debbie's day in court came three years later in 1991, the Streets sat in the witness room with her before the trial began. "I could see Mac [Blackmore, Winston's oldest brother] coming up the walkway, but he couldn't see me," says Faye. "He flung the door to the witness room open. He could only see Debbie but not me. I said, 'What do you want, Mac?' and he said, 'Is this an open court case?' I told him you know damn well it is. He knew damn well it was. He was just there to threaten her."

When Debbie was called to testify, Faye and Steve Street went into the tiny courtroom. Mac Blackmore had stationed himself in the front row and was leaning forward on the railing so close to Debbie that they might have been at adjoining tables in a restaurant. "Debbie had started to shake," says Faye. "So I went and slammed my fat ass into his and moved him to the wall. Then I leaned on the railing and said quietly to Debbie, 'Look at me Debbie. Look at me.'"

Even with the Streets' reassuring presence, Debbie was sobbing before long. The judge ordered a recess to give Debbie time to calm down. The Streets spent the recess with her in the witness room and re-entered the packed courtroom only after Debbie was recalled to the witness stand. Mac Blackmore had ceded the front seat. Instead, he stood at the back of the courtroom, a silent and threatening hulk.

Without the support of friends like the Streets, some of the other witnesses collapsed because of the intimidation. Their testimony was judged to be confused and unreliable. In the end, Marvin was convicted on only one count of sexual assault on Debbie and acquitted of the charges relating to his sexual assaults of others in the family. Before sentencing, Debbie wrote a letter to the judge, saying that she still loved Marvin and that he needed professional help to deal with the abuse he had suffered as a child. The judge ordered a five-year suspended sentence and intensive therapy

Before Marvin's conviction, Winston Blackmore excommunicated him and ordered him out of the house built on United Effort Plan trust land. Blackmore stripped Marvin of his wives, reassigning his sisters and their sixteen children to his close friend, and Marvin's half-brother, Duane Palmer. He ordered Debbie to return with her children to her father's house. Once again, Dalmon Oler was to be her priesthood head. But Debbie had things to do before she moved.

"I cleaned the house all weekend. I cleaned everything. But the house itself was saturated with all the pain that all of us had had," Debbie said. After putting the children to bed, she went to the basement and collected kindling and newspapers. She wadded up the paper and stuffed it with the kindling into the kitchen cupboards. She struck a match and lit the fire.

Debbie says she had no intention of killing herself or the children. But she wanted to destroy the house. Standing outside and watching it burn, Debbie told writer Daniel Woods that she thought about what it says in the Book of Mormon —

that fire from heaven would protect the faithful during the Exaltation and that salvation for one's sins lay beyond. "The fire looked so good to me!" she told Woods. "I'd been told I lived in a protected place in Bountiful, but I learned it was all a lie. When I was three . . . when I was seven . . . all the times I was hurt . . . those memories were in the fire, I told myself. They were burning up, too."

Winston Blackmore's version of Debbie's final years in Bountiful is much different. The only point of agreement is that when Debbie married Marvin Palmer, she was desperate to be loved. "It seemed to me that they took the constitutional privilege of free association a little too liberally and in the end found that they were good medicine for each other," Winston wrote sneeringly in an account he posted on the Internet in 2004. In the account, he alternates oddly between speaking of himself in the first person and then in the third person: "One day he [Marvin] couldn't take it anymore. He came and had a talk with the Bishop and informed him that he was going away for a while."

Winston goes on to say that Debbie was "determined that she was going to do a number on the man so she got him involved in a sexual abuse court case." After Marvin's conviction, Blackmore says she tucked her children into bed, lit her house on fire and phoned him. Winston describes himself as the hero of the evening: "It was around 12:15 in the wee hours of the morning and I ran outside to see the night sky lit up by the blaze. I called the fire department and ran to my car. In no time, I was dragging people out of the blazing fire. Time and again I went in and out of there until all were out. I took Deb out of the house twice, only to find her back in the house . . . She told me there was one boy still in there and so I went in one last time only to find no one. You will never know what it feels like, but I finally made it on my hands and knees to the doorway just a moment before the thing flashed."

Despite his claim that Debbie tried to kill him, Blackmore says he helped her get an insurance settlement and move to Calgary. But his heroic version doesn't square with what Debbie's aunt Carmen Oler remembers. Carmen is Dalmon Oler's younger sister. She was never a polygamist, never lived in Bountiful and scarcely knew Debbie until her niece called in distress, asking Carmen to come from Calgary to rescue her and her children. Carmen remembers them hurriedly packing what remained of their belongings into the trunk of her car; she drove away as fast as possible, looking anxiously in the rearview mirror to see if anyone was following them.

Debbie Palmer was the first woman to leave Bountiful and take all of her children with her. The transition wasn't easy. Debbie and her children had no friends, no family that they knew other than Carmen, no money, no appropriate clothes and no idea of how to live on the outside. They had no school records, so when Debbie enrolled the children in public school all were tested and found to be at least a grade or two behind where they'd been in Bountiful.

One of her sons was sent home from school for refusing to square dance in his physical education class. He had refused because he'd been taught to treat girls like snakes, to stay away from them, just as Adam should have stayed away from Eve in the Garden of Eden. He'd been taught that it was wrong to touch a girl until you were married.

Memory was lonely, disoriented and struggling to deal with the aftermath of her abuse. She wanted to go back to what she knew, even though some of her friends were being prepared for marriage. "She didn't want to be on the outside," says Debbie. "She would attack me and tell me she wished I

Debbie Palmer exemplifies the frustrating paradox of the polygamous sect: leaving can be nearly as difficult as staying.
(Ian Smith / Vancouver Sun)

would die and then she would take the kids back because she said that I had brought them out to hell." It didn't help that Winston kept encouraging Memory to return, helping her to run away from home several times. Several times, Faye and Steve Street were enlisted to help Debbie retrieve her.

After all this, Debbie still loved Marvin. In 1993, six years after she had left Bountiful, and after Marvin's court-ordered therapy and suspended sentence had ended, Debbie and her seven children spent the summer with him in Bountiful. The vacation was uncomfortable, but not so uncomfortable that Debbie didn't end up pregnant.

Debbie Palmer's vulnerability, fear and isolation aren't unique. Cult leaders deliberately create those conditions. They want their followers to be frightened and off-balance. They want them to believe that no one else shares their experience, whether it's emotional or physical abuse or simply doubt. They want them to have little choice but to keep sweet if they want to fit in. Children are especially vulnerable. Their parents put their obedience to the prophet ahead of their responsibilities to their families—and motherless children like Debbie, her sister and her brother get lost in a horde of other kids.

Few children were more vulnerable than Janelle Fischer. She was one of Winston Blackmore's child brides. She ended up there only because her own family lost a custody battle for her and her siblings. The Utah Supreme Court overturned decades of precedents and handed her and her five orphaned siblings to polygamous strangers in Colorado City. Her story is an example not only of the treachery of the FLDS leaders but also of the blindness of the courts and government to the repressive and dangerous nature of the cult.

Janelle's mother, Brenda, wasn't born into a fundamentalist family. In fact, Brenda Johanson Thornton wasn't even a mainstream Mormon until her mother, Marion, remarried when she was ten. Marion was convinced by her new husband, Phil Thornton, to join the Church of Jesus Christ of Latter-day Saints and have her son and daughter baptized there as well. Marion Johanson Thornton became so filled with religious zeal that she later recruited her ex-husband, Calvin Johanson, and his second family to join the LDS. Calvin Johanson and his family went ahead with their baptisms even though Calvin and Marion's son had arrived a few days earlier and told them that Phil Thornton had taken Brenda as a second wife; in other words, that Thornton had married his stepdaughter. Tragically, nobody believed the boy's account of what had happened to his sister; it was discounted as a tale told by a runaway who was angry at his mother and stepfather. But sometimes runaways know better than religious zealots.

Brenda was sixteen when her stepfather began making sexual advances toward her. Although Phil Thornton was still a member in good standing in the LDS, he and his new family had been re-baptized into what would become the Fundamentalist Church of Jesus Christ of Latter Day Saints, and Phil was eager to start practising the Principle. When Brenda sought help after her stepfather's inappropriate advances, she made the mistake of turning to fundamentalist prophet LeRoy Johnson. He asked whether she would be willing to marry her forty-six-year-old stepfather. Appalled, but believing that it was a test of faith, Brenda replied: "If it's what the Lord wants." That night, Phil Thornton claimed his marital rights.

To protect her stepfather/husband's standing in the LDS church, Brenda was forced to sever all ties with the rest of her family and go into hiding, particularly when she was pregnant. She could not tell anyone—especially not her father and his family—that she was married and that she had children whose father was also their grandfather. Isolated, she wrote poetry. "I am a statue, I am a statue, I'm a statue all day long," she wrote in one.

When ten-year-old Brenda had left the Johanson home in Oregon to live with her mother and Thornton in Salt Lake City, her three-year-old half-sister Janet had been devastated. Like her father, siblings and both Marion and Phil Thornton, Janet is deaf, and had depended on Brenda to help her understand and communicate with the hearing world.

The deaf community in general is small and the deaf community within the LDS church is even smaller. So, when word began to circulate that Phil Thornton had taken his stepdaughter as his second wife, the Johansons "heard" about it. They didn't want to believe it, but their attempts to contact Brenda were always rebuffed. Finally, they were able to arrange a meeting with her at the LDS's Temple Square in the centre of Salt Lake City. Brenda refused to say much about her life. They asked her about her stepfather/husband. She denied she was married. They asked her about her children and she just shrugged, "What children?"

In 1975, while Helen Reddy's anthem to the burgeoning feminist movement was playing on the radio, Janet Johanson moved from Oregon to Provo, Utah, to attend Brigham Young University (BYU). She chose the LDS university because she thought that living closer to Brenda might allow her to rekindle their relationship. But Brenda wasn't interested in Janet's overtures. However, when Janet's younger sister, Patricia, came as a freshman two years later, Brenda was keen to spend time with Patricia.

"It was the first time she had reached out to anyone in the family and so I thought I could 'help' her. She wanted to come and see me, which was fine," Patricia says. "She showed up with Phil, her 'husband,' although I did not know he was her husband."

Even though Patricia had been a beauty pageant participant, she was surprised and flattered by the attention. Brenda and Phil started taking her to the section of the BYU library where old church texts are kept and began showing her various passages supporting polygamy written by Brigham Young and John Taylor. They told her how Joseph Smith had meant it to be a permanent principle, not something that could be renounced with a manifesto. "It was seductive in that they were saying they were living the 'higher law' and as a very good Mormon girl who wanted to do the right thing, that was a powerful message," says Patricia. "But I was uneasy with it all. I called my Mom and she told me not to meet Brenda unless Janet was present since Janet was strong and less vulnerable. Turned out it was the opposite."

Patricia did as her mother suggested and took Janet along. It was the last time Patricia met with Brenda and Phil. She heard nothing from them. "I found out Janet was meeting with Brenda alone. I told Mom. She was very upset and contacted a professor at BYU, who called us and asked us what was going on. Janet lied about it all. Then Janet more or less disappeared and I learned she had joined them."

With each step that Janet took towards conversion, Brenda shared more information about her own life. She introduced Janet to her children. She invited Janet to the Thorntons' home. She started taking Janet to the Sunday services at Rulon Jeffs's Cottonwood Canyon church in suburban Salt Lake City. "There were old men standing up and droning on and on with rows and rows of staring, judgmental people," Janet recalls. "We had to pass everybody because we sat right up in the front with the [sign language] interpreter. There were charismatic leaders in the beginning—Joseph Smith, Brigham Young—but after generation and generation of indoctrination and not knowing anything else, there's no charisma now. There's fear."

Even though Janet can't recall any magic emanating from the aging prophet LeRoy Johnson—only a black aura surrounding Rulon Jeffs—she kept going. She did it because of her sister and because, she admits, she wanted to live Joseph Smith's faith to the fullest. Finally, three years after enrolling at BYU, Janet was baptized into the breakaway fundamentalist sect. Dressed in a white temple gown, the nineteen-year-old was fully immersed in the baptismal pool in the basement of Rulon Jeffs's house in December 1978. Years later, Janet still can't quite explain what drew an honours student like her into a cult, other than to say, "Sometimes when you start on a track, it's hard to stop." No one in her family other than Brenda knew about her conversion.

Within a few weeks of Janet's baptism, Brenda was pregnant with Janelle—her fifth child. The sisters took it as God's blessing resulting from Janet's baptism. As the birthdate neared, they went together to Colorado City, where fundamentalist mothers go to give birth to their covenant children, away from the prying eyes and probing questions of gentiles. While they were there, Prophet LeRoy Johnson called Janet to meet with him. He told her that she "belonged" to Don Jacobs, a deaf man thirty-seven years older than she was. The fifty-nine-year-old printer worked at the *Salt Lake Tribune* newspaper and volunteered his time and skills at the Truth Publishing Company, which has published hundreds of pamphlets and books promoting polygamy and fundamentalist doctrine. Janet had seen Don and his wife, Florence, at Rulon Jeffs's church meetings, but she didn't know either of them. All she remembers thinking is that at least she wouldn't have to marry Phil Thornton. Anybody was better than him.

Janet had finished sewing a pastel pink wedding dress by the time Brenda's baby was born on September 12, 1979. Brenda named her daughter Janelle, in honour of her half-sister. The following day, when the three of them returned to Salt Lake City, there was a message waiting for Janet. She was to be married the next day at Guy Musser's house in downtown Salt Lake City.

There was no honeymoon. On their way home, Florence warned Janet that her older sons weren't too happy about the marriage. They'd hoped to inherit the house when their parents died and were now concerned that Janet might steal it away from them. It was a hint of what was to come. On the nights that Don slept with Janet, Florence stormed about the house, flicking on the lights to wake them. For the deaf, light is the equivalent of noise. Florence demanded that Janet's bedroom door be kept open at all times. Once she broke a glass over Janet's hand and, as she tried to "help" Janet get the shards out, she ground them deeper.

After the incident with the glass, Don asked Guy Musser what to do about the awkward relationship between his wives. Musser, who had presided at Don's wedding to Janet, ordered Janet to cut all of her ties to her family, including Brenda. Don was to monitor all her mail and phone calls. Musser also reminded Don that, as a member in good standing at the mainstream Mormon church, he must never be seen with Janet, even at fundamentalist meetings. Janet couldn't even register to vote because that might tip off the authorities that the Jacobses were polygamists. Plus, as Don told Janet, women were incapable of making such important decisions. Musser wanted Janet to be invisible—a "poofer," as the fundamentalists call women like her. Finally, he ordered Janet to stay home and get pregnant.

Even after tests proved that Don was infertile, Janet was blamed for being barren. She was told that she was too strong-willed and not obedient enough. After two years, Janet defiantly went back to college and started sneaking out the window at night to see Brenda. But it was Brenda who left the cult a few months ahead of Janet. Brenda was granted a divorce from Phil Thornton, who had repeatedly threatened to slit her throat and let her bleed to death—blood atonement for her disobedience.

Brenda rented a small house in Salt Lake City; she bought blue jeans and short-sleeved shirts for herself and her children, replacing their pioneer-style clothes. She enrolled the older ones in a public school. All of them hungrily watched television and even went swimming wearing bathing suits like everybody else. Thornton didn't pay child support, and since Brenda had never been allowed to finish high school, she had few job opportunities and very little money. But, for a while, that didn't matter. Brenda revelled in her freedom. But that ended when, not long after she'd left, Brenda was diagnosed with a virulent form of breast cancer. When she had left fundamentalism behind, Brenda had been warned that God would punish her. So she couldn't help but wonder: was this God's revenge?

In the next twenty-four months, Brenda had a mastectomy, as well as radiation therapy and chemotherapy. She got sicker and was ruined by the hospital bills. Brenda asked Janet and Patricia for help with the children. Janet had finished her degree after leaving Don, and had just started a job in Oregon. Patricia was working on her doctorate at George Washington University. Her half-sisters promised to do what they could. Janet began making plans for Brenda to move back to Oregon. But it took time to make those arrangements and Brenda didn't believe she had time.

With only months to live and desperate to find a home for her children, she went to Rulon Jeffs asking for help, both for her eternal soul and for her children. Jeffs said she would only be saved if she moved to Colorado City, married Vaughn Fischer and assigned custody of her children to Fischer and his first wife. Jeffs gave her thirty minutes to decide. Brenda said yes. On June 17, 1987—three hours before her second celestial marriage—Brenda met the forty-seven-year-old groom for the first time. He had twelve children with his legal wife, forty-two-year-old Sharane, two adopted nephews and two children with his second wife, twenty-two-year-old Katrina. Vaughn moved Brenda and her six children into a trailer that had been added on to Fischer's fourteen-bedroom house.

Two weeks after the wedding, Vaughn and Sharane drove Brenda to nearby St. George, Utah, for an appointment with a lawyer in one of the state's largest and most prestigious law firms. Heavily medicated for the pain of the advancing cancer, Brenda signed what is called an instant petition to the court, giving the Fischers permission to adopt her six children. The children's father, Phil Thornton, had already signed the form.

In the meantime, Patricia and Janet had been desperately searching for Brenda, who had followed Jeffs's orders and moved without telling them. When they found her, Patricia rushed to Colorado City and found that Brenda had signed away her children. Patricia insists that Brenda, who was by then too weak to go to an attorney to change her will, begged her in those final days to get the children out. On August 17, 1989, thirty-seven-year-old Brenda Johanson Thornton Fischer died. Her oldest child was eighteen; her youngest only four.

Patricia, Janet and their father, Calvin Johanson, tried to stop the adoption. Their most immediate concern was that fifteen-year-old Vonnie would end up like her mother — married to her new stepfather. They were concerned about the fates of twelve-year-old Julia, eight-year-old Janelle and four-year-old Deanne, as well as the two boys, who had dreams of going to college.

Naively, the Johansons believed that gaining custody would not be difficult. The Fischers were strangers to the children. Vaughn was an admitted polygamist, breaking both state and federal laws. He and his two wives scarcely knew the children, and although his lawyers described Vaughn as a successful building contractor, his annual net income was little more than nine thousand American dollars, which didn't go far towards feeding and caring for two wives and sixteen children.

By contrast, the Johansons were blood relatives. Janet had a master's degree and was an administrator at a college for the deaf in Oregon. Patricia had a doctorate and was staff director of the U.S. Commission on Education for the Deaf in Washington, D.C. Calvin was retired, but willing to help with the financial support of his six grandchildren.

On the Johansons' side was Vaughn's nephew Carl. He had been adopted by Vaughn and Sharane when he was twelve, after his mother had died and after his father was kicked out of the community on what Carl said were "trumped up charges by the polygamists." In his affidavit, Carl said that outside the courtroom before his own adoption, Sharane had threatened that if he didn't consent to it, he would never see his brothers and sisters. His siblings were being adopted by other uncles.

During the two and a half years that Carl lived with Vaughn and Sharane, he worked without pay for his uncle's company. He only saw his brothers and sisters every few months or on their birthdays. "I was treated like an outsider who was a burden to the rest of the family and the only reason I was there was because they couldn't push me off on someone else. They did enjoy the government cheques each month . . . They never showed me any love whatsoever."

Vaughan constantly told Carl that he was "on the road to state prison, like [his] father." Yet Carl was more fortunate than his sister Robynn. When she turned fifteen, Robynn was forced to marry her uncle and adoptive father, fifty-four-year-old Erwin Fischer. In his affidavit, Carl said Erwin had groomed his niece for marriage by "kissing and petting" her as a child.

Despite his testimony, the Utah social services department determined that the Fischers were "highly qualified to take care of these children" and that they were a family where "children are taught good principles." Polygamy was not mentioned in the department's assessment of the family. "The legality of polygamy is not at issue in a home study. The issue is the legality of the home, not their religious practices," department spokesman Terry Twitchell told the *Deseret News*.

To the Johansons' horror, during the custody hearing, all of the lawyers and the judge talked about their own polygamous ancestors. Judge Dean Condor said both his great-grandfathers had been polygamists, adding, "I have some reticence to say, 'Okay, they're criminals.'" The Fischers' lawyer, Steven Snow, a Mormon bishop, bristled at that characterization of polygamy as well. "I'd hate to think that my grandparents or great-grandparents were immoral," he said. Even the Johansons' lawyers—former Utah governor Calvin Rampton and Tim Anderson—chimed in about their polygamous ancestors.

Still, Judge Condor decided in December, 1988 that the best interests of a child can never be met in a home where polygamy is practised, citing a 1955 Utah Supreme Court decision that called polygamists social outcasts without rights to raise children. That unanimous decision calls the practice of polygamy "sufficiently reprehensible, without the innocent lives of children being seared by their evil influence. There can be no compromise with evil."

Condor ordered the Fischers to turn the five minor children over to the Utah family services department—Brenda's oldest son was by then legally an adult. But Condor's order was stayed pending an appeal. So, while the wheels of justice ground slowly, the children lived with the Fischers, who collected six hundred American dollars a month in social security benefits for the children—welcome money for the cash-strapped house-builder.

Patricia and Janet had unmonitored visits with the children. But, by February, the Fischers had turned the children against their aunts. Only five-year-old Deanne seemed genuinely pleased to see them. Twelve-year-old Julia demanded to know why her aunts were asking so many questions. She told them that she was happy there, repeating what she'd written in a badly misspelled and emphatic letter a few weeks earlier.

"My parence aren't stoping us," she had written. "I feel sorry someone is trying to take us from our family. I know my mom wanted us here. She had a choise. She didn't have to marry my Dad. And she wasn't forced! She was afraid to tell you because she knew how mad you can get, she was afraid you would hurt her . . . I think if you realy *love* us, you and the others would not try to take us away from *our family* . . . I hope you'll stop fighting for us and be friends insted of enemies, Love Julia *Fischer*"

Janelle disappeared before the visit ended. The following year, Janelle refused to even look at Janet when she arrived. On another visit, Janelle screamed at Janet: "What are you doing here? Why don't you leave us alone?"

The Utah Supreme Court heard the appeal on July 29, 1989, which included testimony from psychologists and social workers that the children were traumatized by all the uncertainty. Still it took eight months for the justices to reach a decision. Nearly three years after Brenda had died, on March 26, 1991, the Johansons lost in a three-to-two decision. By then, nineteen-year-old Vonnie had also outgrown the court's jurisdiction. Only the four younger children, including eleven-year-old Janelle, were bound by the decision.

Supported by the American Civil Liberties Union, the Utah Supreme Court overturned more than one hundred years of legal precedents and allowed the Fischers to adopt the children. Justice Christine Durham said the trial judge had erred by grafting on to the adoption rules a special category of "wrong-doers" without allowing them a full evidentiary and evaluation hearing. The Utah Constitution states: "Perfect toleration of religious sentiment is guaranteed . . . but polygamous or plural marriages are forever prohibited."

But Durham wrote that this "does not necessarily mean that the state must deny any or all civil rights and privileges to polygamists." Besides, Durham and two other judges decided only Vaughn Fischer was a bigamist. Sharane was not because she was legally married to Fischer.

The two dissenters were the most senior members of the court—Chief Justice Gordon Hall and Associate Chief Justice Richard C. Howe. In the strongly worded minority opinion, Howe echoed the Johanson family's thoughts and fears:

> It would be difficult to conceive of a factor which works more against the "interests of the children" than on-going criminal conduct by the adoptive parents in the home where the children are being nurtured and raised. I cannot conceive of any factor or combination of factors favorable to an adoption or qualities which proposed adopting parents could offer which would outweigh the detrimental effect of felonious conduct engaged in by them.
>
> Teaching and demonstrating to children on a daily basis that the statute proscribing bigamy may be ignored and flaunted [sic] may well breed in the children a disrespect for observance of other laws. Since the children will probably spend their lives in this nation where the voluntary observance of all laws by its citizens is necessary, these six children may never be taught that valuable lesson of citizenship. The state in its role as *parens patriae* of the children owes a high duty to them in approving whoever shall adopt them.

The Johansons could have appealed to the U.S. Supreme Court. The fact that the two senior judges had dissented suggests that they might even have won. But they were exhausted by the fight, broken by the children's rejection and nearly bankrupt. Patricia continued writing to Julia for a few years. But she says, "All I got in return were 'canned' letters talking about how absolutely perfect everything was. I can recognize coached propaganda when I see it so at some point I stopped writing . . . None of them has contacted me."

A few years after the Utah Supreme Court decision, Vaughn Fischer took Janelle and his daughter Marleena, who was the same age as Janelle, to Bountiful. Marleena knew she was getting married, but Janelle thought she was only to be a guest at the wedding. The day after they arrived in Bountiful, during a break in a priesthood meeting, Prophet Rulon Jeffs performed two quick ceremonies, one after the other. Marleena was first, followed by Janelle. The bridegroom was so blasé about his thirteenth and fourteenth brides that he said his vows and went back to the meeting. The bridegroom was Winston Blackmore.

Fourteen years after the Johansons had lost their custody case in Utah and twelve years after Janet had seen the children for the last time, she found a reference to Janelle in Winston Blackmore's Internet newsletter, the *North Star*. Winston wrote that a few weeks earlier, in 2003, he'd taken Janelle and their daughter to Utah to visit Janelle's grandmother Marion Johanson Thornton. The news reopened old wounds that Janet had tried to forget—the foolishness of her own conversion and subsequent plural marriage, the death of her sister, the loss of her nieces and nephews. But Janet emailed to Blackmore and asked him to put her in touch with Janelle. Nothing happened. Janet began hounding him for information about Janelle and a chance to see her. Finally, she confronted him in November 2005 outside a Utah courtroom. Both were vying for a seat on

*Handed over as a child to the custody of a polygamist by a split decision
of the Utah Supreme Court, it was not long before Janelle Thornton
Fischer was taken north to be one of Winston Blackmore's wives.*
(Photo courtesy of Janet Johanson)

the reformed United Effort Plan trust, which had been put into
receivership by the Utah and Arizona attorneys general.

Nearly six feet tall, Janet towered over an uncomfortable
Blackmore, who is stocky, but little more than five-foot-six or
-seven. Flanked by her interpreter and a reporter, Janet asked
him why he refused to let Janelle contact her. She asked him
for Janelle's phone number, her email address. Anything. She
appealed to Blackmore as a family man, telling him that
Janelle's grandfather, Calvin Johanson, was now in his eight-
ies and would dearly love to see his granddaughter again.
Blackmore said he'd pass on the information, but it was up to
Janelle if she wanted to contact her aunt. Nothing happened.

In the spring of 2006, just a few months after Janet had a
cochlear implant and was able to hear for the first time, a journalist got word to Janelle that her aunt was desperately trying
to contact her. Almost immediately, Janelle emailed Janet and

Janelle Fischer with Winston Blackmore and four of his children in Bountiful in the spring of 2006. **(Glenn Baglo / Vancouver Sun)**

invited her to visit on the first long weekend in the summer. On the long drive up to Bountiful from Salem, Oregon, with her two adopted children, Janet alternated between joy and fear. The last time she'd seen Janelle, her niece had angrily accused her of ripping her away from her family—the Fischers. She had no idea what would happen when she pulled up beside the little house in Bountiful where Janelle, a favourite wife, lives alone with her three daughters. Janet was shocked to see Janelle. She was the image of Brenda. When Janet stepped out of her car, Janelle hugged her tightly. It has been too long, Janelle said. It has been too long.

Janet has visited Janelle several times since and they email frequently. Despite Janet's invitations for Janelle to bring her children to Oregon to visit her grandfather, Janelle has yet to do that. And, so far, Janet's attempts to find the other children have all failed.

ELEVEN

IN THE NAME OF GOD

It's not easy to hide forty-eight children and five wives. But, if you live in an isolated sect infatuated with the "begats" of Old Testament patriarchs, it's easy to see how you might be proud of this dubious accomplishment. Perhaps this is why Dalmon Oler was surprised to find himself the focus of an RCMP investigation in the late 1980s, along with Winston Blackmore, who was both his son-in-law and Bountiful's bishop. Despite his surprise, when RCMP officers arrived at his door with a search warrant in October 1990, following a complaint from a neighbour, Oler let them in and showed them around.

He was equally gracious to television reporter Clive Jackson, who knocked on his door a few weeks later. At fifty-seven, Oler was one of Bountiful's oldest residents—only two people in the community were over sixty-five. He was also one of its most prolific, a title not to be discounted in a community where the population had tripled in a decade. The baby boom that Oler had contributed so much to meant that, in 1990, Bountiful's mean age—the midpoint where there are equal numbers of people both older and younger—was six.

Oler took the reporter on a tour of the ramshackle house. The Oler home was massive; fifteen bedrooms, fourteen bathrooms, a gymnasium-sized dining room with two long tables to accommodate everyone. The kitchen was restaurant-sized. It needed to be. The family went through one hundred pounds of potatoes a week and bought thirty dozen eggs at a time. This family had to buy in bulk.

Despite the size of his home, the king of the rundown castle didn't have a bedroom of his own. "I haven't got time for that," he told Jackson. "I just rotate between the wives." He tried to keep to a strict schedule, sleeping in a "different mother's bed" each night. Jackson asked him if the wives ever got jealous. "Well, we're human beings. I don't think you ever solve that problem completely," Oler replied. "You just try to work with it and overcome it."

Oler showed the reporter the hundreds of family photos lining the walls. Some were stapled haphazardly. Others, including a long sequence of photographs of babies sired by Oler, had been taken by professional photographers, framed and hung in sequence along the stairway. Commenting on the photos, Oler said, "Children who were born close together we've tried to name them with the same letter in the first name and it's been kind of fun because we'd have four in a year and they'd all have the first letter of the name the same so we'd call them the As or the Ts or the Js or whatever."

In 1971, R was the chosen letter. In 1973, it was G and, in 1976, it was J. The four children born in 1978 and 1979 all had names starting with S. And the three children born in 1982 shared two initials—R and T. Pointing to one grouping of baby photos, Oler chuckled: "These three were born close enough together that the mothers were all in the hospital at the same time. One was born in the evening and the other the next morning and I attended both of those births and it was really a shock to the doctor to come in the second time and see me trying to work with another birth in the same day and he said, 'Haven't we done this before?' " It seems inconceivable that a responsible doctor would not have reported Oler to police and social workers. But there is no evidence a report was filed.

After the tour, Oler gathered three of his five wives— Memory, Andrea and Wanda—and half a dozen or so little kids around him on the couch. His teenaged daughters lined the staircase wearing their nearly identical pioneer-style dresses with their hair uniformly swooped high in the front and primly tucked into a neat bun or braid at the back. They sang a song one of them had written for their father.

> My Daddy is the best man in the world.
> My Daddy is the best man in the world.
> My Daddy is so good because he does the things
>   he should.
> I love him for he's the best man in the world.

As they sang, the camera caught Oler wiping away a tear.

A couple of months later, Oler told *Vancouver Sun* reporter Douglas Todd that even though he was fifty-seven and recovering from cancer surgery, he had every intention of continuing to follow the Lord's orders to "go forth and multiply": "I'd hate to quit this early. The prime motive of plural marriage is to raise children. It's easier to teach your own children your beliefs than to gather up a lot of people with preconceived notions who don't understand." And then he added, with stunning bravado: "If I just wanted sex, it would be easy enough to come by without procuring children."

Bountiful's bishop, Winston Blackmore, was more grudging in his meetings with the media and, by his account, more aggressive with the RCMP: "There was [sic] three police officers there who wouldn't even let me go to the bathroom by myself," he told one reporter about the 1990 investigation. "They were trying to prove I had more than one wife so I said, 'Right, I do. Now go away.'"

Unlike the easygoing Oler, Blackmore has always tried not to give away any details of what life is like inside his family. He has never answered questions about how many wives or children he has, and feigns horror when asked about how he arranges his sex life. Blackmore tries to rebuff questions by turning them back on the interviewers, chastising them for asking such personal questions or asking them how many men or women they have slept with outside the bounds of marriage. But mostly he insists that to talk about how he services his multiple wives demeans one of the most important principles of his religion.

"Plural marriage, celestial marriage is a very basic fundamental part of our written law that was published and laid down by the founding fathers of our church," Blackmore lectured reporter Clive Jackson in 1990. "It will be remembered in the Bible that Abraham was a man with more wives than one and that he was a man that God greatly loved and he promised him that his posterity would fill the earth so that if you're going to enjoy the blessings of Abraham, you'll have to do the work of Abraham."

His legion of wives might be surprised to learn that Winston thinks of his relations with them as work, especially when it often looks a lot more like pleasure. Though Winston insists polygamy is not about sex, several wives say it is more than incidental. Using the pretense of high blood pressure and the fear of a heart attack, he often calls half a dozen or more of his wives to massage him in his bedroom. Lying almost naked on the bed, he directs which wife should massage where. When he's had enough, one or more of the wives are asked to stay and have sex with him. No one is sure who will be picked until her name is called. And, sometimes, Winston calls more than one.

Winston's wives have been careful to keep the family secrets. The few who do speak to journalists are well coached in how to avoid questions about how their lives are organized. But several of his wives have left, so it's now possible to get a glimpse of what life must be like inside his large home, which has all the charm of a cheap motel. There is no "rotating" from wife to wife on a regular schedule or any pretense at "fairness." Even if there were, it would be almost a month between conjugal visits to each wife. Winston has never attempted fairness. He's always had favourites. But it's also how he controls them.

"I had ulcers because you never knew what day he would call you or when he'd show up," says Shirley Black, who with her baby son was reassigned to Winston in 1999, after she was released from an abusive marriage in Colorado City. Even when Blackmore is with one of the wives, Shirley says he keeps them off balance. "He's the type of guy who's like 'Tell me what you want. Do you want sex? Tell me what you want because I'm busy.'"

He likes to surprise his wives, showing up unannounced. He'll suddenly bestow favours and, just as unexpectedly, withdraw them. Favourite wives have been given homes of their own or places to share with only one other sister-wife. Those who are out of favour sometimes get shifted outside Winston's realm. In Bountiful's equivalent of Siberia, they are left to fret over whether they will ever return to his good graces. Winston has sold houses out from under some of his wives. He's given some only a few days' notice of a change of venue, as if he were a landlord, not the loving husband he purports to be.

A few years ago, one of the wives attempted to bring some order into her chaotic life. She posted a calendar and asked the other wives to sign up for the nights that they wanted to spend with Winston. (Some of the women refused on principle. Others refused because they preferred not to see their husband at all.) The schedule wasn't aimed only at regulating sex. It was aimed at trying to get Winston to spend time with them on special occasions, like birthdays and anniversaries, and also at trying to force him to see his children. Even had all the wives agreed to sign on to a family calendar, it's unlikely that Winston, their god and priesthood head, would have been dictated to by them.

Far from there being solidarity amongst the women, far from this being a loving family unit where sister-wives work together in harmony, the wives' world is a dangerous one, rife with jealousies and conflicts. It's not surprising, since many of the wives weren't women, but girls, when they married. Even now they live in a state of arrested development, capable of all the cruelty and even violence of any teenaged girl. And often the children are caught in the crossfire.

For a while after Shirley Black and her son joined the Blackmore family, the delicate-looking, fair-haired Shirley was a favourite. Her son paid a price for that. One day in the yard, he was surrounded by bigger kids—his new brothers and sisters. They taunted him. One kid picked up a stone and hurled it at him. Then another kid did. When Shirley rushed to help him, the children turned on her, too. As several of her sister-wives watched, the children hurled rocks at her, literally stoning her like a fallen woman in the Old Testament. She got away. Shirley grabbed her son and baby daughter (Winston's daughter), and took one of the vans that Winston allows the mothers to drive. She ended up in a women's shelter in Bonner's Ferry, Idaho. The next day, Winston and another wife, Ruth Lane, drove up and down nearly every street in the town of twenty-five hundred people until they recognized the van. Shirley refused to go back and Winston was too busy to convince her. Instead, Shirley was wooed by proxy. Winston dispatched a couple of his daughters who had participated in the stoning with flowers to beg "Mother Shirley" to come home. Weeks later, Shirley heard them laughing about what they'd done. They called themselves "the stoner girls." It wasn't long after that that Shirley left for good. Even still, Winston tries to exercise some control over her. In 2007, he tried to get her to agree to move back to Colorado City and claim land owned by the UEP. She refused, believing Winston simply wanted the land for himself.

Few outsiders have been given an opportunity to glimpse the daily life of the community. In 1992, Marla Peters got the most intimate look that any outsider has ever had. Winston had rejected her initial request to live with his family, but he agreed to let the University of Alberta sociology student spend several months in Bountiful working in the school as part of the research for her master's thesis on closed communities. Her study is flawed because it wasn't until she was well into her project that Peters realized that, far from being merely an objective observer, she was being treated as a recruit—a potential plural wife. It was his proselytizing and public wooing that led to one of Peters' most cogent observations. She writes: "This reminds me of the Monty Python movie, [*Life of*] *Brian*, in which the mobs proclaim Brian as their leader and messiah. Exasperated, Brian yells at the people that they have to think for themselves. They respond in unison, 'Yes, we have to think for ourselves!' "

Her access to the church meetings and the school sessions gave her chilling insight into the control the bishop exerted on his family and followers. She began to see how people could be naively drawn in by a skilled and charming manipulator like Winston. In the beginning, Peters believed Winston would tell her the truth, and she asked him to instruct her if he ever thought that her behaviour was "inappropriate." Yet, when he later chastised her during church meetings, Peters wrote that she had expected him to have told her privately rather than "announcing it before the members he had told me to befriend." Public humiliation is just one of many tactics cult leaders use to get new recruits to conform and to keep followers in line. It was in part this public pressure to conform that provoked Peters's realization that, from the beginning, Winston had been grooming her as a potential bride— perhaps not for himself, but possibly for one of the other men.

Soon after Peters began her study of Bountiful, she was invited to her first and only Sunday dinner at Blackmore's home. Before dinner, the gregarious bishop insisted that one of his sons show her photos of him on horseback, lassoing a bear. Over dinner and surrounded by the twenty or so silent family members, Blackmore dominated the conversation. After dinner, he strummed his guitar and sang country-and-western love songs and yodelled (an art form perhaps learned from his Uncle Harold). As Blackmore sat there, encircled by his wives and children, Peters described him as "a god sitting in the middle of his domestic kingdom." Blackmore asked one of his daughters to sing with him. And although Winston claims to know the names and ages of all of his 115-plus children, he asked his daughter how old she was. Ten, she replied. The duet he chose was a song about a love for one "too young."

Peters spent most of her time in the school, which Blackmore had built in the mid-1980s in his bid to displace Dalmon Oler as bishop and Bountiful's leader. In Winston's later mythologizing of his role, he wrote that Oler had been content to let the children go to school in a building condemned as a fire hazard. "We fixed it like we always did in those days," Blackmore wrote two decades later. "We pronounced the judgments of God upon them [the government and the fire marshal], took off the red tags and kept on doing school."

After meeting with the fire marshal in 1983, he claims that when he realized what danger his own children were in, he overrode Oler's instructions and "ordered" the principal to send the children home and called a community meeting for that night. At the meeting, Blackmore says he told everyone that until a better place could be found, the children would be taught in the basement of Oler's large home. No one contradicted the upstart Blackmore, not even Oler, whose home had just been commandeered.

Blackmore took out a $47,000 bank loan to renovate Oler's basement and to buy a bus. The provincial government had only recently decided to fund independent schools, but he claims he managed to squeeze $22,000 out of it. The rest was, no doubt, raised through special assessments placed on every family. When the new school was built on an old dumpsite, Blackmore says he convinced the government to accredit the school, which meant that it was eligible for substantial annual operating grants. Then, on the advice of government bureaucrats, he incorporated the Bountiful Elementary-Secondary School Society, put himself in charge and transferred the property title to the society, in order to save on property taxes.

The society's purposes included the usual things—advancing the education of FLDS children, operating as a charity, and soliciting grants, donations, legacies and gifts to help operate the school. But, in an echo of Harold Blackmore's Dumpster-diving frugality, even today, one of the society's stated goals is to "solicit, collect, deal in and dispose of used and salvaged goods and articles of every kind."

Winston has always proved clever at "bleeding the beast," which is fundamentalist slang for bilking governments to support their illegal lifestyle. And he knows it. It was no coincidence that his account of how the school came into being in a 2003 issue of the *North Star* was flanked by this quote from Guy Musser, an earlier fundamentalist leader: "I would lie any day to beat the Devil." As Flora Jessop, an outspoken antipolygamy activist who escaped Colorado City in her teens, says: "They [fundamentalists] find it amusing that Satan is supporting God's work."

Peters gave a sharp indictment of what the government allows to be taught there. "The aim of the school is not so much cerebral as celestial." One teacher could not spell and her mistakes were picked up by the students. Obedience was stressed, Peters wrote, quoting from the school newsletter: "We should all be in agreement that this school is [the prophet] Uncle Rulon's school."

"Uncle Rulon's possession is palpable upon entering the average-looking but neglectfully dirty schools," she wrote. "Pictorial successions of the FLDS prophets dominate the foyers where children may be heard rehearsing song or plays for church and where they gather for morning prayer. Hanging from school walls are computerized banners stating: 'Wickedness never was happiness,' 'Without obedience, learning cannot occur,' 'Be Sweet—it's a matter of life and death' and 'Mind your own business.'"

The main mission of the school, Peters concluded, is to teach the supremacy of plural marriage and prepare students for marriage. Female teachers "are perpetually pregnant" and girls make baby clothes in sewing classes.

Penny Priddy had never heard of Bountiful until after she was elected to the provincial legislature in 1991 and appointed

secretary of state for women's equality. Soon after her appointment, *Vancouver Province* newspaper reporter Fabian Dawson
called her demanding why the New Democratic Party government continued funding a private school where girls
were taught only enough to be good and obedient wives and
mothers. Priddy thought it was a very good question.

Even though Priddy is a feminist, she had no roots in the
women's movement. Before she became a politician, Priddy
had trained as a nurse and worked with children with disabil-
ities. So, despite being the women's equality minister, Priddy
began by asking questions about the children in Bountiful,
not the women. "For me it was always about the kids and not
about polygamy particularly. I was concerned about the ages
of the children when they were married and sent to work
and about the sole expectation that the girls were expected
to marry and reproduce since reproducing was a pretty
important part of keeping Bountiful alive."

Priddy "asked and asked some more" about education.
Nobody seemed to know how many children from Bountiful
were completing Grade 12, or how many children were
being sent off to work in logging camps when they were
barely out of elementary school. It was difficult for her to get
straight answers: "Our party has a principle of not funding
private schools, but that was not a train that anybody would
like to lie down in front of. Besides, I asked Corky Evans [the
local New Democratic Party member of the legislative
assembly] about it and he talked about how important
Bountiful was to the Creston economy, so the issue just sort
of wandered away."

Even though reporters were asking questions about
Bountiful, Priddy doesn't recall any public outcry: "Nobody
was writing to me or to other cabinet ministers saying that
there was a problem." Because of that, she says, Bountiful was

never a priority, even though the government was supposedly committed to public education, equality and defending the downtrodden, and even though the provincial cabinet had never had so many female ministers.

Still Priddy persevered, asking staff in the ministry's regional office whether they could set up a meeting for her with some people from Bountiful. She was told that nobody knew anyone in Bountiful. The regional coordinator suggested she speak to Debbie Oler Palmer and some of the women who had left Bountiful. Priddy did that. "I wanted to know what their experience had been. I asked about the school and I asked about the women there and what I learned was that the community was sending people out to do post-secondary training in things like nursing so that Bountiful could be a self-sustaining community."

But what Debbie and Priddy's officials told her was that it would be a mistake to shut down the school. They argued that as long as the government funded the school, the children would be studying the same curriculum as students in public schools. They argued that education was the only lifeline children had to the outside world.

In early 1992, the RCMP wrapped up its investigation of Dalmon Oler and Winston Blackmore and sent its recommendation to Attorney General Colin Gabelmann that the pair be charged with polygamy. But it turned out that Dalmon Oler had been right not to waste any sleep worrying about being charged. On June 11, 1992, regional Crown counsel Hermann Rohrmoser issued a press release that said no charges of bigamy or polygamy would be laid. He said the decision was based on "exhaustive research undertaken by constitutional experts," who unanimously concluded the relevant sections of the Criminal Code are unconstitutional.

The bigamy section says it is illegal for anyone who is married to go through "a form of marriage" with another person in Canada, or to leave Canada with the intent to marry another person, to marry someone who is already married or to "simultaneously" marry more than one person.

Another section says anyone who "practises or enters into or in any manner agrees or consents to practise or enter into any form of polygamy or any conjugal union with more than one person at the same time whether or not it is by law recognized as a binding form of marriage; or who celebrates, assists or is party to a rite, ceremony, contract or consent that purports to sanction [such] a relationship" is guilty of polygamy.

Rohrmoser said the province's legal experts found the polygamy section to be "in direct conflict with the freedom of religion guarantees in . . . the Charter of Rights and Freedoms and cannot be justified." One of those experts was retired Court of Appeal justice Richard P. Anderson, who was quoted in the press release saying that the polygamy law was "obsolete and apart from being unconstitutional is inadequate to solve the real problems confronting society." Anderson had urged the government "not to persist in expensive and time-consuming litigation."

Before Rohrmoser's press release was issued, Gabelmann—who is not a lawyer—had taken the judge's advice to federal Justice Minister Kim Campbell. Gabelmann asked her to have the antipolygamy sections of the Criminal Code rewritten so that they might withstand a constitutional challenge. Gabelmann's belief that the law wasn't good enough was bolstered by the opinion of Environment Minister Andrew Petter, a lawyer and constitutional expert. But in Ottawa, Campbell and her experts disagreed with the B.C. position.

Campbell—a lawyer who never practised law—had no love for the B.C. New Democrats. She had been a backbencher in British Columbia's Social Credit government before switching to federal politics. Campbell had even aspired to lead the B.C. wing of the party that Winston Blackmore's grandfather had once led nationally. She placed last in that contest, with only fourteen votes on the first ballot. But her speech with its pointed assessment of the eventual winner— Bill Vander Zalm—made national headlines. "Charisma without substance is a dangerous thing," she said. "It raises expectations that cannot be satisfied. Then comes disillusionment and bitterness that destroys not only the leader, but the party." Both Vander Zalm and the B.C. Social Credit Party disappeared a few years later. Yet Campbell's prophetic assessment of Vander Zalm and the SoCreds is eerily applicable to cult leaders.

Before leaving the B.C. legislature, Campbell harshly criticized Vander Zalm's attempts to limit access to abortion. As Canada's justice minister, Campbell burnished her feminist credentials with a revision of the sexual assault law. The so-called no-means-no law recognized that all people have the right to refuse to have sex, including wives and prostitutes. The new act also ensured that victims' sexual histories would be kept private and could not be raised in court.

Campbell urged B.C. to prosecute polygamy and even offered federal help for the case, which would undoubtedly go to the Supreme Court of Canada. Since the Constitution and the Charter of Rights and Freedoms were little more than a decade old, Campbell said a polygamy case would help define the limits of both religious freedom and equality rights. She even offered to share the cost of the prosecution. But Gabelmann refused to lay the charges, even though his refusal effectively legalized polygamy. His cabinet colleagues obviously agreed, even though there had never been so many women and feminists seated around the table.

Three days after the B.C. government had announced its decision, Winston Blackmore claimed "victory over our enemies" in his Sunday sermon to two hundred people in Bountiful, which attacked Justice Minister Campbell. Marla Peters was there and reported that Blackmore questioned how Campbell could support equal rights for gays and lesbians yet make "such a big deal" of "people who live their holy religion." He went on to preach about the rightness of the Principle of plural marriage, reminding his followers of the long-standing decree that not one year should pass when children are not born into a polygamous marriage.

British Columbia's decision not to prosecute the criminal offence of polygamy coincided with Prophet Rulon Jeffs's increasingly frequent revelations about preparing for the coming apocalypse. That preparation included ensuring that righteous men had the requisite three wives to enter the celestial kingdom, even if it meant assigning them girls as young as thirteen.

Soon after the B.C. government's decision, Blackmore framed a copy of the Charter of Rights and Freedoms and hung it on the wall in his office next to a picture of an elk. He also picked up on the constitutional vernacular of the day. Prime Minister Brian Mulroney was attempting to finally get Quebec to ratify the Constitution by offering to recognize the province as a distinct society. Blackmore began asserting not only that polygamy was a legitimate expression of religious freedom, but that fundamentalist Mormons ought to be recognized as a "distinct society."

The B.C. government would have shelved the whole Bountiful mess after Gabelmann's decision not to prosecute, except Penny Priddy wasn't ready to let it go. There was money in her ministry's budget for research, and in February 1992, the

West Kootenay Women's Association asked for $11,500 to "conduct research and write a report on the practice of polygamy and physical and sexual abuse of women in a religious community in B.C." The association promised a report that would provide "a comprehensive analysis of the situation and [that would] be useful for social workers, counsellors and other service providers who have left the colony."

With the RCMP investigation at an end and the government's decision not to prosecute, on August 18, the women's equality ministry staff took the research proposal to Priddy. She reviewed it and agreed that it should go ahead. In November, the ministry and the association signed a contract for $11,500.

The Committee on Polygamous Issues was formed to do the work. It included a psychologist from the area, Debbie Oler Palmer, Debbie's friends Faye and Steve Street, and Lorna Blackmore. In May 1993, it delivered the first and only report that the B.C. government has ever commissioned on the polygamous community. It was called *Life in Bountiful* and it was explosive. Not only did it provide an inside look at the community's beliefs, its organizational structure and the hidden lives of its women and children, the report suggested that the government had failed in almost every way to protect Bountiful's people and their rights as Canadian citizens.

Far from polygamy being the biggest problem, the report said that forced marriages and rigid demands of obedience were graver concerns. It stopped short of calling the FLDS a cult. But it led the government right to the doorstep, saying that the government had failed to consider whether freedom of religion extends to the point of obliterating individual rights. The committee members agreed with Winston Blackmore's assessment that Bountiful had a distinct culture, saying that the religious beliefs are "so encompassing they have shaped a distinct culture." But, they said, "It is a culture that limits

individual rights to the point of virtually eliminating them."
The report pointedly asked: "When does a culture stop being
culture and start being abuse?"

It went on to question whether children raised there could
ever be capable of exercising free choice and of giving
informed consent to sex and assignment marriages. Not only
did children receive an inferior education at the taxpayer-
funded school because the government failed to properly monitor it, the report said the forced marriages of schoolgirls would
continue as long as the government was content to allow child
abuse complaints to go first to Blackmore, not to the police,
social workers or outsiders.

Finally, the committee concluded that leaving Bountiful
was almost impossible because of the web of control exercised
by the church leadership. And, for the very few who do leave,
there is little in the way of services to help them.

Stung by the report's candour, the government disowned
it. The government refused to release it, saying that it was
the property of the West Kootenay Women's Association,
which had initially applied for the government grant to do
the study. The government established a damage-control
committee made up of assistant deputy ministers to deal
with the fallout and appointed a senior communications
manager to the file. Officials scrambled to distance the government, their ministries and themselves from the report.
But, in that scramble, a deep division quickly became obvious within the government ranks.

The Committee on Polygamous Issues and the Ministry of
Women's Equality were on one side. The committee and the
women's ministry viewed polygamy, forced marriages, child
brides and mind control as issues that infringed on individual
rights guaranteed by the 1982 Constitution's equality rights section. The other ministries fell in line with the attorney general's

conclusion that nothing could be done because polygamy was protected by the constitutional guarantee of religious freedom.

At the first meeting between government officials and committee members, there was a debate over whether Bountiful was a cult or a culture. Soon after that, Dyan Dunsmoor-Farley, assistant deputy minister of women's equality, scrawled an "action request" to one of her staff. "I believe it is a fundamentally flawed approach to base everything on the probability of winning [a court case on polygamy] . . . I think this deserves a letter from Minister Priddy to the AG [attorney general] regarding the moral/ethical side of this issue."

Psychologist Harriet Moore, chair of the Committee on Polygamous Issues, spelled it out more clearly in a letter to Anita Hagen, who was not only education minister but minister of multiculturalism and human rights: "It is our hope that the response of the government will address the value of the individual within the context of the community as well as the value of unique cultures within the community of Canada. This is an opportunity for the government to create an innovative, proactive process for approaching a unique culture within the context of its duty to care for the welfare and development of its individual citizens and to end exploitation and oppression."

But that wasn't where the government was headed, even though New Democrats purport to be more concerned about upholding women's rights than other parties. Officials in every ministry except Women's Equality insisted that there was no "rights issue," no urgency to deal with a polygamous community that had existed for more than fifty years. Bountiful was simply one of many unique communities in Canada's increasingly ethnically, religiously and socially diverse landscape. Among those claiming there was no problem were officials in Hagen's ministries: education, multiculturalism and human rights.

Minutes from an August meeting of the assistant deputy ministers noted that the key public relations messages were "respect for cultural uniqueness of the Bountiful community" and "intervention will follow a balanced approach taking into full consideration the needs of the women in Bountiful Community." That echoed a background paper prepared by the attorney general's staff with the message that there must be "acknowledgement of and sensitivity to the 'cultural' norms of the Bountiful community." Yet no one in Victoria, the provincial capital, was as insistent on leaving things alone as the officials on the ground in Creston, where staff were given "cultural awareness training" in the fall of 1993, rather than seminars on human rights, equality rights or cult behaviours.

"We . . . do not view this religious community as being bizarre or particularly cult-like, but instead view it as another manifestation of multiculturalism, a different way of expressing spirituality," O. Gary Deatherage, director of Creston's Mental Health Centre, wrote on July 12, 1993. Deatherage had some expertise in religious matters. He was a contributor to a book published in 1980 titled *Religion and Psychoactive Sacraments*, which looked at the use of LSD in psychotherapy.

Deatherage's notions of multiculturalism and spirituality, which he deploys to defend the Saints, take open-mindedness to new levels and include practices others might find abhorrent, like eugenics. "The prophet in Salt Lake City, Mr. Rulon Jeffs, maintains a large geneology [*sic*] table and participates in the matching of man and women for genetic as well as spiritual reasons. However, he reportedly is becoming more open to the members having more say in the selection of their mates. There is still a possibility of young girls being 'placed' into marriages they do not desire, but hopefully this practice is lessening."

Despite that assessment, the psychologist said that when people from Bountiful came to the clinic they "present no differently than any other member of the broader Creston Valley community. They are bright, verbal people who have strong personal religious views and beliefs. It is very important to understand that each member appears to be free to come and go as he or she wishes and while there are religious strictures on their behaviour, we have never perceived that any person in the community is kept there against their will."

Deatherage noted: "Traditionally, females have been married at the young age of 15 or 16 and this could, in some cases, be considered abusive. It is our perception that . . . young women are marrying at a later age and indeed are finding it possible to participate in the selection of their spouses." Missing from his sunny analysis of the illegal marriages of underaged girls was any reference to the fact that the bridegrooms are usually considerably older than their child brides and that the men are usually senior members of the church's priesthood.

Also missing was any reference to the Criminal Code sections on sexual exploitation or to the B.C. marriage law, which requires children under sixteen to have the written consent of a B.C. Supreme Court justice and children under eighteen to have the signed consent of their parents.

In his three-page letter, Deatherage mentioned that, in the past six years, the centre had provided services to twenty-two sexual abuse victims and three perpetrators from the community of Bountiful, which at the time had a population of about 450. "It has not been our perception that the incidence of sexual abuse is any higher . . . than in society at large," he reported. What Deatherage didn't note—even though he should have been aware of it—is that there is massive under-reporting of sexual assaults, even in mainstream Canadian society. In 1993, Statistics Canada estimated that only 6 per cent of all sexual assaults are reported to the police. The fact that one in twenty girls, boys and women in Bountiful reported having been victims of sexual abuse and that three of 450 people were admitted or convicted abusers was clearly only the very tiniest tip of the iceberg. In fact, extrapolating from the Canadian average, twenty-two victims reporting would suggest that *every* resident of Bountiful may have been abused. That is not likely the case. However, the incidence of abuse was far from normal and very far from benign.

Yet Deatherage felt it important to warn the government to "be careful about accepting the sensational picture of this community" portrayed by journalists and disseminated by Debbie Oler Palmer, whom he described as "a woman who suffered considerable abuse at the hands of the men she was married to and who rightfully feels very vindictive." The psychologist closed his letter by insisting that it be kept strictly confidential because "it would be disastrous if the community members or the community leadership saw our Mental Health Centre as anything but an ally."

Winston Blackmore, Dalmon Oler and Rulon Jeffs couldn't have conjured up a better ally. In the end, Deatherage recommended the government bury the issue—he called it "short-term closure to this issue"—by hiring someone to facilitate a meeting where government officials, the authors of the *Life in Bountiful* report, Winston Blackmore and others from Bountiful would be in attendance. He recommended his wife, also a psychologist, for the job, but he had the good sense to at least acknowledge that perhaps that might be seen as a conflict of interest.

No mediated meeting was ever held. But because of Deatherage's report, his boss in Cranbrook and the entire health ministry took the position that no intervention was

needed, no further study was needed, no additional or specialized resources were needed, no further anything was needed.
But it wasn't only health officials who allied with Blackmore.
There's an unattributed statement in minutes from the August
1993 assistant deputy ministers' meeting that "Winston must
be made to feel respected in his community otherwise he will
feel threatened and this will further entrench the wall of
silence around the Bountiful community."

Education ministry officials went along with the appeasement policy, even though they had been receiving complaints for at least two years about what was being taught at
the taxpayer-supported Bountiful Elementary-Secondary
School. Earlier that month, the minister had received a second copy of the 1990 Grade 11 biology final exam that had
questions clearly not related to the curriculum. A Creston
woman had sent it, along with a letter demanding to know
why nothing had been done since she first sent a copy of the
test two years earlier. In her 1993 letter, the woman repeated
her original query: were similar questions asked in all
taxpayer-supported B.C. schools?

The Grade 11 final exam had only fourteen questions. Of
those fourteen, nine had little or nothing to do with biology or
what is on the standard curriculum:

5. What do the following terms have in common:
   birdie, eagle, divot, greener [*sic*], bogie, handicap,
   "&*%$#!!@??@!!, rough, fairway and woods?

7. What are some interesting and practical applications of biology you have encountered or
   (hopefully) learned this year?

8. In that you have no alternative and will all be
   enrolled in Biology 12 next year, what are some
   topics of concern or interest that you would

like to or hope to study? (No promises or guarantees however)

9. How many goldfish are in the aquarium?

10. What is this year's school motto?

11. Give suggestions to make school life better.

12. Give suggestions to next year's school motto.

13. What does it mean to be committed? What are
you committed to? How can you tell if your
commitments are in tune with the Spirit of God?

14. I want to hear your personal viewpoints on the
following important topics: United Order.
United Effort Plan. Celestial/Placement
Marriage. Obedience. Testimony/Faith. Raising
children. "Come out of her, O ye my people,
and be not partakers of her sins

The Women's Equality staff pressed the education ministry
to do surprise inspections rather than the usual scheduled ones.
Normally independent schools are given six months' notice that
an inspection will be held. Three months before the inspection, the school's administrators are notified of the exact dates
of the inspection, giving them ample time to prepare for those
two days. But in July 1993, the assistant deputy minister wrote
to the Women's Equality officials saying that a "surprise" visit
is unlikely to offer much useful information. Inspections
"require considerable data being provided in advance by the
school" and that, without notice, students may not be at school
that day and "the school might simply say they were on a field
trip or provide some other legitimate excuse why the students
are not present."

Despite that, there was a "surprise inspection" that fall, but
only after the office of the independent school inspector had
advised Winston Blackmore and school principal Merrill

Palmer that unannounced visits were always a possibility. In the subsequent report, Gerry Ensing, deputy inspector of independent schools, wrote: "Interestingly, the principal indicated and the staff confirmed that they had been expecting 'surprise' visits."

When the inspectors arrived, there were no boys in the classrooms. The girls were "diligently working on sewing projects for their home economics program." The inspectors were told that all of the boys were helping at the scene of a traffic accident involving a truck owned by someone from Bountiful. The inspectors concluded that everything at the school was fine.

The problem is, there's a gap in the 1989 Independent School Act large enough to drive several logging trucks through. The act specifically forbids the teaching of racism and hatred, but it says religious schools must be unfettered in their religious instruction. That means inspectors cannot inspect the religious program. It is a clause in the act that the Federation of Independent School Associations (FISA) and its then-executive director—Gerry Ensing—had fought hard for. After the act was passed, Ensing and FISA members had celebrated the fact that while the new act increased independent schools' funding to half the amount given to public schools, it had been accomplished "without any intrusive change in curricular or other obligations."

But, if the inspectors can't examine the religious curriculum, how are they to ensure that racism and hatred are not being taught? And if the inspectors don't enforce the prohibition on teaching racism and hatred, who will?

There is another problem with the oversight of British Columbia's independent schools. The majority of the schools are church-run and most are Catholic schools. Yet with the exception of the first chief inspector, all of the subsequent chief inspectors, the deputies and a disproportionate number of the assistant inspectors come from fundamentalist Christian denominations.

Ensing, who was assistant chief inspector for eleven years and chief inspector for two, is an elder in the Christian Reformed Church, which opposes homosexuality, divorce and birth control. Its members believe in traditional, patriarchal families and creationism. Ensing's successor was James Beeke, a former principal of a school operated by the Christian Reformed Church. Beeke was replaced by Susan Penner, who was principal of the White Rock Christian Academy, where all core subjects are taught from a biblical perspective.

So empathetic is the staff in the independent school office it appears that administrators, such as Winston Blackmore, can go inspector-shopping. Following a 1995 inspection, Blackmore wrote to the ministry with "a grave concern" about one of the inspectors: "It had become obvious to all members of our staff and reported to me that one of your [evaluation] committee members came with a very strong prejudice. Given the nature of this bias, we feel as a group that we have been discriminated against by her. I have requested each member of the staff to document the comments wherein they felt she was prejudicial and I intend to pass these on to our legal counsel for their direction in this matter."

A confidential note about a ministry official's subsequent telephone conversation with Blackmore indicates that among the things that had upset him and the staff were comments to teachers that "women at Bountiful are not valued and are oppressed." In view of the "seriousness" of Blackmore's complaint, two more evaluators went on a scheduled visit in February 1996. Once again, they determined things were just fine in Bountiful.

Little has changed in the way Bountiful children are being educated, other than the fact that there are now two schools. Warren Jeffs controls Bountiful Elementary-Secondary School, while Winston Blackmore is now in charge of another elementary-secondary school named Mormon Hills. Together the two schools receive more than a million dollars annually in government grants, even though they make no secret of the fact that every aspect of the children's schooling is taught through the prism of their religious values and doctrines. What is taught there remains anathema to what is taught in public schools, and to what most Canadians believe, as a selection of questions and answers on Grade 7 weekly religion tests from 2003 to 2004 at Mormon Hills School suggests:

> *The Lord has arranged it so that we can?*
> Gather together. Be unnoticed by the world.
> *What are women promoting by their dress?*
> Immorality in their make-up and actions.
> *How long did Uncle Roy say we have been trying to get our women folk to notice their dresses?*
> The last 35 years.
> *Why shouldn't women cut their hair?*
> Their hair was given to them for a sacred purpose.
> *The Lord said long hair on men was?*
> A shame.
> *Our schools are going to have to change?* From the gentile way of education to the Lord's way of education.

As recently as 2007, the inspectors' report on Bountiful Elementary-Secondary School indicates that nobody in the Ministry of Education has even figured out yet that these are not mainstream Mormons. The inspectors either have no idea or don't care that what the fundamentalists are teaching as "Mormonism" has little connection to the considerably more moderate and modern views of the mainstream Church of Jesus Christ of Latter-day Saints.

They commented favourably on the school's daily assemblies, where taped homilies from "guest speakers" are played. Apparently, they have no idea that students are subjected to Warren Jeffs's often hate-filled rants against blacks, homosexuals and women, rants that are so extreme that the Fundamentalist Church of Jesus Christ of Latter Day Saints is considered a hate group in the United States. The inspectors wrote favourably about the BESS administrator's request to the education ministry to allow full credits for high-school graduation to three of its electives. Those electives are the study of the Book of Mormon, social studies, and "world geography," which "endeavours to provide students with a much broader appreciation of the world, its people, languages, religions and cultures." It's more likely that what's being taught is white supremacy, hatred and the necessity of blind obedience to the prophet, God's messenger.

The inspectors didn't seem the least perturbed that Mormon Hills school has one employee for every 6.5 students — more than double the provincial average — and that the number of students in every single BESS class exceeds the provincial average. If they found it strange that there are only ten teachers, but fourteen other employees with no teaching qualifications, the inspectors didn't write that down. Nor did they suggest that perhaps with such large classes, the teachers and even the principal, who does janitorial work and drives the school bus, might be better off spending time on education-related tasks.

As the *Life in Bountiful* report began trickling out in 1993, Winston Blackmore dispatched some women to dispel the so-called myths and lies about Bountiful. The women not only demanded a meeting with the women's equality minister, they demanded that Penny Priddy dress modestly for the meeting, preferably in a long skirt, so as not to offend their sensibilities. Priddy complied with both requests—although only after briefly considering some shocking alternatives to a long skirt. A handful of women drove a van to Vancouver for the meeting. The primary spokesperson for the women of Bountiful was Memory Oler—Winston's sister, Dalmon's wife and the stepmother who Debbie Palmer says abused her badly throughout her childhood. Memory and the others told Priddy that the women were happily exercising their constitutional guarantees of freedom of religion and freedom of association and would be much happier if people just left them alone.

Memory was the president of the newly formed Bountiful Women's Society, which set about writing its own report (without government funding, they complained). Marlene Palmer—Winston Blackmore's sister, Marvin Palmer's former wife and Debbie Palmer's former sister-wife—was vice-president. JoAnne Blackmore, a teacher at Bountiful Elementary-Secondary School, was communications director.

"We claim to have a perfect system," they wrote smugly in *Bountiful: As We Love It and Live It.* "But we are not a perfect people. We, the women of Bountiful, believe in our system, are willing members of it and intend to protect it with all our traditional and formidable energy. We also defend the rights of all women, Canadian and worldwide, to enjoy the freedom of association. We hope that all, citizens and government alike, will become educated enough to defend each other in the peaceful pursuit of our freedoms. We all tend to want to destroy that which we do not understand."

Having formed the society only after Winston Blackmore had "suggested" it and, no doubt, used the community's money for the legal registration of the society, they wrote, without recognizing the irony, that "Mormon fathers are so far from being tyrannical patriarchs that our bishop suggested we name our women's group Bountiful Organized Sisterhood Society (BOSS)." Somehow Winston Blackmore's sly joke also went over the heads of the deputy ministers on the interministerial committee looking into Bountiful. Throughout the minutes of their meetings, the Bountiful Women's Society is called BOSS.

The "report" depicts an upside-down world, in which women have university educations, financial autonomy and freedom from the threat of domestic violence. In this topsy-turvy world, women do as they please. No one is on welfare. And if people leave, it is because they are lazy. Their fundamentalist Mormon fantasy village bears no resemblance to the reality of Bountiful with its NO TRESPASSING signs, slipshod schools that aren't even accredited up to Grade 12, and industrial-sized families.

Bountiful women countered suggestions of mind control by directly contradicting FLDS dogma: "What if your husband tells you to do something wrong? Simple. Do not do it. No man has a right to command anyone to do wrong and no woman needs to stay married to a wicked or cruel man. There is a procedure in place to handle such cases." They didn't say how that process worked. But they said, "We know the Bishop's authority over us ends if he errs. It is the responsibility of all Mormons to know enough about good and evil and about their religion to know within themselves it they are being led aright."

They argued that in the past twenty-one years, only three women and their children, two girls and two men, had left, proving that everyone else was happy. And they concluded huffily, "In the history of our church and to the best of our knowledge, no man has fathered 80 children"—as if fathering seventy-nine is perfectly reasonable. Of course, Memory Oler and Marlene Palmer had no way of knowing that their own brother was well on his way to changing that.

It's a measure of either stupidity or brazenness, loss of institutional memory or cynical vote-farming that, in December 1997, Health Minister Joy MacPhail appointed Memory Oler to the Creston and District Health Council. Two years later, Penny Priddy, who had moved from the women's ministry to health, reappointed her, possibly mistaking Memory's participation as "interest" in the community rather than another bold manoeuvre to bleed the beast. While Memory was on the board, Bountiful got a $100,000 grant to build the Bountiful Wellness Centre. Far from being a resource for the whole Creston Valley, it became a birthing centre used exclusively by fundamentalist women from that community. What it has meant is that more women—particularly the very young mothers and American women—now have their babies there rather than in Creston's hospital. Because of that centre, teen brides and their much older husbands can hide even further from public view and face fewer risks of being reported.

But, by 1997, when Memory Oler was first appointed to the health board, Bountiful, polygamy and the polygamist pedophiles had fallen off the agenda. Civil servants had found no easy or cheap solutions and no politicians had pressed them to explore the harder and more expensive ones suggested by the *Life in Bountiful* report. Journalists had moved on. Out of sight and out of mind, Bountiful flourished. With polygamy virtually legalized and prophecies about a predicted millennial apocalypse coming fast and furious, so many covenant children were born into polygamous homes that within a decade Bountiful's population had more than doubled from 450 to more than 1,000.

Even though Priddy was the only one at the Cabinet table who tried to do something for the women and children there, she admits she didn't look hard enough to find a way into the community. "Bountiful is like a sleeping snake. Everybody takes a stick and pokes at it once in a while. But nobody takes it out of the place where it lives and hurts the others around it." In retrospect, Penny Priddy believes that she and her government failed. But she said, "Apathy was the single biggest reason."

But Faye Street from the Committee on Polygamous Issues adamantly denies that. "I met with every goddamned minister and everybody I could to talk about what was going on in there. I used to come home and not be able sleep because I kept thinking 'how can this be happening here. We're not from the Ozarks.' We did all that work. We gave them [the government] the damn report and they came back and did nothing. Very few people wanted to deal with it. They all wanted to look the other way. What our society needs is a damned good kick in the ass for that. There are just not enough people who stand up to this."

As a long-time and active member of the Liberal Party, which has governed British Columbia since 2001, Street says she's never quit lobbying for change in Bountiful. As a tax-payer, she resents "every penny that goes to that hell-hole." "They are still living under bloody slavery out there. As decent members of society we should care about what's happening to those kids. If somebody somewhere doesn't draw a line in the sand and stop this, there will be another community and another and another. This is just another disgusting cult like any other."

TWELVE

THE LOST BOYS

The arithmetic is not reassuring for fundamentalist Mormon boys. They are told from early childhood that there is no room for them in heaven without at least one woman at their side, and no room in heaven's highest realm without at least three. The numbers just don't add up for most of them. If one man gets more than one wife, then another gets none. And since you need three wives to get into the celestial kingdom, that means two lonely fundamentalists are on the road to hell.

Males and females are born at near equal rates in virtually every animal species, and we're no exception. There's no starker illustration of that one-plus-one symmetry than Noah marching pairs of animals up the ramp of the ark before the biblical Great Flood. Polygamy goes against the simple arithmetic of life, which means that the Saints' prophets have to cull the boys using every pretense possible. They must be urged out or forced out because, if they are not, the whole power structure will collapse.

While high-spirited girls are trapped by marriage and motherhood, the unsuitable, unworthy boys are forced into freedom. They enter an alien new world alone and often bewildered. No parents go looking for them, even though some of the boys are only twelve and thirteen. There are no court battles fought to have the boys return home. The boys are dead to their families and set adrift in a world that they are totally unprepared for, since few have more than a Grade 8 or 9 education and many lack any experience to help them function among people they've been taught are evil and inferior. Collectively, the boys who are either kicked out or encouraged to leave have come to be known as the "lost boys."

An estimated four hundred or more live in St. George, Utah—the closest urban centre to the twin towns of Colorado City and Hildale. Another four hundred or so live in the Salt Lake City area. And nobody can even guess how many others work in construction or as prostitutes in the Las Vegas area. In Canada, few boys have been forcibly exiled. While absolute power drives Warren Jeffs, money has always been more important to Winston Blackmore. Boys may be turned away when they show up at church or at the weekly priesthood meetings, but they are more than welcome to keep coming to work at one of the Saints' companies. With little education, they live on the margins of fundamentalist society—"eunuchs," as they're called—often living in hope of redemption. Many do the math, find a nice gentile girl and leave by choice.

In Canada, there are dozens, if not hundreds, of boys who have left by choice, and they live throughout British Columbia and Alberta. There are no firm numbers, although at least twenty who have left within the past decade live in and around Cranbrook, B.C., and work for less than union wages at logging companies owned by fundamentalist Mormons.

Among the sad facts about the polygamous Saints is that all children are treated as chattels. Girls are valuable because their fathers can trade them for power, position or property. Boys are the slave labourers who allow fundamentalists' businesses to undercut their gentile competitors who abide by labour laws and pay union wages. It's from the boys' sweat that prophets and bishops buy Cadillacs and planes and support their dozens and dozens of wives.

Without the boys, the fundamentalist communities would sink into squalor—all Saints, by necessity, would be reduced to Harold Blackmore's Dumpster-diving lifestyle. The lost boys are not an unfortunate consequence of Mormon fundamentalism—they are *necessary* to it. Ironically, in mainstream society, many of these boys would be role models. Ethan Fischer and Truman Oler certainly would be. Both are in their mid-twenties and both are bright, hard-working, gentle souls who didn't fit the polygamist mould. They're no longer welcome in Short Creek or Bountiful or in their own families' homes. Their mothers have ripped up and tossed out the family photo albums and baby pictures, all because the prophet says their sons are apostates who have turned their backs on God and the One True Church. And that's worse than being dead.

Unlike many lost boys, neither Ethan nor Truman was particularly rebellious. Both had doubts and had occasionally strayed from the strict practice of their religion. They might have done a bit of drinking and flirted with girls, but they tried to fit in. They regularly attended priesthood meetings and paid their monthly tithe of 10 per cent of their wages. Had Warren Jeffs not started rewriting doctrine and scriptures or mounted a reign of terror that split the FLDS community and even families in two, there's a possibility that both might even have remained among the Saints. Except, of course, their penchant for asking "why" was always going to get them in trouble. Why couldn't they go to school? Why couldn't they be paid as well as gentiles doing the same work? Why couldn't they own their own cars or homes? Why couldn't they choose their own wives?

The question that got Ethan excommunicated was the first one. Why couldn't he go to medical school? Ethan had been one of the fortunate ones. He finished high school before 1998, when Warren Jeffs ordered the FLDS members to take their children out of Colorado City's public schools and teach them at home using tapes he had recorded as principal of Alta Academy. After high school, the then-prophet Rulon Jeffs chose Ethan to train to be an emergency medical technician.

But when Ethan finished the training, he didn't go to work for the ambulance service. He was sent along with all the other men and boys to work for one of the Saints' construction companies. It was a crushing disappointment. "I started taking more classes and I was told that I was not operating directly under the grace of the priesthood. But I wanted to learn more and see more."

Except for clandestinely taking college courses, Ethan seemed on the road not only to receiving the worldly reward of many wives, but to becoming a god. Baptized at eight, he'd become a deacon at twelve. By fourteen, he was a "teacher" in the church and two years later he was a priest. Ethan was on track to take advantage or the Saints' bizarre hierarchy: he was ordained an elder two months before his eighteenth birthday. Until he was told to leave, Ethan still lived at home and obeyed his father's rules—even the one about being home by 10 p.m. He had a girlfriend, but that was one secret he'd managed to keep.

While he worked full-time for an FLDS contractor, in his spare time Ethan helped build a house for his sister and started building a home of his own. He'd helped his mother start a fabric shop in Colorado City—it eventually failed because it was in competition with one owned by the Jeffses. But Ethan also asked a lot of questions, particularly after Rulon Jeffs had a major stroke. Followers were commanded to pay even more money each month and Rulon began making prophecies that contradicted what Ethan believed were basic tenets of his faith: "I was sincere in wondering. I couldn't figure it out. Why would any church that feels it's correct not discuss it with you or feel free to let you look and research what it is teaching?"

As a member of the priesthood, Ethan met with the prophet every month. Before Rulon's stroke, the meetings were part confession, part counselling. "I'd tell him sorry for things I'd done and how I'd try to do better. He [Rulon] always asked how things were going . . . and what you're doing for The Work. He would tell you what to do religiously and what you should do in your personal life. They [the prophet and priesthood] do have full control of your life. But it doesn't seem strange if you don't know the difference. It's just a way of life."

When Warren took over the meetings for his ailing father, the encounters became strained. He didn't want to hear any questions from the young man, questions like why some FLDS members were being told to move to Texas to build the Yearning for Zion temple and await the Second Coming.

> I was taught all my life that according to Joseph Smith, we would move to Jackson, Missouri, to be lifted up and all of a sudden it was Eldorado, Texas. That's when I started wondering what was going on. It was backwards from what I'd been taught all my life. It was not following the script.
>
> Getting closer to the millennium, there were so many drastic changes. We were told they had to

be made. We had to get into a position where we
could be exalted. It triggered the younger brides
because you are in a higher, more exalted state if
you are living the law of plural marriage. And that
triggered so much. A lot of the younger girls were
placed as plural wives and very few were to young
guys. So a lot of guys left within three or four years.
I'd say there were 300 or 400 of them who left. If
you had the right name, though, you'd get a wife.

For years, Ethan's parents—Samuel Fischer and Fayila
Williams—were monogamous. But, in 1994, Samuel was
assigned a second wife and her nine children after the
woman's husband had been excommunicated. That experience taught Ethan to both expect and dread an assignment
marriage. He'd seen from the inside what arranged marriages
looked like. "It [placement marriage] scared the hell out of
me . . . Because I held a position in the church, it was an
absolute no—You could not refuse a blessing [an assignment
marriage]. You didn't have that option. If you fought it, you'd
probably be excommunicated."

What saved Ethan from a forced marriage was his inability
to be blindly obedient, which was the only test that mattered to
Warren Jeffs. Warren, his father and all the senior priesthood
members knew that education makes people stronger, more
independent and less willing to follow orders. They knew
because many of them were educated. And they knew because
of their experience with people like Ethan's uncle—Dan
Fischer—one of the best-known and best-educated escapees.

The priesthood had paid for Dan to go to dental college as
part of a self-sufficiency drive in the 1970s and 1980s. "To go to
college is to go to an evil place and to get contaminated with
unproven science," says Dan. So, before he went to the

University of Utah, he was assigned a second wife to keep him grounded in his faith and in fear. "It was part of locking me to the railway track." Eventually, Dan had fourteen children, seven with each of his wives. But, in 1993, Dan and his whole family left the group: "I had come to a fork in the road. I had to decide what was most important and I felt I had a higher level of responsibility to those people I'd brought to this earth than to my parents, brothers and sisters."

He divorced his first wife, who had been assigned to him, sight unseen—"We were like oil and water"—and legally married his second wife. He continues to financially support his ex-wife and all of their children. Had he not left, Dan believes his children would never have received a proper education: "Warren Jeffs prefers uneducated teachers. The conscious teaching [in the church] is so strong against formal education. Some [followers] are sent to higher education, but none are sent to school to be teachers."

Because Ethan had yet to be assigned a wife, he was not locked into the religion. That's what made it such a sin to sneak out of Colorado City to go to night school. It's something that in a normal society parents and community leaders would applaud. But, instead, Ethan was kicked out of the FLDS and his hometown in the spring of 2005. The powerful bishop William Timpson gave him twenty-four hours to pack up his stuff and leave. He said the prophet knew that Ethan had secretly been taking college classes. And because Warren Jeffs had not approved of it, Ethan had defied both the prophet and God. Having turned his back on God, Ethan was an apostate. Timpson also told him that his family would no longer be able to speak to him. They were to treat Ethan as if he were dead. The expulsion shocked Ethan.

Fortunately, the twenty-three-year-old owned a car. He packed what he could into it and drove north to St. George with no idea of what to do next. It never occurred to him to call his Uncle Dan, even though Dan is a multi-millionaire and patron of the Diversity Foundation, which helps the so-called lost boys of polygamy get the education and training they need. Ethan was still indoctrinated enough to believe Dan was allied with the devil. That's what he'd been taught. So, he never called Dan or his cousin Brenda Williams Jensen (Harold Blackmore's daughter, whose mother, Florence, was Ethan's aunt). The cousins eventually did meet, but only later at the HOPE Organization's office in St. George, where Brenda is one of the volunteers who helps people like Ethan to get settled.

Instead, Ethan got in touch with some other lost boys from Short Creek—"the Crick," as the Saints call it. They helped him get a construction job working with other ex-Crickers. But he spent the first month living out of his car because he had no money for rent. Even with a high-school diploma and specialized training, and even though he'd been going to college in St. George for a couple of years, Ethan's expulsion left him deeply depressed and lonely: "I was polite and decent when I was going to college, but I didn't go out of my way to associate with gentiles. I had no family outside [at least none that he acknowledged], so I had to begin trying to establish a base of friends."

Although Ethan says he's found a new life and hopes to marry a woman he loves, have children and even go to med-ical school, one can't help but feel he has not really left it all behind. He admits to still being intimidated by the prospect of meeting new people because he's not sure how they will treat a guy from the "polyg town." He's still not comfortable wear-ing short-sleeved shirts even in the desert heat. All the swear-ing on construction sites doesn't sit right with him, nor does all the drinking and partying of some of the other ex-Creekers.

And he continues to closely watch the power struggle between Warren Jeffs and Winston Blackmore.

It is an indication of how autocratic and bizarre Warren Jeffs is that Winston Blackmore seems enlightened by comparison. Ethan regards Winston as "a really good guy. I don't think people would necessarily follow him religiously. He's very intelligent and you could probably get a lot of wisdom from him, but not necessarily because he has control from God. He just knows what was happening wasn't right. He didn't assume power and he's not saying that he is in power now. I think he could be a great leader." Ethan stops for a moment, then adds somewhat ruefully, "But I guess I have a conflict of interest because I had everything taken away from me by Warren Jeffs."

Ethan should meet Truman Oler, who would give him an earful about Winston Blackmore. Truman wasn't kicked out of Bountiful. Instead, nearly fifty years after his father, Dalmon Oler, arrived in Bountiful to practise the Principle, the thirty-second of his forty-eight children walked out. Truman was fed up with being controlled and exploited by the likes of Winston Blackmore and the Fundamentalist Church of Jesus Christ of Latter Day Saints.

Before he had even turned fourteen, Truman had worked many summers picking fruit, digging potatoes, doing odd jobs or helping his father look after the local campgrounds. He rarely got paid. If he did, it was a quarter here or a dollar there. The rest was pocketed by Dalmon Oler to help feed his five wives and however many of his children happened to be living at home. When he was fourteen, Truman was deemed old enough to work full-time in the summer for Winston Blackmore's company that manufactured fence posts and poles from logs harvested in the surrounding valleys. Truman "banded" finished fence posts, putting metal strips around the bundles.

Truman Oler began working full-time for an FLDS company when he finished Grade 9. Because Bountiful's kids are routinely pulled out of school to work in FLDS companies for slave wages, the last generation to have had a high-school education was the one that founded the town.
(Brian Clarkson / Vancouver Sun)

One day, a band broke and cut his lip deeply enough that he required four stitches. One of his friends had a couple of toes taken off. None of them filed for workers' compensation. They were told it would cost the company too much. It might also bring on a safety inspection.

Two years later, after finishing Grade 9, Truman went to work full-time for Blackmore. He wasn't told to quit school. "I was told 'Why do you need to go to school? You're just going to be making fence posts.' That was the mentality everybody had. We were just going to be loggers." But if no one ordered him to drop out, no one encouraged him to stay either. There were no other career options suggested to the boys at the government-funded Bountiful Elementary-Secondary School, even though career planning is a required component of the provincial curriculum.

Truman was only sixteen. His father, Dalmon Oler, had just died, and when an important decision had to be made—like whether to quit school—his mother, Memory, told him to consult her brother, the bishop Winston Blackmore.

Memory never encouraged her son to stay in school, even though she had taught at Bountiful Elementary-Secondary School for more than thirty years. She is the same woman who told the government in 1992 that everything was wonderful in Bountiful and that children had the same rights and opportunities as others in the province—the same woman deemed by the government to be such an outstanding member of the community that she was twice appointed to the local health board.

It's astonishing that the last generation in Bountiful to have a high-school education was the community's first generation—its founding generation. Now, their grandchildren and great-grandchildren face dreary futures: the girls will grow up to bear regiments of children for husbands they're assigned to, and the boys will work long hours for little more than slave wages that will be clawed back in tithes demanded by the bishop and prophet.

Only a select few will finish high school. Even fewer are chosen by the prophet to study outside the community. He decides what they can study, and it is always something that will make the community less dependent on outsiders—nursing, dentistry, midwifery, medicine, accounting and, occasionally, teaching. But in Canada, almost all of those who have gone to college are women with children. Some are American-born wives, who have somehow managed to get student visas to legalize their extended stay in Canada (and also qualify them for medical care). The women almost exclusively train to be licensed practical nurses or midwives. Not only are those skills needed within their own community, there are lots of well-paid, unionized health-care jobs in Creston and Cranbrook. These jobs allow the women to contribute substantially to their family's income.

Only a few young Canadian men have gone to college. Winston Blackmore's brother Richard was one of them. He's a qualified teacher and principal of Mormon Hills School. Two other boys Truman's age were sent to the University of Calgary with the goal of getting into medical school. But they were hauled back when Winston ran short of labourers in his logging operation. One of the boys was seriously injured on the job, losing several fingers, which ended any dream he might have had of becoming a doctor. Almost all of the boys, including Winston's forty or more sons, labour for J.R. Blackmore & Sons or other Saints' companies, earning wages far below what they'd earn working for gentiles. The promise is that, if they are righteous enough and pay their tithes, they might be assigned a piece of property where they can build a house. They might get a wife. And, if they continue to work uncomplainingly, they might eventually get another wife and then another. Then, if they are truly righteous, they will be invited into the celestial kingdom, where they will "be as gods" for all eternity.

Despite being the superintendent of a school, Winston never finished high school and doesn't place a high value on education. He doesn't believe in going continuously from kindergarten to Grade 12: "I would like my children to stop at Grade 10 and work for a while. And if they want to go back, they will go back as mature students and they'll get something out of it," he told a TV interviewer, "It's not just a play time."

Of course, whether they want to or not, they seldom do go back. They have tithes to pay, wives and children to care for.

That's part of the reason Bountiful's schools are only accredited to teach to Grade 10. Of course, there also aren't enough qualified teachers in the community and outsiders have never been allowed to teach in the schools. But the problem isn't just a shortage of qualified teachers. People who have left the community say that when secondary-school students show up for classes, they often find that the teachers are away working for Blackmore or for some other Saint's company.

The denial of education was one of Jane Blackmore's primary motivations to leave Bountiful. Even though she had craved education badly enough that she finally got it—after having five children and defying both her husband and the prophet—Jane could never convince Winston to let their own children finish high school, despite his claim that they're all free to go to school if they choose. She remembers all of them crying when their father told them that they had to quit midway through high school. Peter, Susie, Jake, Hyrum, Mary and Joseph were all sent to work in their father's forestry companies. The girls went to Sundre, Alberta, to cook for their father's employees working in logging camps there. Peter, Jake and Hyrum worked as labourers, but now they run some of the family companies. Peter runs the ranch. Jake and Hyrum operate one of the logging companies. Boys with names other than Blackmore aren't as lucky. They'll spend their lives as labourers, driving trucks that aren't as good as what the Blackmores get around in, living in houses that aren't as nice and getting brides that nobody else wants. Jane's half-brother Truman was one of those destined for a lifetime of labour. "They get you to do mindless work and they keep telling you that there is nothing better," says Truman. To numb the boys and men even further to the work, Warren Jeffs's followers are expected to listen to his sermons on their headsets and their vehicles' tape decks.

When Truman went to work full-time for Blackmore, he was sent to Sundre. Throughout the frigid Alberta winter, he and his half-brother Adam lived in an unheated barn with boards laid across the dirt floor. They were paid two hundred dollars a month for working ten-hour days from Monday to Friday and six to eight hours on Saturdays. As terrible as that wage was, it was nearly double what Truman had been paid in the two previous summers working for Blackmore's post-and-pole operation. He never missed a day of work that winter. It wasn't allowed, even though he broke his ankle.

When he found out that other forestry workers are paid an hourly rate, Truman complained to Winston. "Everybody looked at you as if you were shit if you complained. You were just a bad person if you did." But his complaint paid off. Blackmore upped the wages. Still, when Truman quit working there in 2002, he was only earning five hundred dollars a month. But he didn't leave because of the wages. He left because Blackmore had been excommunicated. As a faithful member of the priesthood, Truman couldn't work for an apostate; nor could many others. Truman's half-brother Kendal—Jane Blackmore's and Debbie Palmer's full brother—started a logging company called Oler Brothers. Using labourers who had migrated from Winston's companies, they competed with Blackmore for contracts and often won them, even though Oler Brothers was paying workers 60 per cent more—eight hundred dollars a month. It was a fantastic sum compared to what Truman had been earning. Yet it was still not close to the twenty-two to twenty-four dollars an hour that loggers were paid working for gentile companies. But those other contractors were quickly being driven out of business. They couldn't compete against the Saints' companies when they bid on jobs for companies like Canadian forestry giant Tembec. Yet jobs were so scarce in the forestry industry, even the men whose companies were going bankrupt and whose jobs were disappearing were afraid to complain. And certainly Tembec's managers weren't complaining; nor were Tembec's shareholders, who reaped the benefits of reduced production costs.

But Truman didn't think it was fair. After a few months, he went to his half-brother Kendal and complained. They should be paid an hourly wage like everyone else working in forestry. Kendal said he'd talk to Jim Oler—Truman's full brother, whom Jeffs had appointed as Bountiful's bishop. Even though Kendal's name was on the company registry, Jim was the real guy in charge. But Jim, Jeffs's loyal, unquestioning lieutenant, had to talk to Warren. Eventually, Jeffs told Oler Brothers to pay employees what they were worth. Apparently the Oler Brothers figure their own friends and relatives deserve much less than what gentiles pay strangers. The wages rose to fifteen dollars an hour—still about 40 per cent less than what other local contractors paid.

With about half his men now working for Oler Brothers, Blackmore's companies began to suffer. He was desperate for workers, so when lost boys from the United States, like fourteen-year-old Carl Ream, wandered across the border looking for refuge, Blackmore was quick to put them to work. Carl left Colorado City in 2003 to avoid being kicked out. He had racked up dozens of truancy tickets for failing to go to school in both Arizona and Utah, where it's against the law for children not to go to school or to be home-schooled. But Carl didn't have time for school. His father had sent him to work full-time in construction.

The day after school ended, Carl—who had supposedly successfully completed Grade 7—ran away with his brother

Paul. Together they headed north to see another lost boy who was staying in Porthill, Idaho, just below the Canadian border and within walking distance of Bountiful. When they got to Porthill, Carl called his father to tell him where he and his brother were. His father told him not to come back and not to call. "He told me he'd talked to [Warren] Jeffs and Jeffs had told him, 'They're not worth our time.'" Carl and Paul could never go home again. The prophet had declared them apostates and damned them for all eternity.

After a few days in Porthill, the brothers went to Bountiful. For the past decade, Winston Blackmore had nurtured a reputation, especially among young people, that he was a kinder, gentler alternative to the increasingly erratic and tyrannical rule of first Rulon and then Warren Jeffs. What's curious though is that nobody at the Canadian border was suspicious of the young boys and girls going to Canada alone. Unaccompanied minors are supposed to be asked to produce permission notes from their parents. Nobody asked the boys for notes, even though Carl looked much younger than fourteen.

Carl celebrated his fifteenth birthday a few days later. Duane Palmer, the superintendent of one of Bountiful's schools and manager of one of Winston's forestry companies, bought Carl a pair of steel-toed workboots as a present. Carl went to work the next day: "I got paid $500 or $600 a month, working 12 hours a day. That was good money. Before, I was getting $30 a month in Colorado City, if I was getting paid at all. If I did get paid, I had to give it to my dad." What seemed like good money to Carl and the other boys works out to about $2.50 an hour.

A few months earlier, J. R. Blackmore & Sons had been cited by the Workers' Compensation Board for four violations of the Occupational Health and Safety Standards. The violations ranged from no training for new workers to dangerous equipment being exposed, unguarded or dangerously jury-rigged rather than properly maintained. It was far from the first time that the mill had been cited for infractions.

In 1997, one boy suffered a broken skull when a bundle of posts broke, struck him on the head and buried him. He hadn't been expected to live and, of course, when he did, Winston Blackmore proclaimed it had been a miracle.

So, how was a fifteen-year-old American kid, who was supposedly only visiting friends in Canada, able to work sixty hours a week at a heavy industrial site for wages far below the provincial minimum and not be noticed? How can any kids fresh out of Grade 7 or Grade 8 or Grade 9 work around heavy machinery, green chains, conveyor belts and pits in the type of industrial setting that is listed as one of the most dangerous by B.C.'s Workers' Compensation Board? Lax enforcement and lousy regulations.

British Columbia has among the worst child labour laws in North America, worse than states like Arkansas, Texas and Alabama, which Canadians have traditionally viewed askance. When school is in session, it is legal for B.C. children as young as twelve to work up to twenty hours a week. When school is out, children twelve and older can work as many as forty hours a week. Not only that, children under twelve can work if an employer gets permission from the B.C. employment standards director. Not only does British Columbia have fewer restrictions for child labourers than most other jurisdictions in the developed world, the B.C. government made hiring children more attractive in 2003, when it instituted a training wage that is two dollars an hour less than the going rate for adults.

The B.C. government also eliminated many of the restrictions on where children can work. It's legal for children to work in mines in British Columbia as long as they're trainees.

The only jobs that the Workers' Compensation Act forbids children aged fifteen and under from doing are mixing, loading and applying toxic pesticides or working with explosives. Apparently, serving alcoholic beverages is more dangerous to children than handling dynamite and pesticides or working with explosives and heavy equipment. You have to be eighteen in British Columbia to work in a bar.

About the time that Carl was working in Canada, Truman went south to Colorado City to do construction work with a couple of his brothers-in-law. As Truman recalls, "It was my little self-test. I went to church. I didn't do any partying. I wanted to try it before I left for good and I knew up here [in Canada] I wouldn't try. My friends were into partying too much." Three months was enough.

"I called up Jimmy [Oler, his brother] and told him I was coming home. He said I should talk to Warren. But I didn't call him. I got a couple of my brothers to come and get me. I didn't want to get stuck there. Jimmy wanted me to see Warren, but I went there of my own free will and I didn't want somebody to tell me I had to stay." It took another couple of weeks before Truman finally made the decision to walk away from Bountiful, all that religion and even his family. But he says, "When I left I felt I'd rather go to hell than be there."

He told two of his younger nephews that he was done with it all, but he didn't tell his mother. He drove back to Sundre and went back to work for Oler Brothers. A few weeks later, after Kendal realized that his brother was no longer paying his tithes or going to the monthly priesthood meetings, he told Truman to repent; if he did, he could come back to work. If he didn't, he was fired. Kendal didn't offer him any enticements to stay. Instead, he warned him that people had tried leaving before, but they soon found out that they didn't like it on the outside. However, Truman knew that wasn't true. Both of Kendal's full sisters—Debbie Oler Palmer and Jane Blackmore—had left and had no regrets.

"I've thought about why [the FLDS] think they're so right," says Truman. "They think they are the only ones going to heaven and that is so wrong. There are so many more ways to live. I don't need to give money to a church to be a good person and I don't have to repent. I know I'm a good person."

Jane's sons, Jake and Hyrum Blackmore, hired Truman even though he was no longer a believer. They were desperate for workers. When their father, Winston, transferred the company to their names, he also transferred hundreds of thousands of dollars in debts. They were struggling to stave off corporate bankruptcy. But, in addition to handing them the financially troubled company, Winston had assigned them second wives, which had put more strain on their personal finances. The Blackmore boys' company didn't pay as well as Oler Brothers, but Truman says it covered the cost of buying enough beer to keep him drunk every weekend. Truman no longer needed to go to Bountiful for weekly priesthood meetings and church services, but he kept making the long drive back to Creston each week.

He and a clutch of other lost boys went to Lorna Blackmore's little house on the edge of Bountiful—the house that Harold Blackmore had bought for her using money that her aunt Florence Williams had saved. From the time Truman's "Grandma Lorna" left Bountiful, she has patiently endured lost boys coming to her house, partying and drinking. They remind her of the difficulties her own sons had when she left Bountiful more than thirty years earlier. Lorna says drinking and partying seem the inevitable first step before these young men get sorted out enough to make a new life. The boys believe they are damned for eternity. They believe they are worthless. They no longer know what the truth is.

Lorna Blackmore tells them they are wrong. They are good boys and she loves them regardless of what they do. Without her, Truman says he would never have survived: "She was very kind to us. She never kicked us out."

But, because they have never been allowed to think for themselves, it takes time for the boys to fully adjust, Truman says. Everything in his life had been circumscribed by the priesthood. He wanted to play hockey in Creston, but Winston Blackmore had told him he couldn't mix with gentiles (even though Winston and many of his sons did play in organized hockey leagues there). Truman wanted to buy a Jeep, but he was told he couldn't. If he wanted a vehicle, he could just drive one of Winston's company trucks. Their accommodation when away from Bountiful—foul as it was—was all taken care of, as were their meals.

The first thing Truman says he had to learn was how make a decision on his own. "It's a lot of mind control [by the leaders]," he says. "You just look at them [the FLDS members] and they don't even know how the world actually works. They don't have TV. They don't read newspapers. They're naive about how things work. But they sure know how to use government and milk it for all it's worth."

Truman rewarded Grandma Lorna's patience. After a year of partying, Truman was done with that. He'd figured out that if he was going to do more than just survive on the outside, he needed more education. He asked his half-sister Jane Blackmore for help. Jane is a midwife with a very large and successful practice in Cranbrook. And though she left her husband, Winston Blackmore, her fundamentalist faith and her five older children in Bountiful, Jane continues to play an important and influential role in her children's lives. She persuaded Jake and Hyrum to help Truman and some of the other young men and women who had left Bountiful finish high school by giving them time off work to attend classes. She asked some local people to donate computers and raised enough money to hire a teacher for about a dozen students. Jake and Hyrum then set up a makeshift classroom at the back of their company's office.

When Truman told his mother that he was doing his Grade 12 equivalency, she didn't respond. "My mom didn't call me once all year. She's a teacher and she didn't even ask me two questions about how I was doing in school." Truman got his high-school certificate and then enrolled in the heavy-duty mechanic's course at Selkirk College in Cranbrook, where he got the highest marks in his class. He also met a young woman there who was studying to be an electrician. He'd been taught to treat girls "like poisonous snakes"—a reference to Eve in the Bible. But, for the first time in his life, he started dating. There was so much that he didn't know about how differently things work in the outside world that it's difficult for Truman to articulate them. But one thing he mentions is that he had no idea that the common practice of cousins marrying cousins is actually both illegal and dangerous.

Truman says he never embraced the notion of polygamy, which he rejects as "morally wrong," along with underage marriage. "A lot of what they do goes against human nature and polygamy definitely goes against human nature," he says. "I can't see taking a 16-year-old for myself and it's not right for them [the older men]. It's also not right for the girl. What kind of life will she be able to have? There's not even a little bit of a love life [in plural marriages] and I think people really only want to be with one other person."

Although he constantly fought for fair wages before he left Bountiful, it was only in 2004 that Truman realized the full extent of how Winston Blackmore had taken advantage of him and others. Revenue Canada had audited Winston and his company, J. R. Blackmore & Sons. It was like peering under a rock.

Some of what the audit determined is that none of the employees had ever paid income tax either. They had been led to believe that it was being deducted from their pay-cheques. But it wasn't. Truman needed to pay a few thousand dollars, but some of the long-time employees got bills for as much as twenty thousand dollars. That's a huge sum and almost impossible to repay when it's more than double what your annual wage has been for many years and you have no house or property to use as collateral for a loan.

Truman paid what he owed. But it meant he had to delay his plan to buy a house and delay marrying the young woman he'd met at college. It reignited memories of how Winston Blackmore had "repaid" Dalmon Oler for helping him set up J. R. Blackmore & Sons by never lifting a finger to help as his father-in-law's businesses slid into bankruptcy, and even orchestrating Oler's humiliation by shoving the patriarch aside and grabbing the title of bishop. Now, in his greed, Winston had no qualms about throwing his own sons, brothers, nephews and cousins under the bus.

Truman Oler is trying to organize a class-action suit against Winston, involving all of the others who had been exploited, not just for himself and others, but also for his father.

Typical of almost everyone who has left the patriarchal cult, Truman reveres his father and has little good to say about his mother. When asked what he hopes for in his life, Truman says, "I hope to be a good person like my dad. He was a real good man. He helped everybody he could, he worked himself to death for his family . . . My Dad's favourite saying was 'There's always room for one more at the back of the bus.'"

Getting a class-action suit organized is difficult for any-one, let alone a young man with so little experience and so many other dreams to take care of. But a civil suit in the United States, filed in September 2004 and financed by Ethan's uncle Dan Fischer, focused attention on the fact that boys are victims of the cult as much as girls are. Six boys and twenty "John Does" filed the suit, claiming that Warren Jeffs, the Fundamentalist Church of Jesus Christ of Latter Day Saints and the church's United Effort Plan trust "have established the secret, cruel, abusive and unlawful practice of reducing the surplus male population by system-atically expelling young males." The suit goes on to claim that Jeffs and the church's patriarchs "purposefully and completely shielded them [the boys] from the outside world and intentionally deprived them of the necessary skills, knowledge and education one would need to function in mainstream society."

What the boys wanted was compensation for damages they had sustained as a result of "the defendants' pattern of unlawful activity, fraud, breach of fiduciary duties, breach of assumed duties, alienation of parental affections, infliction of emotional distress, invasion of privacy and civil conspiracy, which arose from the defendants' unconscionable conduct, including the practice of expulsion to further the illegal prac-tice of polygamy."

In a stunning display of self-interest, Winston Blackmore filed an affidavit supporting the lost boys' call for the United Effort Plan to be reformed. He put himself forward as "a per-son interested in the well-being of families who have spent their lives building up the UEP trust and who are dependent on its existence." He said he would ensure that the boys and other beneficiaries of the trust got what they deserved, having in the past spent "countless hours as a trustee administering the UEP trust and its assets for the benefit of the people." He graciously offered to serve without compensation.

The civil suit forced the Utah and Arizona governments to increase their scrutiny of the FLDS and of Hildale and Colorado City, the twin towns that straddle the state border. It prompted questions about how the charitable United Effort Plan trust was being administered on behalf of its beneficiaries, and it led the two state governments to force the trust into receivership.

The lost boys' civil suit also provoked the state governments into reconsidering what they could do to help the thousand or so castaway boys. What was clear was that they couldn't take all of them into government care. There were simply too many of them. In an attempt to address that problem, the Utah legislature passed a child emancipation act in 2006, which allows children to effectively "divorce" their parents and gives children under eighteen the rights and responsibilities of an adult. Included in those rights is the ability to apply for government financial assistance, such as welfare and medical care.

The publicity generated by the suit also helped groups like Dan Fischer's Diversity Foundation and the St. George–based HOPE Organization raise more money to help the boys and girls leaving polygamy. It's expensive trying to help them, and Dan Fischer has wasted lots of money trying to figure out how best to do it. Initially he ran the Diversity Foundation himself and liberally doled out money for every sad story, only to learn later that the money had been used for drugs, not rent. He's hired a succession of people to deal with the boys. Some were like him, too gullible, soft or trusting to last. Another was too much like the overbearing prophet that the boys had already rebelled against or been rejected by.

But some of Dan Fischer's lost boys have graduated from college. Others have completed technical courses and high school. A number of them work at his company. Others have moved on to other companies.

HOPE has a much smaller budget than the Diversity Foundation and its successes are more of the day-to-day kind. Its volunteers make sure that the boys and anyone else leaving polygamy have clothes to wear and food to eat. The volunteers help them find schools, places to live and jobs. They also help the fugitive young people open bank accounts, get car insurance and driver's licences.

In 2007, another lost boy, who had been kicked out at thirteen, filed a civil suit in Utah demanding that the FLDS disclose where his mother was. Eighteen-year-old Johnny Jessop said that all he wanted to do was see her, "give her a big hug and tell her how much I love her."

In Canada, very little help is available for the lost boys or anyone else leaving polygamy. There are no foundations to assist them. There's no government recognition of their special plight, not even the recognition that provincial labour laws encourage the lost boys' continued exploitation. And while Truman Oler despises the label "lost boy"—he believes himself to be anything but lost—a civil suit might be just what is needed to get Canada's victims of polygamy the help they so desperately need.

—

THIRTEEN

FALLEN PROPHET

For Warren Jeffs, his father's stroke was too good an opportunity to pass up. Warren seized the moment and began knocking out his competitors, starting with Winston Blackmore. In September 2001, he ordered the bishop of Bountiful to appear before a priesthood court in Colorado City. They assembled on September 12, the day after terrorists had attacked New York's World Trade Center. Warren was armed with a list of complaints and pages of charges were read out. Blackmore has never said what those charges were, nor has anyone else, but he insists "most of them were laughable." Warren told Blackmore that he and Fred Jessop, Rulon's most senior and respected adviser, had spent hours wondering how to deal with Blackmore. But, when the time came for Uncle Rulon's verdict, the debilitated prophet said: "Why don't you all just love one another?"

A teenaged girl named Vanessa Rohbock was the excuse for Winston Blackmore's trial. As Winston later wrote, "She became a very important way for Warren to dispose of Ron

[Rohbock, her father] and myself: Two potential threats." A year before the religious trial, Winston called Warren to see how Rulon was doing. Warren gave him an update and then asked whether Winston had heard from Ron Rohbock, one of Rulon's bodyguards. Rohbock was on his way north to Bountiful. From this point on in the story, there are varying versions.

Winston's version is that Rohbock brought his married daughter Vanessa to Bountiful to stay in Blackmore's home for a while. She was unhappy, taking two different antidepressants and potentially suicidal. It was only after Ron and Vanessa arrived that Winston says he learned that Vanessa was the third wife to her father's close friend. She had tried to run away, but when she got to her sister's home, her sister told her to go back to her husband. Vanessa did. But, after that, she started sneaking out at night to meet her friends, including a young man her own age. The young man would drive with his lights off to the house where Vanessa lived and off they'd go. One night they were followed. Winston's account doesn't say who followed the couple—it was probably the religious police, the Sons of Helemon, who are more commonly known as Warren's God Squad.

Vanessa and the young man were taken before a church court. Vanessa was found completely to blame: she had bewitched the young man into acting foolishly. Warren ruled that Vanessa—like her older sister before her—should be cast out, shunned and never allowed to return. But, when Ron Rohbock appealed to the prophet, Rulon said she could go to Canada.

Ron Barton, the Utah attorney general's closed-communities investigator, told another version of the story to *Phoenix New Times* reporter John Dougherty in December 2003. He said Vanessa had fallen in love with a young man and refused to become the third wife to a man who was not only her father's age, but one of his friends. For that, Barton says, she was hauled before a church court with Warren Jeffs as judge and jury. "Warren wanted Vanessa blood-atoned," Barton said. In terror, Vanessa fled to Canada and found sanctuary in Winston's home. The investigator noted that while blood atonement doesn't always mean that the sinner will be killed, Blackmore had told him that he and Rohbock had been instructed to pray day and night for the girl's destruction. Barton said Rohbock had been ordered by the prophet to retrieve his doomed daughter and bring her back to Colorado City.

Barton took it all very seriously. He told Dougherty that around that time Jeffs had preached about Brigham Young's 1856 sermon in which the Mormon patriarch had said there are sins for which people can atone only by having their blood spilled. Jeffs's father, Rulon, had preached about blood atonement quite often in 1997. In one sermon that was later printed and published, Rulon said:

> I have seen scores and hundreds of people for whom there would have been a chance if their lives had been taken and their blood spilled on the ground as a smoking incense to the Almighty, but who are now angels to the devil until our elder brother Jesus Christ raises them up—conquers death, hell and the grave.

He went on to say that blood atonement fulfills God's commandment to "love thy neighbour as thyself": "If he needs help, help him; and if he wants salvation and it is necessary to spill his blood on the Earth in order that he may be saved, spill it. . . . That is the way to love mankind."

There are two versions of how the story ends. According to Barton, Vanessa was saved from blood atonement only by agreeing to marry the fifty-something-year-old man to whom she had been assigned. Barton considered charging Warren Jeffs with conspiracy to commit murder in 2003, after Vanessa went back to Colorado City. But because she was apparently safe and not willing to testify, Attorney General Mark Shurtleff told him to wait for "more prosecutable crimes from the prophet."

On a polygamy blog site in 2004, Joseph L. R. Williams, who claims to be Vanessa's brother, denied that blood atonement had been threatened or that Vanessa had been coerced into anything:

> I know Warren Jeffs personally. He taught me High School all four years. He is a wonderful guy and would never do anything to hurt anyone. You people think those girls down there are sentenced to their doom? My sister is Vanessa Rohbock . . . She left and had a boyfriend, then she realized that their way of life was so much higher than the way of life the world today is living, and so she and her boyfriend went back to the church. She is living there now and she is as happy as ever. These horror stories you hear of the girls being forced to do this that and the other thing are a bunch of lies.

Vanessa Rohbock may have been saved by Winston Blackmore, or at the very least by Warren Jeffs's fear of prosecution. And Blackmore himself was rescued by Rulon Jeffs's invocation that everyone should just love one another. But it was only a reprieve. After the prophet had uttered his verdict, Blackmore says Warren took him into a back room. "If you ever question one more thing I do or say, then you will be just like Bill Roundy," Warren threatened. Warren had already excommunicated Roundy, stripped him of his wives and children and expelled him from the community. Warren could as easily have used Rebecca Musser's father as an example. Lloyd Wall had been Rulon Jeffs's business partner and lived in a large home within Rulon's Cottonwood Canyon compound. But after Rulon was stricken with his stroke, Warren excommunicated Wall and reassigned his wives and children while Wall was away visiting Bountiful. "No trial, no mercy, no defense and all while Uncle Rulon was in his bed and asleep," Blackmore later wrote in his newsletter.

Blackmore's reprieve ended May 30, 2002. Under the influence of his son and with wobbling, crabbed writing, Rulon Jeffs removed Blackmore as a director of the United Effort Plan, stripping him of access to the US$110 million fund and all of the properties that it had accumulated in Colorado City, Hildale, Bountiful and dozens of other communities. Over the loudspeaker at a church meeting in Bountiful on June 2, the aging prophet pronounced Blackmore's fate: "Dear brothers and sisters, this is Rulon Jeffs speaking. I want you to know that Winston Blackmore is dismissed. He is no longer in that position that he has assumed. Is that sufficient? Okay, God bless you."

Rulon's first councillor, Fred Jessop, spoke next, recounting how as a young man he had heard Joseph Smith's advisor Lorin Woolley speak. Jessop said he had learned from the Spirit of the Lord that Woolley was a man of God, just as he later learned from the Spirit that both John Y. Barlow and LeRoy Johnson had been chosen by God to be fundamentalist prophets. Finally, Jessop said, "The same Spirit that bore witness to me that Joseph [Smith] was a prophet bears witness to me that the responsibility has fallen upon President Rulon T. Jeffs."

Then Rulon came back on the line. "Amen. Winston Blackmore is dismissed. That is the latest and most final word regarding Winston. God bless you. Amen." After a pause, Rulon asked, "That reach them? You understand that Winston is dismissed. Warren is now in my position and following me and he stands with me every way. God bless you. Amen." According to Blackmore, throughout the whole broadcast, Warren could be heard in the background, coaching his father on what to say.

A couple of days after that phone call, Blackmore sat down at his computer to write Warren a letter. Just as Blackmore finished it and before he had a chance to save the final version, there was a power failure. It lasted about fifteen minutes. "To my great surprise, there was my letter back on the screen. It was different this time," Blackmore revealed in his newsletter in 2005. "Someone had edited it in cyberspace. The hard things that I wanted to say to Warren were not there. The kind things that I was saying to his Father were still there." Blackmore called it a "miraculous event . . . a blanket of peace came over me and I knew that God was still with me in this thing."

But before Winston's miracle letter reached Colorado City, Rulon Jeffs had sent a letter of his own to the Canadian Saints reiterating what he had said in the broadcast. "The Lord has instructed me to dismiss Winston Blackmore as bishop and president elder in Canada. And I call on you to support me in this. I call on Brother Winston to stand as a faithful member and elder and support me, along with all the members there. Let the spirit of criticism and dissension cease."

Rulon went on to say that both Warren and Fred Jessop were "one" with him and that they did his will. Rulon ended by telling Blackmore to "remove Vanessa Rohbock from his home and to stop spreading the lie that Warren and I are not one." Addressing the Saints, he said, "Winston is wrong on these issues. And I call on him to repent and continue as a faithful member with his family." Rulon's signature at the bottom is shaky and scarcely legible. It was witnessed by Fred Jessop and by Rulon's other favoured son, Leroy Jeffs.

In September, the ninety-two-year-old president, prophet, seer and revelator of the Fundamentalist Church of Jesus Christ of Latter Day Saints died, leaving behind another failed prophecy. Rulon had told his followers that he would live to witness the Second Coming of Christ and live 350 years into the new millennium. More than five thousand people attended his funeral in the meeting house in Colorado City on September 12, 2002. They came in their large family groups, with many men holding the hands of two wives while other wives and flocks of children trailed behind. The women—including Rulon's seventy or more widows, some still in their teens—wore pastel, floral-printed pioneer dresses and their hair was swept up at the front and braided at the back, in exactly the manner that Rulon Jeffs had decreed.

Among the mourners were Winston Blackmore and some of his wives. "When we went there we were flanked by Warren's armed guards as we went up through the viewing line and down to our seating," Winston later wrote. "His guards were posted to watch us as we were considered a 'high risk' for his security."

Eight of Jeffs's sons were pallbearers. Another twenty-two sons (including Rulon F. and Rulon H.) were named as honorary pallbearers, along with "all other sons and grandsons." Rulon's sons sang two hymns titled "Our Prophet's Will" and "This One Man." Warren Jeffs and his older brother LeRoy both spoke at the service in the meeting hall and Warren dedicated the grave. But, according to the leaflet handed out to followers, the service had "President Rulon T. Jeffs Presiding, Bishop Fred M. Jessop Conducting."

On the back of the leaflet were nine quotes from the prophet. The first established Rulon Jeffs's legitimacy as the prophet: "I sprang from John Y. Barlow and LeRoy S. Johnson."

The other quotes, all from 2002, were orders to obey the leader and his family. "My constant message to my family is to keep sweet and we have a heaven on earth. I suggest that for you, brethren," says the first one, attributed to Rulon on March 17. "My family is united as one and they all love me and I love all of them and I am constantly telling them, 'Keep Sweet no matter what.' God bless you, brethren, I have a love and unity in my family that is grand and glorious."

That Sunday, four days after the burial, Ethan Fischer remembers Warren's younger brother Seth standing up in church. "He said he felt inspired, that he had had a revelation about the next leader and it was his brother Warren. Then one of Rulon's wives [Naomi] stood up and said she felt she had had a revelation as well that Warren should be the leader." Strangely, none of Warren's relatives or followers had "revelations" suggesting anyone other than Warren should claim the role of prophet.

There were no dissenting voices at all, even though within Mormon tradition the leadership falls to the most senior member of the priesthood hierarchy and does not follow family or dynastic lines. The person next in line was ninety-two-year-old bishop Fred Jessop, followed by Winston Blackmore. But no one objected and no one stood up to say that they had been impressed by the Lord to proclaim either Fred Jessop or Winston Blackmore the next prophet.

Two weeks later at the Sunday meeting in Colorado City, Steven Harker—a retired U.S. military man—pledged total obedience to Warren Jeffs. "I testify that he is God to us, Warren Jeffs. His father does lead and guide us through his son. I want to rededicate my life and all I have to help the kingdom of God," he said, according to notes taken by Winston's sister Marlene Palmer, which were later entered as evidence in a B.C. Supreme Court case involving Bountiful's school.

Bishop Fred Jessop spoke next, urging people to work harder, be sweeter and put more energy into their faith. Then Warren Jeffs rose to speak: "The Lord and Father have told me to come here today to deliver a particular message to the Saints in Canada and the Saints here. There has been a day of calling, but the time has come for a day of choosing." Jeffs preached to both the followers in the hall and to those listening to a broadcast of his speech in Bountiful: "This is a sweet invitation from our Prophet to repent and stand as one . . . He who is not with me is against me."

Warren buttressed his sermon with quotes from Joseph Smith and the Book of Mormon before returning to this theme: "There is a division particularly in Canada . . . Choose ye this day whom ye shall choose. Come—follow the word of the Prophet . . . The word and will of God to this people is to keep sweeter and sweeter . . . [But] the spirit of apostasy is filtering down to this people."

The message was clear. The spirit of apostasy was being fed by Winston Blackmore. Warren had already urged Blackmore's wives to leave him and return to Colorado City to be reassigned. At least one did. Warren told his followers to shun Blackmore, his family and anyone who sided with them. Twenty-seven employees quit their jobs with J. R. Blackmore & Sons, crippling the forestry company and severely damaging its profitability and viability.

About seven hundred of Bountiful's 1,200 people stuck with Blackmore. The split in the community didn't run along family lines as much as it did on the basis of past hurts and offences. Among those who abandoned Blackmore were his two older brothers Macrae and Brandon, who believed Winston had deprived them of a share of their father's estate. Winston's sister Memory Oler, who had been president of the Bountiful Women's Society, stuck with Warren Jeffs as well. Memory hadn't forgotten how Winston had abandoned her husband, Dalmon Oler, in his time of need. But, perhaps more important, her son Jim is now the FLDS bishop. She is now the mother of a man who could be a god, which will enhance her own chances in the fundamentalist hereafter.

Like everyone else in Bountiful, Jim Oler is related in some way to them all. He is Dalmon and Memory Oler's son, which makes Debbie Palmer and Jane Blackmore his half-sisters. Winston Blackmore is both his uncle and his brother-in-law. Lorna Blackmore is his mother-in-law. Truman Oler is his full brother.

Bountiful churned with bad feelings and ill will. Families split apart. Mothers shunned their children. Grandparents were cut off from grandchildren. Brothers broke with brothers; sisters shunned sisters. But it was the government-funded school that became the battleground for the fight between Jeffs and Blackmore.

It's not that education was important to Jeffs or Blackmore. Jeffs revealed his negative attitude towards education at Alta Academy, when he established a doctrine-laden curriculum, and then again in Colorado City, when he ordered parents to take their children out of the public school and teach them at home. Blackmore simply didn't think education was important, since girls would only be wives and mothers and boys would only be loggers and millworkers in companies he controlled.

But at the time the school provided cash flow—more than half a million dollars a year of government money. And because the school only operates four days a week, it provides ready access to a pool of young workers. On Fridays, the boys do their mission work—free labour—which also counts as job experience under the education ministry's career-planning program. But, just as important, school provides the best opportunity to program the children into a belief system that will keep them obedient to the prophet.

In short, the school, more than the church, is the community's command and control centre. If Winston Blackmore was to have any hope of ever being a leader and prophet, he needed not only to retain his following, but also to ensure that his businesses remained viable. Even if it meant having to go to a gentile court and airing the community's laundry for all to see and using every devious method that the priesthood had honed over the years, the school was worth the fight.

The battle came to a head the first day of the school year, which happened to be the first anniversary of the September 11 attacks on the United States. Winston's followers had occupied one part of the school, which is an old barn that had been retrofitted into two classrooms, along with thirty-two children and some teachers. Winston described what happened that day as "a terrorist action" against the children: "A mob of men and observers complete with a hired bailiff demanded that they [the students, parents and teachers] immediately leave the premises. Two of the leading mobocrats commenced to pick a quarrel with some of the teachers, stating their willingness to do anything—'I mean anything that the prophet tells me to do'—indicating that they were on the mission of their leaders. They further stated that it was not breaking the law for priesthood to enter any place on the UEP [United Effort Plan] property."

Among the "mobocrats" were Jim Oler and principal Merrill Palmer, Blackmore's former ally and friend, who had switched sides in the mistaken belief that Warren Jeffs and Oler cared more about education than Blackmore. When school resumed a few weeks later, children from families loyal to Blackmore were told they were wicked. At least that's what affidavits and documents filed in the B.C. Supreme Court by Blackmore said. One affidavit quoted Merrill Palmer as saying that Bountiful Elementary-Secondary School is now "Uncle Warren's school and we will teach his ways." Grade 5 teacher JoAnne Blackmore wrote that during prayers one morning a student prayed that "everyone who didn't believe in Uncle Warren would get discouraged and leave."

Even though the school is funded by the B.C. government, the "terrorist" incident escaped the education ministry's notice. Somehow Winston, the school's superintendent, had neglected to report it to the ministry and so had the parents and the "mobocrats." The only hint the ministry got that something had changed at the school was a terse note from Warren Jeffs dated October 26. It stated that Jim Oler had been appointed as the church's representative "to act as it's [sic] authority for the church's school . . . He is replacing Winston Blackmore effective immediately."

Less than a month later, Blackmore was in Victoria meeting with James Beeke, the government's inspector of independent schools. Blackmore claimed that at that meeting he told Beeke that Jeffs had sanctioned the teaching of racism in the government-funded school and that Jeffs's taped sermons were being played to the children, teaching them that "negroes" came from a war in heaven and they were turned into "negroes" because they were "fence-sitters" who would not choose sides in the fight between good and evil. Beeke reportedly responded by reading aloud the Independent School Act regulation that forbids promoting or fostering doctrines of "racial or ethnic superiority or persecution, religious intolerance or persecution, social change through violent action or sedition."

Then, according to Blackmore, Beeke urged him to get legal advice and "deal with any accusations before a complaint gets to this office." Blackmore claims Beeke also urged him to form another society and set up another school. BESS would continue to get funding, but because the new school would have many of the same trustees and teachers who had been affiliated with BESS, the new school could be immediately accredited and would be eligible for funding within a year.

The day after the meeting in Victoria, Blackmore was at his lawyer's office. He transferred the title to the school property from the school's society to his own company, J. R. Blackmore & Sons. When the dispute over the land's ownership and control of the school went to the B.C. Supreme Court a few months later, Blackmore claimed that he had never meant for the school to own the property. Rather he had transferred the land title from his company in trust to the school society to reduce his own taxes, on the advice of friendly folks in the government's assessment office.

The same day that Blackmore transferred the school property to his company, Warren Jeffs's supporters held an annual general meeting of the Bountiful Elementary-Secondary School Society. Blackmore had not been invited, nor was his brother Guy, another trustee. To make sure that the new bishop, Jim Oler, and the others did what they were told, Jeffs sent a few of his bodyguards to Bountiful. At the meeting, Warren's brother Leroy Jeffs, Jim Oler and Jim's brother Macrae Oler were elected to replace former trustees Rulon Jeffs, Winston Blackmore and Guy Blackmore.

Two weeks later, there was another annual general meeting of the Bountiful Elementary-Secondary School Society. This time, none of Jeffs's followers or trustees were invited, since Blackmore was the organizer. Predictably, Winston Blackmore got himself re-elected along with his new bishop, Duane Palmer, and Cyril Colonel, who replaced Rulon Jeffs and Leroy Jeffs.

The court battle was on. But by then, Winston's own large brood of children and those of his followers—ninety-five children in total—were being taught in a makeshift classroom set up in a former woodworking shop at Winston's farm. It was intended to be a temporary measure until they regained control of the school. But on April 3, the B.C. Supreme Court ruled that Warren Jeffs and his followers were the rightful owners and operators of the school. Blackmore had to return the school property to the Bountiful school society.

It was an expensive defeat for Blackmore. Not only had he lost control of the school's curriculum, he'd lost access to the nearly $500,000 in government grants for the school each year. Starting a new school would be expensive and Winston no longer had access to the money tithed by everyone in the community or to United Effort Plan land.

What is surprising, however, is that once again the government seemed happy to ignore what was happening in Bountiful. Despite the allegations raised in court and in private meetings with the government's independent school inspector, the issue of racism and white supremacy being taught to the nearly two hundred students at Bountiful Elementary-Secondary all but disappeared. It wasn't until after the B.C. Supreme Court ruling that the education ministry's independent school inspector bothered to ask Blackmore for evidence, and even then it was only after a reporter had called asking Jim Beeke for comment. Beeke wrote to Blackmore on April 9. His letter made no reference to the issue's having been raised at the November meeting. But he did note that Blackmore had made that claim when they met in March.

Blackmore responded haughtily to the inspector's request for more details about Jeffs's teachings. "Forgive me if I am wrong, but it seemed to me that you came a little bit short of wondering if I was just dealing in sour grapes." Rather than providing evidence, he blustered that he didn't want his children being taught that their parents were "wicked apostates and going to hell" or that "we are the best people on the face of the Earth" or that "the negro race came because they could not choose sides in the war in heaven. I don't know what you call that Jim."

Blackmore refused to make a formal complaint against the school or its teaching—"I am just happy that my children do not have to be exposed to that . . . I am sure that when [deputy inspector] Susan [Penner] pays the school a visit at the end of April she will find everything in order and I hope she does."

Small wonder Blackmore didn't rat out Warren and his followers. Rulon Jeffs's and other earlier prophets' sermons, which form part of the religious curriculum at both BESS and Blackmore's new school, which was later named Mormon Hills, are also rife with references to black people being allied with the devil.

But after Blackmore refused to provide more details, the independent school inspector was apparently satisfied with his "investigation." And, four years later, in 2007, when a government evaluation team went to Bountiful Elementary-Secondary School, they favourably reported that every morning the children assembled and listened to taped homilies from "guest speakers" and that the curriculum being used was from the Alta Academy, where Warren Jeffs had been principal. The evaluation team seemed unaware that the tapes are of Jeffs's sermons. In fact, the team didn't even seem to know that these were fundamentalist Mormons and not members of the mainstream Church of Jesus Christ of Latter-day Saints.

Fashioning himself as a kinder, gentler prophet, Winston held church meetings in an old cabinetmaking shop at his farm down on the flatlands of the Creston Valley and made plans for a new school that was to be called Mormon Hills. Once again, Winston was abetted by British Columbia's ever-helpful inspector of independent schools. Jim Beeke had agreed to accredit the new school, even before it physically existed. Even after another arm of government—the Agricultural Land Commission—had threatened legal action for setting the school up on land specifically set aside only for farm use, Beeke never once suggested decertifying the school.

The only reason Blackmore has been able to retrench and attempt to challenge Warren Jeffs's control is that Blackmore has more resources than most FLDS members. Despite having convinced his mother to sign over all that she'd inherited from his father to the United Effort Plan trust—a transaction that assured his elevation to bishop and a seat on the UEP board—Blackmore had shrewdly amassed his own considerable land reserve outside the trust.

Throughout his eighteen years as bishop, he had constantly urged Canadian Saints to dedicate their "time, talents, money and materials to the Lord's storehouse." As one of the UEP's directors, Blackmore had reduced the trust's beneficiaries to nothing more than tenants, who were allowed to stay in houses they built only at the pleasure of their lords and masters. All the while, Blackmore accumulated his own portfolio of property in the Creston Valley, Cranbrook and just across the border in Idaho. His Canadian property alone was worth an estimated six million dollars in 2005, not including the 1,500 acres of farmland that he had under long-term lease from the Kootenay Indian band, as a result of his close friendship with the band's chief.

Blackmore's assets included a grain elevator used for canola storage in the middle of Creston, an airport warehouse, a retail store/office building, another store, industrial land in Cranbrook, eight houses, a duplex and three mobile homes. In addition to the six million dollars worth of property, Blackmore and his companies had managed to secure several substantial contracts with Tembec, one of Canada's largest forestry companies, by undercutting other contractors who didn't have access to such a large pool of cheap indentured workers.

Of course, Blackmore also had considerable debt. His name was on a long list of mortgages as the sole owner, joint owner or signatory for companies such as Blackmore Farms, J. R. Blackmore & Sons, Kootenay Wood Preservers, Rocky Pine Contracting and Prairie Holdings. One mortgage, signed just two weeks after Rulon Jeffs's funeral, carried the stunningly high rate of 18 per cent, nearly three times the posted commercial rate. His signature was also on pages and pages of loans for tens of thousands of dollars worth of specialized equipment as well as loans for twenty-seven trucks and/or four-wheel-drive vehicles and two cars.

Blackmore was not unique among the upper-echelon Saints. Almost all of them had carved out substantial worldly wealth in their search for salvation, using their easy access to cheap labour and the church's collection plates. Rulon Jeffs and his sons also controlled countless numbered and named companies that they kept separate from the United Effort Plan. In a 1989 court deposition, Rulon Jeffs admitted that for twenty years he had deposited tithes to the Rulon T. Jeffs Trust, a chequing account over which he had sole signing authority.

Having lost control of the school, access to the community's meeting house and half his followers, Winston Blackmore began an electronic ministry in January 2003, using an Internet newsletter to bolster his depleted and disheartened flock. From his pulpit as the editor of the *North Star*, he spread his own version of fundamentalist doctrine and attacked his rival. Of course, he wasn't reaching any of Jeffs's followers. Jeffs had long ago banned computers except for his own use. But Blackmore's newsletter reached a lot of young people and quite a few of the disaffected and excommunicated. He also didn't restrict himself to the *North Star*. Blackmore blogged late at night on his own site and on other polygamy blogs, giving mini-sermons using Old Testament language that was strangely incongruous in cyberspace.

"I had rather be a fallen prophet than a false prophet." Joseph Smith's quote was prominently featured in the *North Star's* inaugural edition and again in June. Blackmore must have found comfort in those words. He had been so close to glory. Second in line to replace Rulon Jeffs, after ninety-two-year-old Fred Jessop, Blackmore had been only a few years away from being the prophet. But Warren Jeffs had disrupted the succession plan.

Blackmore was so certain of his gift of prophecy and his own claim to leadership that in the newsletter's premiere edition he laid out his revelations for the year ahead. He predicted "hundreds, if not thousands" would leave the FLDS and would "return to the iron rod, the word of our Lord Jesus Christ." Blackmore promised to be that iron rod.

He warned Warren Jeffs and all who stuck with him that they would be punished in the coming year. "The chastening hand of the almighty God shall fall upon the crook, the liar, the scam artist and the thief . . . I tell you in the name of God that if we are wicked and ungodly we shall not escape His hand."

In the *North Star's* early editions, there are frequent references to Nephi, the Book of Mormon's favourite son who brought the gold plates to America around 590 BC and settled the place he called Bountiful. Prophet LeRoy Johnson had likened Blackmore to Nephi when he had given him his priesthood blessing. In a January 31 issue, Blackmore quotes Jesus from the Book of Mormon:

> Behold thou art Nephi and I am God. Behold, I
> declare it unto thee in the presence of mine angels
> that ye shall have power over this people and shall
> smite the earth with famine and with pestilence
> and destruction according to the wickedness of this
> people. Behold I give unto you power that whatso-
> ever ye shall seal on earth shall be sealed in
> heaven; and whatsoever ye shall loose on earth
> shall be loosed in heaven; and thus shall ye have
> power among this people.

In a later issue, a whole page is devoted to Nephi and the long-running war with the Lamanites (who Mormons believe are the ancestors of American Indians). Blackmore writes that Nephi was called "an usurper of authority, a murderer, a thief and a liar. They [the Lamanites] were jealous beyond anything that you can imagine for he had built ships, tools, weapons, homes, lands, roads and schools . . . Remember that an angel appeared . . . telling them that the Lord had in mind for Nephi to be the leader over them and commanding them to be obedient to them." Blackmore's story ends with Nephi preaching, baptizing and attempting to make peace and with this line: "But oh, how history repeats itself."

In another edition, Blackmore claims his priesthood authority directly from God through Prophet LeRoy Johnson. Coyly—and in a clear case of what cult expert Willa Appel has labelled "messianic etiquette"—Blackmore always denies any aspiration to lead. Yet his newsletter is salted with quotes from previous prophets saying that true prophets don't proclaim their titles. Blackmore went out of his way to draw parallels between himself and Brigham Young, and quotes the Mormon prophet on the topic of succession:

The brethren testify that Brigham Young is Brother Joseph's [Smith's] legal successor. You never heard me say so. I say that I am a good hand to keep the dogs and wolves out of the flock. I do not care a groat who rises up. I do not think anything about being Joseph's successor. That is nothing that concerns me. I have asked yet, or had a feeling as to what kind of a great man, O Lord, are you going to make me? . . . I do not trouble myself as to whose successor I am.

Whether or not Young is to be taken at his word when he says he has no interest in seizing the reins of power, there is little reason not to think that Blackmore was being more than a little disingenuous when he made the same claim.

In March 2003, Blackmore made a forthright assumption of leadership. He announced that on April 6—the date in 1830 that Joseph Smith officially founded the Church of Jesus Christ of Latter Day Saints—he would re-baptize anyone who was willing. Baptism, he wrote, is "the gateway that God has required everyone to go through that [sic] have any intentions at all of entering into the Kingdom of God." Blackmore accurately predicted that he would be roundly criticized for exercising what he believed was his right to do baptisms in the name of God and Joseph Smith. "There will be a howl from the sidelines. The mockers will mock, the cursers will curse, the priests will cry treason."

He rhetorically asked and answered the question of under whose authority he was performing that ritual. "Well bless your soul," he wrote. "God commanded everyone everywhere to forsake their sins, to be baptized and then keep all of His commandments. It is unto this end that this opportunity is provided by God."

In the same issue, Blackmore announced the appointment of two bishops and directed his followers to pay their tithes directly to his bishops—Duane Palmer and Shem Johnson. Palmer was named bishop for Bountiful (in addition to being superintendent of Mormon Hills School) and Shem Johnson (one of the former prophet LeRoy Johnson's progeny) was appointed as Blackmore's bishop over his growing flock in Idaho. Johnson had left Colorado City just a few months earlier and moved to Bonner's Ferry, a century-old town about a forty-minute drive south of Bountiful. Johnson and Blackmore are multiply related. Seven of Blackmore's wives are Johnsons, and Blackmore's oldest daughter, Susie, is married to a Johnson, although Susie's husband Ben remained in the FLDS.

Initially, Shem Johnson's children and the children of Blackmore's other Idaho followers were bused daily to Mormon Hills School. But soon there were so many children that Blackmore and Johnson set up another school in Johnson's large home.

But Johnson wasn't only Blackmore's bishop. He is sole director and shareholder in J. R. Blackmore & Sons Idaho division, which purchased a bankrupt post-and-pole company located outside Bonner's Ferry. Johnson's employees are other ex-FLDS men who had moved north to be closer to Blackmore. Johnson also put them to work at his own company, S & L Underground, digging trenches and doing excavations. With a ready supply of cheaper labourers, S & L Underground was soon undercutting local contractors and winning bids on municipal projects.

Mayor Darrell Kerby of Bonner's Ferry isn't happy about fundamentalist Mormons moving into his community. His town had only recently seen the end of the Aryan Nations, who had finally been bankrupted and moved away. Kerby really wasn't happy about S & L Underground winning those contracts, but there was nothing he could do about that either. Idaho state law requires municipalities to go with the lowest bidder.

While Blackmore was doing what he could to increase the number of his followers with a kindly message, Warren Jeffs became more tyrannical and autocratic. Recognizing the threat, Jeffs continued his attacks on Blackmore. He accused Blackmore of "sinning against knowledge." "Father told me the whole world has denied God and yet they call themselves Christians by the hundreds of millions," Jeffs said in one sermon in Colorado City. "The only true Christians are those who come under the rule and guide of God through His living Priesthood." That is, the FLDS and its prophet.

While Blackmore promised "free agency," the themes of almost all of Jeffs's sermons were strict obedience to the prophet, keeping sweet and never questioning. In his January 28, 2003, sermon, later printed under the title "Live so you never disturb the spirit of God," Jeffs amended the closing of the Lord's Prayer to suit his needs, praying "Father, Thy will be done through the Priesthood over me."

That month marked the beginning of Jeffs's pogrom against his own people, starting with men deemed unworthy and unfaithful. He expelled them from their homes and stripped them of their wives and families, whom he quickly reassigned to his loyalists. Jeffs then culled boys and single young men, who were surplus to his vision of Zion and polygamy's unnatural arithmetic. In unprecedented numbers, boys—some as young as twelve and thirteen—were driven out of town and left to fend for themselves, often having done nothing more than talk to a girl their own age or watch a forbidden movie.

In the *North Star*, Blackmore countered Jeffs's increasingly messianic message by asking, "Who said Warren was giving new training? It was taught by Chairman Mao, Adolf Hitler, Benito Mussolini, Saddam Hussein and many others just like them, and his name will be enshrined in history along with them as leaders who brutally robbed, pillaged and destroyed the very people who trusted, served and revered them. Higher teachings don't get any lower than that."

Jeffs finally made his position as the church's president, prophet, seer and revelator official on August 5, 2003. Warren had his brother Leroy ordain him just moments after Warren had blessed Leroy as the patriarch. After his ordination, Warren said that the time for choosing sides had come, adding, "There is only one side and that is the Lord's side." He warned of a coming conflict and recounted a conversation he'd had with God, in which God had said: "Verily I say unto you my servant Warren, my people have sinned a very grievous sin before me, in that they have raised up monuments to man and have not glorified me."

He told his followers to repent their idolatry lest God unleash a scourge to "purge the ungodly from among you." A few weeks earlier, on the fiftieth anniversary of the Short Creek raid, descendants of the prophets John Y. Barlow and LeRoy Johnson—some of whom were more sympathetic to Blackmore's leadership aspirations than to Warren's—had unveiled a monument inscribed with Uncle Roy's words that the polygamists' survival was "the greatest miracle of all time." Within days of Warren's denunciation of idolatry, the monument was destroyed. Three years later, in the same Colorado City park, Winston Blackmore unveiled another monument to the 1953 raid. It, too, was vandalized within days and destroyed within weeks, even though by then Warren Jeffs had not been seen for three years.

—

What Warren Jeffs hadn't told his followers at his ordination is that he had had a revelation that Short Creek was no longer the place from which the righteous would be lifted up. It wasn't Missouri either, as Joseph Smith had prophesied. Jeffs's search for the New Zion had begun in early 2003, soon after both Arizona and Utah had stepped up their investigations into the FLDS and the twin towns of Colorado City and Hildale. As FLDS lawyer Rodney Parker later explained, Jeffs was looking for a new "outpost and retreat" for about five hundred of the most righteous.

Establishing a new community would be expensive. But unlike Winston Blackmore, Jeffs was not strapped for cash. He began stripping the assets of the United Effort Plan Trust. He upped the special assessments. Some businessmen in Canada and the United States were asked for as much as US$15,000 a month in addition to their tithes. Those who couldn't meet the payments were stripped of their businesses and some subsequently lost wives, children and homes.

On October 3, 2003, David Steed Allred bought one hundred acres near Pringle—population 125—in the Black Hills of South Dakota. By spring, behind high walls and a guard tower, a twenty-bedroom, 7,200-square-foot log home was built, along with a smaller two-storey log garage with a loft apartment and a cellular phone booster antenna. The buildings looked just like what Jeffs's followers had built in Bountiful. Local people who asked Allred about the new owners' plans were told it was going to be a hunting lodge for executives. Harold Blackmore must have spun in whatever part of the heavenly kingdom he's in to hear them use the same hoary old excuse that they'd used to steal his property in Bountiful.

An FLDS guard tower in South Dakota. Local residents find the silhouettes of guard towers in the trees more menacing than spiritual. **(Photo courtesy of HOPE)**

In November, Allred bought 1,700 acres near another dot of a town called Eldorado, Texas. Population: 1,800. A pilot flying over the property in March 2004 reported to Schleicher County authorities that he had seen three unusually large buildings under construction. Again Allred said in response to questions that the owners were building a hunting lodge. But a couple of months later, when the local paper, the *Eldorado Success*, broke the news that fundamentalist Saints were ditching Short Creek and moving to Texas, Allred finally admitted that it was the site of a new community. In fact, Warren Jeffs had earlier ordered construction of the first fundamentalist Mormon temple there; the temple's design was to be based on Joseph Smith's temple, which the Mormons had been forced to abandon in Nauvoo, Illinois, in the 1880s. Randy Mankin, the *Success*'s editor and publisher, as well as the town's administrator and hospital board member, told the *Washington Post* that the arrival of the FLDS was "like a UFO [had] landed north of town."

Texans were highly sensitive to the Saints' arrival. In 1993, twenty law enforcement officers and seventy-five followers of cult leader David Koresh—including twenty-five children under the age of fifteen—were killed in a gun battle. Two government investigations into the incident determined that the FBI had provoked the shootout because agents failed to listen to the agency's behavioural experts, who warned against going into the compound. The reports recommended that both the FBI and the U.S. Justice Department needed to develop specific policies to deal with "unconventional groups," which is no doubt one of the reasons that the FBI did the premillennial Meggiddo Report on cults.

The *Success* has closely followed the construction at the armed and guarded site, which is called the YFZ Ranch. YFZ stands for Yearning for Zion. The paper posts frequent aerial-photo updates of the colony on its website, which illustrate the startling speed at which the Saints are working. Huge, prefabricated log houses were trucked in from Idaho and British Columbia—the largest house reportedly belonging to the prophet. The site has many other buildings, as well as a meeting house, rock quarry and grain silo. While legions of men did the construction, legions of women in pioneer dresses cleared the fields and planted crops. But what is most amazing is the temple. There are unconfirmed rumours that it contains a crematorium in the basement. Estimated to be ninety thousand square feet, it is larger than the new temple in Nauvoo that the Church of Jesus Christ of Latter-day Saints only completed in 2002 near the site of the original Mormon landmark.

Even after the Yearning for Zion ranch was under construction, Allred continued to buy land. On September 10, 2004, he got title to sixty acres in Mancos, Colorado (population 1,119), at the base of rugged mountains near Mesa Verde National Park. The site had a home, two cabins, a large metal shed and several ponds. Once again Allred told locals the owners were building a hunting retreat. Within weeks, construction crews had hauled in trailer-truckloads of supplies, including a satellite dish, solar panels and generators. Within the walled compound, two large log homes were built and the barn was turned into a dormitory-sized home. It was all done so secretively that Deputy County Assessor Scott Davis, a former bail bondsman, told the local paper, "He [Allred] was acting so strange I thought he had a meth lab in there."

One of the first people to be moved to Mancos was ninety-four-year-old Fred Jessop, the man who should have been prophet. It was done in secret. Not even his family was told where he had gone and, as a result, a missing persons report was filed by worried relatives in August 2004. The first news they had of his whereabouts was the report of his death on March 15, 2005, at Skyline Medical Center in Lone Tree, Colorado. Jessop, who had more than one hundred children and somewhere between fifteen and thirty-seven wives, was buried in Colorado City.

More than three thousand people attended his funeral. Others, including Winston Blackmore, were denied entry. "Many made an attempt to go to his funeral service," Blackmore reported in the *North Star*. "Macrae Oler [Bountiful bishop Jim Oler's brother] was stationed at the front door to identify those who came from above the 49th parallel that were not a part of the Warren Regime. When they were identified, [police officers] Sam Roundy and Willie Jessop went into action." According to Blackmore's account, people had their arms wrenched behind their backs as they were moved away, while others had "a keep sweet experience with Sam Roundy."

It must have been a bitter occasion for Blackmore, and not only because of the way he was treated. Except for Warren Jeffs, Winston Blackmore might have had it all. He could have been God's mouthpiece on earth—the prophet with absolute control of close to ten thousand people eager to do his every bidding, and unchallenged access to the US$110 million United Effort Plan trust.

—

FOURTEEN

BORDER BRIDES

The last two decades of the twentieth century were among the best of times to be a god in training. But they were trying times for unexalted Saints like Ruth Chatwin.* She said a final goodbye to her brother Craig a few weeks after her thirteenth birthday in 1999. Ruth was the seventh of Craig Chatwin's sisters sent north to become brides in Bountiful. Marsha and Zelpha were the first to go in 1995. Marsha had been seventeen and Zelpha was twenty when they married thirty-nine-year-old Winston Blackmore on the same day.

After that ceremony, Craig says the bishop of Bountiful had asked which sister wanted to have sex with him first, adding, "We are in the business of making babies." Zelpha pushed Marsha forward. "The next night it was Zelpha's turn," Craig told reporter John Dougherty in 2003. "That was the extent of their romance." Before Zelpha left for

---

*Ruth Chatwin is a pseudonym.

Winston Blackmore with American wives Edith Barlow, Marsha Chatwin (middle) and her sister Zelpha (right). The Chatwins married Blackmore the same day. One of his first questions was "who wants to have sex first?" (Glenn Baglo / Vancouver Sun)

Bountiful, Craig told her that, because Blackmore had so many wives, she'd probably spend less than three years of her life with him. A few months later, Zelpha wrote: "Craig, you were so wrong about what you said. I spend far less time with him. In reality, I'm married to the other women."

In 1999, at the age of thirteen, Ruth was driven north from Colorado City, across the world's longest undefended border, to Bountiful. She was too young to drive, too young to buy cigarettes or liquor. Yet a few days later, she was married in a celestial ceremony to Bishop Winston Blackmore's nephew. Even though Ruth was a first wife, the marriage was still illegal. She was too young to have been married without the written consent of a B.C. Supreme Court judge. And even though Canada's age of sexual consent is among the lowest in the developed world, Ruth was still too young to be deemed legally able to consent to intercourse. Urged on by religious leaders, her husband was a child-rapist.

"She was just a kid and assigned to marry someone in Canada," Craig told a reporter in 2004. "I haven't seen her since. She was just a kid and they married her to a guy who was 28." Ruth's husband wasn't twenty-eight, but he was in his late teens or early twenties.

In Rulon Jeffs's orgy of marrying and assigning child brides before the predicted millennial apocalypse, former members have accounted for more than fifty teenagers, including very young girls like Ruth, who were traded across the Canada–U.S. border so that "righteous men" could make their way into the celestial kingdom. In a bride exchange of unprecedented numbers, nineteen American girls were married to Blackmore alone. In exchange, Bountiful's bishop shipped dozens of daughters, nieces and granddaughters to Colorado City.

"Almost every girl I thought was the best student, Winston got. Or Warren. Or Rulon," Colorado City teacher Deloy Bateman told a reporter in 2001. "The leaders take the best girls. No overweight ones. None with family problems. The beauties, the virgins, the smart ones." When the girls returned home a year later with babies, Bateman said they'd shyly smile and tell him, "Winston said to me, 'We're in the business of making babies.'"

Lenore Holm raised the alarm in 1999, when her sixteen-year-old daughter, Nicole Knudsen, was assigned to a thirty-eight-year-old man with ten children. Lenore and Milton Holm were monogamous by choice, but they were FLDS and didn't oppose Nicole becoming the thirty-eight-year-old's second wife. What Lenore didn't want was Nicole getting married before she was eighteen. When she confronted Warren Jeffs, he agreed to delay the wedding on the condition that Nicole would live in his home, where she could be properly trained to be an obedient wife. Lenore found that to be a less than satisfying solution. As a means of getting Nicole out of Jeffs's grasp, Lenore wrote to Nicole's biological father, Paul Knudsen, transferring custody of Nicole to him.

Within an hour of Nicole's leaving for her father's home in LaVerkin, Utah, Milton Holm was ordered to appear before Jeffs. When he refused to divorce Lenore, Milton was stripped of his priesthood—excommunicated—for allowing his wife to rule over him. He was fired from his job. And because he was no longer deemed a member in good standing, the United Effort Plan's trustees began a court action to evict the Holms and their ten children from their home, which they had built on trust land. The Holms eventually won the right to remain in their home unless the UEP agreed to buy it from them at market rate.

Nicole stayed for a few weeks in LaVerkin before she ran away to Canada. Like many others before and since, Nicole got across the border without attracting any suspicion from the authorities, and moved into Winston Blackmore's home. Her mother filed a complaint with the RCMP. "I would like an investigation for rape of a child and I want to see the written paper trail that permitted immigration to allow an unsupervised juvenile into your country." She told *Province* newspaper reporter Fabian Dawson, "This is all about older men wanting young teens and church leaders getting their pick of the crop." Yet Lenore never once made a fuss about the fact that her daughter might end up in polygamy and, in the end, Nicole went back to Colorado City and married the thirty-eight-year-old man she'd been assigned to.

In the frantic process of trying to locate her daughter, however, Lenore mentioned to both the *Province* reporter and the RCMP that in 1998—a year before her sixteen-year-old daughter had disappeared—Nicole's classmate Lorraine Johnson had been assigned to marry Blackmore. Lenore's complaints sparked an investigation by the Utah attorney general's office. There's no indication that the RCMP or the B.C. attorney general's office did anything more than file it along with the hundreds of other missing persons reports received each year.

But Lenore's complaints prodded Winston Blackmore into responding. In October 2000, he invited local media to the Grade 2 classroom of Bountiful Elementary-Secondary School for his first-ever press conference. Flanked by four women from the community, he gave an "aw shucks, I'm just a simple farm boy" performance. He expressed wonderment that a reporter had come all the way from New York to inter- view him. "I can't imagine why anyone would come from New York to have an interview with me," he said. "I don't con- sider that I'm any more strange than people are in New York and no more strange than they are in the world in general. We don't feel like we're any better or any worse off."

The ninety-minute press conference was a classic example of what fundamentalist Saints have always been encouraged to do with outsiders: speak but don't speak. "I don't have any 15-year-old wives and I don't have any 16-year-old wives," Blackmore replied when asked about Lorraine Johnson, who was by then seventeen or maybe eighteen. "I'm not going to comment on my family life and I'm not going to comment on Lorraine Johnson because you should probably have a discus- sion with her." Of course, Lorraine was nowhere to be found. Blackmore may not have been lying—at that very moment none of his wives may have been fifteen or sixteen. But a few years later, Blackmore readily admitted that several of his wives had been fifteen and sixteen when he consummated his "marriages" with them.

The reason he'd called the reporters was to assert his belief that the practice of polygamy is fully protected by the

Winston Blackmore before ascending
to his roles as prophet, local potentate,
and husband to scores of wives.
(Photo courtesy of the Blackmore family)

Canadian Charter of Rights and Freedoms. It's the same Charter, he said, that protects gays, lesbians, common-law relationships and "unfaithful husbands," and "the same one that protects unfaithful everybodies."

He denied that there had been anything illegal in the way the American brides had entered Canada. "They present themselves to the Canadian customs and then at Canadian customs there are customs and immigration officers and those people let them into Canada, not me. They don't sneak across the border . . . Every under-age person that comes across here has a letter from their parents giving them permission to cross an international boundary and certainly has upon them photo identification."

But it soon became clear that very few of the brides immigrated legally. They had taken advantage of the provision that allows Americans to visit Canada for up to six months without applying for a visa, even though the brides had no intention of going home. Their visits to Bountiful were meant to last a lifetime. The job of Canadian immigration officials became more complicated after 1992. Officials were confounded by the B.C. government's failure to prosecute Blackmore and Dalmon Oler and that may be why the border service seemed reluctant to either stop the women and girls from entering or deport them once they were here.

Several women who had lived in Bountiful long enough to have borne five or more children each applied for landed immigrant status in the early 1990s. They were given the right to citizenship because of the children resulting from their illegal polygamous marriages. With that decision, the trickle of brides became a flood. In 1993, Blackmore had three wives. Four years later, "Uncle Wink" (as Blackmore is called by his admirers) had seven wives. By 2002, he had twenty-six wives—only seven of whom were Canadians—and close to ninety children born in Canada and entitled to both Canadian and U.S. citizenship.

In the security-tightening frenzy after the September 11, 2001, terrorist attacks on the United States, border guards had to pay more attention to everybody, including the oddly dressed young women going back and forth. But Immigration Canada may also have begun realizing the problems being created by its own contradictory policy of allowing the Saints' wives to stay in Canada on humanitarian grounds while routinely denying entry to the multiple brides of Muslims who had legally married in their homelands and taken the legal route to try to get into Canada.

In 2005, three of Blackmore's wives were ordered deported. Marsha and Zelpha Chatwin, the first of Craig Chatwin's sisters to be sent north, had their humanitarian and compassionate appeals denied, as did Edith Barlow. Among them, they had sixteen of Blackmore's children. In a last-ditch effort to have the deportation orders overturned, Blackmore tried to stir

*Elissa Wall was forced by
Warren Jeffs to marry her
nineteen-year-old cousin when
she was only fourteen.*
(Photo courtesy of Elissa Wall)

up public sympathy for the women and children. He held a
second press conference in May 2006 at his compound near
the entrance to Bountiful—just beyond the NO TRESPASSING
sign at the top of the road.

Among Blackmore's invited guests was Roger Hoole, the
Salt Lake City attorney who acts for the "Lost Boys" as well as
for Elissa Wall, who was the star witness in both Utah's and
Arizona's cases against Warren Jeffs for the forced marriage of
underage girls. Wall had been fourteen when Jeffs assigned
her to marry her nineteen-year-old first cousin.

Hoole expressed surprise that the Canadian government
would deport Blackmore's wives. Coming from Utah and a
member of the mainstream Mormon church, Hoole said he
found it confusing that Canada had legalized same-sex marriage a few months earlier, yet was willing to split up families

like Blackmore's. He contended, "The United States wouldn't do it." It seems that to Utahns, the definition of *family* is somewhat more expansive than it is in other parts of the developed world.

Hoole had arrived with Sam Brower, a Utah private investigator who works for him and for the Utah attorney general's office. Both Brower and Hoole said they had come to observe and support Blackmore, who they said had been very helpful in providing evidence for their civil cases and for the criminal cases being investigated by the state's attorney general's office. Blackmore had been so helpful that Hoole said Blackmore had been offered, but declined, immunity from prosecution in the state of Utah. It's a claim that Utah Attorney General Mark Shurtleff denies.

The pair was fulsome in their praise of Blackmore. "I wish everybody was as progressive as he [Blackmore] is," Hoole said. "In terms of the religious spectrum I see Warren Jeffs and those people's inability to think freely on one side and Winston and these people on the other because I think they're free to do that [think freely]."

Even though Hoole is fully aware that Blackmore has had a number of underaged brides and has underpaid his youth workforce, he went on to say: "I can tell you there is a big difference between a family like this [Blackmore's] and the abuse we're trying to correct [in the United States]. I see huge problems with Warren Jeffs and the way he compels people to do things and destroys families. I don't equate what is happening up here with what Warren Jeffs is doing."

While Hoole and Brower were being scrummed by reporters and anxiously trying to get away, Blackmore ignored the journalists and made a show of playing with his children for the assembled photographers and cameramen. Along with his wife Janelle Fischer (another likely candidate for deportation), he played on the wide gravelled parking lot with a handful of blonde daughters. Other blonde and blue-eyed daughters picked dandelions, forcing another delay in the start of the press conference while wives obeyed Winston's request and scurried off for a jar to place them in. Blackmore wanted the flowers on the table, where he sat flanked on his left by the three wives facing deportation and on his right by two other wives.

At the press conference, Blackmore picked up on Hoole's suggestion that Americans would never stand for such heartless deportations, noting that the U.S. chief consular officer in Vancouver had offered assistance to the wives and children. The consular officer said later that the Blackmore wives weren't getting any special favours. The consular staff was only fulfilling its mandated responsibility to help any Americans who get into legal trouble in Canada. Still, the deportation order prompted the U.S. consulate to dispatch passport officials to Bountiful the following year. They determined that as many as half of Bountiful's 1,200 residents were either American citizens or eligible for citizenship.

Blackmore and his wives painted a picture of their sixteen children wailing as they were torn from their mothers' arms by brutish Canadian Border Service guards and warned of a resulting backlash by tolerant Canadians. It was a scenario that didn't withstand scrutiny. Even if the wives were deported—which they eventually were—the children could go with them. They were entitled to American citizenship, after all. And they would not have to move very far: Blackmore and his companies own four acres of land—five lots with houses on them—in Porthill, less than a thousand yards from the Canada–U.S. border. Porthill is so close that his wives and children could practically walk to Bountiful from there every day to go to school and take part in the family's daily life. But Blackmore's wives said that couldn't possibly happen. Their husband couldn't bear to be separated from his children. What nobody said is that if the children went to the United States, Blackmore would lose out on a lot of money available from the Canadian government.

The Child Tax Benefit and the B.C. family bonus at the time amounted to $360 each month for every child; $5,760 for all sixteen children. If the children lived in the United States, they also wouldn't be covered by provincial medicare. And even if they were bused to Mormon Hills School, as American residents the children could not be counted for the school's per capita grants.

Conversely, had the women been allowed to stay in Canada as immigrants, it would have been an economic windfall for Blackmore. The wives would have been eligible for free health care, daycare subsidies, the Canada Pension Plan and the Old Age Security pension. Because none of the three women is legally married, they might also be eligible for welfare as single mothers.

No one challenged Immigration Canada's assessment that the women did not meet any of the requirements for legal immigration. All three women confirmed they had no special training that qualified them as skilled workers. None was well-enough educated to qualify for a student visa to attend college or university. And they could provide no evidence that their lives would be at risk if they went back to the United States, so they couldn't qualify as refugees. The best they could do was say that they would not be allowed to return to their families because they are now deemed apostates by Prophet Warren Jeffs and the FLDS.

The women admitted to having skirted the law for close to a decade by taking quick trips down to Utah every six months to visit family, which then reset the clock on their visitor's visas when they returned. "Literally thousands cross our borders each day from coast to coast on just the same conditions, for it is plainly known that you do not need printed documentation to be a visitor of less than six months," Blackmore wrote in the *North Star* that month. At the press conference, he likened his wives to "snowbirds"—Canadian retirees who spend winters in the warm southern states. Of course, he didn't bother to mention that it would be the very rarest of snowbirds who went south for a couple of months in the sun, became a plural wife and had half a dozen or more kids.

Oblivious to the fact that people can't move to Canada simply because they want to and that polygamy is a criminal offence, Marsha Chatwin asked plaintively: "Why would Canada want to deport us? I have never had a speeding ticket in my entire life. I have no criminal record and we have added to the Canadian population, 16 beautiful children . . . We raise our children to be respectful of people and their differences and we want them to be a valued part of the Canadian society."

Edith Barlow said she felt "hurt, betrayed and violated" by the immigration process and the interviews with immigration officials. One might have thought that would more aptly describe what it must have been like to have been a teenager when she was separated from her family and friends and sent north to marry a man nearly thirty years older than her.

A teary and distraught Zelpha Chatwin read a singsongy plea to Canadians to be compassionate. "Oh Canada don't break the hearts of our children, your children. Oh Canada, your children . . . have the right to be raised by their parents; the right to ethnic and cultural diversity and they have a right to be raised in the country of their birth."

The women railed against the Canadian government's "religious persecution" and "cultural genocide." Edith's sister Leah Barlow, who is also married to Blackmore, claimed fundamentalist Mormons have a "rich cultural heritage that adds to Canada's diverse tapestry." Yet, far from adding to the tapestry,

Winston Blackmore with one of his American-born wives, Leah Barlow, at the 2005 polygamy summit. Barlow is quick to claim that polygamy should be protected under Canada's Charter of Rights and Freedoms, even though the sect is unapologetically racist and homophobic.
(Ian Smith / Vancouver Sun)

God's Chosen, the Saints, pray for its destruction. They are anxiously awaiting the day that the rest of us will be cleansed off the earth in preparation for Christ's Second Coming. It's because of their contempt for and suspicion of the "tapestry" that their contact with mainstream society is limited.

They seem to despise almost everything about Canadian society, from its tolerance of divorce, abortion, homosexuality and birth control to its television, books, movies and even science. Their belief that government is a tool of the devil encourages them to flout the laws they disagree with (though they eagerly accept public money). Their teachings about blacks, and particularly Warren Jeffs's sermons about them being the "seed of Cain" and "uncouth or rude and filthy," not only run contrary to the letter and the spirit of the Canadian constitution, they have landed the FLDS on the U.S. Southern Poverty Law Center's list of hate groups, along with the Ku Klux Klan. None of which is a very helpful contribution to our "cultural tapestry."

Winston Blackmore and his wives wanted Canadians to believe they were victims of religious persecution, even though only a handful of the more than one thousand applications for entry to Canada on humanitarian and compassionate grounds are accepted each year. At the heart of their complaint is the belief that, in the name of religion, fundamentalist Mormons should be allowed to do exactly as they please. As if to prove this, Blackmore and his wives confidently cited this religious freedom as their constitutional right, guaranteed in the Canadian Charter of Rights and Freedoms.

But as it happened, a Supreme Court of Canada decision written by Chief Justice Beverley McLachlin just a few months earlier suggested that that is a highly debatable assertion—particularly when it comes to polygamy. Ironically, it was raised in a case that legalized swingers' sex clubs in the dissenting opinion written by Justices Michel Bastarache and Louis Lebel.

"According to contemporary Canadian social morality, acts such as child pornography, incest, polygamy and bestiality are unacceptable whether or nor they cause social harm," they wrote. "The community considers these acts to be harmful in themselves. Parliament enforces this social morality by enacting statutory norms in legislation such as the Criminal Code."

While in most cases evidence must be heard to establish harm, the chief justice said that some acts are by their very nature unacceptable—not just because individuals disapprove of them, but because they lead to "societal dysfunction or to the creation of a predisposition to anti-social conduct." Polygamy is one of those.

She quoted from a landmark 1985 Supreme Court of Canada decision that sets out the concept of religious freedom as "the right to entertain such religious beliefs as a person chooses, the right to declare religious beliefs openly and without fear of hindrance or reprisal and the right to manifest religious belief by worship and practice or by teaching and dissemination." But that 1985 decision went on to say that freedom is primarily characterized by "the absence of coercion or constraint" and that limits on *religious* freedom are "necessary to protect public safety, order, health or morals or the fundamental rights and freedoms of others."

The rulings suggest that the B.C. government had at least a fighting chance of convincing the courts in 1992 that the practice of polygamy is not protected by the constitutional right to freely follow one's religious beliefs. And what's a bit perturbing is that in other contexts, the B.C. government hasn't been at all squeamish about testing the limits of religious freedom. In the spring of 2005, the Ministry of Children and Family Development got a court order forcing a fourteen-year-old Jehovah's Witness to have a blood transfusion that was deemed necessary to treat her life-threatening cancer. It did it again, in 2007, to force transfusions on sextuplets born to Jehovah's Witnesses.

In the most recent ruling, B.C. Supreme Court Justice Mary Boyd determined that the court has the authority to protect the life and safety of children. She said that the right to freedom of religion is not absolute. Although people can't be denied their right to hold their beliefs, Boyd said, religious beliefs cannot override a person's Charter-guaranteed right to life and security of person.

"The preservation of the life of a child . . . is foremost," the judge wrote. "All children are entitled to be protected from abuse and harm . . . Ultimately, her [the child's] religious beliefs don't override her right to life and health."

And while the Supreme Court of Canada has singled out polygamy in other rulings as clearly anathema to Canadian society, for two decades or more, Canadian immigration officials have differentiated between polygamous Muslims and polygamous Mormons. Until recently, illegally arrived Saints have had their appeals on humanitarian and compassionate grounds granted, while the Federal Court of Canada has consistently upheld Immigration and Refugee Appeal Board rulings that deny polygamous Muslims entry to Canada, on the grounds that they will likely continue the practice in Canada, where it is illegal.

In 1995, Palestinian Bahig Mohamed Shaik Ali, his two wives and five children were denied entry. Ali had been living in Kuwait, where both marriages—the first in 1965 and the second in 1987—were legal. "There is no pretense by either the applicant or his two wives that they did not wish to continue the same family relationship they had in Kuwait," a federal court judge wrote in his 1998 ruling on the case. "There was no evidence of any intention by the applicant or either of his wives to divorce . . . The mere fact of the existence of polygamous marriages and legal marriages of the male applicant to two different spouses constitutes reasonable grounds to believe that the parties would be practising polygamy in Canada." And that alone, he said, is grounds for inadmissibility to Canada.

In a 1968 case involving a Muslim couple, an Ontario provincial court judge said that simply by stating an intention to move to a country where polygamy is illegal, immigrants choose to subject themselves to monogamy. His ruling was upheld by the appeal courts.

It's an odd twist on what Sir John A. Macdonald had promised in 1890, when he told Parliament, "Her Majesty has a good many British subjects who are Mohammedans, and if they came here we would be obliged to receive them; but whether they are Mohammedans or Mormons, when they come here they must obey the laws of Canada."

If fundamentalist Mormons are being discriminated against by Canadian immigration policies, it is in a way that is unlikely to cause Winston Blackmore much upset. Since 1993, when Canada was one of the first countries in the world to list rape, forced marriages, polygamy and genital mutilation as gender-based persecution and reasons for granting refugee status, Canada has not only granted refugee status to women fleeing forced polygamous marriages, it has deemed them in need of special assistance and has provided them with money and training to help them settle in Canada. Most have been Christians and have come from Africa.

No similar help has ever been offered to Canadian or American-born girls and women fleeing polygamous marriages forced upon them by their fundamentalist Mormon fathers or the groups' leaders.

In 2002, a federal court judge overturned the deportation of a Zimbabwean woman who had fled a polygamous marriage because the board failed to follow the 1993 gender guidelines. In 2006, another federal court judge similarly overturned another Immigration and Refugee Board decision to deny safe haven to a Nigerian woman. The board had found it "implausible" that Christians would practise polygamy. The two judges were apparently unaware that polygamy is widely practised in North America by fundamentalist Mormons who claim to be Christians.

In the first case, the judge ruled the refugee board was wrong when it said that it is "universally known that any Christian sect . . . does not permit marriage to more than one person and that a Christian man would not arrange a forced marriage for his only daughter to a considerably older man." It's not that the judge believed that polygamy is practised by Christians, which fundamentalist Mormons claim to be. Rather, he indicated that the board had failed to take into account "cultural differences in Zimbabwe and [had] imposed a *western* view of Christian practices in evaluating the applicant's allegations."

Winston Blackmore's news conference and the appeals of the wives had little effect. The wives left Canada, deported by the end of 2006, and are now living in Idaho. But by then, the immigration tribulations of Blackmore's wives had taken a bizarre and unexpected twist.

Five months after Canada legalized same-sex marriage in June 2005, two of Blackmore's celestial wives purchased a marriage licence from the B.C. government agent in Creston. On a Tuesday evening in December, Lorraine Johnson married Shalina Palmer. Both brides had been in their mid-teens when they were married to Blackmore in a religious, but not legal, ceremony. Lorraine Johnson had been only fifteen or sixteen when she was assigned to marry Blackmore. Shalina is a few years younger than Lorraine. She was born in Creston and was also only in her mid-teens when she married Blackmore a few years after Lorraine did. As the bishop of Bountiful's brides, the pair became fast friends. For several years now they have lived together in trailer on the outskirts of Cranbrook, where Blackmore's company manufactures poles and fence posts. Shalina works while Lorraine keeps house and looks after their nine or more children. Was it love that prompted the marriage? Or fear of deportation? Was it their choice? Or Winston Blackmore's sly calculation?

It seems implausible that two barely educated young women, struggling to raise so many children without daily help from their husband, would be so attuned to current events and changing public policy that they would have come up with the idea on their own. It seems impossible to believe Winston Blackmore's claim that he had nothing to do with the marriage and didn't even know about it until after it had taken place. RCMP officers, who were in the middle of an investigation into abuse and sexual exploitation, knew about the marriage within hours. So did B.C. Attorney General Wally Oppal.

Even if Blackmore hadn't known about it, how could the former FLDS bishop square the same-sex marriage with Mormon belief—fundamentalist *and* mainstream—that homosexuality is a sin? Even in the mainstream Church of Jesus Christ of Latter-day Saints, homosexuals are excommunicated. But in an email response to the question about homosexuality and his beliefs, Blackmore wrote: "I have some friends that are openly gay and I have decided a long time ago (say around 1986–87) that I was not going to be their judge in their private life. I also have many friends that live common law and I don't judge them either." Blackmore went on to say that the Canadian constitution protects the equality rights of homosexuals just as it guarantees religious freedom.

While the women's marriage surprised people in Creston, it shocked Saints on both sides of the border. It was one more reason for the FLDS to discredit the excommunicated bishop. Not only could Blackmore not control his wives, he now condoned homosexuality, which Prophet Warren Jeffs has called "the worst evil act you can do, next to murder. It is like murder. Whenever people commit that sin, then the Lord destroys them."

Until her same-sex marriage was reported in the media, Lorraine Johnson had stayed below immigration officials' radar. But, at some point, Immigration Canada may be forced to investigate whether she is legally in the country. And, if she is not, immigration officials will be asking Lorraine, and both her spouses, questions that are much more pointed than anything Edith Barlow was faced with. To claim the right to stay in Canada as the legal spouse of Shalina Palmer, Lorraine

Johnson will have to prove that their marriage is not an immigration dodge but an intimate, conjugal relationship that is sexually exclusive.

But, more important, their civil marriage dumped a huge mess into the laps of provincial and federal politicians. Wittingly or not, by marrying one another, the two young women linked polygamy and same-sex marriage in a way that no one—neither evangelical Christians opposing same-sex marriage nor gay-rights activists—could ever have imagined.

FIFTEEN

CALL TO ARMS

Politicians might have let the Saints coexist on the fringes, out of sight and out of mind, if it were not for the wild-eyed wackiness of polygamist Tom Green. According to the bearded, pot-bellied Green, in the late 1980s, he was awakened one morning in his decrepit trailer on an isolated tract of Utah desert by a voice telling him, "Don't hide your light under a bushel, but let your light so shine before men so that they will see your good words and glorify your Father in Heaven."

What Green says he did next was wake the wives and tell them that God wanted them to be an example of how plural marriage can work. With that, Tom and his five wives began to seek what was to be much more than just fifteen minutes of fame. "We just want people to realize that polygamists are not a threat, we are not fanatics, we are not criminals," Green told author Jon Krakauer.

Green had ties to people in both Short Creek and Bountiful. One of his wives had been married to FLDS prophet LeRoy

Johnson. Another of his wives and Green had honeymooned in Bountiful, B.C. But Green didn't follow the other prophets. He believed himself to be one.

Green and his family had been on trash-TV shows like the *Sally Jessy Raphael Show* in 1989, bragging about his bizarre family and his five wives, who included two pairs of mothers and daughters. Green made no secret of the fact that he'd married his one stepdaughter when she was only thirteen and he was thirty-seven. After that, the Greens were frequent fodder for the grocery-store tabloids and on other tabloid-TV talk shows like *Jerry Springer* and *Queen Latifah*. But it wasn't until 1999, when they were featured on the National Broadcasting Company's *Dateline* that their story caused a sensation in serious newspapers and other sober current events shows, and forced the attention of law enforcement.

Except for his revelation, Tom Green might have quietly lived his depraved life as a polygamist pedophile without interference. Unfortunately for him, his coming out in the mainstream media was badly timed. Salt Lake City was preparing for the 2002 Winter Olympics, and Utahns—especially Mormons, who make up the state's majority—were already extremely sensitive to the international media's focus on polygamy in the pre-Games coverage. The state was in full damage-control mode after the news had broken that bribes had been paid to secure the Games. But polygamy! It not only tarnished the state's reputation, it damaged the Church of Jesus Christ of Latter-day Saints' efforts to project itself as a modern, moderate and mainstream religion.

David O. Leavitt was one of millions who watched Green brag about his child brides on *Dateline*. Leavitt was the district attorney for Joab County, where Green and his family lived. As the media frenzy about the Greens grew, Leavitt felt he had little choice but to lay charges. Sex with a minor is a first-degree felony in Utah, with a minimum penalty of three years in jail and a maximum of life in prison. Both bigamy and polygamy are illegal, with polygamy specifically prohibited in the state's constitution.

In April 2000, Leavitt charged Green with rape of a minor and four counts of bigamy. But Joab County didn't have the money for what Leavitt knew would be a difficult and expensive prosecution, since none of Green's wives was likely to testify against him. Fortunately, he had a good connection in the state capitol; his older brother Mike was Utah's Republican governor. In November 2000, David Leavitt went to see Mark Shurtleff, who just been elected attorney general. He is another Republican, and had served as an LDS missionary before joining the navy and its Judge Advocate General's Corps. From Leavitt, Shurtleff began to understand why there hadn't been a single prosecution for polygamy or bigamy since Arizona's failed raid in 1953. Astonishingly, there were now about thirty-eight thousand polygamists living in and around Utah. The more Shurtleff learned, he says, the more difficulty he had sleeping at night. Polygamy was an uncomfortable topic for Shurtleff. Like 90 per cent of Utah legislators, Shurtleff is a devout Mormon. Like David and Mike Leavitt, Shurtleff's ancestors include Mormon pioneers and polygamists.

But the attorney general couldn't shake what David Leavitt and his own staff were telling him about young girls forced to marry old men, women treated like chattels, children denied the opportunity to go to school, and boys tossed out of the community like garbage. The rookie attorney general felt he had a duty to do something about it. But he concluded that, unless Utah taxpayers were prepared to build dozens and dozens of new prisons, there weren't enough jail cells to accommodate all of the polygamists. He decided not to go after polygamy, but after the other crimes polygamists commit, especially those against women and children. Shurtleff denies that this is tantamount to decriminalizing the only criminal offence specially forbidden by the state's constitution. If police and prosecutors have a good case with a strong witness, Shurtleff says he wouldn't shy from prosecuting either bigamy or polygamy. So far, the attorney general says that case hasn't come along.

Within a few weeks of taking office, Shurtleff appointed a full-time "closed communities" investigator, whose job was not to root out polygamy, but to search out rape and sexual abuse, as well as welfare fraud, tax evasion and any other violations involving the misappropriation of public money. During the 2001 sitting of the Utah legislature, Shurtleff shepherded through a "child bride" bill that toughened penalties for parents and others who forced girls under the age of eighteen to marry.

With the assistance of the attorney general's office, David Leavitt got the evidence he needed to convict Tom Green. Green, the father of twenty-nine, was convicted in 2001 on four counts of bigamy and one count of criminal non-support of his children and sentenced to five years in jail. In 2002, Leavitt made the unprecedented decision to rely solely on birth certificates of the mother and child—not victim testimony—to secure Green's conviction on a child-rape charge.

After serving six years in prison, fifty-nine-year-old Green was released on parole in August 2007. As a condition of his parole, he was to have contact only with his one legal wife and none with his other "celestial" wives. It's a condition that courts have imposed before on polygamists leaving jail, but one that's rarely obeyed. The parole board decided against other conditions, even though one of Green's ex-wives asked that Green be allowed only supervised visits with their children and be barred from sharing his religious views with them. She told the parole board, "When the state of Utah turns its back on him . . . he can influence my young children into a life of polygamy, which from my experience is a life filled with pain and agony and long-lasting social consequences."

The flurry of national and international media attention to polygamy and Tom Green's trial had scarcely died down when fourteen-year-old Elizabeth Smart was kidnapped from her bedroom in an upper-middle-class home in suburban Salt Lake City. Nine months later, in March 2003, she was found wandering the streets with self-proclaimed prophet Brian David Mitchell and his spiritual wife, Wanda Barzee. Smart was wearing a wig, sunglasses and veil. The details of what happened to the fourteen-year-old girl have never been made public because neither Mitchell nor Barzee was found fit to stand trial. But it was widely reported in Utah that Mitchell, another self-proclaimed fundamentalist prophet, had abducted the young girl to become his second wife.

Arizona's legislators also felt the heat from Tom Green's decision not to hide his light under a bushel. In August 2002, Arizona's Attorney General Terry Goddard and Shurtleff, his Utah counterpart, co-sponsored a "polygamy summit" in St. George, Utah. They invited polygamists, antipolygamists, law enforcement officers, social workers and the public to talk about what could or should be done. Winston Blackmore was one of the polygamists who showed up to hear Shurtleff and Goddard explain that they were unlikely to prosecute polygamists who didn't take child brides, abuse their wives and children or flaunt their lifestyle.

A few months later, Arizona charged Colorado City police officer Rodney Holm with bigamy and unlawful sex with a minor. As part of its investigation, Arizona's attorney general's staff compiled a list of more than forty teenaged girls it suspected had been coerced into polygamy. In the summer of 2003, a group called the Citizens' Coalition to Protect the Children had formed and quickly collected nearly five thousand signatures on petitions aimed at prodding the government into enforcing child-abuse laws. The group was based in Mohave County, which includes the town of Colorado City, and one of its members was county supervisor Buster Johnson. He wanted state and police to "put an end to this mess once and for all." The former cop told the *Arizona Republic*, "Maybe federal agents are going to have to go and knock on every door, collect birth certificates and do DNA testing. But we've got to get to the bottom of this situation."

State Senator Linda Binder, a Republican, joined the chorus. "I couldn't care less what consenting adults do with their lives in Colorado City. But we've got to stop the abuse of children and women," she told a reporter, adding, "There's enough abuse of government services like welfare fraud up there to cure the budget deficit. For every $1.14 we get from up there [in taxes], we deliver $8 in services." The "beast" had finally begun to realize it was bleeding.

A decade after virtually legalizing polygamy, the B.C. government was also being prodded into action by citizens outraged by what they were learning, not only from the American media but also from the Canadian media, about the polygamists living in southeastern British Columbia. In June 2002, Jancis Andrews was reading the *National Post* in the neat little drawing room of Jenny Wren Cottage in Sechelt on British Columbia's Sunshine Coast, two ferry rides and six hundred miles away from Bountiful. "'Word is out' Canada is a safe haven: Prosecutors fear any case would fail Charter of Rights test," the headline said.

The story went on to explain how fundamentalist Mormons

were fleeing to Canada to escape prosecution in Utah and Arizona, in the belief that since B.C. had decided not to prosecute polygamists, it was a safe haven for them. It quoted Debbie Oler Palmer saying that in the past few years at least forty-five teenaged girls had been shipped across the border to marry men in their forties. The story also quoted Joab county attorney David Leavitt. "No one ever looks at what happens to the women," he said "They never see the heartache or the inward soul of the women who are dragged into it."

Andrews couldn't believe what she was reading. That day, she fired an email off to federal Justice Minister Martin Cauchon demanding to know why the government assumed it would lose the case when the Canadian Charter of Rights states that women are men's equals. She sent a copy to Prime Minister Jean Chrétien and her local member of Parliament, John Reynolds. "With all the trust of a babe in arms, I waited for a reply, naively confident that the government would correct this wrong immediately," Andrews says.

While she waited, she began doing research. Even in her seventies, Andrews is a formidable campaigner. After the Second World War, she joined the Women's Royal Naval Service at eighteen and has never shied from a battle since. But she had more or less retired from social activism after a long, bitter—but successful—battle in the 1980s to get the B.C. government to stop Vancouver's Red Hot Video stores from distributing illegal tapes of women being raped.

The more Andrews read about Bountiful, the madder she got. In September, she went to the monthly meeting of the Sunshine Coast chapter of the Canadian Federation of University Women, armed with what she'd learned about the United Nations Convention on the Rights of the Child and its Convention on the Elimination of All Forms of Discrimination against Women (CEDAW). Bountiful was added to an agenda already filled with issues such as Middle East peace, pesticides and the dearth of women in politics.

Over home-baked cookies and tea, the women—mostly grandmothers—agreed that someone ought to defend the rights of the women and children in Bountiful. The Sechelt group began emailing, mailing and phoning politicians in Victoria and Ottawa. No one wrote to more of them, more often or more stridently than Andrews. Emboldened by Canada's ratification of CEDAW that October, the group wrote B.C. attorney general Geoff Plant in December, warning that if he didn't do something, they would take a complaint to the UN's human rights commission.

In mid-January 2003, the Canadian Broadcasting Company aired a television documentary called *The Bishop of Bountiful.* The documentary galvanized a new generation of journalists and inspired a burst of activism that had been so oddly absent a decade earlier. In the documentary, Winston Blackmore was smug, sanctimonious and sneering as he diverted interviewer Hana Gartner's questions about his bizarre living arrangements by lecturing her about how she ought to treat her husband. But he did admit to having more than one wife and to marrying some girls when they were only fifteen. Still, he was no Tom Green, no "peacock polygamist," as the *Salt Lake Tribune* had described Green as he flaunted his young wives.

What touched off the storm of outrage was Gartner's interview with Blackmore's gaunt-faced ex-wife Jane. It was not only revealing, it was painful to watch. Her flat, halting delivery contrasted sharply with Winston's braggadocio. Her haunted look only made what she had to say all the more searing, reinforcing the sense that she must be telling the truth.

When Gartner told her that Winston said no fourteen-year-old had ever been married, Jane lifted her eyebrows, turned her head to one side and laughed. "You mean Winston is lying?

He's not telling the truth?" Gartner asked. "Not in all instances, no," Jane replied with a wary smile. "It's not the truth."

Jane talked about what it had been like working as Bountiful's midwife. "There was this 15-year-old girl who was married and she became pregnant just very soon after she was married and she was crying and she didn't want to be married. She didn't want to be pregnant. She was 15 . . . This girl's mother was married to Winston . . . I said, 'Winston, weren't you supposed to be this girl's parent?' "

When Jane asked Winston why he had allowed the girl to be married so young, he told her to mind her own business. She was not the bishop. He was.

B.C.'s attorney general says he didn't see the disturbing documentary, but Plant soon began hearing a great deal about it and about Bountiful.

The summer before the CBC documentary was broadcast, Audrey Vance had been vacationing at Kootenay Lake, near Creston, when a windstorm sent a tree crashing through the roof of her R.V. The R.V. was destroyed, but seventy-one-year-old Vance miraculously survived with only minor injuries. She believed she had been spared for a reason. What that was, she had no idea until she saw Jane Blackmore's pain-etched face on television.

Vance has lived in Creston most of her life, raising her four children there. She has always been active in the community and had only recently retired as a school trustee. For years, all the pregnant young girls in long-skirted, long-sleeved dresses with their babies had troubled Vance. But she didn't want to make a fuss and break Creston's unspoken live-and-let-live rule, even though that attitude had led to some very strange things happening in Creston, from mass murders to a revolving door of cults.

After seeing Jane interviewed, Vance concluded that what was happening in Bountiful wasn't about religion, it was child abuse. That spring Vance went to hear Mary Mackert speak at the Baptist church about her experiences growing up in Colorado City, which she detailed in her book, *The Sixth of Seven Wives: Escape from Modern Day Polygamy*. Mackert was born in Short Creek and had been a plural wife for fourteen years before she fled. Within days of her escape, Mackert was abducted by men from the community, locked in a bedroom and threatened with blood atonement. What stuck with Vance from Mackert's presentation was her description of the fundamentalist Mormons as being no better than the Taliban.

At the end of the meeting, Vance made an announcement. Anyone interested in getting together to talk about what could be done about Bountiful could leave their names and phone numbers with her. If there was enough interest, Vance said, she'd organize a meeting. At that first meeting in January 2004, twenty women showed up. Linda Price was one of them.

When Price and her husband had moved to Creston from Calgary in 1999, she had never imagined that a polygamous community could exist in Canada. Like Vance, Price has a history of activism that includes spending three months as an "international accompanier" for Guatemalan refugees returning from Mexico in 1997. During those three months, she taught many of the widows to knit, a skill that would provide them with some income. Since then, she and her husband, Don, have gone back to Guatemala almost every year. While he helps build houses, she teaches knitting. In Creston, Price was co-chair of the Save Our Community Coalition, which was lobbying the provincial government to reverse its cuts to health care. Audrey Vance was on another committee that was trying to keep the government from closing the town's long-term care facility. They met at a joint meeting of those two

Since leaving Bountiful, Winston's ex-wife Jane Blackmore has become a powerful critic of the group and a source of hope and support for people fleeing the wreckage of polygamous families.
(Douglas Pizac / Associated Press)

groups, and Vance mentioned that she was organizing a meeting to talk about Bountiful. At that first meeting, Price and Vance were chosen to co-chair the unnamed group.

By the next meeting, in mid-February, the core group had shrunk to about ten women—again, mostly grandmothers. For the first few months, it was more like a book club than a lobby group. They assembled a library of books, statutes and the relevant Criminal Code sections and passed them along to one another. As part of the information gathering, Vance called Debbie Palmer and got in touch with Jancis Andrews and Jane Blackmore. Another woman in the group knew Lorna Blackmore, who eventually met with the group and joined.

Jane Blackmore met with them and filled in more gaps in their knowledge. They asked her what they could do to help. Her answer was clear. Focus on education, not polygamy.

Focus on the children, not the women. Jane told them that change was possible only if the children were allowed to get an education. The group soon had a name—Altering Destiny Through Education.

Vance quickly found out just how divisive the issue was in small-town Creston. People who used to stop and visit when she met them on the street now said hello and kept walking. Some women quietly told Vance they supported what she was doing, but couldn't join the group because their husbands did business with Blackmore or were friends of his. But she was determined to keep fighting to see whether something could be done to help Bountiful's young brides and their children.

Meanwhile, Andrews and the Sechelt group kept writing letters. They got in touch with the heads of the Anglican, Catholic and United churches, asking them to join the lobbying. In September 2003, the president of the B.C. conference of the United Church of Canada wrote to the B.C. attorney general expressing "profound concern for the welfare of young women and female children" in Bountiful. Anglican archbishop Michael Ingham also wrote to Plant urging the government to "enforce the law with respect to this commune."

In his letter to Ingham, Plant said that he'd asked the federal justice minister to consider amending the Criminal Code section on polygamy to ensure that a prosecution would not be contrary to the Charter of Rights. "Unfortunately, he has refused that request," Plant wrote. "This means if there was a prosecution of polygamy, there would have to be a determination of the constitutional validity of the Criminal Code section by the courts." That would require that "significant resources be expended by the police, Crown and court services, but also that witnesses, victims, the accused, their families and their communities would be put through considerable strain without any reasonable assurance that a conviction would result." B.C.'s attorney general closed with the bromide that the government remained concerned about the alleged offences against women and children, and if tangible complaints were received, they would be prosecuted just as they had been in the past. Just what would count as tangible is difficult to imagine, given the mountain of information, including the lists of underage brides that activists had provided to the RCMP.

The archbishop had sent copies of his letter to a number of people, including Merrill Palmer, the principal of Bountiful Elementary-Secondary School. In response, Palmer wrote a rambling, at times incoherent, three-page letter that was studded with biblical references and included a threat to sue the Anglican archbishop.

"Shame on you! As a man 'professing' to represent our Lord and Saviour, you do not have a monopoly on the interpretation of the truth or the character of God. And yet you have read or listened to some of these media-sponsored allegations and bold-faced lies about our community and you have felt compelled to act under the guise of your faith to attack our way of life. You would condemn our great Father Abraham and all the other biblical prophets who practiced polygamy as contemptible lunatics based on your lack of understanding?"

The school principal demanded to know what the archbishop wanted and cast the millionaire patriarchs as the victims. "What would make you happy, sir? To do as the state of Arizona attempted to do exactly 50 years ago? Put all the men in prison. Put the women in detention homes, adopt out all the children, burn and destroy all the Church records and books . . . Doesn't this sound an awful lot like something that a certain leader in Germany tried to do to a race of people in

World War II? I sense in your fear of our lifestyle that is what you would proscribe: Eliminating a people who you do not agree with."

Somehow Bountiful came to the attention of Oprah Winfrey. In October 2003, she mentioned it on her hugely popular television show, noting the B.C. government's failure to prosecute polygamy and uphold the rights of the women and children. Premier Gordon Campbell wrote back to the TV diva. Except for the signature at the bottom, the letter was almost identical to Plant's response to the archbishop.

By spring 2004, the activists had had enough of letter-writing and waiting for action. Jancis Andrews, Debbie Palmer, Audrey Vance, Linda Price and some unnamed women from Bountiful filed a complaint with the B.C. Human Rights Tribunal. They filed on April 1—April Fool's Day, Andrews bitterly noted three years later, when they were still waiting for their complaint to be heard. They accused the attorney general, the education minister, the women's services minister and the minister of children and family development of having failed to stop plural marriages in Bountiful.

They alleged the government had failed to protect teenaged girls who are "forced or coerced into marrying men old enough to be their father or grandfather." They accused the government of allowing open discrimination against women and girls. "Female children are groomed to be housewives, concubines and mothers," the complaint said. "Females are taught they are inferior to males and their role is to obey males."

Prodded by the activists, newspaper journalists started to comment on the issue in their columns and editorials. Radio talk-show hosts devoted hours to the issue. Several school boards in various parts of the province sent letters supporting

Altering Destiny's demands that something be done about the education Bountiful's children received. The B.C. Teachers Federation had a petition on its website. The National Council of Women passed a resolution at its annual meeting in May 2004 opposing polygamy, "the immigration and emigration of women and female children for sexual and breeding purposes; and the abuse of women and children in polygamous communities." It called on the Canadian government to enforce the antipolygamy law, to prevent the movement of women and girls across the border and to make certain that the constitutional guarantees of protection, freedom and equal rights are extended to women and female children in polygamous communities. And it called on all of its members to lobby politicians at all levels to draw attention to the issues.

The B.C. branch of the Canadian Federation of University Women passed a resolution as well that spring, asking the provincial government to enforce the antipolygamy law. It had been prompted by Jancis Andrews's initial interest. But, by the time it passed, Andrews had been long gone from the organization. It simply moved too slowly and had too many rules and regulations for her fiery nature.

The West Coast branch of the Legal Education and Action Fund (LEAF) began doing its own research. They organized a two-day consultation in December 2004 that included lawyers, activists and representatives from different religious communities, including the Muslim community, to determine what role, if any, LEAF might play. The fund's mandate is to advance women's equality in the law and to ensure that their rights are fulfilled in a substantive way.

In Cranbrook, Nora Mennie and her husband, Nick Ronaldson, had also started demanding answers from the government and from the giant forestry company Tembec. Ronaldson had been earning $27.50 an hour plus health and pension benefits when he was laid off. The contractor he worked for had been underbid by one of Winston Blackmore's companies. What Ronaldson, Mennie and others wanted to know is why the government refused to prosecute polygamists. But, more important, they wanted to know why a publicly traded company like Tembec was hiring lawbreakers when its corporate "guiding principles" are to uphold all laws and regulations and make a positive contribution to the community by supporting local employment.

Even the B.C. Civil Liberties Association, which had supported the government's decision not to prosecute in the 1990s, called for an investigation into the child brides.

Attorney General Geoff Plant was swamped with citizens and journalists asking "Why aren't you doing something?" The previous summer, at Mark Shurtleff's instigation, Plant had met with his Utah counterpart to talk about polygamy, Warren Jeffs and the split between Jeffs and Winston Blackmore that had divided Bountiful into two camps. Shurtleff left the meeting unimpressed. "He didn't seem to have much knowledge," Shurtleff said later of their hour-long meeting.

Unlike his Utah counterpart, Plant had no familial connections to polygamy. And unlike Shurtleff, Plant—who had been a corporate lawyer before entering politics—seemed largely unmoved by the allegations of child brides, assignment marriages or even polygamy. But it was becoming more and more obvious that the B.C. government would have to do something. There was too much media coverage, and too many letters and emails.

On June 14, 2004, Plant asked the RCMP to investigate all of the allegations of criminal conduct in Bountiful. But the attorney general's message was a muddled one, since he continued to insist that the antipolygamy law was unconstitutional.

Plant was also asking the RCMP to do the investigation without ponying up any additional money for the investigation. The RCMP took six months to appoint an inspector to run the investigation, and he was more than four hundred miles away, not in Creston.

One can only imagine what Plant was thinking that October when, intentionally or not, he sent a message that could only be encouraging to B.C.'s polygamists. More than fifty years after the B.C. government had rounded up the Doukhobor children from the Sons of Freedom sect and placed them in residential schools, Plant rose in the legislature to issue an official apology for having divided families from 1953 to 1959. He expressed the government's deep regret for what it had done to the Doukhobors. He didn't mention that parents who had their children taken away had been responsible for bombing and terrorizing the province for two decades.

The apology was welcomed by the children, who were now in their late fifties and older, but was not widely reported or analyzed. No one pointed out what author Simma Holt had concluded in her 1964 book, *Terror in the Name of God*. As traumatic as the breakup of those Doukhobor families was, Holt said, the educated sons and daughters of those Freedomites did not grow up to perpetuate their parents' reign of terror.

So the question was: If the government was sorry for that, what plan did it have for the children of Bountiful? Of course, nobody was answering questions about Bountiful anymore. Plant and his Cabinet colleagues had a perfect excuse now. There was an RCMP investigation underway.

—

SIXTEEN

LYING FOR THE LORD

The polygamists had learned as much about the power of the media as the politicians had. The followers may not have been allowed to watch, read or listen to the popular media, but the patriarchs like Winston Blackmore knew that when they needed to, they could really pull in a crowd. In 2003, with pressure building on politicians in both the United States and Canada to do something about polygamy, and with the RCMP investigating Bountiful, Blackmore began a public relations offensive.

He'd gone to St. George, Utah, in August 2002, and had met with both the Utah and Arizona attorneys general at the polygamy summit they'd sponsored. After that, he began ingratiating himself with Mark Shurtleff and the staff in the Utah attorney general's office, offering help to whoever might also be an enemy to his enemy, Warren Jeffs. He made himself useful to Salt Lake City attorney Roger Hoole and Joanne Suder, a Baltimore attorney whose firm has filed more than two hundred cases involving sexual abuse and Catholic priests. In the early 1980s, Suder came to public attention as one of the first lawyers to make the controversial recommendation to a judge that pedophiles and sexual predators ought to be chemically castrated if they are placed on probation or released from prison.

Suder and Hoole were gathering evidence for civil suits involving boys whom Jeffs had kicked out of Hildale and Colorado City. In July 2004, the lawyers set up shop for a week in the five-star Grand America Hotel in Salt Lake City, a hotel where staff guilelessly brag about the ballroom's spectacular chandeliers, which they say were plundered from Hitler's bunker. Blackmore checked in that week as well. So did both U.S. vice-president Dick Cheney and Taufo'ahau Tupou IV, the King of Tonga. (Coincidentally, polygamy is widespread in Tonga, an island nation in the South Pacific.) The lobby buzzed with an assortment of secret service agents, large black Pacific Islanders in expensive suits with earphones and microphones up their sleeves, and polygamists, past and present.

Hoole and Suder were interviewing anyone with information about Jeffs, the FLDS or the United Effort Plan. Blackmore wasn't the only one who showed up. Several dozen lost boys and runaway girls tearfully told their stories. Debbie Palmer was there. So was Arizona activist and former FLDS member Flora Jessop, along with two sixteen-year-olds, Fawn Broadbent and Fawn Holm, whom she had rescued eighteen months earlier. Carolyn Jessop was there, and so was Jon Krakauer, the author of *Under the Banner of Heaven*, a bestseller about the fundamentalist Mormons. Private investigator Sam Brower, who works with Hoole, was in the hotel. Former Colorado City sheriff Sam Roundy, the enforcer of the KEEP SWEET imperative made an appearance. But it's most likely he was there to intimidate rather than to help Hoole and Suder.

Blackmore was nowhere to be found at the end of the week when close to fifty lost boys and runaway girls held a news conference on the steps of the state legislature. They were there to mark the launch of the non-profit Diversity Foundation, which was raising money and looking for mentors to help dislocated children of polygamy. The foundation's patron is Dan Fischer, the dentist who had left the FLDS in 1992. The first two mentors to sign up were Krakauer and Utah attorney general Mark Shurtleff.

At the rally, the lost boys also announced that two civil suits would be filed against Warren Jeffs, the Fundamentalist Church of Jesus Christ of Latter Day Saints and the church's United Effort Plan Trust. The one filed on behalf of twenty-one-year-old Brent Jeffs claimed that from the time he was six and started school at Alta Academy, he had been repeatedly sodomized and sexually abused by his uncles—Warren Jeffs, Blaine Jeffs and Leslie Jeffs.

The other suit was filed on behalf of six young men who were named and twenty "John Does," who were collectively referred to as "the Lost Boys." They were suing Jeffs, the church, the UEP and twenty unnamed church officials for the "cruel, abusive and unlawful practice of reducing the surplus male population by systematically expelling young males from the FLDS communities in which they were born and raised." (Blackmore could well be included in that group of unnamed officials.) They claimed that Jeffs, the church and its elders had "purposefully and completely shielded them from the outside world and intentionally deprived them of the necessary skills, knowledge and education one would need to function in mainstream society."

The strategy of going after not only Jeffs but also the church and its trust is similar to what Suder did in suits involving Catholic priests. It's also the strategy the Southern Poverty

Law Center used after the Aryan Nations' security guards assaulted a pair of black motorists in 2000. The centre sued the group until it was bankrupt and eventually disbanded.

The Lost Boys' lawsuits received little attention in Canada and none in the local *Creston Valley Advance*. But that was no real surprise. The *Advance* also hadn't reported the B.C. attorney general's announcement in June that the RCMP would investigate Bountiful. What the local newspaper did publish that summer was an opinion piece by editor-in-chief Lorne Eckersley focused on "the hounds [who] are attacking the Bountiful and Mormon Hills communities." He conceded that there are "legitimate reasons to question what goes on in the FLDS communities." But he continued, "Plural marriages, high birthrates, questionable teaching practises, teen girls marrying, cross-border movement of members: they have all been an issue since we came to the Creston Valley in 1979 and they become issues about every five years, usually when some enterprising journalist from Vancouver decides the story has the potential to win an award for investigative reporting."

Contrary to what the Lost Boys' lawsuits claimed and to a growing international consensus that polygamy violates women's rights to be free from all forms of discrimination, Eckersley concluded that there is no need to do anything about polygamy because it is a "victimless crime."

Two days after Eckersley's piece appeared, Marlene Palmer—Blackmore's sister and the secretary for his companies—told the Canadian Press that the women of Bountiful were planning a media blitz to get the word out about how they freely choose polygamy and how happy they are with their choice. Within a few weeks, various journalists were invited to visit. Unfortunately for some of us who did, the welcome mat wasn't out.

When I went to the J. R. Blackmore & Sons' office at the scheduled time, Marlene refused to speak to me. Winston

Marlene Palmer shaking her pompoms on the day Winston Blackmore ducked an interview with the author. Palmer is Blackmore's sister and secretary. (**Ian Smith** / *Vancouver Sun*)

Blackmore was in his office, but he ducked out the back door after I refused to leave the office unless someone talked to me. Eventually Marlene and a few other women agreed to talk, but only after a number of whispered telephone conversations with, presumably, Blackmore. To illustrate just how "normal" the women of Bountiful are, Marlene agreed to be photographed at the local gym doing her usual routine—bouncing on a trampoline in her long dress and shaking cheerleader's pompoms.

But when it came time for the promised tour of Bountiful, there was no way. So *Vancouver Sun* photographer Ian Smith and I went on our own. For nearly an hour, as women and children ran away, hid in the bushes, scurried into houses or shouted insults at us, we were followed at a distance by Cherene Palmer—Marvin Palmer's widow and one of Blackmore's many wives. Eventually, Cherene invited us to her home, where she lived alone, and showed us photographs of her fourteen children and their families. (She has since moved out of the home she was so proud of, to make way for her son's family.)

That same summer, Duane and Susie Palmer filed a complaint with the B.C. Human Rights Tribunal against the B.C. Teachers Federation for its petition. Their complaint urged the government to do "an all-encompassing investigation into the community's independent schools" and "respond to the persistent and serious allegations of abuse." The Palmers were hardly objective observers. Susie Palmer, a teacher at Mormon Hills School, is Jane Blackmore's and Debbie Palmer's half-sister. Susie's brother is Jim Oler, Bountiful's FLDS bishop. Duane is the school's superintendent and Winston Blackmore's bishop in Bountiful. Among Duane's wives are two of Winston's sisters, Marlene and Miriam.

Meanwhile, Blackmore not only was being scrutinized by the RCMP, he and his companies were being audited by Revenue Canada. On October 19, 2004, the Federal Court of Canada ordered one of his companies—J. R. Blackmore & Sons—to pay $196,032 owing in income tax and another $73,395 owing in unpaid goods and services tax. And Revenue Canada charged 6 per cent interest for every day that any part of the $269,395 remained unpaid. It was June 2005 before the GST debt was repaid and April 2006 before the income tax was paid. The total—including the compounded interest—was never disclosed in court documents.

But there was more bad news for Bountiful. *Keep Sweet: Children of Polygamy* was published that year. It's a graphic and disturbing account of Debbie Palmer's childhood, co-written by Dave Perrin, a "gentile" veterinarian who was once married to a woman from Bountiful. It was a bestseller in British Columbia, although it was not readily available in Creston. Stores were afraid to stock it, fearing a boycott by the Bountiful Mormons.

Debbie Palmer was the keynote speaker in February 2005 at a Winnipeg conference on child brides and forced marriages sponsored by the non-profit group Beyond Borders. To intimidate her, and to rebut whatever she or any other activists might say about Bountiful, Blackmore dispatched two van-loads of women to drive across the Rockies and the Prairies, despite the risk of winter blizzards. It was minus thirty-one degrees Fahrenheit and the wind was howling when they showed up en masse wearing what one of the organizers described as their "Holly Hobby" dresses.

Half a dozen of them were Blackmore's wives—among them were Cherene Palmer and Marsha and Zelpha Chatwin. Marlene Palmer was also there. She had been Debbie's sister-wife when both were married to Marvin Palmer and had even testified against Marvin when he was on trial for sexual assault and abuse. Two of Debbie's half-sisters had been sent—Nola Oler and Susie Palmer, who had brought her fourteen-year-old daughter Pamela with her.

In addition to being there to challenge Debbie, Blackmore's surrogates were armed with orders to pledge support for Beyond Borders' long campaign to have Canada's age of sexual consent raised from fourteen to sixteen. (At four-teen, Canada's age of consent is among the lowest in the developed world.) The women also carried the message that Winston Blackmore's group would no longer allow girls to marry before their eighteenth birthdays. They almost imme-diately went back on their word. But it was a good strategy.

It was conciliatory and helped deflate Debbie's message that polygamous communities are inherently unresponsive, rigid, abusive and misogynist.

But, wittingly or not, Zelpha Chatwin stole the show. During the discussion, several of the Bountiful women contended that underage girls were so strong-willed that they could not be dissuaded from marrying much older men. They said parents and even the priesthood leaders were powerless against the wishes of these amorous young girls. Zelpha Chatwin put the lie to that when she blurted out that her husband had married several underage girls, including one who was only fifteen. She said Blackmore—the once powerful bishop of Bountiful, second in line to succeed the prophet—had no choice.

He was only following orders, she said, echoing the defence of miscreants through history. He was only doing his duty. He was only following the orders of his prophet and obeying what was purportedly the command of God. If he couldn't say no, how could a fifteen-year-old girl?

After the Winnipeg conference, Winston Blackmore got his wives to revive the Bountiful Women's Society and organize a polygamy summit for the spring of 2005 in Creston. Blackmore engaged the help of Principle Voices, a propolygamy group formed two years earlier by Anne Wilde and Mary Batchelor. At the height of the Tom Green media frenzy in 2000, the pair had published a book called *Voices in Harmony*, a compilation of essays written by one hundred women about their experience of polygamy. Although Wilde and Batchelor have literally become the principal voices speaking in favour of polygamy, neither is in a polygamous marriage. Wilde had been a plural wife until she was widowed, but now lives alone. Batchelor had been a second wife. But the first wife left when the attractive and much younger Batchelor joined the family.

The first wife was Vicky Prunty, who helped found Tapestry Against Polygamy in 1998 to raise awareness, in the lead-up to the 2000 Winter Olympics in Salt Lake City, of the "horrific" abuses within polygamous societies. Tapestry was established to fight statutory rape, underage marriages, trafficking of minors, neglect, domestic abuse and mental torture.

It's indicative of just how starkly different women's experiences in plural marriage can be that this one polygamous family generated both a strident apologist for and a powerful advocate against plural marriage. It's also interesting that Batchelor, the polished propolygamy activist, lives monogamously.

With the help of Principle Voices, the Bountiful women invited the attorneys general of British Columbia, Utah and Arizona; members of the B.C. and Idaho legislatures; the mayor of Creston; other municipal and regional government officials; local RCMP officers and the general public. None of the attorneys general attended.

Batchelor did what she could to help Blackmore and his wives upgrade their images. Bountiful is a century away from the public face of polygamy that Principle Voices promotes, and even a bit of an embarrassment. It said as much in its glossy magazine, *Mormon Focus: Exploring the Diversity of Mormon Culture*, which was handed out at the summit.

"Even though there has been a remarkable increase in population in Bountiful during the past decade, one still feels that he is going back in time when visiting this community," its profile of Bountiful said. "The women wear long dresses, have clean, long hair, and use little or no makeup, and many are pregnant with toddlers in tow."

The magazine featured Brent Davis, his three wives and twelve children from Salt Lake City. The Davises may well have been the model for the polygamous family on Home Box Office's television series *Big Love*, which premiered in 2006.

In the article, the Davises are depicted as the apex of American family values, with Brent the hero of their story.

By summit night, Blackmore's wives didn't quite measure up to the *Mormon Focus* cover-girl wives with their stylish hair-cuts and clothes. But most had come a long way from wearing pastel-coloured dresses, puff sleeves and swooped-up hair with braids. They were still conservatively dressed from neck to toe to wrist, but quite a few wore makeup. No doubt it was from Mary Kay, since several of Blackmore's American wives—unable to work in Canada—had recently signed up as beauty consultants for the door-to-door cosmetic company, whose phi-losophy is "faith first, family second and career third."

The women had not only prepared a PowerPoint presenta-tion, they had baked and laid out dozens of cookies and cinna-mon buns on a table at the entrance to the hall for the 350 or so people who attended. The parade of articulate, well-groomed wives spoke of their contentment and joy in their chosen "lifestyle." They spoke of the importance of family, the beauty of their culture and their constitutionally guaranteed rights to freedom of religion and freedom of association. The underlying message was the old polygamist adage: Better to have 25 per cent of a 100 per cent man than 100 per cent of a 25 per cent man. They didn't articulate exactly what made their men so special, but a scan of the polygamist men in the audience—some of them sitting with very young wives who bounced babies on their knees—suggested their appeal is more than skin deep; their talents are well hidden under plaid shirts and expansive bellies and behind the dulled eyes of yes-men.

Everything about the summit was aimed at enhancing the perception that Winston Blackmore wasn't scary and secre-tive like his rival, Warren Jeffs. Dressed in a dark blue suit, Blackmore was a modern polygamist, a businessman and a pillar of the community. He feigned the slightly puzzled air of a man unable to fully account for his great good fortune to have so many beautiful young wives—girls who had prayed to be married to him. He joked that he planned to write *Winston Blackmore's Guide to All You Need to Know about Women.* No doubt, he said, a willing publisher could be easily found. Playing the role of henpecked husband, Blackmore then asked whether anyone really believed that he could really keep all his wives in check. It was a clever move that elicited more than a few empathetic chuckles from monogamous men in the crowd.

It's always been the mantra of polygamists that polygamy is a burden that men have to carry, a challenge put before them by God. The men have always contended that it's women who are the beneficiaries because they have sister-wives all happily pitching in to keep a perfect house, raise perfect children and keep their man perfectly happy. As Brent Davis is quoted as saying in *Mormon Focus,* "You have to have Christ-like love to overcome your own selfish desires. Plural marriage forces you to focus on a spiritual lifestyle. If you judge everything through temporal eyes, you will fail . . . I can't be equal, but I can be fair. In setting the schedule, I treat my wives with consideration for the individuals that they are." It must be a great comfort to his wives to know that their husband's gracious recognition of their individuality is tied to the time of the month that they're ovulating.

Compared to the highly scripted and polished performance of the wives, Blackmore's keynote speech was rambling, often incoherent and slightly bizarre. He talked about taking his NHL hockey hero Bobby Orr bear-hunting. He likened himself to Pope Benedict. He disingenuously claimed that he hadn't known polygamy was illegal until 1990, when "the media came grouching around."

Near the end of his rambling monologue, Blackmore gave a revisionist version of the story of Noah's ark, a biblical metaphor for monogamy with God ordering Noah to load pairs of animals onto the ark before the Great Flood. Blackmore talked about "a whole herd of cats" coming off the ark. "You couldn't tell if they were loving or fighting . . . love happens in families in some of the strangest ways." Strange love indeed. In Blackmore's family it includes everything from marrying step-daughters and first cousins to becoming your own grand-mother. His speech ended with Rudyard Kipling's poem "If," an ode to Victorian values and manhood.

Blackmore then answered questions that had been vetted by Mary Batchelor. Blackmore was asked how many wives and children he had. He refused to say and could have left it at that. But the loquacious preacher couldn't stop himself. "I have married several very young girls in my life," Blackmore confessed. "That doesn't mean that the day after that all the things that you can imagine happened." He claimed he waited an appropriate length of time before having sex with the youngest, who was fifteen. Blackmore claimed the girls "went to the authorities over my head . . . I remember getting called to participate in that. That's the way it happened in our society. We had a change of thinking in the very early 1970s. We didn't know that we had a right to say if we had someone on our minds [to marry]. The first question is do you have someone in your mind. But it is not as much with someone in mind to marry as someone in mind who you definitely do not want to marry." There was more. "One girl was married one day short of her 15th birthday. She married my son . . . That's the youngest case that I know anything about."

He had confessed to having committed several criminal offences and knowing about at least one other. He did it in the presence of more than 350 people, including some politicians and police officers, who know that sex with minors is illegal in Canada and that it's a serious offence that could land the

Winston Blackmore expounding the advantages of plural wives at the 2005 polygamy summit he convened. Though he admitted in a room full of witnesses, including media and police, to having had sex with minors, he has never been charged.
(Ian Smith / Vancouver Sun)

older person in jail for up to ten years if he is in a position of trust, power or authority.

So, why did Blackmore say that? Was he seeking absolution? Does he really believe that it's a defence to say he was only following orders? Had he had a revelation like Tom Green to no longer hide his light under a bushel? Or was Winston Blackmore begging to be prosecuted? Central to fundamentalist Mormons' self-image—and even mainstream Mormons—is that they are a persecuted people. Misunderstood because of their claims to be God's Chosen, their history is studded with ill-treatment, beginning with the murder—or martyrdom, as they perceive it—of Joseph Smith. As Debbie Palmer says, fundamentalist leaders' credentials are burnished by a stint in jail. It proves to their followers that the devil—embodied by the government and police—believes that particular leader is worth going after.

The RCMP didn't arrest Blackmore that night. What one officer dressed in civvies did do that night was help escort a heckler out of the hall, after he went toe-to-toe with Creston Mayor Joe Snopek, demanding: "When are you going to clean up this mess?"

Blackmore's confession didn't elicit much reaction at all. Nobody gasped in surprise or horror. And there was no rising up of indignant and outraged citizens demanding that Blackmore be taken away in handcuffs. But why would they? Polygamy has been normalized in the Creston Valley. The sight of pregnant teens in polygamist dresses is so common that nobody notices any more. Between 1998 and 2004, the B.C. Vital Statistics Agency reported sixty-nine Bountiful girls were eighteen or younger when they had babies. A third of the girls were impregnated by men ten or more years older than them. Three-quarters of the girls were impregnated by men at least five years older. According to Vital Statistics, Bountiful's daughters are two to seven times more likely to get pregnant than teenaged girls anywhere else in the province.

Over the previous decade, more than half the New Year's babies born at Creston Hospital were children of the Saints. Ironically, given that their prophet had said the world would end on January 1, 2000, even the millennium baby was born to a couple of Saints.

Outside the hall, few people heard or read about Blackmore's confession. It wasn't widely reported, even though the summit was covered by journalists from all of the major national media outlets, several American television stations, German television and a wide selection of journalists from local and regional newspapers and radio and television stations. Why it was not widely reported isn't clear, since confessions of sexual misconduct by powerful men usually make sensational headlines. Why journalists chose to ignore Blackmore's revelation about his illegal and inappropriate behaviour is surprising. Journalists have not been squeamish about reporting on sexual misconduct by church leaders from almost every known Christian denomination or sexual abuse involving public school superintendents, principals and teachers. Maybe the novelty of polygamy was enough of a story. Maybe the government's own confusion about whether polygamy is illegal or just unusual played a role in their decisions.

But the result was that most media didn't have a story the next day saying that Canada's best-known polygamist had admitted to having sex with underage girls. What Canadians got on almost every national television and radio newscast and in every newspaper—save the *Vancouver Sun*, the Vancouver *Province* and CBC Radio—was a feature about how Blackmore's wives, children and close to eight hundred followers are perfectly happy with their polygamous lives and fed up with the hounding and "grouching" of the media.

The local *Cranbrook Townsman* pronounced the summit a "bravo performance," focusing its report on how the women of Bountiful had "turned the tables on their tormentors . . . striking at the critics." Midway through, it did quote one sentence from Blackmore's confession before returning to the theme that the women gave a spirited defence of their lifestyle.

The *National Post*, the *Globe and Mail* and the local *Creston Valley Advance* ignored the confession completely. A few weeks after the summit, the *Advance*'s new editor-in-chief, Brian Lawrence, claimed Blackmore had not said anything at all that night about taking underage girls as wives. He went to bat for the polygamists, recounting Marlene Palmers's claim

The twenty-first century or the nineteenth? Winston Blackmore has never been averse to exploiting the media value of his sect's greatest resource: children. He coached them to pose for the cameras at the polygamy summit in 2005 and again in 2006 when he called a news conference to decry the Canadian government's decision to deport three of his American wives, who had been illegally in Canada for close to a decade. (**Glenn Baglo / Vancouver Sun**)

that she had been called "the scum of the earth" at the local fitness club, where she liked to wave her pompoms. He lamented the ostracism of another woman who worked as a cashier at a local grocery store, who said that since all the negative media coverage, customers had been avoiding her till, preferring to stand in long line-ups rather than have her put though their groceries. "That shameful attitude is spreading beyond the Creston Valley, thanks to media sensationalism and anti-polygamy groups," Lawrence scolded.

Advance readers and most Canadians got the very message that Blackmore had wanted to send. Polygamists are just like everybody else. On summit day, he had opened Mormon

Hills School to the greedy eyes of the media. The children spent most of the day on the playground posing for photographers and videographers and providing quotes. Far from scattering like birds, as they did only a few months earlier, or taunting the outsiders, they chattered about their dreams of being rock stars, pilots and fashion designers and of travelling to Paris and New York. One little girl let the façade drop when she suddenly blurted, "Oh, I wasn't supposed to say that." But she hadn't revealed any deep secret. To all appearances, they were all healthy and happy looking—the little girls in their dresses and the boys in their J. R. Blackmore caps, jeans and long-sleeved shirts.

That evening, before the meeting began, teenaged boys and girls from Bountiful in jeans and long-sleeved shirts hung around the edges of the media scrums outside the Creston Recreation Centre, intimidated and attracted by the cameras and microphones. Their youthful good looks and energy provided a sharp contrast to elderly protesters from a local church who quietly carried signs with slogans like "Sex with children is called pedophilia, Religion does not change this," "God's Watching" and "One Man, 26 Wives, 100 Kids, Ungodly."

There was one bold girl who stepped in front of the cameras with her friend Pamela Palmer at her side. Cindy Blackmore, Winston Blackmore's sharp-tongued blonde and green-eyed fourteen-year-old niece, stormed into a room that Altering Destiny Through Education had rented and stuffed with posters and pamphlets denouncing polygamy and Blackmore. In her jeans, sweatshirt emblazoned with a beer manufacturer's slogan (WE ARE CANADIAN) and flip-flops that revealed her painted nails, Cindy went toe-to-toe with Audrey Vance, the co-chair. Vance, whose granddaughters are older than Cindy, was wearing a logoed t-shirt as well. Hers said: SILENCE GIVES CONSENT.

The *National Post* never printed Blackmore's confession, but it did run a large photo of Cindy with the protesters' signs behind her and a description of her confrontation with Vance. "Every time I come into town, I feel like everyone hates me. They treat me like I'm an alien or something. Well, guess what? I'm normal," she told Vance. According to the *Post's* story, an "elderly" woman shouted, "How many wives does your father have?"

"One," snapped Cindy. "My mother. And I'm not getting married for another ten years and no one can make me." Then she stormed outside. "Wow," said one of the other antipolygamists. "I've never seen anything like that in all my time here."

Winston Blackmore himself couldn't have written a more eloquent description of the new faces of polygamy than fearless, fresh-faced Cindy or her pixie-faced friend Pamela, who had her first taste of media exposure at the Winnipeg conference. The pair were the summit's poster girls, providing a compelling storyline: attractive, modern young women asserting their rights and standing up to a bunch of old fuddy-duddies from the church.

If journalists go back looking for those spirited poster girls, they'll find that they have changed. The day after her sixteenth birthday, Pamela Palmer married her nineteen-year-old cousin in a civil ceremony. Her mother, Susie Palmer, says her daughter begged to be married. But Susie, a teacher at Mormon Hills School, could have stopped it and should have stopped it. In British Columbia, sixteen-year-olds can marry only with the written consent of both parents.

Pamela, the quietly defiant young girl who'd worn a cute little bikini to the hotel swimming pool in Winnipeg, is a subdued wife. Since Pamela's husband began exercising his priesthood authority over her, she's retreated. She is finishing high school, but she's been told she can no longer speak to rebellious friends like Cindy. Pamela doesn't wear full-skirted, ankle-sweeping dresses like her mother does, but she still dresses conservatively. No bare arms or legs. When she's in a crowd of strangers, she holds her mother's hand.

Along with the other women from Bountiful, Susie Palmer had pledged at the Winnipeg summit that there would be no more child brides. She and the others promised that they would not allow these underage marriages, nor would Winston Blackmore. But Pamela's father—Blackmore's bishop and the superintendent of Mormon Hills School—must have signed his name to his daughter's marriage licence. Pamela's marriage showed the hollowness of the promises, the power-lessness of the mothers and wives and the mirage presented as reality at the polygamy summit. In 2007, Susie Palmer also left Bountiful and joined activists Debbie Palmer, Jancis Andrews, Jane Blackmore, Audrey Vance and Linda Price in their human rights tribunal complaint.

Even before the Winnipeg conference and her son's polygamy summit, Anna Mae Blackmore had expressed her concern about the ages of the brides. In 2003, she wrote to one of her hundreds of grandchildren, urging that teens wait until they are at least eighteen. "I have been so sad about the girls who got married and didn't know what they wanted. It is so sad to prove yourself foolish because you married too young . . . I'm so sorry I get carried away when I think of young marriages."

The real Bountiful is the one that Cindy Blackmore left in 2006. She didn't run away. She convinced her parents to let her go. With their consent, Cindy lives in the United States. Because she is still a minor, she has a guardian—Sara Hammon, the daughter of a former prophet who escaped from polygamy as a teen nearly twenty years ago. Cindy's blazing anger at outsiders is gone now; it's an anger she now admits was misplaced. All the time she was defending Bountiful and polygamy, she says she was desperate to leave. Cindy says that's the way it is for most people on their way out. That was certainly true for Ruth Lane.

Lane was Winston Blackmore's tenth wife. She was twenty-one when she moved from Arizona in 1995 to marry him. Like Cindy, Ruth is fierce. At the polygamy summit, she had cheekily answered on Blackmore's behalf when someone asked if women were treated equally. Women were more than equal, Ruth said. How could they not be? There are so many of them, the husbands have no choice but to do what they're told. After the summit, TV's *Dr. Phil* show flew Ruth to Los Angeles, where she told psychologist Phil McGraw and his audience how much she loved her polygamous lifestyle, her husband and her faith. "I have a great deal of love and respect for my husband. But I feel free to make my own choices," she said. Later, she'd angrily complained to some of the others interviewed for the show about how few of her comments had actually aired. In October 2005, she was featured in the Canadian edition of *Time* magazine along with her sister Diana, another of Blackmore's brides. "It's a lifestyle I chose. I wanted it," she was quoted as saying.

Ruth had been one of the most aggressive and outspoken members of the group that had been in Winnipeg and in Vancouver, when she and some of the women from Principle Voices had crashed a meeting that antipolygamy activists had organized with Utah attorney general Mark Shurtleff. At the 2006 news conference that Blackmore held to elicit sympathy for the wives who were being deported, Ruth was pregnant with her seventh child and staunchly defended her community as an important "cultural minority" within Canada's mosaic.

But, like the others, her final performance in Bountiful went unrecorded. A few months after the news conference, she left Bountiful and Canada without any intention of ever returning to live with Blackmore or practise polygamy again. She lives in Utah and has gone back to Bountiful a couple of times. In the summer of 2007, she was there for the Blackmore reunion with her seven children. She went back to Utah with only her baby; she left behind the other six with their father and her sister-wives. She had no way to support them all.

Ruth had been living in Canada legally on a student visa. But having seven children in eleven years and earning some spending money selling Mary Kay cosmetics didn't leave her much time to go to college. As a result, she didn't finish college. Ruth doesn't have the skills to do the kind of well-paid job a parent needs to raise seven children. Her pride may also be getting in the way of her asking for the kind of help she needs, say some other refugees from polygamy who have spoken to her. Leaving her children behind must have been a heart-breaking decision. Because of all the things she said, it was impossible to doubt her conviction that children must be protected from harm.

In spite of what those women and girls professed at the Creston polygamy summit, at other conferences and meetings and in interviews, polygamy didn't work for them and doesn't work for most women. Dozens of academic studies and books have noted for decades that women are hard-wired for the kind of intimacy that's impossible to find in a plural marriage.

International research overwhelmingly concludes that polygamy negatively affects the health of women. Researcher Alean al-Krenawi has studied Arab Islamic women and found that polygamous wives more commonly face family stress and mental health issues than monogamous wives, with the risk of psychiatric illness particularly acute for first or senior wives, who experience a sense of mourning or loss when their husbands take other wives. They suffer from feelings of failure and low self-esteem that are often reinforced within the family. Research work from other parts of the world indicates that none of that is unique to Arab or Islamic cultures.

It is also now widely accepted that the practice of polygamy is inconsistent with the Universal Declaration of Human Rights; the Convention on the Elimination of All Forms of Discrimination against Women, which guarantees the right to freely choose a spouse and enter into a marriage with free and full consent; and the International Covenant on Civil and Political Rights, which requires states to ensure both men and women have equal rights and responsibilities within marriage.

Four Canadian studies of polygamy and the law commissioned by the federal government came to that conclusion. In *Separate and Unequal: The Women and Children of Polygamy*, the Alberta Civil Liberties Association described Bountiful as "an authoritarian, theocratic culture where many individual rights are so limited that they have little or no meaning when measured against the bundle of rights and liberties that other Canadians enjoy . . . Polygamy as practised in Bountiful is harmful to children, women and society because it perpetuates a value system premised on the idea that women have no place in a community as fully equal citizens."

The libertarians noted that under Canadian and international law, there is a difference between a guarantee of religious *belief* and a guarantee of religious *practice*. And what the courts have determined is that religious practices can and should be outlawed if they cause harm to others.

Political scientist Tom Flanagan goes back to the simple arithmetic of polygamy and argues that the greater harm of polygamy may be to society itself. "As they [the surplus men] search for reproductive opportunities, they are likely to become criminals or to be hired as soldiers, militiamen or retainers of wealthy polygamists. The most likely result is a brutal society dominated by a warrior cult of violent masculinity—unpropitious conditions for democracy and the rule of law."

It's an ugly picture and it bears no resemblance to Winston Blackmore's chimera, just as Bountiful bears no resemblance to the Potemkin village that many politicians and others choose to see.

—

SEVENTEEN

FLDS UNDER SIEGE

L ori Chatwin sits on the steps of her Colorado City home and gazes out at the Vermilion Cliffs. Her skin seems impossibly white and delicate given the harsh desert sun. Her blue eyes are fierce. As we talk, a boy who looks no older than eight or nine drives by on a tractor with a flatbed trailer attached. A toddler stands on the trailer while the boy alternately speeds up and brakes, apparently trying to knock the baby over. It's a game, but a dangerous one that helps explain why there are so many graves in the nearby Babyland cemetery. Lori's own toddler plays behind the house in a mud puddle, watched over by a sister who is only a few years older. At one point, they both come careering around the corner, the baby covered head to toe with muddy red water.

Lori and her family are outcasts, shunned by most of the people who live here and by the eight thousand or so devout followers of Warren Jeffs. It's all because she stood up to the church and refused to do what she was told. When her husband, Ross, a building contractor, was told to move out of their church-owned house in January 2004, he refused. Lori was not listed on the eviction notice. She was ordered to leave Ross, take their six children and go to the bishop, William Jessop.

Had she left, Lori and the children—like the house— would have been reassigned to some other man. Instead of being Ross's first and only wife, Lori would have likely become a plural wife. Her children would have been urged to forget their father and call her new husband "Father." It's not that Lori objects to plural marriages. For the past couple of years, she has yearned for a sister-wife. Ross is often away working on construction jobs in St. George or Las Vegas, and Lori's weariness is palpable. A sister-wife would be a companion on the long, lonely nights in a community where she no longer feels entirely safe. Another woman could help out with all the housework that never seems to end with six children under the age of ten. A sister-wife could help with the child-minding, the garden-tending and the cooking and baking. That would free up some of Lori's time so she could do what she really loves. She proudly says that the dress she's wearing with its cowboy-fringed bodice is one of her own designs. Some day, Lori says, she'd maybe like to have a small business designing clothes for others.

It's hard not to empathize with her desire for another wife. How often have other North American women juggling family and career lamented, only half in jest, "I wish I had a wife!" Of course, what they're really saying is that they want someone else—their husband, perhaps—to do half the unpaid work at home. But if they can't get their husband to do an equal share of the family's unpaid work, there seems little chance that Lori or other fundamentalist women could convince their priesthood heads to pick up a mop or learn how to run the washing machine.

—

*Lori Chatwin and two daughters. Lori and
husband Ross became outcasts from the FLDS
when they disobeyed Warren Jeffs's orders,
which would have meant that she and her
children would be "assigned" to a new man.*
(Rick Wright / Vancouver Sun)

Around 6 a.m. on January 10, 2004, eight thousand men,
women and children were shaken out of their beds in
Colorado City and Hildale. They were told that Father
wanted them to fast for two days and pray every fifteen minutes. Nobody needed to be told that "Father" was FLDS
prophet Warren Jeffs. So, they hurriedly dressed and rushed
to join their families in prayers and readings of the scriptures.

The Sons of Helemon, the religious police, patrolled the
twin towns. The sheriff and his officers, all more loyal to
Jeffs than to the laws they'd sworn to uphold, didn't bother

knocking on doors as they began rounding up the twenty-one men whom the prophet planned to excommunicate and evict from the towns. Ross Chatwin was one of them, along with his brother Isaac Wyler, four of Warren Jeffs's brothers and some of the town's leaders, including Dan Barlow, who had been mayor for nineteen years.

Ross didn't really know why he had been rounded up with the others. But when they were asked to write a list of their sins, Ross and the others enumerated the ones they could think of, without any idea that the consequence of missing one or two would be the loss of their homes and families. When they were through, Jeffs took their lists and compared them to ones that he said had been dictated to him by God.

"My list of sins obviously did not match up with the list of sins Jeffs put together," Ross said a few weeks later during a news conference in front of his home. He had decided that his best defence against Jeffs, the FLDS and its trust was to speak to the media.

> James Zitting, a member within the FLDS organization, came to my home on Wednesday, the 14th [of January] and told me that he was sent to deliver a message as a trustee of the UEP [United Effort Plan trust]. He then told me to leave my home immediately.
>
> James said that he was doing what he was sent to do and that he wasn't there to philosophize or to listen to me. At the conclusion of the meeting I told him that I knew what I had to do. He answered, "Good, so let's get doing it." I want James Zitting to know that what I have to do is stand up to Warren Jeffs and to the UEP. My family and I do not plan on leaving our home anytime soon.

Ross told the assembled journalists that he hoped to be the first of many who would fight the prophet's order:

> Almost all the families in the society are really good and hard working people. They are just taught—brainwashed—from infancy to just trust, believe, follow like sheep and not to ask questions. If we don't understand something then we were told just put it on the shelf of beliefs.
>
> Well, I'm tired of being kept ignorant . . . We need your help to stop Warren S. Jeffs from destroying families, kicking us out of our homes, and marrying our children into some kind of political dollar brownie-point system. This Hitler-like dictator has got to be stopped before he ruins us all and this beautiful town.

Over the next few weeks and months, Jeffs excommunicated and expelled more than one hundred men, dividing up their wives and children among men he trusted. Some fled Colorado City and moved to places like Bonner's Ferry and Porthill in Idaho, to be close to Winston Blackmore, whose form of fundamentalism had begun to look much kinder and gentler next to that imposed by the increasingly erratic Jeffs. But the Chatwins decided to stay. "I love this place. I love these people. If it were just us, we would have left like the others," says Lori. "But we felt it was our mission to stay . . . There are a lot of good people here who have been misled and greatly abused. And it's all—in their minds—in an effort to become perfect. But until they recognize they are abused and misused, they will continue to empower Warren."

After the Chatwins decided to stay and fight, a few others refused eviction orders and several others returned to their homes. "It's been hard," says Lori. "This [the FLDS] was something I really believed. But the more restrictive Warren got, the more I thought it wasn't right."

Despite all that's happened, the Chatwins remain committed to their faith. Lori doesn't object to polygamy or all of the other things she's been taught. What she objected to was being told what to do. "To be under [prophet] Warren's rule is to have no freedom," she says. "I feel free now to choose my own actions and accept the responsibility for the consequences of those actions . . . Warren has made the public call for people to stand up if they were willing to give their lives for him and there are a percentage that would do that even without peer pressure."

Ross and Lori now get their spiritual guidance from Winston Blackmore, as do several other members of Ross's family, including his father, Marvin Wyler, and his brother Isaac, whose wife and four children left him after he was excommunicated. The Chatwins/Wylers and Blackmores are multiply related through marriage. Seven of Ross's sisters are married to men in Bountiful, including his sisters Marsha and Zelpha, who are Winston's wives, and a sister who was only thirteen when she married another Blackmore.

As painful as the excommunications and the dividing up of families have been, they provided the break that the Utah and Arizona attorneys general had hoped for. Slowly, informants and witnesses began coming forward. Arizona was better prepared than Utah to take advantage of it. Attorney General Terry Goddard, pushed by a group of twenty-seven legislators, had already provided money to Mohave County for an office in Colorado City, a special investigator and a child-protection-service worker. The office opened in the summer of 2004 and, a few months later, Gary Engels was on the job.

Engels is a fire hydrant of a man. He'd taken early retirement seven years earlier from the Bullhead, Arizona, police force after being wounded in a shootout. Working alone in a double-wide trailer that sits in plain view on a desert knoll, Engels is straight out of central casting as the Wild West sheriff. He's a modest, plain-spoken guy with a firm sense of right and wrong. "I took this job because I didn't think anyone else would do it. It takes somebody who is not scared off easily and I wanted to get back into investigating."

He's alone there. Up until 2006, all of the Colorado City police were FLDS members. In late 2006, a non-FLDS officer was hired. But even he says he doesn't entirely trust his co-workers. Engels's office is constantly watched. Engels keeps the blinds tightly closed and he peeks through them whenever a car drives up or there's a knock at the door. Until recently, his office was broken into and rifled through so regularly that the only things he leaves in it are some battered furniture, a phone and a phone book. Before Engels leaves his office, he straps on a small standard-issue handgun.

For the first couple of years, Engels was hassled all the time by Jeffs's youth militia, the Sons of Helemon, and by young FLDS guys trying to prove their mettle. The locals would routinely throw mud or rocks at his four-wheel-drive vehicle when he patrolled the Arizona side of the twin towns. If he turned to follow them, they would race across into Hildale because Engels has no jurisdiction in Utah. Now the FLDS are used to him, and leave him alone.

Still, it's too dangerous for him to live in Colorado City or Hildale. So, he keeps a place nearby. He won't say where his family lives, only that they are close enough that he can see them every weekend.

"I'm committed to trying to find if there is truth to any of the rumours," he says. "We know that by doing this we are making martyrs out of some people. I think Jeffs has done everything in his power to bring law enforcement here. But we have no choice in the matter."

In little more than a year on the job, Engels had gained the trust of people like the Chatwins, the Wylers and local historian Ben Bistline. He'd also gathered enough evidence to lay charges against Warren Jeffs and eight others for "sexual conduct with a minor" and conspiracy to commit sexual conduct with a minor. In June 2005, an Arizona grand jury indicted Jeffs and the others. Jeffs didn't show up for the hearing and, as a result, federal prosecutors in Arizona charged him with unlawful flight to avoid prosecution. Jeffs had rarely been seen in public since 2003 and, since the excommunications, only rarely in the twin towns.

In July 2005, the attorneys general of Utah and Arizona added to the sense of Wild West justice. They posted a US$10,000 reward for information leading to Jeffs's arrest. In August, the FBI posted the reward and Jeffs's photo on its "Ten Most Wanted" list, with a warning that he was dangerous and likely armed.

But it wasn't just Jeffs's arrest and prosecution that Arizona and Utah were after. Without the forced separation of church and civic institutions, the attorneys general believed Short Creek would remain a theocracy—a place outside the American mainstream, its laws and its values. They began retaking control. Utah revoked the certification of Police Chief Sam Roundy and Officer Vance Barlow in March 2005. During interviews with Arizona investigators, Roundy admitted to having two wives and Barlow admitted to having three wives and eighteen children.

Roundy also admitted that during his ten years on the job, he had never once notified child-welfare authorities of the approximately twenty-five sexual abuse cases he had investigated, including a recent one that involved the rape of an eight-year-old. "I didn't know I was supposed to, to be just frankly honest with ya," Roundy said in the interview, which was transcribed and released to reporters. "They said [it] was protocol, but I didn't even know about it . . . Maybe I've been in a Hicksville too long and not looking out at what's coming in."

Following Roundy's decertification, Fred Barlow was promoted to marshal even though he was blindly loyal to Warren Jeffs. He said as much in a letter to Jeffs dated October 2005 and found by the FBI in late 2006. "Dear Uncle Warren," Barlow wrote: "I fill [*sic*] that without priesthood I am nothing . . . I do not know exactly what we have ahead of us, but I do know that I and all the other officers have expressed our desire to stand with you and the priesthood." In his letter, Barlow went on to say that he was praying that God would protect the fugitive prophet and keep him from arrest. "I love you and acknowledge you as my priesthood head. And I know that you have the right to rule in all aspects of my live [*sic*]. I yearn to hear from you . . . Your servant Fred J. Barlow Jeffs."

A few months after Roundy and Vance Barlow lost their jobs, the local judge was disbarred. Walter Steed had been appointed to the municipal court by the Hildale city council in 1980. In a written ruling, the Utah Supreme Court concluded: "It is of little or no consequence that the judge may believe a criminal statute is constitutionally defective. A judge ignores the clearly stated criminal prohibitions of the law at his or her peril."

While the police decertification and the judge's disbarment were proceeding, Arizona attorney general Terry Goddard began staunching the flow of public money to Colorado City. The twin towns have guzzled millions of dollars in taxpayers' money through food stamps, welfare and grants that have been misappropriated to aid the leaders.

Goddard got a bill passed by the state legislature allowing the state to take control of elected school boards. The day after the law took effect in August 2005, Goddard went to court and had the Colorado City school district placed in receivership and the trustees removed for gross financial mismanagement. The FLDS trustees had squandered millions of dollars, including US$200,000 on a plane. In his first report, in December 2005, the receiver said the school district owed more than US$2 million and it had no way to repay it.

The plan to cut Prophet Warren Jeffs's access to money included both Goddard and Utah attorney general Mark Shurtleff going to a Utah court in spring 2005 to freeze the assets of the US$110-million United Effort Plan trust and replace the trustees with an independent receiver. Jeffs had been plundering the trust to pay for the new compounds being built in Texas, Colorado and South Dakota and to pay for his expenses while he was on the lam. Their decision to go after the trust was prompted by the Lost Boys' lawsuit. The attorneys general wanted to make sure that the interests of the other beneficiaries of the trust were represented and protected, since Jeffs and the other trustees had never responded to the various claims against it in the civil lawsuits. To do that, Judge Denise Lindberg had to parse both the law and the fundamentalist Saints' religion. That spring, she began what she called a "reformation"—a process that will still take many more years to complete.

Goddard and Shurtleff went to court together because the UEP's assets and beneficiaries are in both states. The trust also owns most of Bountiful's townsite, but British Columbia's newly appointed attorney general, Wally Oppal, was not a party to the court action. But that didn't mean that Oppal shared his predecessors' hands-off approach to Bountiful or polygamy.

The former B.C. Court of Appeal judge had been elected in the mid-May provincial election. Within weeks of becoming

B.C.'s top lawman, Oppal said he wasn't content to just sit back and do nothing. While prosecuting cases of sexual exploitation and abuse in the community was his priority, he said he wouldn't shy away from prosecuting polygamy as well. "It smacks of slavery, if there's no evidence of consent. There's no question about that. But we need evidence."

Even though Geoff Plant had initiated an RCMP investigation a year earlier, it would be a long time before Oppal had any evidence to look at. It was not until mid-September 2005 that the RCMP named two investigators to the file. It took another fifteen months before their investigation was completed.

With the UEP in receivership and the judge actively seeking new trustees, Winston Blackmore and his supporters hoped he would be among them. Blackmore's name was on the slate proposed by the Lost Boys' attorney, Roger Hoole. Also on Hoole's slate were Margaret Cooke, an interior designer who had left the FLDS more than a decade earlier; Carolyn Jessop (Harold Blackmore's granddaughter who had escaped with her eight children); two prominent businessmen from Centennial Park (which had splintered off from the FLDS nearly three decades earlier); and John Nielsen, one of the men Warren Jeffs had evicted.

Flora Jessop and her Child Protection Project also proposed a slate, which included Carolyn Jessop as well as Janet Johanson, the former plural wife whose niece is married to Winston Blackmore. But for Jessop and her group and many other activists, what was more important than getting their trustees appointed was making sure that Winston Blackmore was not.

In a petition filed with Lindberg, Jessop pointed out that Blackmore was under investigation in Canada for crimes similar to what Warren Jeffs was charged with. "Blackmore has raped under-age girls in the name of marriage, desecrating that institution so important to building solid community . . . When a man believes he can break the laws as he chooses and yet still asks this court to believe that he will be honourable in his dealings, it is a farce and an insult to this court."

She went on to say: "Blackmore could never be trusted to cooperate with the 'Beast' [as fundamentalists call the government], but would be engaged in solidifying his own base of polygamists once Warren is arrested."

In late August 2005, Winston Blackmore was in a lineup with a whole slew of lawyers, journalists, polygamists, antipolygamists, former polygamists, activists and prospective trustees waiting to go through the metal detectors at the entrance to Salt Lake City's Scott Matheson Courthouse. Judge Denise Lindberg was expected to pick the trustees that day who would eventually replace the court-appointed fiduciary, Bruce Wisan.

When it was Hoole's turn to speak, he told Lindberg that Blackmore "has been vilified in the press, he has the ability to affect hundreds of people in those communities." Hoole also noted that Blackmore had come to the hearing at his own expense.

The so-called vilification was the reporting of Jessop's affidavit and the close to one hundred letters sent to the judge about the former bishop of Bountiful—letters that were almost equally split between people supporting him and those opposing him. His supporters were mainly his family. But it wasn't just antipolygamy activists who opposed Blackmore. He was also the lightning rod for polygamists forced out of their homes nearly twenty years earlier, after Blackmore and the other trustees had amended the trust and taken away beneficiaries' security of tenure.

Blackmore himself was coy. He said he wouldn't mind being a trustee if it meant getting back the title to his father's property, property that he'd persuaded his mother to hand over twenty years earlier. But, he said, it would be a lot of work and would cost a lot of time and money to fly back and forth for meetings.

Blackmore sat next to John Nielsen in the courtroom. Nielsen had been evicted even though his father, Wendell Nielsen, is a close confidant of Warren Jeffs. Wendell is often described as Jeffs's enforcer and bodyguard, and sometimes as a possible successor to Jeffs. Wendell Nielsen ran Western Precision, a high-tech machine shop that manufactured components for everything from bicycles to military aircraft. It was once Colorado City's biggest employer. During the court recesses, Blackmore was surrounded by admirers, including Ross and Lori Chatwin.

Judge Lindberg didn't appoint any trustees that day. It was clear she was dealing with an unholy mess. It was a full year before she appointed six advisers—not trustees—to help the special fiduciary. Blackmore was not among the chosen, even though during the year he had met several times with Hoole, Wisan and Attorney General Mark Shurtleff. But Blackmore's friend John Nielsen was appointed, and so was Carolyn Jessop. Along with Wisan, they began the complicated process of determining who the beneficiaries were and figuring out how best to divide up the trust's assets.

In the end, the decision was to privatize the trust. That means all of the land in Arizona, Utah and British Columbia must be surveyed. Most of it has never been legally divided into lots, so the various municipal and regional governments will have to approve those subdivisions. So far the FLDS-controlled councils in Colorado City and Hildale have refused. Dividing the property in B.C. is even more complicated. Most of the land is in the Agricultural Land Reserve, a land bank intended to protect valuable farmland, and some of the houses were built illegally on that land.

On October 28, 2005, the Pueblo County sheriff's office got a call about 3 a.m. from a citizen reporting someone driving erratically on Interstate 25 in southern Colorado. A sheriff's deputy was dispatched. He found the van and pulled it over. In the van was Warren Jeffs's younger brother Seth Steed Jeffs, who had been "inspired" by the Lord to stand up after Rulon Jeffs's death and "reveal" that Warren was the true prophet. Also in the van was Warren's nephew Nathaniel Steed Allred. Seth Jeffs, thirty-two, was arrested after Allred, twenty-five, told police that his uncle had paid him US$5,000 for oral sex.

When the sheriffs realized who Seth Jeffs was, they got a search warrant for the van and found US$142,000 in cash, seven cellular phones, prepaid credit cards, phone cards and a glass jar labelled "Pennies for the Prophet," which was filled with coins. There were also piles of documents and hundreds of envelopes addressed to "The Prophet" and "Warren Jeffs." (The seized items were the subject of a subsequent court hearing, with Warren Jeffs's lawyers arguing that the FBI were not entitled to read or use the letters and documents in the other cases against the FLDS prophet.)

Seth Jeffs told the police he was "a messenger" for the FLDS church on his way to deliver the items to the FLDS compound in Eldorado, Texas. He told them that he knew his brother was a fugitive. Seth said he didn't know where Warren was hiding and that he had no intention of helping investigators find the fugitive prophet. Seth Jeffs was charged with harbouring, aiding and abetting a federal fugitive and freed after posting a US$25,000 bond. But what set the polygamy blogs across North America alight was the suggestion of illicit homosexual activity, even though Seth was never charged with procuring a prostitute and Allred was never charged with prostitution.

Seth Jeffs pled guilty and was sentenced in May 2006 to three years' probation for aiding and abetting the harbouring of his fugitive brother. He was also ordered to pay a US$2,500 fine and a US$100 special assessment that goes towards a victims-of-crime fund.

The circle was tightening around Warren Jeffs. In December 2005, a month after Seth Jeffs was arrested, Utah's attorney general Mark Shurtleff was in Vancouver. He'd come to take the measure of his new B.C. counterpart and get Oppal's agreement that the state and province would work more closely. Shurtleff brought the paperwork for an international arrest warrant for Warren Jeffs. The attorneys general signed reciprocal agreements to enforce court orders from each other's jurisdictions. These agreements cleared the way for Utah to subpoena witnesses from British Columbia and vice versa.

But even with their reciprocal agreements, which could force witnesses into court, Shurtleff told reporters that there was still no guarantee of a successful prosecution. He noted that Arizona had lost a case against a man charged with child sexual assault — the prosecution had birth records as proof — when his underage bride swore in court that she had impregnated herself with a turkey baster. "The FLDS, I tried to trust them," Shurtleff said. "But they are liars. They're taught it's okay to lie to people like me because we are the monster, the beast."

Still, Shurtleff made a point of meeting with women from Bountiful before his meeting with Oppal. Two of Blackmore's American wives, Leah Barlow and Ruth Lane, along with Anne Wilde and Mary Batchelor from Principle Voices of Polygamy, had breakfast with Shurtleff before his scheduled breakfast meeting with members of the Bountiful Roundtable, a coalition of women's groups. At the suggestion of Shurtleff's communications director, Paul Murphy, the Bountiful women then tried to crash Shurtleff's meeting with the Roundtable members. The Roundtable members refused to let the women join them for their meeting with Shurtleff, but they met with them later, after Shurtleff had gone off to meet with Oppal.

The attorneys general's meeting attracted a large crowd of journalists, including one sporting a newly minted press card. The journalist was Winston Blackmore, who had a business card that described him as a reporter for the *North Star*, his Internet newsletter. He didn't ask any questions during the scrum with the attorneys general. But he ended up answering quite a few. Blackmore didn't think much of the reciprocal agreements. Although he had initially volunteered information to Utah officials, now Blackmore and others could be forced to testify.

Blackmore hedged when he was asked whether he'd encourage other people to help the police find Warren Jeffs or help in prosecutions of domestic abuse or sexual exploitation. "I certainly wouldn't encourage them not to go forward," he said. "I have been accused for some many years of controlling people's lives, but I have no interest in being the conscience, mind or will of other people. So I'm not going to stand up in church and tell them what to do." Of course, Blackmore has never had any qualms about telling boys to quit school or girls to get married or demanding men pay 10 per cent in tithes from their meagre wages.

Although the attorneys general have agreed to work together, their approaches to the problems posed by polygamous communities are clearly very different, even though both said their primary concern is abuse in the communities, not polygamy itself. Their problems are also very different.

Shurtleff's office estimates that there are 38,000 polygamists living in and around Utah, although some activists estimate the number could be 100,000 or more. British Columbia has at least 1,200 and maybe as many as 2,500 polygamists. Shurtleff's state is dominated by Mormons; British Columbia is the most secular of the Canadian provinces and territories.

Shurtleff's efforts have been focused on appeasement and engagement of the polygamous communities, not prosecution. He established a "safety net committee" with members from various fundamentalist groups, as well as representatives from groups that work with the refugees from polygamy. Its goal is to provide education to stop domestic abuse and to offer access to services for victims from those closed communities. It's an odd goal for a committee funded by the state's top cop. It's also hard to measure the committee's success, because after two years membership had dwindled to only the polygamists, who seemed intent on using the committee as a platform to push for decriminalization.

Oppal is concerned only about legal remedies. But, unlike Shurtleff, who is reluctant to condemn polygamy both for practical reasons and because some of his ancestors practised it, Oppal calls polygamy "abhorrent" and says allegations that underage girls are forced to marry older men "smacks of slavery." He's not interested in appeasement or engagement, and he's left it to his Cabinet colleagues to deal with the victims, the schools or any other issues arising in Bountiful. Few people are more cognizant of the challenges of diversity and the balancing of religion, rights and values than Oppal is. Some of it is personal. Oppal is a Sikh, born in Canada to parents who emigrated from India. And he's also the province's multiculturalism minister.

There was no more tangible illustration of the difference of approach than what happened following Oppal's meeting with Shurtleff. Shurtleff commandeered Oppal's boardroom for a brief private meeting with Blackmore. When that ended, Blackmore tried to get in to see Oppal and was firmly told that the B.C. attorney general would not be meeting with him.

EIGHTEEN

THE ROAD TO PURGATORY

Nevada Highway Patrol officer Eddie Dutchover was not expecting to arrest one of the FBI's Ten Most Wanted men on a hot August night in 2006 when he pulled a red Cadillac Escalade over on a routine stop. Dutchover hadn't been able to see the numbers on the temporary licence for the Colorado-registered luxury sport-utility vehicle as it cruised north along Interstate 15, with the gaudy neon of Las Vegas behind it. So, he flipped on the cruiser's lights.

It was just after 9 p.m. when the driver, Isaac Jeffs, pulled the SUV off to the shoulder near the exit for what billboards claimed was the world's largest discount sex shop. Dutchover asked Isaac to step out of the vehicle. There were two other people in the car—a man in the front and a woman in the back. Dutchover asked the driver a few questions, but something about Isaac's answers just didn't seem right. After a few minutes with Isaac, Dutchover went around to the passenger side.

Warren Jeffs, the fugitive prophet, was sitting with a salad on his lap. He had been hiding for more than fourteen months, moving from state to state and occasionally venturing into Canada and Mexico. He had fled after an Arizona grand jury had indicted him on five counts of sexual conduct with a minor and one count of conspiracy to commit sexual misconduct with a minor. The charges related to his assigning underage girls to older men. His failure to appear to face the charges resulted in federal prosecutors charging him with unlawful flight.

After those initial charges in April 2006, Warren Jeffs was charged in Utah with two counts of being an accomplice to rape for his part in forcing a fourteen-year-old girl to marry her nineteen-year-old first cousin. When Jeffs didn't appear in court to enter a plea, the federal prosecutor added another unlawful flight charge. Then, rather astonishingly, in May 2006, Jeffs had been added to the FBI's Ten Most Wanted list, along with terrorist Osama bin Laden, drug lords and mobsters. Jeffs became the subject of the longest segment ever to run on the television show *America's Most Wanted*. Despite that, Dutchover didn't recognize the fugitive.

"He [Warren] was nervous. He didn't make eye contact with me. He was eating a salad, staring straight ahead," Ditchover told *Vancouver Sun* reporter Chantal Eustace. "It was even to a point where I asked him if everything was okay because he was extremely nervous. I even told him, 'You're making me nervous.'"

Dutchover asked his name. Jeffs replied, "John Finley," and dug out a drugstore receipt with that name on it. By that point, the prophet's artery was jumping in his neck. "It was just that nervousness; obviously there was some type of criminal activity afoot. We just didn't know what it was." Dutchover called for backup.

When two other officers arrived, he and one of them searched the Cadillac. The other talked to Isaac. By some fluke, the two officers responding to the backup call had stopped some of Jeffs's associates just a month earlier. They'd questioned them and let them go. With that still fresh in their minds, they couldn't help but think that the guy in the passenger seat looked a lot like the photo of Warren Jeffs on the FBI poster, where he was listed as possibly armed and dangerous. Suspicious about John Finley, they notified the FBI.

Meanwhile, Dutchover and the other officer had found a letter addressed to "President Warren Jeffs." In the luggage, they also found twenty-seven bundles of money—US$54,000 when it was all counted. There was another US$10,000 in gift cards, along with fourteen cell phones, a global positioning system, four portable radios, a police scanner, four computers, a dictating machine, recording devices, religious books and writings, a collection of sunglasses, three women's wigs and a photograph of Warren with his father, Rulon.

When the FBI arrived, an agent asked the passenger his name. "He said, 'Warren Steed Jeffs' just kind of like a sigh. He didn't seem upset," Dutchover said. "It was more like, he knew he was—he was caught."

It was an ignominious capture for one of America's Ten Most Wanted, especially after his months of choreographed movement throughout North America. Besides, it wasn't supposed to have happened at all. Jeffs had told his followers that God would never allow his capture. But it wasn't just the fact of his capture that was so disturbing to his followers. When the fugitive prophet was caught, there was proof of his hypocrisy.

His sport-utility vehicle was red—a colour he'd banned as too attention-grabbing and off-limits because it is the colour Christ will wear for his Second Coming. Worse, Jeffs, his brother and his wife Naomi were dressed like apostates. For years, even little children had been forced to conform to the rigid dress code that required men and women to be covered from neck to toe to wrist, with temple garments—the so-called holy underwear—underneath. Yet here was the prophet wearing a white short-sleeved T-shirt with a logo on it and cargo shorts. His brother was dressed similarly. And Naomi— one of Warren's favourites among his more than forty wives, who had also been one of his father's favourite wives—was wearing a bright pink short-sleeved T-shirt and tight jeans. Jeffs had recently excommunicated young men and disciplined young women for less brazen violations.

Police allowed the prophet to change his clothes before his arrest photo. It's an unusually flattering picture compared to the gaunt face on the wanted poster and the hollowed-out man who later appeared in court. Many of his followers refused to believe news reports that described what the trio had been wearing when they were arrested. They accused the police and reporters of making it up. But on the eve of Jeffs's preliminary hearing in December 2006, the highway patrol released a photo taken at the scene. The photo ran on the *Salt Lake Tribune*'s front page on the same morning that a dozen television trucks were parked next to the courthouse in St. George, Utah, and close to fifty journalists were milling about waiting for the doors to open.

Jeffs had waived an extradition hearing in Nevada—an odd protocol required in the United States—and was transported from Las Vegas to the aptly named Purgatory Correctional Facility in Utah, where he was held without bail. The attorneys general of Utah and Arizona agreed that Jeffs would be tried first in Utah, where the charges carry a higher penalty—from five years to life in prison—and then in Arizona. One of the odd things about the Utah charges was that even though Jeffs was being tried as an accomplice to rape, the alleged rapist was charged only after Jeffs's trial was over.

—

On the red cliffs behind the courthouse, police snipers, dressed in black with bulletproof vests, had taken up their posts long before Jeffs was driven in from Purgatory for his day in court. Two officers, who normally patrol the quiet town on bicycles, spent the day in a truck wearing bulletproof vests and holding semi-automatic weapons in their laps. More officers milled around in the crowd of journalists while they surveyed the growing line of people anxious to get one of the few unassigned spaces available in the courtroom. It wasn't clear who the authorities thought was in more danger—Jeffs or the prosecutors. It wasn't even clear where they thought the threat might come from—Jeffs's own people wanting to martyr him, someone seeking revenge or just some lunatic.

Inside the packed courthouse, the state's key witness, Elissa Wall, sat in the jury box with her two sisters and her lawyer, Roger Hoole. White-blonde and pale complexioned, the twenty-year-old was only weeks away from delivering her second child. Jeffs sat at the defence table flanked by his three lawyers—two from Utah and one from Nevada, where he was still fighting to regain control of the documents seized from the Cadillac Escalade.

The fifty-one-year-old prophet was not shackled at the wrists and ankles as he had been at previous court appearances, nor was he wearing his orange and white striped prison jumpsuit. He wore a dark grey suit, white shirt and tie. His jacket draped over his shoulders and bulged at his shoulder blades, suggesting that he too had on a bulletproof vest. He was almost morbidly thin. Looking past the two rows of journalists, Jeffs acknowledged his family and supporters with a hint of a smile and a nod before the proceedings began. They had all risen as one when the prophet entered the courtroom.

Because Jeffs hadn't been charged with rape itself, but with being an accomplice to the crime, the question of his guilt turned on a single point: would the rape have taken place if not for the Prophet's involvement? Since the crime for which Jeffs was facing justice was nothing more or less than the way the FLDS handles its most important theological activity—marriage—what was on trial was the sect's entire hierarchy of values and beliefs. Utah's case rested almost solely on the credibility of its star witness. That knowledge was almost as heavy a burden on the young woman as the stress of confronting her tormentor.

Elissa's sisters testified first, setting the scene. Rebecca Musser talked about growing up in Salt Lake City and attending Alta Academy, where Jeffs had been the principal and primary instructor in the importance of obedience and keeping sweet. Every morning, Jeffs had led the students in prayers and preached homilies. On Fridays, when boys went to work at unpaid construction jobs, Jeffs taught the girls how they could become mothers in Zion. He had told them that husbands are women's lifeline to God and the prophet, and that wives must never question their husband's decision, regardless of whether it was about what to eat for dinner or whether to have sexual intercourse. If men make a wrong decision, he told them, it is because their wives haven't prayed hard enough.

Sex education wasn't taught at Alta Academy. Girls were told that their husbands would instruct them when the time came, and both the boys and girls—like their Canadian cousins—were taught to treat the opposite sex as if they were snakes.

"We were told that God would talk to the prophet and tell him who that girl belonged to. Dating would cloud that revelation to the prophet because the girl had sinned," Rebecca explained, adding that they were told that courtship came after the wedding. So would love, if the wife prayed enough and was obedient and submissive.

Rebecca was one of the "blessed." When she was nineteen, Warren Jeffs performed the marriage ceremony that joined her to his eighty-six-year-old father, Rulon. That made her Warren's stepmother, even though she was nearly twenty years younger than him. Soon after their marriage, Rulon had a stroke and Warren excommunicated the girls' father, Lloyd Wall, who had been Rulon's business manager. Rebecca's mother, Sharon, and younger siblings were reassigned to Fred Jessop, the octogenarian patriarch who already had fifteen wives and more than one hundred children. Elissa was twelve and Jessop was now her priesthood head, the man she must obey as she would the prophet.

Two years later, in April 2001, Fred Jessop announced at a family gathering that God had revealed to the prophet that three of his daughters were to be married later that week. He didn't say which three, but it never occurred to fourteen-year-old Elissa that she might be one of them. Sure, she'd thought about marriage and having children. "It is the highest honour you can imagine. It's what we live for. It's our dream. It's what we're taught," she said in court. "But I was so young and I was scared. I trusted them, but I thought Uncle Fred [Jessop] had mistaken me for someone else because several girls were much older than me."

She went to Jessop. "Are you sure?" she asked. "I'm only fourteen. He told me to go and pray." When she asked Jessop whom she was to marry, he said it would be revealed at the time of the ceremony. As she prayed, her conviction grew that the marriage was a mistake. She again went to Jessop, this time to ask if the marriage could be delayed. She told him she needed time to grow up.

Naturally, her pleas meant nothing to a hierarchy that had only one answer to any of their followers' questions, especially those of a disoriented young girl: submit. Jessop sent her to Rulon, but the incapacitated prophet delivered her into the hands of his usurping son. The outcome was predictable. The scared, sobbing fourteen-year-old was married to her burly, naïve, FLDS-indoctrinated cousin in a brief, awkward cere-mony in a Nevada motel. When she balked at sex, she was raped. When she asked to be released from the marriage, she was sent back to her husband—and was raped again. This was how Elissa Wall spent her early teenage years.

Elissa was pregnant in November 2002 when she went to see Warren Jeffs again and asked for permission to leave her husband. She'd kept the pregnancy a secret from everyone, including her husband and Jeffs, who was now the prophet. Jeffs refused to dissolve the marriage, but he did agree to let her to go to Bountiful to visit her sister Teressa, who as a rebel-lious seventeen-year-old had been sent to Canada and forced to marry. Her groom was Roy Blackmore, a nephew of the then-bishop Winston Blackmore.

While Elissa was visiting, she began bleeding profusely. She had no medical insurance. The midwife, Jane Blackmore, did what she could, but Elissa had a miscarriage in 2003. Her recovery was slow. Elissa wanted to stay in Bountiful. But only a few weeks after the miscarriage, her hus-band ordered her to come home. She had no options and a few days later, the seventeen-year-old was on her way home to Hildale and the husband she loathed.

Jeffs's attorney, Tara Isaacson, picked holes in the testimony, getting Elissa to admit that she never directly told Jeffs or anyone else that she had been raped. Isaacson got into the record that the victim had filed a civil suit against Jeffs before she went to police with her claims of rape, and that Utah had paid for her to move to another city, paid her rent and paid her for lost wages. Isaacson tried to discredit Elissa's testimony by getting her to admit that she had a sexual relationship with another man while she was still married, and that when Elissa left her husband, the FLDS and Hildale, she was pregnant with the other man's baby. Elissa subsequently married the baby's father.

Isaacson was clearly satisfied with her cross-examination. As one reporter dryly commented, she'd all but high-fived her co-counsel, Walter Bugden. But it wasn't enough. In mid-December, 2006, Judge James Shumate ruled that there was sufficient evidence to go to trial. Outside the courthouse, Bugden and Isaacson issued a terse statement claiming that the trial was religious persecution. It was clear they would have to pull their own rabbit out of a hat at trial to counteract Elissa's confident, credible testimony. The expectation was that they would need to call her ex-husband, the alleged rapist to testify. The trial promised to be sensational. But between the preliminary hearing and the trial, the defense case nearly fell off the rails as the long days and nights in Purgatory took its toll on the prophet in his solitary cell.

Warren Jeffs began fasting in early January, refusing all food and liquids as he spent hours on end kneeling in prayer, so many hours that he developed ulcers on his knees. By mid-January, the already skeletal prophet, who is six feet, four-inches tall, had lost nearly thirty pounds and weighed only 130 pounds. He was receiving frequent visits from God. While he was in Purgatory, all of his conversations except those with his attorneys were recorded. And in those conversations, Jeffs was telling his family and followers that God had urged him to repent his sins and renounce his claims on the priesthood.

In a series rambling telephone conversations with an unknown person on January 24, Jeffs described himself as "a damned soul." He confessed to having "committed immoral acts with a sister and a daughter" when he was twenty years old. Who those women were, Jeffs didn't make clear. When his favourite wife, Naomi Jessop, came on the line a few minutes later, Jeffs repeated that he'd been "immoral with a sister and a daughter when I was younger." He told her that he had not held the priesthood since that time and ordered her to destroy all of his dictations, but not his revelations. He told Naomi she and all the other "ladies"—his wives—and their children needed to be rebaptized by the bishop, William Jessop. In another phone call that day, he ordered some members of his family to pack up and relocate and ordered the others to take their direction from presiding elder Merril Jessop.

The following day, Jeffs's brother Nephi was dispatched to Purgatory to check up on him by the bishop and presiding elder, who had also phoned Jeffs's lawyers expressing their concerns about Warren's mental health. They had asked the attorneys whether a doctor could be dispatched. But during his conversation, Nephi assured his brother "you're perfect in every way." A glass wall separated them as they spoke via the in-house jail telephone. The conversation was punctuated by pauses ranging anywhere from a minute or two to thirteen minutes. At one point, Warren hung up the phone and just sat mutely. Eventually, Jeffs told Nephi that God had offered him a compromise to mitigate his damnation: if he dictated a message to Nephi for his followers outlining his sins, he would be granted a place in the telestial kingdom, a realm that offers no glory in the afterlife (the Doctrine and Covenant 76 says its inhabitants include "liars, and sorcerers, and adulterers, and whoremongers, and whosever loves and makes a lie," who are "cast down to hell to suffer the wrath of Almighty God until the fullness of times when Christ shall have subdued all the enemies under his feet and shall have perfected his work"). But it is a step up from eternal annihilation.

Jeffs told his brother to take this message to his followers: "I am not the prophet. I never was the prophet and I have been deceived by the powers of evil. Brother William E. Jessop has been the prophet since Father's passing, since the passing of my father. And I have been the most wicked man in this dispensation in the eyes of God," he explained. "As far as I possibly can be, I am sorry from the bottom of my heart. And write this. The Lord, God of Heaven, came to my prison cell two days ago to test and detect me and he saw that I would rather defy him than obey him because of the weakness of my flesh. I am hesitating while I'm giving this message as the Lord dictates these words to my mind and heart."

Jeffs told Nephi that he yearned for people's forgiveness for his "aspiring and selfish way of life, in deceiving the elect, breaking the new and everlasting covenant and being the most wicked man on the face of the Earth in this last dispensation." Jeffs was in tears as he continued his instructions to Nephi, who tried to reassure his brother that this was simply God testing him. "You are the prophet," Nephi said. Before Nephi left, Warren's attention turned from the metaphysical to the decidedly mundane; he asked his brother if he wouldn't mind putting a little money in his account at the prison commissary. "We will not forsake you," Nephi replied.

As Nephi was about to leave, Warren said, "Just a minute. The Lord is still dictating. This is not a test. This is a revelation from the Lord God of Heaven through his former servant, who is never his servant . . . that you may know this is not a test. I say farewell again, to all who qualify for Zion. Farewell."

Three days later on January 28, Jeffs attempted to hang himself in his cell and was rushed to hospital. After he was returned to his cell, psychiatric consultants were brought in from Dixie Regional Medical Center as well as Southwest Mental Health Center. They described Jeffs as "somber and dull" and placed him on a suicide watch, which meant moving him to a cell adjacent to the booking area where the lights are left on. The psychiatric consultants determined that the suicide attempt was "a cry for help," and that Jeffs was experiencing "elective mutism as a sign of catatonia." Two days after the suicide attempt, Jeffs began throwing himself against the wall and was given Ativan to calm him down. On February 2, Jeffs started banging his head against the wall. He denied he was having hallucinations. He was anxious, he said. He was prescribed more antidepressants and a tranquilizer. Jeffs began to improve and by mid-February, contrary to the psychiatrists' orders, Jeffs discontinued the medications.

On March 27, he was back in Judge James Shumate's courtroom with his attorneys. They tried, but failed, to have the case quashed on the grounds that the charges were "unconstitutionally vague." The attorneys argued that the charges should be thrown out because the statute does not define the criminal offence with "sufficient definiteness that ordinary people can understand what conduct is prohibited and in a manner that does not encourage arbitrary and discriminatory enforcement."

They then tried, but failed, to have the trial moved to Salt Lake City. It would be would be impossible to get an impartial jury in southern Utah, they argued. As proof, they provided a poll they had commissioned that found that 52 per cent of the people surveyed in the county surrounding St. George believed Jeffs was "definitely guilty" and 23 per cent believed he was "probably guilty." Of the 628 people surveyed, the poll found,

94 per cent knew of the case from the news media and 78 per cent believed that what they had heard and read was true.

There was little news in the legal manoeuvring. What drew headlines was Jeffs's radically altered appearance. He was no longer gaunt; he was emaciated. His skull seemed almost visible beneath his tightly drawn skin. Jeffs fell asleep several times during the proceedings, at times even drooling on his fresh white shirt and dark suit. As the judge was getting ready to leave the courtroom, Jeffs suddenly stood up and raised one hand. "May I approach the bench? I need to just take care of one matter." Judge Shumate warned him to stay away, urging him to speak to his attorneys. Jeffs bent over and scribbled something on a piece of paper, which he feebly tore from the pad. Sheriffs' deputies swarmed around him and ordered the courtroom cleared.

His lawyers took the paper from him, but not before the pool photographer—a staffer from the *Deseret News*—had taken a number of photos. Those photos were later enlarged and the *News* and other media reported that what Jeffs had written was a confession. "I am not the Prophet" is the one phrase that they were able to make out.

His attorneys filed a motion a few days later asking the judge to order a competency hearing because their client "lacked the mental clarity to engage in meaningful conversation" with them. They described Jeffs as "detached, confused and unclear about everything transpiring in the court." In addition, they said he had difficulty standing.

The judge granted their request and two psychologists interviewed Jeffs to determine whether he was capable of understanding the court proceedings and the possible punishment he faced. They were also to determine whether Jeffs was capable of consulting and directing his lawyers. Both psychologists concluded that Jeffs was fit to stand trial. Eric Nielsen determined that he suffered from a "substantial mental illness." Nielsen said the most appropriate diagnosis was "depressive disorder NOS, which includes significant features of agitation and depression." The NOS stands for "not otherwise specified," a vague diagnosis at best.

The other evaluator, Tim Kockler, also concluded that Jeffs was suffering from an unspecified depressive disorder. But he wrote that it "does not appear to be negatively impacting the defendant's competency status." Kockler described Jeffs's intelligence as being in the "average to above average range." In explaining how he reached that conclusion, Kockler inadvertently reported another of Jeffs's hypocrisies. Although Jeffs had banned television from his community and had presided over schools that didn't teach current events or anything other than church history, the psychologist found that Jeffs was up to date. He was able to recite the names of the past four American presidents and correctly identify current news events before completing a test that also included interpreting a simple proverb, copying two geometric figures and following a simple, three-step command. And even though Jeffs had attempted to kill himself and had told his brother and others about God visiting his cell, Kockler wrote that Jeffs had not had any delusions, had not experienced any hallucinations and didn't consider himself "special."

So the prophet was not the prophet and mouthpiece of God. But if he didn't consider himself special, where did that leave his followers, who had been told both that Jeffs's incarceration was a sign of just how badly the Devil wanted to harm their powerful leader and that Jeffs was so special that his incarceration was God's way of protecting him from harm? And if Jeffs didn't believe he was the prophet or even a member of the priesthood, that tore a hole in his legal team's argument that Jeffs was a victim of religious persecution.

Jeffs and his attorneys were in a bit of a bind. Like the Wizard of Oz, Warren Jeffs was sane enough to know that when the curtain came down he was nothing more than a man and that what he'd been doing was wrong.

But even had the psychologists found Jeffs not mentally competent to go to trial, there is no provision in Utah for a defendant to be found not guilty by reason of insanity. In Utah, accused deemed not mentally competent are sent to psychiatric facilities and periodically tested to determine whether they have improved enough to stand trial. David Mitchell, another fundamentalist prophet, who abducted Elizabeth Smart to groom her as a second wife, undergoes just such a regimen of tests.

As a result of the psychologists' conclusions, the prophet went back to court in May. He'd gained weight by then and seemed alert. He smiled and waved to his friends and family in the courtroom. Judge Shumate set the trial date for September.

While Jeffs was struggling with his demons in February, the U.S. Supreme Court denied Rodney Holm's request to have his bigamy conviction overturned on constitutional grounds. Holm was a thirty-two-year-old Hildale police officer when he married his wife's sixteen-year-old sister in a religious cere-mony performed by Warren's father, Rulon. The bride, Ruth Stubbs, was in Grade 6 when she was forced to become Holm's third wife. She had wanted to marry a young, single FLDS man. But Rulon said no and ordered her to marry Holm instead. According to Assistant Utah attorney general Laura Dupaix's brief filed to the high court, Holm and Ruth "consummated their marriage on their wedding day."

The U.S. Supreme Court's refusal to hear the Holm case validated the Utah Supreme Court's ruling that constitutional guarantees of religious freedom do not shield polygamous practices from state prosecution. One might have thought that would open the floodgates to prosecutions. But, so far, Utah hasn't laid a single charge.

Still, Utah attorney general Mark Shurtleff was on a roll. With Jeffs in a Utah jail, Shurtleff had been on every national newscast in the lead-up to the preliminary hearing and frequently after that with each twist in the story.

The prophet's legal problems were good news for Winston Blackmore, who was still making frequent trips to Utah and courtesy visits to Hoole, the Crown prosecutors and Bruce Wisan, the special fiduciary who was getting ready to divide up the United Effort Plan trust. The only place Blackmore had not been spotted was in the St. George courthouse.

Of course, Blackmore was still expecting the RCMP to knock at his door with an arrest warrant. Officers had interviewed his wives, taken boxes of files from the midwife's clinic and DNA samples from almost everyone in Bountiful. It's not that Blackmore was worried. He may not have been eager to have to pay the high cost of mounting a legal defense. But he seemed ready for a chance to finally get his day in court and a chance to proclaim his constitutional rights, because even if it meant a stint in jail, that could only polish his credentials as a martyr for the cause.

NINETEEN

WHOSE RIGHTS?

During U.S. National Victims' Rights Week in April 2007, the Utah and Arizona attorneys general held a daylong session to provide social workers, law enforcement officers and government lawyers with tools to help victims in "isolated, authoritarian groups." That's the politically correct code in Utah and Arizona for polygamists, which encompasses the FLDS, Winston Blackmore and his followers and dozens of other discrete polygamous groups.

Paul Murphy, the communications director for Utah attorney general Mark Shurtleff, opened the session with a shocking, inaccurate and ridiculous analogy. He likened the 1953 raid on Short Creek that resulted in the arrests of two hundred men and the separation of mothers from their children to the Holocaust. The raid has taken on iconic significance to the Saints, but it was far from genocide. It was a police action taken against lawbreakers in which not a single person died. And, if anything, the raid improved the lives of polygamists. It strengthened the resolve of fundamentalist

Mormons to continue their lawless ways, and frightened politicians so badly that Murphy and his boss still feel compelled to tread gently.

Murphy noted that Utah had a two-track approach to polygamy: prosecuting polygamists who marry underage girls or abuse their wives and children, while engaging, integrating and providing services for "law-abiding" polygamists—which assumes that there is such a thing as a law-abiding lawbreaker. Since Utah's recent prosecutions have amounted to a single one—Warren Jeffs—the focus is clearly on what in international circles would be referred to as "constructive engagement," which amounts to lots of talk and lots of money thrown around in the hope that the other party will change by osmosis. While Murphy spoke about how the "safety net committee" was helping polygamous communities, he didn't dwell on the consequences of normalizing and, in effect, legalizing polygamy's practice. That was left to Deputy Darrell Cashin of the Washington County sheriff's office.

Cashin is the only one of four sheriffs patrolling Hildale and Colorado City who is not a member of the FLDS. All of the others either believe in or practise polygamy. He isn't concerned that they are the people backing him up on routine calls. "But," he says, "on a serious incident involving a prominent citizen of their community, I wouldn't let them get behind me . . . We have some trust issues."

When Cashin started working there in November 2006, children ran away from his patrol truck. People avoided him; no one would answer the door when he tried to serve legal papers. "They told me not to take it personally. People are afraid." What they are afraid of is the scenario that they have been programmed to fear.

It goes something like this. Men wearing badges and carrying guns break open the door of a home while a man's wives are cooking breakfast and his kids are just waking up. There is yelling and crying. The wives and children are lined up outside and have their photos taken as they hold a card with numbers on it. Then they are herded into a chicken coop and a door is closed behind them. This is the last memory that a man has of his family, until he is released from jail two years later.

Cashin said he didn't know if the story was true, though it echoes what happened in 1953. That doesn't really matter. What matters is that the polygamists believe it and the story has become their leitmotif of persecution and fear. It animates not only their actions but also their belief in who and what they are. As Canadian communications theorist Marshall McLuhan noted, "Only the vanquished remember history."

The deputy sheriff said he "doesn't subscribe either for or against polygamy . . . There are those in higher positions than I'm in that make decisions that direct the prosecutions and policies toward polygamy." But what his experience has taught him is that "the only way to be fair is to hold fast to the laws already set forth by our legislatures, to obey and enforce court orders in place, to follow the police officer code of ethics and to uphold the state's and U.S. constitutions."

Social worker Livia Bardin, a cult expert who led the day's training, has studied the fundamentalist Saints and has no doubt that they are persecuted. It's why they've formed closed and isolated communities and are afraid to seek outside help. But what should be done about it? Like Cashin, she is uncomfortable with governments cherry-picking which laws to enforce since that approach offers no safety to polygamists. As long as polygamy is illegal, the amnesty could end suddenly and without warning.

Mark Shurtleff said as much that night at a town hall meeting after LeAnn Timpson, a high-school principal and plural wife, likened the polygamists' struggle for recognition with

Martin Luther King's freedom marches. Quoting from the Church of Jesus Christ of Latter-day Saints' profession of beliefs, which the fundamentalists also use, she said, "I believe in being subject to kings, presidents, rulers and magistrates and in obeying, honoring and sustaining the law. But I hope to defeat this unjust law [against polygamy] . . . I am practising civil disobedience [as a polygamist]. I am committed to changing the law. I am not engaged in a criminal act."

Shurtleff curtly responded that lobbying to change a law is fully within her right. Until then, he reminded her, polygamy is a criminal offence, albeit one that he has so far chosen not to prosecute.

But is it right for countries, provinces or states not to enforce laws out of some perverse notion of tolerance?

No, was the unanimous conclusion of three studies on polygamy commissioned in 2005 by Status of Women Canada. The studies focused not only on fundamentalist Mormons but also on Muslims. While estimates of the number of polygamous Saints in the United States range wildly from 38,000 to one million, there are probably fewer than a couple of thousand in Canada; this compares with 580,000 Muslims, or 2 per cent of the population, at last count in 2001. Islam is Canada's fastest-growing religion, with the number of adherents doubling between 1991 and 2001. And while there is no estimate of how many practise polygamy, Islamic women's groups have recently noticed an alarming increase.

"There is no neutrality in maintaining a stance of official indifference to the practice of polygamy, however attractive that may be from an administration of justice perspective," the Alberta Civil Liberties Association concluded in its report for Status of Women Canada. "Tacit tolerance" could lead to a patchwork of rules and laws, undermine the notion of equality under the law and "pose a potential challenge to the social

*Wally Oppal and Mark Shurtleff. The Canadian and American
Attorneys General have agreed to cooperate to get convictions.*
(Bill Keay / Vancouver Sun)

cohesion of our country . . . In effect, we would be saying that
equality for all without regard to gender is not an absolute or
intrinsically Canadian value."

In one of the other studies, Queen's University law professor Martha Bailey wrote, "Accommodating cultural practices that differ from the practices in mainstream society
may seem the fair thing for a modern, pluralistic, democratic nation to do, all in the name of tolerance and respect
for cultural diversity. However, the accommodation of all
practices of a minority cultural or religious group may in
some cases create a situation where the vulnerable members of that group are subjected to harm . . . The reality of
culture-based gender discrimination is such that the most
insidious forms of it are practised in that private sphere of
life where historically the highest bar was raised against
remedial state action."

—

So how do liberal societies deal with this dilemma in which, by being tolerant, they can become unwitting accomplices in endangering, oppressing or persecuting some of the very groups they ought to be protecting? The answer lies in core values and beliefs. And, in Canada, the United States and all liberal democracies, equality is at the top of the list, not diversity. Merely being different isn't enough to override another person's human rights.

France's response to diversity has been what might best be described as radical secularism. Equality trumps everything else. In 2001, it strengthened its laws, giving police and the courts the power to disband cults and jail cult leaders for offences committed by their followers. But what is a cult? As theologians will tell you, one person's cult is another's new and emerging religion.

In September 2004, France banned all religious symbols in public schools. Muslim girls may no longer wear scarves or veils, but nuns aren't allowed to wear their habits either. Priests may wear only small, discreet crosses and crucifixes had to be taken down. Jewish men and boys are not allowed to wear their skullcaps. Sikhs can't wear turbans. The government is so convinced that equality is more important than diversity that it went ahead with the ban even though Iraqi militants abducted two French reporters in retaliation.

Over time, France's policy might yield the kind of integration the politicians are aiming for. But in the short term it may have worsened tensions. In November 2005, twenty nights of rioting began after two Muslim boys were accidentally electrocuted in a Paris suburb when they hid from police in a power station after climbing a fence. Nearly 9,000 cars were burned and 2,888 people were arrested. France's employment minister

Gérard Larcher said polygamy was at the root of the problem. He estimated that there are twenty thousand polygamous families living in France and he contended that polygamy was the cause of the racial and economic discrimination against Muslims. Because polygamous families are so large, Larcher said, children lacked the strong influence of their fathers.

France, Britain, Australia and the Netherlands all have what they call loyalty tests aimed at stopping new citizens—immigrants—from eroding societal values. Dutch officials require prospective citizens to watch videos of gays and lesbians as a means of gauging whether they can accept Holland's liberal attitudes towards same-sex couples. The videos aren't pornographic by Dutch standards, but they might be in other countries.

Fortunately, Canada has avoided the kind of violence that ripped through France, even though Toronto and Vancouver are the two most ethnically diverse cities in the world and close to one in five Canadians was born somewhere else. Here, tolerance has prevailed, even if it means that safety might be compromised. Sikhs have won the right to wear turbans if they serve in the RCMP and the right not to wear helmets when they ride motorcycles and bicycles or work on construction sites.

While French schools were taking down crucifixes, Canada's most populous province very nearly approved the use of Islamic or *sharia* law. It took an international campaign that included petitions and demonstrations by a coalition of women's groups before the Ontario government was dissuaded from becoming the first Western jurisdiction to allow an Islamic body to arbitrate family disputes, including divorce, division of property and child custody, using a legal code that in most interpretations does not recognize the equality of men and women.

As women were demonstrating in the street, the Ontario Court of Appeal reached the same conclusion as the protesters: there are limits to religious freedom. It rejected a Muslim man's defence of the so-called honour killing of his wife. There is no cultural or religious justification for stabbing someone nineteen times, the three justices ruled. They rejected the cultural/religious argument because it is "premised on the notion that women are inferior to men and that violence against women in some circumstances is accepted, if not encouraged. These beliefs are antithetical to fundamental Canadian values, including gender equality."

Canada and all liberal democracies guarantee religious freedom, freedom of association and freedom of expression. That's what confounded the B.C. government in 1992. Where does religious freedom end? Law professor Martha Bailey doesn't believe that it ends with polygamy. In her report to Status of Women Canada, she recommended decriminalizing polygamy for the purposes of immigration—people legally married in other countries should not be barred. To deny plural wives entry into Canada, she argued, could result in less favoured wives and their children being left behind. Although Bailey said that criminalization may not be the most effective means of dealing with gender inequality in plural marriages, she stopped short of recommending decriminalization within Canada, which would leave polygamists who do immigrate in an odd legal limbo.

But other studies commissioned by the federal government disagreed with Bailey's assessment that the antipolygamy law is unconstitutional and that decriminalization in any form is appropriate. Both the Alberta Civil Liberties Association and Rebecca Cook, co-director of the international reproductive and sexual health law program at the University of Toronto, make a distinction between religious *beliefs* and religious *practice*. What is protected by the Constitution and international treaties that Canada has signed are beliefs. Practices, the two studies contend, can be circumscribed if they result in harm or violate the rights and freedoms of others.

"Polygamy," Cook concluded, "constitutes an unjustifiable violation of the rights of women and children." Violations include the loss of rights to family life, security and citizenship. Among polygamy's harms are "competitive co-wife relationships, mental health harms, sexual and reproductive health harms, economic harms, [and] harms to the enjoyment of one's citizenship." Because of the Constitution and commitments to United Nations conventions (including those outlining the rights of women and children), Cook says Canada has no choice but to strive to eliminate polygamy.

But the same analysis doesn't apply to the United States. Even though Americans were instrumental in drafting the Convention on the Elimination of All Forms of Discrimination against Women, which was unanimously adopted by the United Nations General Assembly in 1979, the United States is the only industrialized nation that has never signed it. Among the reasons American politicians opposed CEDAW is that the definition of discrimination against women is too broad.

The convention defines discrimination as "any distinction, exclusion or restriction made on the basis of sex which has the effect or purpose of impairing or nullifying the recognition, enjoyment or exercise by women, irrespective of their marital status, on a basis of equality of men and women, of human rights and fundamental freedoms in the political, economic, social, cultural, civil or any other field." American politicians might better have opposed it for being badly worded and punctuated.

The U.S. Constitution also has no guarantee of women's rights. An Equal Rights Amendment (ERA) was approved by both the U.S. House of Representatives and Senate in 1972, but has yet to be ratified by thirty-eight states, as is required for it to become law. Among the holdouts are Arizona and Utah, where legislators were influenced by a massive mobilization of the mainstream Mormons against it. The leaders of the Church of Jesus Christ of Latter-day Saints said ERA is antithetical to traditional family values where men are the heads of the household. Among the amendment's most vociferous opponents was Arizona's Senator Orrin Hatch, an LDS member who once played the organ at an FLDS meeting in LeRoy Johnson Hall in Colorado City.

A month after the 2007 polygamy meeting in St. George, lawyers in the B.C. attorney general's office finally concluded their review of the mountain of evidence the RCMP had collected from Bountiful. Their recommendation went to Wally Oppal, who has refused to say what it was. But he clearly didn't like it. Oppal appointed a special prosecutor to do another review. His choice was Richard Peck, a respected criminal lawyer who had worked on a number of controversial cases, including one that resulted in the Canadian government's rewriting its child pornography law.

Oppal gave Peck a wide scope with which to evaluate the evidence, urging him to consider "any and all potential criminal or quasi-criminal charges including, but not limited to, polygamy and any offence of a sexual nature." Although initially the review was expected to take only a month, Peck soon found that the task was considerably more complex that he'd thought. He got a thirty-day extension.

Peck's recommendations were both distressing and encouraging. Winston Blackmore would not be charged, nor would anyone else. Peck had concluded that there was no substantial likelihood that any of the men investigated could be convicted of sexual exploitation—even though Blackmore had publicly confessed to having sex with minors, even though there was DNA evidence that he and others had fathered children with underage girls and even though the Crown had all of the records from the midwife's clinic. What was lacking, Peck said, were witnesses.

He concluded there was also no substantial likelihood that anyone could be convicted on any of the other applicable Criminal Code offences. Among the sections he had considered were parent or guardian procuring sexual activity; trafficking in persons; bigamy; procuring feigned marriage; pretending to solemnize marriage; and marriage contrary to law. And after reviewing the B.C. Independent School Act, Peck found that the only offence it lists is operating a school without a licence. Both of Bountiful's schools have valid licences.

But his other recommendation offered a way to unstick the legal and bureaucratic logjam. "Polygamy itself is at the root of the problem," Peck wrote. "Polygamy is the underlying phenomenon from which all the other alleged harms flow, and the public interest would be best served by addressing it directly." It was long past time that the legal uncertainty about polygamy was dealt with, he wrote. "The integrity of the legal system suffers from such an impasse."

Peck disagreed with the government's previous legal opinions that the polygamy section of the Criminal Code would likely be found unconstitutional. "Religious freedom is not absolute," he said. "Rather it is subject to reasonable limits necessary to protect public safety, order, health or morals or the fundamental rights and freedoms of others."

Peck recommended that the B.C. government go directly to the B.C. Court of Appeal and ask a panel of justices to hear arguments on the constitutionality of the polygamy law. From there, the government has an automatic right of appeal to the Supreme Court of Canada.

Peck argued that it would be faster than a test case in which one or two men were charged. Plus, he said, there is a chance that the constitutional issue might never be heard at all. He suggested that a good lawyer might even get the case thrown out of court: "given the unique history of this matter, including the lengthy passage of time since the first expression of police interest in Bountiful and the existence of prior Crown opinions regarding the constitutionality of section 293 [the polygamy prohibition]." This is another consideration he didn't mention. If B.C. took a case to trial and lost on constitutional grounds, polygamy would be legal and lawmakers would then be in the same politically uncomfortable position as they were with same-sex marriage. They would have to either legalize it or scramble to rewrite the law.

Even so, a court reference would take several years before it reached the Supreme Court of Canada. By then, dozens more babies will have been born in Bountiful; dozens more young women married to bishops, teachers, school principals and superintendents, to say nothing of cousins, uncles and stepfathers; and dozens more young boys forced out of this community and into penury. Besides, if a reference to the court was all that was needed to finally start prosecuting the men who prey on women and children, it seemed inconceivable that nobody thought of it earlier, and amoral that no one had the courage to act on it.

EPILOGUE

Five weeks after the report of the first special prosecutor assigned to Bountiful, B.C., Attorney General Wally Oppal hired a second one. The first, Richard Peck, had been appointed after Oppal's staff had determined that there was no substantial likelihood of winning a case against polygamists. Peck had concluded that while Canada's polygamy law would likely be found to be consistent with the Constitution's protection of rights and freedoms, he would not recommend testing it in a criminal trial. Instead, he recommended referring the law to the B.C. Court of Appeal for what he said would be "an authoritative and expeditious judicial resolution of the legal controversy surrounding polygamy."

Oppal, a former Court of Appeal justice, was not convinced that handing it off to someone else was the best way to go. From experience he knew that judges hate to rule on things in the absence of evidence and without some context for those facts. They also hate doing politicians' work for them—and determining the borders and limits of laws is just the sort of thing Oppal thought governments should do. Besides, he said, it would put the onus on the polygamists to raise the constitutional defence rather than on the government to make all the arguments. But Peck had convinced Oppal that polygamy was at the root of all evil in Bountiful. It was a dramatic conversion. Until then, Oppal had repeatedly said his greatest concern was abuse, not polygamy, although he had said that if there were a strong case, he would consider adding a polygamy charge.

Oppal was well aware of the problems of finding victims willing to testify. Testifying to abuse can be a harrowing experience for anyone; for the victim of a closed religious sect, it means turning your world upside down. However, finding polygamists was likely to prove simpler. After all, Winston Blackmore was both highly visible and vocal.

The second prosecutor was another highly regarded criminal lawyer, Leonard Doust, who had a reputation for being a tenacious street fighter—just what Oppal needed if charges were to be laid. While Peck's terms of reference had been extremely broad, with instructions to consider "any and all potential criminal or quasi-criminal charges, including but not limited to polygamy or any offence of a sexual nature," Doust's assignment was limited to sifting through the boxes of evidence the RCMP had collected nearly two years earlier with the aim of finding and prosecuting someone with the offence of polygamy—"if at all possible."

Oppal was tired of having polygamists flout the law and angry that a polygamist had recently taunted him on a radio talk show, asserting a constitutional right to all manner of religious practices. "I want to get this done," he said. "We're going to do something. The mere fact that nothing has been done in seventeen years [the last time the government refused to lay charges] does not mean that the government condones illegal activity. People in Bountiful are not immune from prosecution just because they've been lulled into a sense of security."

Some of Oppal's detractors were quick to criticize, accusing him of yet another delay. But what no one gave him credit for was playing a small but significant role in the high-profile trial of Warren Jeffs. Because of the agreement he had made two years earlier with Utah attorney general Mark Shurtleff, Utah was able to subpoena witnesses from British Columbia. At a time when the world's media were focused on a small courtroom in St. George, Utah, where the fundamentalist Mormons' dirty laundry was laid out for all to inspect, it was a B.C. witness who at least one juror said convinced him that Jeffs was guilty.

—

On the same day that Oppal appointed Doust, jury selection for the Jeffs trial began. On September 7, 2007, 230 potential jurors met in the Dixie Convention Center in St. George, Utah. It was the first step to finding twelve men and women to sit in judgment on the FLDS prophet, who was charged with being an accomplice to the rape of a fourteen-year-old girl.

Prospective jurors were handed a seventy-five-question survey that included the usual queries about age, sex, marital status, employer, education and health-related limitations. Then there were some very pointed and personal questions. What political, religious, civic, social or charitable organizations do you belong to or donate to? Do you have any religious beliefs, moral feelings, political views or philosophical principles that would interfere with fairly judging Jeffs? Are you currently a practising member of the LDS church? In the end, only two Mormons were chosen.

On Monday morning, the first thirty-six were called to the courthouse. Eighteen were excused based on their answers to the questionnaire. The remaining eighteen were interviewed individually, not in open court, as is the usual practice, but in the judge's chambers or the tiny jury room down the hall. Crowded into the small rooms were the three prosecutors, the three high-paid defence lawyers, Jeffs, Judge James Shumate, a court reporter, the judge's clerk, several bailiffs and sheriffs (Jeffs was considered dangerous and a flight risk), a court reporter and two journalists on a pooled basis. Prospective jurors were asked to expand on the answers to the question-naire. At least one woman was asked by Jeffs's lawyer Walter Bugden to look his client in the eye and tell him she believed he was innocent. She did and eventually wound up on the jury.

Surprisingly, given the amount of media attention sur-rounding the case in every major newspaper in the country and on CNN and every major network's nightly news, some of the potential jurors had no idea that the gaunt, pale man sit-ting in the corner was Warren Jeffs, one of the FBI's Ten Most Wanted. When one woman was asked whether she recog-nized Jeffs, she pointed to Deputy County Attorney Ryan Shaum. Everyone laughed—even Jeffs, who up until then had seemed either not to understand or not to appreciate some of the light-hearted remarks between the attorneys and prospective jurors. Whatever medical or mental problems Jeffs had suffered earlier in the year, the so-called prophet seemed to have recovered.

During the jury selection interviews and throughout the trial, it became clear that the FLDS's certainty in the superi-ority of their own way of doing things did not extend to legal expertise. In addition to Nevada attorney Richard Wright, Jeffs was flanked by two lawyers with whom he and his sect had nothing in common. Jeffs had interviewed all of Utah's lead-ing criminal attorneys before choosing Bugden and Tara Isaacson. Bugden is an atheist. His Syracuse, N.Y., upbringing is evident not only in his faint East Coast accent: he wears bow ties, which he ties himself, and his round tortoiseshell glasses and deliberately mismatched socks enhance his professorial style and air of cultivated eccentricity.

Tara Isaacson is the antithesis of a good FLDS woman. She is well-educated, stylishly dressed, confident and articulate. Close to six feet tall without her high heels, she commands attention in an ordinary crowd, but she was a walking revelation to the FLDS men who attended the trial every day. Whenever Isaacson strode through the courthouse lobby, they stopped talking, turned and hungrily followed her with their eyes.

—

The jury selection was a painstaking process. No one believed that Jeffs would be judged by his peers, since the questionnaire and interviews were aimed at screening out all other prophets- and gods-in-waiting. The best Jeffs and his attorneys could hope for was an unbiased jury. At the end of the first day of interviews, seventy-four people had been excused and only thirteen qualified to go on to the final selection. Given the number of challenges allowed to the prosecutors and defence attorneys, twenty-eight would be needed in order to choose the final twelve. It seemed that Jeffs's attorneys may have been right—for months they had argued that it would be impossible to find such a jury in St. George.

St. George is about an hour's drive from the twin towns of Hildale and Colorado City. It is named not for the dragon-slaying patron saint of England, but for Brigham Young's cousin George Albert Smith. Smith was known as "the potato man" because he shared his food supply with other Mormon migrants on the long trek from Illinois to the Salt Lake Basin.

Smith ate only the peels and distributed the potatoes' white flesh to the others. Unfortunately for the others, the peel has the most nutrients, and many died of malnutrition. Whether or not he had been aware of the nutritional properties of potato skins, Smith survived and was rewarded for his generosity by being canonized.

St. George was the winter home of Brigham Young, the LDS church's second president and prophet. The desert climate eased his rheumatism, according to the volunteer guides at his home, which is now a national historical site. The guides are all LDS, and they'll tell you that whenever Young was there, he brought only one of his fifty-five wives—his youngest, Amelia. She was thirty-eight years younger, but the guides insist that the couple never slept together. Their pairing, so they say, was a spiritual one. However, across the street there's a bed and breakfast slyly named The Seven Wives.

The overwhelming majority of people in St. George and those in surrounding Washington County are LDS. The temple is the oldest in Utah, predating the grander and better-known structure in Salt Lake City. The tabernacle also has an illustrious history. Its staircase was carved by the great-grandfather of Mitt Romney, who is only the second Mormon ever to take a run at becoming president of the United States (Joseph Smith was the first, and that ended badly). The climate that attracted Young is now a magnet for retiring baby boomers. St. George is one of the fastest-growing cities in the United States. Its population grew by nearly 35 per cent between 2000 and 2006, to just under sixty-eight thousand.

It's only because of that recent increase in diversity that the attorneys were able to find twenty-eight people deemed sufficiently fair-minded and willing to accept the premise that Jeffs was innocent until proven guilty. That group was whittled down to seven women and five men on Wednesday afternoon. Four were alternates, but none of the twelve knew which they were.

—

The trial began Thursday afternoon. After the opening statements, the prosecution didn't waste any time — it called its star witness. There was another surprise. Although Washington County attorney Brock Belnap had done a credible job of leading Elissa Wall through her testimony at the preliminary hearing, Craig Barlow, Utah's assistant attorney general, led Elissa through her testimony this time.

On Friday morning, Attorney General Mark Shurtleff sat in the courtroom's front row behind the prosecution bench. Utah's chief prosecutor and law enforcer had flown in from Salt Lake City to hear Elissa testify how at fourteen she had been forced by Warren Jeffs to marry her nineteen-year-old first cousin, who subsequently raped her. When Elissa finished her gruelling and teary testimony, Shurtleff put his arm around her and comforted her, undeniably signalling that this was no ordinary prosecution. It was not only political; it was personal.

With the attorney general present, security was tighter than usual. Rather than being driven in a multi-vehicle convoy from Purgatory Correctional Facility, as he was every other day of the trial, Jeffs came in by helicopter in shackles and wearing an orange and white striped prison jumpsuit. The jury, however, never saw Jeffs that way. Every day before court began, he was allowed to change into a dark suit, white shirt and tie, with a bulletproof vest underneath.

Every day, Jeffs was in the courtroom before the jury came in. They never saw him turn with a thin-lipped smile and a nod to acknowledge family, friends and followers as they filed into their assigned seats in the third and last row of the tiny courtroom. The jurors may not even have seen the handful of other followers who, after standing in line early each morning with antipolygamy activists, got one of the few, highly sought after public passes to sit in the glassed-off anteroom.

Those who came were the FLDS elites—Jeffs's brothers, his enforcers and henchmen. Dressed in dark Western-style suits, they were a solid, silent and brooding force leavened only by a couple of women in their pastel pioneer dresses. The only outsiders they spoke to were Jeffs's lawyers. And they had nothing to say to Elissa Wall or any of the other prosecution witnesses. They simply glared at the apostates, whose only purpose seemed to be to betray the community's secrets.

When Elissa took the stand, she made a point of looking directly at Warren Jeffs. He stared back at the pale blonde twenty-one-year-old expressionlessly. Even though it was the all-powerful prophet who was on trial, Jeffs was little more than a bystander. That was partly due to the nature of the charges, but it was largely because he and his attorneys had decided that the prophet should not take the stand. The case focused instead on two young people—two of Jeffs's many victims—Elissa Wall and her ex-husband Allen Steed.

Because Steed had never been arrested or tried for rape, if the jurors were to find Jeffs guilty they had to believe beyond reasonable doubt that Elissa had been raped, not once but twice. Then they had to believe, beyond reasonable doubt, that the rapes would not have been committed except for Jeffs's actions. They had to reach their unanimous conclusion based almost entirely on the faces, voices, demeanour and testimony of the young couple. The state's case rested almost solely on Elissa's credibility, while the defence case rested almost entirely on Steed's. The only words that jurors heard

Jeffs speak loudly and clearly were taped sermons played by both the prosecution and the defence.

—

Elissa Wall was well-prepared—almost too well-prepared. Occasionally she slipped in some legal language, no doubt picked up from her frequent contact with lawyers over the past couple of years. The prosecutors had coached her. She'd had intensive counselling, and Elissa's retelling of her story was more detailed and less raw than at the preliminary hearing. Even so, her recounting of how she was betrayed by the people she loved and trusted most was heart-wrenching.

Elissa, her younger siblings and her mother had moved to Short Creek after her father, Lloyd Wall, had fallen from grace. Wall had been Rulon Jeffs's business partner and one of his most trusted advisers before Rulon's stroke and before Warren excommunicated him. The same day that Wall was excommunicated, his wife and five youngest children—including Elissa—were moved from Salt Lake City to Hildale, Utah, and reassigned to Fred Jessop, Short Creek's bishop and patriarch, who already had fifteen wives and forty-five people living in his home.

After Elissa's mother told her she was to be married, Elissa went to Jessop and asked whether he hadn't confused her with one of the many other girls in his home who were older and more ready to be married. Jessop said no. She asked her stepfather to speak to the prophet, and eventually, on her own, persuaded Warren Jeffs to arrange a meeting with Rulon. She'd blurted out her story through tears, which seemed to confuse Rulon, who asked her to repeat what she'd said. Warren interrupted and told his father that the young woman wanted to defy the prophet and God by refusing the marriage.

But Rulon patted the fourteen-year-old's hand and told her to follow her heart.

Elissa believed the prophet had given her a reprieve. But Warren would not hear of it and told her that she couldn't know her own heart. The wedding would go ahead. "I felt like I was getting ready for death," Elissa told jurors about the days leading up to her wedding.

On April 23, 2001, Elissa was married to Steed in a motel room in Caliente, Nevada. Rulon Jeffs was at the ceremony, but Warren officiated. When Elissa twice refused to say "I do," Warren ordered Elissa's mother to stand beside her daughter and take her hand. Elissa said her mother "squooze" her hand so hard that she finally pronounced the fatal words that bound her to Steed. Jeffs pronounced Elissa and Allen husband and wife, exhorting them to "Go forth and multiply and replenish the Earth with good priesthood children."

Having babies is what every FLDS woman lives for, but fourteen-year-old Elissa had no idea how they were made. She'd never dated or kissed a boy, never even held a boy's hand. She had been taught that when she married, her husband would be her priesthood head and would instruct her in all matters, including sex. She was to obey him as he was to obey the prophet, who was like God on earth. Elissa had been taught that her salvation was tied to that of her husband and that she was to follow him "as obediently as if I was led by a hair, meaning that if I refused in any way, it [the hair] would pop." Even so, submission did not come easily. Although she knew nothing about sex, Elissa said, "I felt horrified that I would have to do that with Allen."

Jurors saw photos from the wedding and honeymoon. She is smiling in some, hinting that she may have been a typically happy bride. But Elissa said she'd felt "robotic," smiling when the people taking the photos told her to. In other photos,

Elissa appears distressed and very uncomfortable. In one, Allen Steed is carrying her across the threshold of their motel room, and Elissa's hands are over her reddened face. She said she tried to laugh to mask the sobs. In another, Steed has her buried in a tight embrace; her hands are on his chest. She said she was pushing as hard as she could to get away from him. In another, it's not the image of Elissa and Steed in the horse-drawn carriage that's so disturbing, it's the couple in the front seat. The groom appears to be in his forties. His bride is Elissa's diminutive fourteen-year-old half-sister Ruby.

Elissa refused Steed's sexual advances during the honeymoon, telling him that she didn't want him touching her and even that she hated him. But a few weeks after the wedding, she testified, Steed told her it was time for her to be a wife.

"I wasn't completely sure what he was saying. But I said, 'Please don't do this.' He just ignored me and came over and undressed me. The entire time I cried and started to get very afraid and he undressed himself and made me stand there. I said, 'Allen, I don't know what you are doing, but I am really uncomfortable with this so please stop. I had never seen a grown man naked and I had never been naked in front of a man. He came over and we went over to the bed. I said, 'I can't do this. Please stop.' I was sobbing. My whole entire body was shaking because I was so scared. He just lay me on the bed and had sex."

"It hurt," she continued, with her eyes closed as she tried to keep back the tears. "I so extremely hurt," she said, pausing between each of those four words. "I didn't understand why he had done what he had just done. In my mind I felt it was evil. I didn't know he had to do that sort of thing to have a baby. It was horrible. When he was done, he rolled over and went to bed. I was numb, shocked, and I felt dirty and used."

Elissa went into the bathroom and swallowed the contents of a bottle of Tylenol and a bottle of ibuprofen, which she later threw up. "I just wanted to die. I didn't want to have to deal with [her husband] any more or with Warren or with the prophet or my mother or Fred [Jessop, her stepfather]," she said emphatically, with tears in her eyes. "I was so hurt by them."

Elissa didn't tell anyone about the rape or her aborted suicide attempt, not even her mother, who lived in the room next door to where the newlyweds were sleeping. "I felt I was such a terrible person. I thought my mother would judge me. I felt I was a disgusting, evil person for having done that." She had no word to describe what had happened to her. She had heard the word *rape*, but thought that it meant physical, not sexual, abuse.

Elissa went to Warren Jeffs after Steed raped her and told Jeffs that her husband was touching her in private places where she didn't want to be touched. She asked to be released from her marriage. But Jeffs refused and told her to repent. "He said I was not living up to my vows. I was not being obedient, not being submissive to my priesthood head [her husband]. He told me I needed to go home and give myself to [her husband] mind, body and soul." A few days after that meeting, her husband raped her again.

Elissa also didn't tell anyone until a few years later that just days before she was raped the first time, her husband had exposed his genitals to her one night in a park. "I turned away. I shut my eyes. I said, 'Put that away. I don't want to see it.'"

Throughout Elissa's testimony, Jeffs stared at her almost unblinking and slack-jawed, his mouth slightly agape, as is his habit. He gave no indication of whether he agreed or disagreed with what she related, although he occasionally gave a wan smile to his attorneys, who leapt up frequently—and mostly successfully—objecting to Elissa's testimony, arguing that it was hearsay.

After Elissa finished testifying on Friday afternoon, prosecutors made the curious decision to play close to an hour's worth of Jeffs's soporific sermons for "young ladies." These were taped at Alta Academy and are still used in FLDS communities and schools, including Bountiful's. "If a woman rules over the man, both will lose the spirit of God," Jeffs says in his monotone. "Pray for him, seek his counsel. When you approach your husband, always do it with a prayer in your heart."

With temperatures close to 100 degrees Fahrenheit outside, the St. George courtroom was stuffy. As Jeffs's mind-numbing monotone played on, the judge and a bailiff nodded off briefly. It had a similarly somnolent effect on some of the jurors, and at times even Jeffs seemed to struggle to stay awake.

"Success is to give yourself to your husband, mind, body and soul, so that the Lord will guide him right in teaching you . . . Seek out that oneness early in your marriage," he advised in one sermon, adding that it is possible for a woman to attain "oneness" with her husband only if she submits to his will. It's not a very complicated theology, especially if you're a girl: submit and let the men take care of things. The sermons are so mesmerizing and, apparently, familiar-sounding enough to mainstream Mormons that not only did Jeffs's supporters murmur "amen" when one tape ended, so did one of Elissa's civil lawyers, who was sitting in the gallery.

With that, the week came to an anticlimactic end. However, the prosecutors had left Jeffs's defence team no time to cross-examine their key witness. It meant that all weekend long, jurors had time to think about uncontested testimony about the rape of a fourteen-year-old, the eerie, creepy monotone voice of the man who allegedly sanctioned it, and Jeffs's blank, expressionless face as he watched Elissa testify. The jury was not sequestered but had been instructed not to listen to or read any media reports or talk to anyone about the trial. But coverage of the trial was everywhere on the national, regional and local media, and the prosecutors had seen to it that they could report only Elissa's side of the story.

—

It's a tricky business attacking the testimony of a victim, especially one as young as Elissa Wall. Tara Isaacson did what she could to raise some reasonable doubts in the jurors' minds when the trial resumed Monday morning. Other people, including Elissa's mother, stepfather and even her sisters, had encouraged her to marry, Isaacson noted. Why weren't they charged as accomplices to rape?

Isaacson asked Elissa whether Jeffs had ever told her that she must consent to rape. He hadn't, Elissa said. Why hadn't Elissa ever told Jeffs that she'd had been raped? Elissa said she couldn't have—"We didn't use those words in our society." Why hadn't Elissa told her mother? Isaacson wanted to know. Elissa fired back: "Who wants to tell anyone that they are being raped?"

Even though Elissa described herself as trapped in marriage, Isaacson got her to acknowledge that she had spent nearly four months in Bountiful without her husband, that she had visited her sister Rebecca alone in Oregon, and, most troublingly, that she had sneaked away with another man for a weekend in Las Vegas. Elissa was forced to admit that Steed had found photos of her with her lover, Lamont Barlow, and that this is what had provoked Steed to ask Warren Jeffs to release him from the marriage. Elissa admitted that by then she was pregnant with Lamont's baby. (After Elissa left the FLDS, she married Lamont, who was in the courtroom every day. They have two children.)

Isaacson insinuated that Elissa's decision to report the rape to police was motivated by money and revenge. Jeffs's attorney pointed out that Elissa had first gone to a civil attorney and filed a lawsuit against Jeffs, the FLDS and the United Effort Plan, claiming millions of dollars in compensation. Isaacson noted that both Elissa and Lamont had received financial help from Utah's victim services programs. Even victims have their dirty laundry.

But whatever damage Isaacson had done to Elissa's credibility was repaired by the testimony of her two sisters. Elissa and Steed had gone to Bountiful within weeks of the first rape to visit her sister Teressa, who had been in Grade 10 when she was sent north to marry Winston Blackmore's nephew Roy. During the visit, Elissa never used the words *sex* or *rape*, but Teressa said Elissa told her Steed was doing things that she didn't want done to her. "She was so extremely sad," Teressa said. "She was just a terrified little girl."

Teressa had bolstered Elissa's story, but it was the frank and dynamic testimony of Rebecca Musser that won over many of the jurors. Warren Jeffs had performed the assignment marriage when Musser became one of his eighty-six-year-old father's eighty-some wives. "At 19, I had no idea of sex," said Musser. "I was taught by Rulon in the first two months after we were married." Even though Rulon was still the prophet after his stroke, Warren Jeffs was deeply, disturbingly involved in the intimate lives of people in the community. Musser told how several times Warren had called her into his office and upbraided her for refusing Rulon's commands in the bedroom. "Warren would tell me under no circumstances do you ever, ever, ever say no to your husband. He would never be led by God to do something wrong."

After Rulon died in September 2002, Musser said Warren had called her into his office to tell her that she was going to be reassigned. Looking straight at Jeffs, Musser testified: "He said, pointing at me, 'I will break you and I will train you to be a good wife. You have had too much freedom for too long . . . I will always have jurisdiction over you.'" Before Warren had a chance to take her as a bride (as he did with many of his father's wives) or reassign her, Musser left Hildale and the FLDS and moved to Oregon.

When Musser completed her testimony, the prosecution abruptly closed its case against Warren Jeffs, one of the FBI's Ten Most Wanted, even though its witness list had fifteen more names on it. Jeffs's three defence lawyers had been told that the prosecution's case would take just two days. Still, they were surprised. Walter Bugden asked the judge to dismiss the charges, arguing that the prosecution had failed to provide enough evidence. The motion was denied. Even so, Jeffs's attorneys believed the prosecution had provided them with an unexpected opportunity.

They believed that they might first be able to discredit Elissa and her sisters as angry and vindictive, and then humanize and "normalize" the FLDS by providing an unprecedented glimpse into the daily life of the community. The risk, however, was that their witnesses would only reinforce just how far outside the mainstream Jeffs had taken his followers, and how powerless and obedient he had rendered them.

First up was Jennie Pipkin, a twenty-six-year-old mother of five, whose two most extraordinary features were a surprisingly crown-like swoop of hair and an iPod loaded with 769 of Warren Jeffs's sermons, religious teachings and songs. Pipkin spoke in a childlike voice and rested her head on her folded arms, as a little girl might in school. She explained how at seventeen she had "turned herself in" to the prophet when she felt she was ready to be married and told Rulon

Jeffs how she'd been "impressed by the Lord" that she was to marry Jonathan, another seventeen-year-old.

The marriage foundered after eight years and five children. Pipkin's last pregnancy had been a difficult one, and she told her husband that she needed to "take a break from having children." Since the FLDS teaches that sexual intercourse is for procreation, not recreation, that meant no more sex, and Pipkin's husband was anything but happy with her decision. "He [Jonathan] mumbled something under his breath. I was furious and said he could no longer hug or kiss me. He followed me around the house saying that it was wrong and 'I need it' and 'It's your duty to comfort me.' I didn't fight with him, I just said no."

Pipkin said her husband kept "nagging" her about sex. She prayed and listened to scriptures and sermons. She wrote Jeffs and had the first of two meetings with him. After the first meeting, when Jeffs apparently told Jonathan to leave his wife alone, Jennie testified that she woke up one night. "He had taken my clothes off and was touching me intimately . . . I reported him to Warren and 2 1/2 days later, I was released from the marriage."

Under cross-examination, Pipkin said she probably told Jeffs something about being touched on her "private parts," just as Elissa had.

"You expected Mr. Jeffs to understand that he had made unwanted sexual advances?" assistant attorney general Craig Barlow asked.

"Yes," she replied. In other words, if Jeffs knew that Pipkin was being abused, it followed that he was capable of understanding that Wall was as well. Pipkin also subsequently agreed that her situation was very different from Elissa's — Pipkin had asked to be married and had been seventeen, and her groom was a boy she had chosen.

Ben and Margaret Thomas both testified how they had come to love each other after marrying at ages twenty-three and twenty respectively. Their first child was born eleven months after the wedding. Both said they were taught that a husband should never force his wife to have sex. Both said they were raised to be obedient. But not blindly obedient, Margaret said: "Blind obedience means you don't have a brain. We were taught that intelligence inspires obedience."

But under cross-examination, Ben said he would follow the prophet "no matter what."

"Whatever Mr. Jeffs says is something that you would do?" prosecutor Ryan Shaum asked him.

"Yes," Ben replied.

"You would be led by the prophet and even give your own life?" Shaum asked.

"Correct," Ben said.

Joanna and John Keate had never met until a day before their wedding. Like all of the women testifying for the defence, Joanna exuded a childlike sweetness and, like Pipkin and the others, she had "turned herself in" to the prophet for an assignment marriage. She had been nineteen and determined not to have children before she loved her husband, so they lived "like roommates" for several months. Joanna said he'd "try things" and she'd push him away. "I knew I wasn't doing what I promised to be and that was a wife," Joanna said, even though both she and John testified that it was up to the woman to determine the timing of sexual intercourse. When they hadn't consummated their marriage after a few months, John said they went to Jeffs for counselling because "I felt I needed some correction." They have now been married for six years and have one son, in a society where most women have a child every two years.

Of the defence's nine witnesses that day, the final one was the most tragically compelling and disturbing. Merril Shapley had been forced to leave school at age eight to work for his father's construction company. Now twenty-four and barely literate, he struggled to spell his own name. He met his wife only minutes before their marriage. Merril said he'd been told to wait until she was ready for sex. Then how did you happen to have two children in four years? prosecutor Ryan Shaum asked. Red-faced, Shapley stammered that he and his wife never talked about it. "It just happened. I didn't ask for it. I didn't bring it on. She wanted to."

With the notion of male victimhood established, the defence had set the stage for its own star witness, the alleged rapist Allen Steed, who strangely had never been charged. On Wednesday morning, Walter Bugden began by asking Steed whether he was aware that by testifying he might be incriminating himself. Steed said yes and acknowledged that his lawyer was in the courtroom.

The twenty-six-year-old truck driver's demeanour was in striking contrast to Elissa's. She had walked confidently to the witness stand in tailored suits and was feisty under cross-examination. Steed wore a long-sleeved shirt with no jacket, and spoke so softly that at times the judge repeated his answers for the jury. Steed was urged so many times to speak up that finally Bugden asked if he'd rather testify standing up. Steed stood for nearly three hours with his hands folded in front of him. It's how men give their testimony in church when they're called upon to speak.

Before the marriage, Steed said, Fred Jessop—the bishop, Steed's employer and Elissa's stepfather—had counselled him to "be slow, take a long time, to be kind, considerate and respectful" of his child bride. Steed claimed no memory of teasing Elissa about her weight before they married, no memory of the wedding, of Elissa refusing to say her vows or her crying. Growing up in that repressive society, Steed said, he had not been given any sex education or been allowed to date. He described the first few months of their religious marriage as "rough and rocky." He wept as he talked about how he didn't know how to talk to Elissa, didn't know how to court her or make her fall in love with him. Because communication was difficult for him, he said he sent her notes and occasionally flowers.

Of course, he had also exposed his genitals to her in a park as part of the courtship. "In my own clumsy way, I tried to make her feel more comfortable to help move things along," he said.

Steed testified that Elissa had told him she didn't want to have children for maybe as long as five years, and that they'd waited a couple of months before having intercourse. And when they did, Steed says, his fourteen-year-old bride initiated it.

"I came home. I was putting in long hours at my job and I was really, really tired," the sturdily built Steed said. "I went to sleep in my work clothes and as the night progressed, she woke me up and asked me if I cared about her and I said I loved her. She rolled up close to me and asked me to scratch her back and one thing led to another." He found himself "guided to her" and they had sex.

Steed's testimony fell apart under cross-examination. Barlow showed him a photograph dated three weeks after the wedding. The couple was on their way to Bountiful to visit Elissa's sister Teressa. Steed admitted that they'd already had intercourse by then. But hadn't Elissa said she didn't want to have children for five years? Barlow asked.

"She said maybe a couple of weeks, couple of months or maybe five years," Steed replied.

"So you took the earliest date?" Craig Barlow asked.

"Wouldn't you?" Steed replied.

"I'm not you," said Barlow, asking again whether Steed chose the earliest date.

"Of course I did. I wanted to have a child. I wanted her to know I loved her. I didn't want her frightened."

"Why was she frightened?" the prosecutor asked.

Steed said he'd never asked.

Barlow asked if Steed's idea of going slowly was having sex three weeks after marrying a fourteen-year-old who had no idea how babies were created and who had told him she didn't want him touching her. "It seemed like a long time to me," said Steed.

Barlow hammered away at Steed, getting him to admit that he didn't believe state laws, such as the marriage age of sixteen or the one forbidding polygamy, applied to him and the FLDS; only God's laws applied. Barlow harkened back to the 1940s, when polygamists—including his own great-uncle, the fundamentalists' first prophet John Y. Barlow—had lied to authorities, falsely signing papers agreeing never to practise polygamy again if they were released from prison.

Would Steed be willing to disobey the laws of man if he were commanded to? Barlow asked.

"Yes, sir," Steed replied.

Barlow noted that since Steed's release from Elissa, he had never been assigned another wife, and that without several wives he wouldn't be allowed into the highest realm of heaven. Steed agreed and said that he would get another wife or wives only if Warren Jeffs decided he was worthy.

—

Bugden tried to repair some of the damage. He manoeuvred Steed into saying that he would never lie, even to protect the prophet, because lying is against God's law. With that, the defence abruptly ended its case, even though it had filed a list of seventy-one potential witnesses, including Elissa's mother, Sharon, and several of her sisters and brothers who remain committed to Jeffs. (The defence list was a compendium of the families and lives Jeffs had broken in the name of God. For every person who had left the FLDS and was named as a possible prosecution witness, the defence listed six or seven family members willing to speak against them. Carolyn Jessop, for example, was on the prosecution's list. Her oldest daughter, Betty, who had returned to the FLDS that spring, just a few days after her eighteenth birthday, was on the defence list.)

The prosecution called a single rebuttal witness, Jane Blackmore. Because one of her daughters is married to an FLDS strongman, Blackmore was there under court order, which had been made possible by the agreement Shurtleff and Oppal had signed. Winston's ex-wife had been the midwife in Bountiful for four years, and Elissa had come to her as a patient in December 2002. According to Blackmore's records, Elissa was pregnant, had had a miscarriage in June, and had received no medical treatment. Elissa had not told her husband about either the miscarriage or the pregnancy. Blackmore said Elissa spent most of the time in her office crying. She didn't want a baby, didn't want to be married, and didn't want to go home to her husband. "I asked her about abuse and she said she felt she was being forced," Blackmore testified. "She said, 'My husband won't take no for an answer.'"

In February 2003, Blackmore said, Elissa had a second miscarriage. Second-trimester miscarriages can be dangerous, and Blackmore was uncomfortable managing it outside a hospital, but she had no choice—Elissa had no medical insurance. Within days of the miscarriage, Elissa's husband had ordered her to return home. She reluctantly complied. What options did she have? Elissa was sixteen, and an unaccompanied minor in Canada on a visitor's visa. More importantly, within the FLDS she had no choice but to obey her husband. Elissa still believed her salvation depended on it.

With all of the evidence in, the four alternate jurors were excused. County Attorney Brock Belnap closed the state's case by urging the five men and three women on the jury to find that Warren Jeffs knowingly, intentionally and recklessly put Elissa and Allen in a bedroom together and encouraged Elissa to submit to her husband's will. "He is the one who turned Allen Steed into a person of authority," Belnap said. "He taught Elissa Wall to obey and drop her resistance to her priesthood head . . . At very least, he disregarded a known risk of which he should have been aware." Belnap pointed out that under Utah law, Elissa at fourteen was too young to legally consent to having sex with someone in a position of special trust. And he parried the defence's suggestion that Jeffs had not enticed Elissa into marriage but had done it as part of his sincere religious belief.

"Let's suppose that in some little corner of America, there is a little town where the community believes that every year in order to appease the god of the harvest they have to sacrifice a fourteen-year-old," Belnap said. "They prepare a special dress and decorate things for her. There are flowers, pictures and everyone tells her it is a wonderful honour. When they take her up on the mountain, the leader of the community says, 'Sweetheart, this is what God wants you to do.' It doesn't matter if you are motivated by love, if you persuade someone against their better will, it's enticement."

Walter Bugden closed for the defence. He suggested that the State of Utah's prosecution of Jeffs was misuse of the broad and sweeping power of the state. Bugden noted that even though the alleged rapist had never been charged, his client was being tried as an accomplice. "The state has gone crazy for political reasons." Far from this being a rape case, Bugden said, Jeffs and his church were on trial for their religious beliefs. But rather than Utah's officials having the courage to charge Jeffs with polygamy, unlawful marriage or the marriage of an underage girl, "the state dropped a nuclear bomb on the FLDS community and charged Warren Steed Jeffs with rape. There was not rape. There was no accomplice liability because there was not rape."

Allen Steed was not a rapist and a monster, Bugden said. Just the opposite, the attorney suggested. Fourteen-year-old Elissa had been a strong-willed temptress, "no shrinking violet," in control at all times during the marriage. She concocted the story of the rape only after she had fallen in love with another man, abetted by her two equally strong-willed, combative and protective sisters. Bugden suggested Elissa had been driven to testify in order to improve her chances of getting a large settlement in her civil suit against Jeffs, the FLDS and the United Effort Plan. "Money changes everything," he told the jurors.

But the jurors believed Elissa Wall, not Allen Steed. They believed that she was raped and that it would never have happened had Warren Jeffs not put them into a bedroom together and told them to have children or risk eternal damnation. Even though the prosecution never clearly spelled out when the second rape occurred, the jurors found Jeffs guilty on both counts of being an accomplice to it

But the decision had taken four difficult days. At one point in the deliberations, one juror threw a marking pen at another. At another, a female juror cowered in the bathroom, fearing that fists might fly. After nearly eight hours of deliberations, the jurors had told the judge they had reached a stalemate on the second count. Shumate reread his instructions on how the deliberations were to be conducted and sent them back to try again, urging them to have open minds. After nearly thirteen hours of deliberations, at 8 p.m. on Monday the jury foreman indicated they were close to a decision but wanted to go home and "sleep on it."

But the next morning, a juror was expelled. She had fudged an answer on the questionnaire about whether she or anyone close to her had been a victim of sexual assault. An alternate had to be brought in and deliberations had to start again from the beginning. However, within three hours there was a verdict. It was September 25, the 117th anniversary of the mainstream Mormon church's manifesto outlawing polygamy.

When the verdict was read out, the prosecutors' sighs were audible. Several of Jeffs's followers, including Rodney Holm, the convicted polygamist pedophile and former police officer, seemed shaken. The FLDS women left the courtroom redeyed. None of the FLDS responded to reporters' questions. Jeffs's three defence attorneys made no comment other than to say that they expected there would be an appeal.

Jeffs went back to Purgatory in shackles and again traded his business suit for the green-and-white-striped prison jumpsuit. In late November, Judge James Shumate handed down the maximum sentence—two consecutive terms of five years to life in prison with credit given for the fifteen months he had already served. In addition to the jail term that could be as little as nine years or as much as two lifetimes, Jeffs was assessed fines amounting to $37,000.

Arizona planned to have Jeffs transported from Purgatory Correctional Facility to a jail in Mohave County after his sentencing. And while jailed FLDS men are hailed as heroes and martyrs for the cause, it may be harder for a jailed prophet to recklessly manipulate and intimidate young women like Elissa Wall, or even young men like Allen Steed.

The jurors had no reticence about talking to the media. All eight spoke to journalists in the cleared courtroom after the verdict. They said they never doubted that Elissa was raped the first time. Jerry Munk said it had been midwife Jane Blackmore's testimony that had convinced him of the second rape. But what persuaded Munk and the others to find Jeffs guilty on both counts was the incredible power Jeffs wields over every aspect of followers' earthly and eternal lives. Munk described Jeffs as Elissa's "only ticket for getting out of the marriage," and blamed him for failing to help her.

Another juror, twenty-six-year-old Ben Coulter, said he was one of the three who had initially argued for Jeffs to be found not guilty. But in the end, Coulter concluded, "[Jeffs] ultimately held all the keys to say [to Elissa], 'You don't have to be in this marriage,' and there would be no consequences."

After the verdict, County Attorney Brock Belnap called Elissa "a pioneer." With Elissa beside him on the steps of the courthouse, his voice cracked with emotion. "One of the high-lights of my entire life will always be the courage of Elissa Wall. It has been an honour to stand alongside a woman who spoke out to stop the practise of abuse against enormous odds and enormous power." He said he hoped Jeffs's conviction would shine a light of hope for others who are in circum-stances that they believe they have no power to control.

Elissa, who now goes by another name, then read a pre-pared statement. "When I was young, my mother told me that evil flows when good men do nothing. The easy thing is to do nothing. But I have followed my heart and spoken the truth." She had a conciliatory message for her mother, Sharon Wall, her sisters who were on the defence's witness list, and others who remain in the FLDS. "Mother, I love you and my sisters unconditionally. I understand and respect your convictions and I will not give up on you. I still have very tender feelings for the people of the FLDS. There is so much good in them. I pray they will find the strength to step back and re-examine where they've been led."

The case was not about religion or about a vendetta against Jeffs or the FLDS, she said. "It was simply about child abuse and about preventing future abuse." Elissa urged others in the FLDS to recognize that they don't have to surrender individual rights or give up their "spiritual sovereignty." She also pledged to continue to fight for those rights and the FLDS people. That fight will come sooner rather than later. Elissa is also the key witness in Arizona's case against Jeffs on ten sex-related counts, including incest, sexual conduct with a minor and conspiracy to commit sexual conduct with a minor.

The day after Allen Steed testified, he was charged with one count of rape. Elissa Wall issued a statement through her civil lawyers: "Allen Steed was both a victim of Warren Jeffs and a perpetrator of child abuse. We have seen the justice system bring out the truth, and I am confident it will again." Bail was set at US$50,000. If convicted, he faced between five years and life in prison. A week later Steed turned himself in to police and was released on US$5,000 bail. His preliminary hearing was set for early November 2007.

The FLDS moved swiftly to retaliate. Teressa Blackmore was served with a civil lawsuit from her ex-husband, claiming custody over their four children. She had left her husband and the cult eighteen months before the Jeffs trial. Initially she had left the children in Bountiful while she got settled in Idaho and found a job so that she could support them. She didn't have the money to hire a lawyer. The fund set up to help lost boys get re-established, which is controlled by Elissa's civil lawyer, Roger Hoole, gave her $1,500 to hire a lawyer and ensure that her ex-husband would not get a default judgment.

Richard Holm, whose family and home were taken from him by Jeffs, sat through several days of the trial. His reaction was perhaps the only rational one—grim satisfaction. "If Warren Jeffs even spent one day in jail for each of the people he's hurt, it would be several dozen years. He was portrayed [in court] as a kind man and a religious leader. That's nonsense. He's left a trail of blood and bones."

—

There can be no rejoicing in the fact that Jeffs was convicted. A fourteen-year-old girl had been raped and Jeffs had turned a nineteen-year-old into a sexual deviant and a rapist. Close to eight thousand people still believe him to be God's infallible messenger. How many of them are victims of child rape is impossible to know, since there's nothing new in what Jeffs did. Since the 1950s, FLDS prophets have assigned underage girls ostensibly on orders from God. Even before placement marriages it wasn't uncommon for girls to be married shortly after puberty. It's impossible to guess how many more will become victims.

Equally impossible to quantify is how many FLDS boys and young men have been put in the terrible position of Allen Steed. Raging with hormones, Steed had been taught that he had authority over Elissa, that she was his chattel and that it was his duty to impregnate her and "bring forth priesthood children." Perhaps he really believed that rape was all right. After all, FLDS teachings have rendered him so socially and emotionally backward that he believed exposing his penis in a public park might encourage his child bride.

Even though politicians will take some share of the credit for Jeffs's conviction, Warren Jeffs wasn't put on trial because of Utah's crusading attorney general or county prosecutors.

Charges were laid only after Elissa Wall found civil attorney Roger Hoole, who believed her and filed a civil suit. The question is whether the conviction will result in more prosecutions or whether politicians will return to the status quo—tolerating both people who so adamantly remain outside societal boundaries and their "infallible" prophets.

What is worth celebrating about Jeffs's Utah conviction is that ordinary people are not willing to tolerate the abuse of women and children. The jurors—five men and three women—knew rape when they heard about it. They understood how a cult leader like Jeffs could be an accomplice by recklessly putting a fourteen-year-old and a nineteen-year-old in bed together with the expectation that they have children. They rejected the defence attorneys' suggestion that Jeffs's conviction would open the door for prosecuting all religious leaders or even marriage counsellors who suggest couples try to work through a difficult marriage. The jurors concluded that this was different. It took a lot of talking, arguing, reading and rereading the law over nearly sixteen hours of deliberations. But in the end, eight people decided that it can never be right for anyone to do what Jeffs did, regardless of religion.

—

While the North American war on polygamy's abuse and inequities has lurched a few steps forward in the six years since George Bush argued for invading Afghanistan to improve the lives of that country's women and children, little improvement has been made there. There was a flurry of burkas being thrown off after the initial invasion. A few schools for girls are open again, but students and teachers are threatened—all schools in Afghanistan remain suspect by Taliban insurgents. In the fall of 2007, three hundred schools did not reopen in the most volatile and violent regions of the country. Since 2005, thirty-six schools have been burned and seventeen teachers killed in Kandahar province alone.

Far from winning a quick victory in the war on terrorism and for equality rights, six years of fighting has claimed thousands of lives and disrupted thousands of families, homes and schools. Tens of thousands of women have been widowed, tens of thousands of children left fatherless — in Afghanistan as well as in the United States, Canada and other nations that have troops there.

Six years after the American president promised to eliminate the Taliban, the number of foreign soldiers in the country was at its highest level ever. Fifty thousand troops were fighting in Afghanistan with the North Atlantic Treaty Alliance–led International Security Assistance Force in the fall of 2007, including twenty-five thousand Americans and twenty-five hundred Canadians. In mid-September, within days of Warren Jeffs's conviction, Afghanistan's president Hamid Karzai once again pleaded with the Taliban to join his government and work towards peace. But the powerful warlords refused. They won't join until the international troops leave the country. Like all tyrants, they want the way clear so that they can exercise their terrible destructive power in secret.

Getting rid of bullies and rapists and child abusers who act in the fanatical certainty that God is directing them is difficult. The international coalition has been fighting to eradicate the Taliban in Central Asia longer than it took the Allies to oust the Nazis from Europe. Whether denominated in lives, dollars or political capital, the cost has been staggering. Yet we fight on, convinced that it is the right thing to do. Imagine if Canadian and American governments stood up for their own citizens with the same moral certainty, refusing to back down from petty tyrants such as Warren Jeffs, Winston Blackmore and all those who preceded them. How long would it have taken to bring our polygamist zealots to heel? It is impossible to say. In all these years, we've hardly tried.

ACKNOWLEDGEMENTS

Except for an angry email from Jancis Andrews in April 2004, I would never have written about Bountiful at all. Jancis was responding to a series of columns I'd written for the *Vancouver Sun* on the illegal trafficking of Asian women and children into Canada. Why didn't I write about Canadian girls being trafficked to become concubines to polygamist men? she angrily demanded. The answer was simple: I didn't know anything about it. Jancis set me on the road to finding out.

Telling the story was possible only because so many brave women and men—both members and former members— agreed to talk to me. To all of them, thank you. Special thanks to Debbie Palmer, whose help has been invaluable. She spent hundreds of hours explaining the religion, culture and family relations. She provided documents, insights and access to other escapees. Her own award-winning biography, *Keep Sweet*, helped fill in some other blanks.

Jane Blackmore's pain-etched face convinced me when we first met that what goes on in Bountiful is simply wrong. Since then she has generously shared her careful, conscientious and considered evaluation of fundamentalist Mormonism, the FLDS and her own life.

I owe an enormous debt to Harold Blackmore's daughters Lorna Blackmore and Brenda Williams Jensen. Their memories of the early days of Lister and their parents, plus their boxes and boxes of documents, photographs, letters, diaries and newspaper clippings, allowed me to follow one family's journey through polygamy. They have been unstintingly honest in their assessments of their lives and family, even when they have rekindled extremely painful memories.

Janet Johanson also bravely revisited some of her darkest hours and dragged down from her attic boxes of court documents, photos and newspaper and magazine articles that she had been unable to bear looking at for nearly twenty years. I am grateful for her generosity, strength and reluctance to throw anything out.

Others who have helped in the making of this book are the activists, including Jancis Andrews; Audrey Vance and Linda Price, the co-chairs of Altering Destiny Through Education; Elaine Tyler and Sara Hammon of the HOPE Organization; Flora Jessop of Help the Child Brides; Mary Plant of the University Women's Club of Vancouver, chair of the Bountiful Roundtable; Alison Brewin, executive director of the West Coast Legal Education and Action Fund (LEAF); Linda Calahan; Gary Pharness; and Debbie Quesnel.

I would also like to thank B.C. Attorney-General Wally Oppal, Utah Attorney-General Mark Shurtleff and his aide Paul Murphy, Nancy Volmer of the Utah Court's public information office, Arizona Attorney-General Terry Goddard, Gary Engels, and Roger Hoole, who all took time from their busy schedules to answer my questions.

The book has been enriched by the fine reporting of my

journalistic colleagues, particularly Jon Krakauer, whose *Under the Banner of Heaven* opened many people's eyes to the atrocities being committed; Brooke Adams of the *Salt Lake Tribune*, who must surely be the world's only full-time polygamy reporter; Jennifer Dobner of the Associated Press; Ben Winslow and Nancy Perkins of the *Deseret Morning News*; Patrice St. Germain of the *St. George Spectrum*; and Arizona freelancer John Dougherty.

This book could not have been written without the support of two editors-in-chief at the *Vancouver Sun*. Neil Reynolds gave me a dream job, asking only that I write two interesting pieces a week. His successor, Patricia Graham, continues to allow me to do that. Patricia has been wonderfully supportive during the writing of this book, and her kindness and caring helped sustain me through my father's long illness and death in early 2007.

Much of my reporting was based on research done by the *Sun*'s fine library staff, and particularly librarians Joel Minion, Sandra Boutilier and Kate Bird.

Stevie Cameron is this book's godmother. She insisted it needed to be written, and her help and advice ensured that it was. Claire Sowerbutt kept me sane by insisting that the two-member Harbour Cove Ladies Swim Club meet regularly for laps and the occasional glass of wine. My apologies to the Alpha-bettes and other friends whom I neglected during the writing.

But my special thanks goes to wonderful editors, who really are writers' best friends. Anne Collins and Nick Garrison at Random House should be cloned and given to all authors, first-timers like me in particular. Thanks also to copyeditor Susan Folkins and proofreader and indexer Gillian Watts. To my in-house editor, John Skinner, thank you for reading and improving on draft after draft after draft and for your patience and love.

SOURCE NOTES

PROLOGUE

The speeches by George and Laura Bush and the report on the Taliban and Women dated Nov. 17, 2001 are available on the U.S. State Department's website (http://www.state.gov/g/drl/rls/index .cfm?id=4804). The B.C. government's response to polygamists in its midst comes from a news release in 1992 and from contemporaneous news coverage in the *Vancouver Sun* and the *Vancouver Province* (*Vancouver Sun*, editorial June 16, *Vancouver Province* editorial and news stories June 14, 1992, as well as news stories on June 12). The B.C. Supreme Court decisions are from two separate cases involving children of Jehovah's Witnesses. The one is B (S.J.) v. B.C. (Director of Child, Family and Community Services) in 2005 (BCSC 573). The other case involves sextuplets born in 2007 (*V.M. and C.M. v. The Director of Child, Family and Community Service for British Columbia*, 2007 BCSC 552).

Information about Joseph Smith's revelation about polygamy comes from numerous sources listed in the bibliography. The quote from Orson Pratt was taken from *Solemn Covenant: The Mormon*

Polygamous Passage by B. Carmon Hardy.

Winston Blackmore's confessions about having "married" several girls who were 16 or younger comes from my notes from the polygamy summit held in Creston in 2005 and from the transcript of *Larry King Live!* (Dec. 8, 2006). Information about Blackmore's wives and children, Warren Jeffs's arrest and the investigations and various court proceedings come from interviews with Debbie Palmer, Jane Blackmore, Lorna Blackmore, Brenda Williams Jensen, Flora Jessop, Utah Attorney General Mark Shurtleff, Arizona Attorney General Terry Goddard, Mohave County Investigator Gary Engels, court documents and reporting (both my own in *The Vancouver Sun* as well as news reports mainly from Brooke Adams in the *Salt Lake Tribune*), Ben Winslow and Nancy Perkins in *The Deseret Morning News*.

CHAPTER 1—THE POLYGAMY CAPITAL OF CANADA

Interviews done during half a dozen visits to Creston between 2004 and 2007 are the basis of this chapter. Among those interviewed are the members of the lobby group Altering Destiny Through Education, Mayor Joe Snopek, Lower Kootenay Indian band Chief Chris Luke, John Kettle (an elected member of the regional district board), current and former members of the legislature of Corky Evans, Ann Edwards, Bill Bennett and Blair Sufferdine as well as current and former residents of Bountiful including Marlene Palmer, Cherene Palmer and Susie Palmer. Alex Ewashen's letter to the editor was published in the *Creston Valley Advance* on Sept. 2, 2004.

CHAPTER 2—IN THE BEGINNING

A *Logan Herald Journal* article from May 25, 2006 titled "Through the Eyes of a Pioneer" provided much of the background about Charles O. Card's contribution to that community before he became a fugitive. Biographical information about Card and other historical information came from: *The Diaries of Charles Ora*

Card: The Canadian Years, 1886–1903; The Mormon Presence in Canada; Mormon Polygamy; A History of the Mormon Church in Canada; Regional Studies in LDS History; an article by Brian Campion titled *Mormon Polygamy: Parliamentary Comments, 1889–90* that appeared in the spring 1987 edition *Alberta History* magazine; D. Michael Quinn's essay *LDS Church Authority and New Plural Marriages, 1890–1904;* and the Alberta Online Encyclopedia.

Two recent biographies on Joseph Smith were particularly useful: Richard Lyman Bushman's *Joseph Smith: Rough Stone Rolling* and Robert V. Remini's *Joseph Smith.* Other information was taken from another biography, *Mormon Enigma: Emma Hale Smith,* and from Martha Beck's autobiography, *Leaving the Saints: How I Lost the Mormons and Found My Faith.*

Biographical information about John W. Taylor comes from several sources including *Mormon Polygamy* and *Solemn Covenant.* The Archives of Canada is the source of the letters between Taylor and the Government of Canada, Taylor's affidavit dated 1902 and other documents relating to Taylor's part in the emigration of Mormons from Utah. Robert Scott's letter to Sir John A. Macdonald as well as Northwest Mounted Police Officer Sam Steele's reports are also from the Archives of Canada.

The story of William and Mary Blackmore comes from two unpublished family histories. One was written by John H. Blackmore and the other by Harold Blackmore. Another source was Harold Blackmore's self-published book, *We Three in Polygamy.* All of those, plus the letter to John H. Blackmore congratulating him on his election to Parliament, are from the private collection of Brenda Williams Jensen, Harold Blackmore's daughter.

CHAPTER 3 — THE PROMISED LAND

John Blackmore's excommunication is taken from contemporaneous reporting in *Newsweek* magazine and *The Toronto Star.* The context of the time was helped by reading *America's Saints: The Rise of Mormon Power* by Robert Gottleib and Peter Wiley, while Harold Blackmore's self-published books, *Patriarchal Order of Family Government, All About Polygamy: Why and How to Live It!* and *We Three in Polygamy* provided details as did extensive interviews with Harold's daughters, Brenda Williams Jensen and Lorna Blackmore. Harold's letter to his father was from Jensen's collection of family papers.

The wording of Doctrine and Covenant 132 is taken from the Church of Jesus Christ of Latter Day Saints' website (http://scriptures .lds.org/en/dc/132). Richard S. Van Wagoner's Mormon Polygamy and Ben Bistline's *The Polygamists: The History of Colorado City* provided context and details about polygamists in the early 20th century.

Simma Holt's excellent reporting both in *The Vancouver Sun* and in her book *Terror in the Name of God* are the sources of information about the Doukhobors. Articles from the Library and Archives of Canada's "Moving Here, Staying Here: The Canadian Immigrant Experience" were also useful in providing context.

CHAPTER 4—PERSECUTION, PROSECUTION AND BETRAYAL
Interviews with Lorna Blackmore and Brenda Williams Jensen provide much of the detail in this chapter. What they remembered was supplemented by letters and papers from their family collections as well as *All About Polygamy: Why and How to Live It!* and *Patriarchal Order of Family Government*, both of which were self-published by Harold Blackmore. The confidential appendix to *Life in Bountiful,* a report done for the B.C. government in 1993, as well as Debbie Palmer's autobiography, *Keep Sweet: Children of Polygamy*, provided other details.

I relied on Ben Bistline's book, *The Polygamists: The History of Colorado City* for some of the information about Joseph Musser as well as Musser's own books and others published anonymously by

Musser's Truth Publishing Company for a detailed description of the 1953 raid. Richard S. Van Wagoner's *Mormon Polygamy: A History* was another source of information about the raid as well as a transcript of Arizona Governor Howard Pyle's radio broadcast.

CHAPTER 5—A CHOSEN SON AND A CHILD BRIDE

Interviews with former members of the Bountiful community including Lorna Blackmore, Brenda Williams Jensen, and Jane Blackmore as well as some who did not want to be identified are the basis for much of the information in this chapter. Debbie Palmer's genealogy is the source for the family connections and her autobiography, *Keep Sweet: Children of Polygamy*, provides some other details. Other information comes from court documents filed from several legal actions involving the United Effort Plan trust (Harold Blackmore's lawsuit against the United Effort Plan trust in the Utah Central Division, Civil No. 87-C-1022J; Bountiful Elementary-Secondary School Society v. J. R. Blackmore & Sons Ltd. and Winston Kaye Blackmore, B.C. Supreme Court, 2003, L023719 Vancouver Registry; and J. R. Blackmore & Sons Ltd., Guy Blackmore and Leona Blackmore v. Bountiful Elementary-Secondary School Society, Cranbrook Registry 147560) and from Winston Blackmore's newsletter, *The North Star* (www.sharethelight.ca), as well as letters to his father that are posted on that website.

The quotes about plural marriage were taken from *Purity in the New and Everlasting Covenant of Plural Marriage*, first edition published by Rulon Jeffs in 1997. The story of Sarah and Hagar was taken from the Church of Jesus Christ of Latter Day Saints' website.

Brigham Young's quote about blood atonement was found in the book *In Mormon Circles: Gentiles, Jack Mormons and Latter-day Saints*. *In Mormon Circles* and a feature at www.crimelibrary.com provided details of Rulon Allred's murder, while the story of Ron and Dan Lafferty was compiled using *In Mormon Circles* and Jon Krakauer's *Under the Banner of Heaven*.

CHAPTER 6—THE NIGHT OF LONG KNIVES

J. R. Blackmore's quote in the first paragraph comes from the first edition of Winston Blackmore's Internet newsletter *The North Star* dated Jan. 15, 2003. His letters to his father are also from the website (www.sharethelight.ca) as are the descriptions of his wife, Jane Blackmore, and her sister, Debbie Palmer, from the website's article "Tale of Two Sisters".

Interviews with Lorna Blackmore, Brenda Williams Jensen, Jane Blackmore and Debbie Palmer all contributed to this chapter. Dalmon Oler's favourite saying was quoted in a *Vancouver Sun* story by Douglas Todd on Feb. 14, 1991. Court documents, including a copy of J. R. Blackmore's will and Harold Blackmore's affidavit, were provided by the family. Winston Blackmore's affidavit claiming that the school property had been given in trust was part of a lawsuit filed in 2004 against the Bountiful Elementary-Secondary School Society by J. R. Blackmore & Sons Ltd., Guy Blackmore and Leona Blackmore.

The transcript of Ross Chatwin's news conference in January 2005 is from the *Mohave County Supervisor's* website Mohave-CountyNews.com.

CHAPTER 7—GOD'S MOUTHPIECE

Biographical information about Rulon Jeffs comes mainly from reports in the *Salt Lake Tribune* and, in particular, a profile by Tom Zoellner published June 28, 1998.

The psychologists' reports on Warren Jeffs were filed to Judge James Shumate on April 18, 2007 following a competency hearing to determine whether Jeffs was fit to stand trial. I also relied on the excellent reporting of two Utah reporters—*Salt Lake Tribune's* polygamy reporter Brooke Adams and her March 14, 2004 profile, and the *Deseret Morning News's* Ben Winslow's reporting on the videotapes of the school concerts.

Brent Jeffs's affidavit was filed to the Third Judicial District

Court in Salt Lake County on Sept. 4, 2004.

Quotes from Warren Jeffs's sermons are from tapes provided to me by former members of the Fundamentalist Church of Jesus Christ of Latter Day Saints. LeRoy Johnson's sermon from 1984 is from the website www.mormonfundamentalism.com. Rulon Jeffs's sermon about videos and rock music is from *Purity in the New and Everlasting Covenant of Marriage*.

John Dougherty was the first to report on birth defects in Colorado City/Hildale in the *Phoenix New Times* on Dec. 29, 2005.

CHAPTER 8 — DOWN AT THE "CRICK"

The misuse of government money was first reported by John Dougherty in the *Phoenix New Times* in a story headlined "Polygamy in Arizona: The Wages of Sin" on April 10, 2003.

Rebecca Musser's descriptions of life in Rulon Jeffs's household come from her testimony at Warren Jeffs's preliminary hearing in St. George, Utah in November 2006.

Information about the Rodney Holms case comes from various news sources including the *Salt Lake Tribune*, *Deseret Morning News*, *St. George Spectrum* and the *Associated Press*.

Winston Blackmore's *North Star* newsletter noted that FLDS members had been told to dispose of televisions even though Warren and Rulon Jeffs continued to watch theirs. Ethan Fischer provided more details about the increasing tyranny of Warren Jeffs during an interview in St. George in November 2006.

The United Effort Plan trust documents were filed in the B.C. Supreme Court in 2003 as part of the case between Bountiful Elementary-Secondary School Society v. J. R. Blackmore & Sons Ltd. and Winston Kaye Blackmore.

The description of the gathering of the faithful in 2000 in preparation to be lifted up comes from John Llewellyn's book, *Polygamy Under Attack*, while the second gathering was described by Ben Bistline in his book, *Colorado City Polygamists*.

The report on Doomsday Cults by the Canadian Security Intelligence Service is on its website (http://www.csis-scrs.gc.ca/en/publications/perspectives/200003.asp). The Megiddo Report is available on the FBI website (http://permanent.access.gpo.gov/lps3578/www.fbi.gov/library/megiddo/Megiddo.pdf).

CHAPTER 9—THE OTHER SIDE OF UTOPIA

Interviews with Harold Blackmore's daughters, Lorna Blackmore and Brenda Williams Jensen done over many hours on several different occasions provide the basis of this chapter along with letters from the family's collection. They also invited me to go with them when they first met their niece, Carolyn Jessop, in the fall of 2006. I had met Jessop a year earlier and first reported her story in *The Vancouver Sun* in December 2005.

CHAPTER 10—GOD'S BROTHEL

Rulon Jeffs's quote at the beginning of the chapter comes from *Purity in the New and Everlasting Covenant of Plural Marriage*.

Debbie Palmer's story comes from personal interviews I have done with her as well as from the account of her life in Jon Krakauer's *Under the Banner of Heaven*, the CBC documentary *Leaving Bountiful* (which first aired in 2002 and again on May 13, 2004) and Daniel Woods's article in *Saturday Night* magazine on Aug. 4, 2001.

David Livingstone's cult was described in an Alberta Provincial Court decision dated Aug. 25, 1978 in the matter of LAM and KK.

Interviews with Janet Johanson and Patricia Johanson plus the mountains of material including court documents, judgments and affidavits collected during their custody battle over their half-sisters' children are the sources of the story of Janelle Fischer.

I also relied on some of the contemporaneous reporting on the case done by Kathryn Casey for the *Ladies Home Journal* in February 1990, the *Deseret News*, *Network* magazine and *Sunstone* magazine.

CHAPTER 11 — IN THE NAME OF GOD/THE RELIGIOUS "RIGHT"
Clive Jackson generously gave me access to the raw footage of his
visit to Bountiful in October 1990. I am also grateful for the reporting of my *Vancouver Sun* colleague Douglas Todd and the great
investigative work on Bountiful done in the early 1990s by my friend
Fabian Dawson of the *Vancouver Province*.

I interviewed Shirley Black in April 2007, who corroborated
some of the information that other wives had given me previously
on the basis that their names not be used, while Penny Priddy provided her perspective in an interview in March 2007.

Marla Peters's thesis "Pearls Before Swine: Secrecy in a Mormon
Polygynous Colony" was completed in 1994.

Minutes from the assistant deputy ministers' meetings, memos,
letters and O. Gary Deatherage's report were all obtained under a
Freedom of Information request.

The Grade 7 religion tests from 2003/04 were provided by someone who wishes to remain anonymous.

CHAPTER 12 — THE LOST BOYS
I interviewed close to a dozen lost boys in Canada and the United
States between 2005 and 2007. Some interviews were done in Salt
Lake City, others were done in St. George and still others in
Cranbrook and Creston. I have also interviewed Dan Fischer on sev-
eral occasions as well as Elaine Tyler, executive director of the HOPE
Organization, Jane Blackmore and Lorna Blackmore. Some of the
information comes from the so-called Lost Boys' civil suits filed in the
third judicial district court, Salt Lake County (Civil No. 040918237).

CHAPTER 13 — FALLEN PROPHET
Winston Blackmore's *North Star* newsletter and court documents
filed in the B.C. Supreme Court case of the Bountiful Elementary-
Secondary School Society v. J. R. Blackmore & Sons Ltd. and
Winston Blackmore are key sources. Interviews with people who

have left both Bountiful and the FLDS provides the context of the times as did CBC-V's documentary, *The Bishop of Bountiful*, which first aired on Jan. 15, 2003.

Blackmore's financial worth is based on reporting I did for *The Vancouver Sun* with the invaluable assistance of librarians Joel Minion, Sandra Boutilier and Kate Bird and staff at the land titles office in Bonner's Ferry.

The description of Warren Jeffs's ordination and quotes from his sermon were taken from Ben Winslow's Aug. 30, 2006 profile in the *Deseret Morning News* titled "From Nerd to FLDS chief," while the information about the Mancos ranch and the quote from Deputy County Assessor Scott Davis is from a July 16, 2005 story in the *Rocky Mountain News*.

CHAPTER 14 — BORDER BRIDES

Rose Matjasic did the reporting on Winston Blackmore's news conference in October 2000 for the *Cranbrook Daily Townsman*. I relied on my notes and digital recording from Blackmore's news conference in May 2006 and interviews with Roger Hoole, Sam Brower and U.S. consular officials.

I first reported on the marriage of Lorraine Johnson and Shalina Palmer in January 2006 based on information provided to me by a number of sources.

CHAPTER 15 — CALL TO ARMS

Tom Green's story is a compilation of material taken from various sources including Jon Krakauer's book *Under the Banner of Heaven*, a transcript of the *Sally Jesse Raphael* show and the *Arizona Republic*.

Utah Attorney-General Mark Shurtleff has spent many hours speaking to me about polygamy and the laws in his state. Arizona's Attorney-General Terry Goddard has also spoken to me several times about various legal issues as has Buster Johnson, the Mohave County supervisor.

Jancis Andrews is the person who urged me to write my first column about Bountiful and the fundamentalist Mormons. I have spent hours speaking to her over the years and she provided me with access to her unpublished book manuscript, *The Bountiful Conspiracy*, about the efforts she has made to end polygamy as well as her voluminous files.

Audrey Vance and Linda Price have spent hours sharing what they have learned about Bountiful, while Nora Mennie and Nick Ronaldson have spoken to me numerous times about the financial hardships they've suffered because of the polygamists undercutting logging contractors.

CHAPTER 16 — LYING FOR THE LORD

Several people directly involved in helping Roger Hoole and Joanne Suder described the atmosphere at the Grand Hotel that week.

The description of Marlene Palmer's public-relations drive is the result of her inviting me to Bountiful, which resulted in my first trip there. The quotes and descriptions from the Beyond Borders conference on child brides and the Creston polygamy summit come from my notes, a tape of the proceedings and interviews at those meetings.

The B.C. Vital Statistics Agency's report on teen births in Bountiful was first reported by CBC Radio reporter Gregor Craigie, who got the information under the B.C. Freedom of Information Act.

Dozens of interviews with people who do not wish to be named were used to piece together what has happened to the women and girls who were such outspoken advocates at the polygamy summit, but have since left.

CHAPTER 17 — FLDS UNDER SIEGE

Gary Engels introduced me to Lori Chatwin, who generously invited me into her home during my first visit to Colorado City in 2005. She and her husband, Ross, have since spoken to me several times during various court hearings in Utah.

Fawn Broadbent filled in some of the details of what it was like the day that Warren Jeffs began excommunicating men. Broadbent and her friend, Fawn Holm, were both sixteen that day, which was the same day that they ran away.

The diligent reporting by the *Deseret News, Salt Lake Tribune, St. George Spectrum* and *Arizona Republic* provided the information about the marshal being decertified and the judge disbarred.

Descriptions and quotes from the August 2005 hearing on the United Effort Plan trust is from my notes and interviews I did at the Salt Lake City courthouse.

Details of Seth Steed's arrest are from a U.S Department of Justice press release dated July 14, 2006.

The turkey-baster quote is from an interview with Mark Shurtleff while he was in Vancouver. Other quotes and descriptions from the Utah attorney-general's meetings that day are from my notes and from digital recordings.

CHAPTER 18 — THE ROAD TO PURGATORY

My *Vancouver Sun* colleague Chantal Eustace was responsible for getting Eddie Dutchover's detailed description of Warren Jeffs's arrest. Her information is supplemented with subsequent police reports and other news reporting from that day by Reuters, BBC and the *Deseret News.*

The descriptions and quotes from the preliminary hearings in St. George are from my notes.

CHAPTER 19 — WHOSE RIGHTS?

The information is taken from my notes from the day-long training session, the evening townhall meeting and interviews with Deputy Sheriff Darrell Cashin, Utah Attorney-General Mark Shurtleff and

Arizona Attorney-General Terry Goddard, pro-polygamy activists and anti-polygamy activists at the meeting.

The definition of cult and a description of French laws comes from work done by the Montreal-based Info-Cult, while information about the riots in the fall of 2005 are from BBC News and the *Financial Times*.

Information about Ontario's flirtation with sharia law comes from my own reporting at the time for *The Vancouver Sun* as well as news reports by the *Canadian Press, Toronto Star, The Globe and Mail* and CBC.

Both B.C. Attorney-General Wally Oppal and special prosecutor Richard Peck spoke to me at length about Bountiful and their concerns about the success of a prosecution and the rationale for doing a reference to the court versus a test case.

EPILOGUE

Interviews with B.C. Attorney-General Wally Oppal and special prosecutor Richard Peck done in September 2007 as well as news releases from the Criminal Justice Branch of the Attorney General's Ministry are the sources for the section on British Columbia.

The descriptions and quotes from Warren Jeffs's trial are from my notes taken in the courtroom and interviews done in St. George, while I was reporting on the trial for *The Vancouver Sun* and the CanWest News Service.

The information about Afghan women and girls comes from several sources. Asne Seierstad's fine reporting in her internationally acclaimed *The Bookseller of Kabul* provided a general understanding, while an Oct. 7, 2007 Canadian Press report provided the details about the schools. The number of allied troops in Afghanistan was reported by The Associated Press in a story on Oct. 7, 2007, while the Canadian number is from the National Defence Department.

BIBLIOGRAPHY

Appel, Willa. *Cults in America: Programmed for Paradise*. New York: Holt, Rinehart and Winston, 1983.

Arendt, Hannah. *Eichmann in Jerusalem: A Report on the Banality of Evil*. New York: Penguin Books, 1964.

Battle, Kemp. *Hearts of Fire: Great Women of American Lore and Legend*. New York: Harmony Books, 1997.

Beck, Martha. *Leaving the Saints: How I Lost the Mormons and Found My Faith*. New York: Three Rivers Press, 2005.

Bistline, Benjamin. *The Polygamists: A History of Colorado City*. Agreka Books LLC, 2004.

Blackmore, Harold. *All About Polygamy: Why and How to Live It!* Hurricane, Utah: Patriarchal Society, 1978.

———*Patriarchal Order of Family Government*. Hurricane, Utah: 1974.

Braun, Nathan, ed. *The History & Philosophy of Marriage: A Christian Polygamy Sourcebook*. San Francisco: Imperial University Press, 2005.

British Columbia Royal Commission on Doukhobor Affairs. *Interim Report*. Victoria, B.C.: 1948.

Bushman, Richard Lyman. *Joseph Smith: Rough Stone Rolling.* New York: Alfred A. Knopf, 2005.

Coates, James. *In Mormon Circles: Gentiles, Jack Mormons, and Latter-Day Saints.* Reading, Mass.: Addison-Wesley, 1991.

The Coming Crisis: How to Meet It. Salt Lake City, Utah: Truth Publishing, 1968.

Dahl, Larry E., and Donald Q. Quinn, eds. *Encyclopedia of Joseph Smith's Teachings.* Salt Lake City, Utah: Desert Book Company, 1997.

Enroth, Ronald, ed. *A Guide to New Religious Movements.* Downers Grove, Ill.: InterVarsity Press, 2005.

Fulton, Gilbert A., Jr. *Dear Bill, About That Polygamous Wife, Gil.* Eagle Creek, Ore.: 1977.

Gottleib, Robert, and Peter Wiley. *America's Saints: The Rise of Mormon Power.* New York: Harcourt Brace Jovanovich, 1986.

Hardy, B. Carmon. *Solemn Covenant: The Mormon Polygamous Passage.* Urbana: University of Illinois Press, 1992.

Hawthorn, Harry B., ed. *The Doukhobors of British Columbia: Report of the Doukhobor Research Committee.* Vancouver: University of British Columbia Press, 1952.

A History of the Mormon Church in Canada. Salt Lake City, Utah: Truth Publishing, President of the Lethbridge Stake of the LDS.

Holt, Simma. *Terror in the Name of God.* Toronto: McClelland and Stewart, 1964.

Krakauer, Jon. *Under the Banner of Heaven.* New York: Doubleday, 2003.

Kraut, Ogden. *Revelations 1880–1890.* [n.p.], 1970.

Llewellyn, John R. *Polygamy Under Attack: From Tom Green to Brian David Mitchell.* Agreka Books LLC, 2004.

Mackert, Mary. *The Sixth of Seven Wives: Escape from Modern Day Polygamy.* Salt Lake City, Utah: www.expolygamist.com, 2000.

Miller, Timothy, ed. *When Prophets Die: The Postcharismatic Fate of New Religious Movements.* New York: State University of New York Press, 1991.

Moore-Emmett, Andrea. *God's Brothel*. San Francisco: Pince-Nez Press, 2004.

Noddings, Nell. *Women and Evil*. Berkeley: University of California Press, 1989.

Palmer, Debbie, and Dave Perrin. *Keep Sweet: Children of Polygamy*. Lister, B.C.: Dave's Press, 2004.

A Priesthood Issue and the Law of Plural Marriage. Salt Lake City, Utah: Truth Publishing, President of the Lethbridge Stake of the LDS Church.

Quan, Holly. *Sam Steele: The Wild West Adventures of Canada's Most Famous Mountie*. Canmore, Alta.: Altitude Publishing Canada, 2003.

Remini, Robert V. *Joseph Smith*. New York: Viking Penguin, 2002.

Shermer, Michael. *The Science of Good and Evil: Why People Cheat, Gossip, Care, Share and Follow the Golden Rule*. New York: Henry Holt, 2004.

Smith, Joseph. *The Book of Mormon: An Account Written by the Hand of Mormon Upon Plates Taken from the Plates of Nephi*. Salt Lake City, Utah: Church of Jesus Christ of Latter-day Saints, 1981.

Solomon, Dorothy Allred. *Daughter of the Saints: Growing Up in Polygamy*. New York: W.W. Norton, 2003.

Stackhouse, John G., Jr. *Finally Feminist: A Pragmatic Christian Understanding of Gender*. Grand Rapids, Mich.: Baker Academic Press, 2005.

Tarasoff, Koozma J. *Plakun Trava: The Doukhobors*. Grand Forks, B.C.: MIR Publication Society, 1982.

Utah Attorney General's Office and Arizona Attorney General's Office. *The Primer: Helping Victims of Domestic Violence and Child Abuse in Polygamous Communities*. July 2005.

Van Wagoner, Richard S. *Mormon Polygamy: A History*, 2nd ed. Salt Lake City, Utah: Signature Books, 1989.

Wood, V.A. *The Alberta Temple: Centre and Symbol of Faith*. Calgary, Alta.: Detselig Enterprises, 1989.

INDEX

Award-winning journalist Daphne Bramham has been a columnist at the *Vancouver Sun* since 2000. She won a National Newspaper Award for her column in June 2005. She was honoured by the non-profit group Beyond Borders in 2004 for a continuing series of columns on the polygamous community of Bountiful, B.C. Born in Saskatchewan, Bramham lives in Vancouver with her partner, John Skinner.

A NOTE ABOUT THE TYPE

The Secret Lives of Saints is set in Electra, designed in 1935 by
William Addison Dwiggins. A popular face for book-length work
since its release, Electra is noted for its evenness and high legibility
in both text sizes and display settings.